Working *with* Midpoints

Your Key to Predictive Precision and Astrological Insight

KATHY ALLAN

foreword by MICHAEL HARDING

Published in 2024 by Ibis Press, an imprint of Nicolas Hays, Inc.
P. O. Box 540206
Lake Worth, FL 33454-0206
www.nicolashays.com

Distributed to the trade by
Red Wheel/Weiser, LLC
65 Parker St. • Ste. 7
Newburyport, MA 01950
www.redwheelweiser.com

ISBN: 978-089254-230-7
Ebook ISBN: 978-0-89254-697-8

Library of Congress Cataloging-in-Publication Data available upon request

Book design and production by
Sky Peck Design

Charts generated using Solar Fire and Nova Chartwheels software

Printed in the U.S.A.
MP

Contents

To Reinhold Ebertin,
upon whose shoulders I stand,
gazing at the future.

Foreword

"If we listen, we can start to hear the midpoints making themselves heard."

—MICHAEL HARDING AND CHARLES HARVEY
Working with Astrology

B efore the contract for our book *Working with Astrology* was signed with Routledge Publishing on February 17, 1988, my coauthor Charles Harvey and I had discussed with their editor Howard Sasportas the possibility that the three central topics included in the book (Midpoints, Harmonics, and Astro*Carto*Graphy) might best be served by publishing the work in three separate volumes. While Howard was okay with this idea, the publisher was not. As it turned out, Routledge did not print the work at all and eventually sold their rights to Penguin, who published the book in 1990 under the Arkana imprint (which Erin Sullivan was later to edit).

However, with the initial contract signed—and with the understanding that Routledge planned on publishing the work in a single volume—Charles and I set to work trying to cover as much of the three techniques as possible within the limits of this single volume. One of our discussions was about the quality of both the historical and extant books that had introduced us to astrology and what we felt was needed *now*. In my case, there were two books that I bought a couple of days after I attended my first astrology class on September 22, 1979 at 4:00pm BST London.

One of those books we had been instructed to buy for the class: Jeff Mayo's *Teach Yourself Astrology,* published in 1964—a rather ambiguous suggestion, I thought. But while looking for it in the elusive section of the bookstore where astrology books tended to find themselves, I came upon John Addey's *Harmonics in Astrology.* Thus, right from the beginning, I had two very different views to absorb: first, Jeff's worthy introduction that followed a relatively mainstream path; and second, John's dense questioning of the assumed centrality of signs and houses with his focus on the intricacies of planetary relationships that went far beyond the usual list of suspects.

Our class took the Jeff Mayo route—albeit with a strong psychological twist—but I kept Addey's book of waveforms beside me and tried to fit it all together. While I now find Addey's search for a system that is "coordinated, simplified and unified" a bit suspect (this sounds a bit like Steven Hawkins' wish for a Grand Unified Theory of Everything), there is still a vast amount to explore within the basic idea of harmonics, as the work of Hamblin, Cochrane, and others have demonstrated. "Unified" the theory might be, but "simple" it is not.

Consider: harmonic charts generally map the planets' positions from 0° Aries as in the natal chart; they can also be set in the diurnal circle with the Ascendant as 0° degrees, or in the aspect circle where every planet's conjunction with every other planet is the starting point. And how many harmonic charts are there for each possible circle/cycle? Each possibility gives us a different picture to interpret and generally the wish is for the one that is most useful (for all are accurate in their own way) but not always helpful.

However, there is one use of harmonic charts where patterns within the 2nd, 4th and 8th harmonics can be particularly valuable in terms of their observed expression in life (though some ramp the number up to the 64th, as did the late Theodore Landscheidt.) Yes, we've arrived at midpoints, and in particular the work that Kathy Allan has given us here.

For some reason, midpoints have the reputation of requiring a mathematics degree and fluency in German when actually there are typically just 13 factors and 8 aspects to consider. That's it. No houses, signs, falls, dignities, exaltations, detriments, rulerships, planetary hours, or arcane systems of tertiary progressions too terrible to countenance.

In short, Kathy Allan has written exactly the sort of book I would love to have read when starting to study midpoints.

Very well written, clear and comprehensive, *Working with Midpoints* covers all the key points with some excellent examples based on Kathy's obvious experience with the subject—and she also includes some detailed case studies. This book takes us through the subject step by step with clear diagrams and lucid explanations, and at the end of each chapter the author invites the reader to reflect on the significance of how their own midpoints have worked out in life. This last suggestion is particularly valuable since keeping a brief record of the midpoints that are triggered by ordinary events in life (and the occasional dramatic ones) imparts a deeper understanding of how they reveal themselves within the circumstances of our lives.

Charles Harvey was always ready to share personal experience and anecdotes, generally coupled with their midpoints, and to this end noted the times of all sorts of events, once telling a class how he had fainted but "fortunately looked at my watch before I passed out." He was pleased to find out later that, yes, the MC was on his Ur/Ne midpoint at that precise moment, for which Ebertin gives "the elimination of the waking consciousness." For my part, a couple of accidents occurred with MC = Ma/Ur, one of them involving electricity. For a while, I kept a computer file of such events under the title Quirks until a quirk of computing deleted it.

Using examples from today's world, Kathy brings much of the tradition up to date. I particularly like the way in which some of the original patterns described by Ebertin are amplified and engaged with, both in terms of their history and their current applications, many of them obviously drawing upon Kathy's considerable experience working with clients. Charles Harvey used to say that COSI should come with a health warning, reminding us that many of the interpretations arose from events observed in 1930s Germany where such midpoints as Ur=Ma/Pl frequently found expression in "cruelty, violence, brutality, sudden disasters and calamities." At other times in history, this midpoint could be seen in the charts of those who broke with convention and attracted strong censure and resentment for doing so, such as Martin Luther King, Galileo, Germaine Greer, Piet Mondrian, Philip Glass, Kurt Vonnegut . . . okay, and the Concorde crash and the St Valentine's Day massacre, if you must.

What first attracted me to the use of midpoints was their potential for specificity, of seeing a chart factor that pictures what can be observed in life, be it a mundane event or some characteristic of personality. True, there are Taurus qualities and Aquarian events—and so on—which often capture the sense of the moment, but signs can sometimes paint with too broad a brush while midpoints have the ability to depict something more precisely. Here one still needs to recognize that in order to understand a particular expression one must be aware of its circumstances and the different ways its language—like all languages—can describe possibilities.

Again, COSI can sometimes dwell on one potential outcome, such as the Sa/Ne midpoint that Kathy draws attention to. Sure, it can accompany periods of ill health or when boundaries dissolve with depressing consequences, but it can also "earth a vision" as Charles would say, such as finding its form in the fashion world where Christian Dior, Georgio Armani, and Gianni Versace all had natal So=Sa/Ne.

In demonstrating the calculation of midpoints, Kathy has addressed an omission in our own book: she places strong focus on the use of dials. At the time when Charles and I were writing *Working with Astrology*, computers had yet to feature the mouse-controlled dial on the screen, although they printed midpoints in a variety of degree sorts—an addition often particularly requested by Charles. Calculating midpoints and drawing them on dials is not the easiest introduction to the technique, and its demands often put students off. Hence we decided to omit dials altogether in favor of using the computer's printout directly as "trees" of sorts, and working from there. However, the ability to use the dial on the screen is a wonderfully visual way to see midpoint clusters and also the sequence in which they can be triggered by transits.

This book gives some very good examples along with a thorough series of illustrations which graphically show the build up of midpoint patterns and their manner of interpretation. Kathy follows this through with her work on Solar Arc and its place on the dial. Again, clear examples abound of how directed planets emphasize natal positions or act as time markers for predicting possible life changes. Many of the examples show both directed and natal planets on the same circle, though some computer programs like Janus allow for inner and outer circles in the style of Uranian astrology. Considering predictions, we are obviously going to focus on patterns that are yet to be and the different ways in which these transits can be depicted. Here, again, the dial plays its part, although the use of the Graphic Ephemeris is also emphasized, and again the computer has liberated the astrologer; some of the older amongst us can recall painstakingly transcribing ephemeris positions into their graphic equivalents, if only for the planets from Jupiter out.

While the computer can set a graph for any harmonic, the 45° graphic ephemeris remains the choice here and Kathy's introduction to the use of that ephemeris is very detailed, clearly explaining what is being portrayed and how it can be read. The graphic diagram is a particularly powerful way of watching events unravel, and I am often surprised at how many astrologers do not use it. They've no excuse here, as everything is made plain—how the lines are read, how the graph can be set for any time period from one minute to one century, or longer—always with the ability to select or delete lunations, ingresses, planets, or midpoints at will. This allows the astrologer to focus on specifics in the moment, or see patterns over many years. The latter is particularly useful for those interested in mundane astrology when the interactions of the outer planets over long periods can be scanned in a matter of seconds.

In addition to forecasting, Kathy also provides us with examples of how midpoints can be used to interpret an event chart and then applied to a client's natal positions as a transit, even if there is no exact time for the event. This situation is very common in an astrologer's practice, with clients often saying it happened "sometime in the morning" when the all-important Asc and MC cannot be relied on as they travel so quickly in midpoint terms. When exact times are known, everyday events can be used to rectify a chart to see what midpoints are triggered, albeit this is a slow process as it relies on quite a number of timed events. Here the Asc or MC may be seen to consistently fall ahead or behind an appropriate midpoint combination, suggesting a birthtime error. It's a long process and probably only done by the astrologer for their own chart. Which is where it should always start. As Kathy puts it: "I went back to Ebertin and reread his books. I noted what he said, and followed what he did. At times, these were not the same. He had theoretical information and practical application. In the end, I did my own research, and I suggest you do yours."

Kathy's book is a wonderful introduction to using midpoints in ways that develop and enrich your own understating of astrology. Let the journey start now!

—Mike Harding

Introduction

This is a textbook on midpoints. They are simple to use, yet few astrologers take advantage of them. One reason may be that few current books explain how to use them. I first noticed their importance when a beloved dog died under a nice transiting trine to natal Jupiter in Scorpio. While Jupiter is in the sign associated with the underworld and rules my 6th house of small pets, I didn't understand why a soft aspect from the Sun transpired as a sad unexpected death. That is until I realized the transiting Sun was simultaneously triggering the natal death Mars/Saturn midpoint and the highly personal Sun/Moon midpoint. Thus began my study.

Midpoints have been used sporadically in the distant past and are related to the Arabic Parts. Historically, two separate schools of astrology used midpoints, Uranian Astrology and Cosmobiology. Uranian astrology was developed in Germany in the early 1900's by Alfred Witte, who was one of first to recognize the importance of midpoints in the chart as the place where combined energies of two planets manifest, thus forming a "planetary picture" (hence the book's title.) He was the first to develop the 90° dial, as well as an ephemeris for eight hypothetical trans-Neptunian planets (TNPs). His *Rules for Planetary Pictures* (1928, 1932) is the basic text of Uranian astrology. Witte's approach was revolutionary in that his method placed less importance on the aspect (i.e., whether it is "good" or "bad" as had been the traditional approach) and greater importance on the nature of the planets involved in the aspect. His *Rules for Planetary Pictures* is basically a compendium of keywords for groupings of planets—the pictures they create. All books on midpoints invariably flow from Witte's system.

Witte's system was simplified by his student Reinhold Ebertin in 1940, who established Cosmobiology, which focuses on midpoints. Ebertin ignored the TNPs, zodiac signs, and houses. He emphasized the combined symbolism of planets. The basic Cosmobiology text—fundamentally, the "bible" of delineations—is Ebertin's *The Combination of Stellar Influences,* commonly abbreviated as the COSI. The COSI outlines the principles of Cosmobiology and provides midpoint definitions—taking Witte's keywords further. It is used extensively by many astrologers and is highly recommended.

Today in the United States, Uranian astrology is alive and vibrant. The fine astrologers working at Astrolabe who developed the software program Solar Fire and the dial program, Nova Chartwheels, are highly accomplished Uranian astrologers, as was my excellent teacher, Penny Bertucelli, based in South Florida. In contrast, Cosmobiology has largely faded into the background. Ebertin published many books on midpoints and solar arcs, but these were written before the advent of personal computers. Consequently, he spent an inordinate amount of effort outlining how to construct a dial, unnecessary in this age of personal computers.

Throughout this book, Ebertin is my primary source of information, although we have some differences in our methodology and application. (I will expand on these differences in Part 4 of this book.) Just as Ebertin's delineations flowed from Witte's keywords, so too do the delineations in this book flow from Ebertin's. While still staying true to the heart of COSI, I have adapted Ebertin's interpretations to both clarify them and bring them more in line with contemporary language. Both Witte and Ebertin were men of their generation (early 1900s), and both originally wrote in German. Many keyword terms are now archaic, and subtle differences of word choice can get lost in translation.

Notable and more contemporary books on midpoints have been written, but many are out of print. An exceptional hands-on book is *The Life Blueprint*, written by Jane Reynolds in 1978, but it is rare and hard to find. Rob Hand has a chapter on midpoints in his 1981 text *Horoscope Symbols*, but that is only a chapter, albeit an excellent one. The essential modern text, *Working With Astrology*, was published by Michael Harding and Charles Harvey in 1990, over thirty years ago. However, because Ebertin dedicated one of his books to solar arcs, they excluded this technique from their text. In 1991, Michael Munkasey published *Midpoints: Unleashing the Power of the Planets*, which is a superb reference that delineates the combined meaning of the planets and chart angles. Munkasey also developed Weighted Midpoint Analysis (WMA), a feature in the astrological software program Solar Fire. That same year, the NCGR Journal published the Uranian/Cosmobiology Issue.

In this century, Doris Greaves, based in Australia, wrote *Cosmobiology Beyond 2000*, a book currently out of print. Carole DeMott Devine's book, *Solar Arc Directions*, was published that same year. Noel Tyl's book on midpoints, *Solar Arc*, came out in 2001, as did the second edition of Maria Kay Simms' *The Dial Detective*, which mixes Uranian and Cosmobiology, and explains how to manually find and use midpoints on the dial. The Oct/Nov 2005 Issue #123 of The Mountain Astrologer was dedicated to Uranian astrology and Cosmobiology, and the following year Eleanora Kimmel published her fourth book on Cosmobiology, *Altered and Unfinished Lives*. To my knowledge, the most recent book, *Midpoints*, was written by Don McBroom in 2007. No new books on this technique have been published in English since then—and that was seventeen years ago.

I thought it was time we had a new book. As an astrologer, I would hate for this technique to be lost. The information that midpoints provide is astonishing. The way they mirror what is going on in the world is astounding. In many cases, they provide the missing links that explain what is really happening when traditional astrology fails. Just as you would never ignore a t-square of the Moon, Saturn, and Pluto, the midpoint of Moon = Saturn/Pluto should not be overlooked either.

This is a beginner's text on midpoints which assumes an intermediate understanding of astrology. I start at the beginning, explaining what midpoints are, how to find them, and how to interpret them in a 360° chart. I examine midpoint axes to see how these influence the focal planet and how to add this information to natal chart delineation. Next, I look at these techniques on the dial. If you don't know how to use it, I'll explain in Chapter 7. The dial is the best tool for finding midpoints and 8th harmonic aspects. I use the dial as an addition to the chart, not a replacement.

From there, we'll move on to solar arc directions. We'll see how to find and interpret them, as well as identify years when significant solar arcs are active. The transits are triggers. We'll look at the 45° graphic ephemeris, an aid that enables us to visualize transits over time and pinpoint eventful dates. In a timed transiting chart, we'll see how midpoints enhance the interpretation of eclipse, ingress, return, lunation, and diurnal charts. We'll examine timed events in the lives of famous people to see how solar arcs work with transits.

No astrology text can be read as a novel. I advise drawing the charts and dials as we go along and finding the aspects and midpoints for yourself.

You can check your results against mine. There are suggested exercises at the end of each chapter so that you can practice the technique on your own chart. By studying the example charts and dials, and doing the exercises as you go through the book, by the time you reach the end, you will know how to use midpoints. It is my hope this textbook will generate a resurgence of interest and application in their use.

—Kathy Allan
11/17/2021
Mimbres, New Mexico

Glossary

(Learning the Language of Midpoints)

Midpoints

The following midpoint terms will be used throughout this book:

Midpoint: a combination of three planets with one planet equidistant to the other two

Completed midpoint: a synonym for "midpoint" and confirms that three planets comprise the configuration

Occupied midpoint: another synonym for a midpoint confirming that three planets are contained in the configuration

Midpoint pair: refers to two planets that comprise a midpoint

Incomplete midpoint: synonym for a "midpoint pair," and assumes there is no third planet at the midpoint degree; (i.e. there is no focal planet)

Unoccupied midpoint: a synonym for a "midpoint pair" or "incomplete midpoint"—there is no focal planet at the midpoint degree

Direct midpoint: a midpoint planet that is in conjunction or opposition to a midpoint pair

Indirect midpoint: a planet that is in hard aspect (square, semisquare, sesquisquare) to a midpoint pair

Mixed midpoint: a midpoint that involves three planets formed by placements in two different chart types. For example, a midpoint formed with natal Venus and natal Mars with directed Saturn at the focal point, or one formed with natal Venus and directed Saturn, with natal Saturn at the focal point. I also call this "mixing levels" or "crossing levels."

Mixed-level midpoint: synonymous with "mixed midpoint": a midpoint comprised of a natal/directed or natal/transit pair completed by a third planet. I do not use them in this book

Exception Midpoint: in biwheels, there are no midpoints formed by mixing pairs across charts, with one exception. Ebertin noted that when the same planet forms a pair with its directed or transiting counterpart, and the pair forms a completed midpoint, it is active. For example, tMo = Su/dSu would be a valid midpoint, with the symbolism of the Sun repeated twice for emphasis.

Midpoint Axis: a term used by Ebertin to denote the midpoint degree of a planetary pair, recognizing the midpoint degree forms an axis, rather than a single degree point. His term for a planetary pair was a midpoint axis.

Midpoint Tree: shows a multitude of midpoint pairs configured with a focal point. It is a synonym for a midpoint axis.

Midpoint Variant: these are three midpoints comprised of different combinations of the same three planets, such as Ve = Me/Ur; Me = Ve/Ur, and Ur = Me/Ve. The variants give variations of a single theme.

Special Midpoint: the most important are Su/Mo and As/Mc. The list is given in Appendix 2.

Terminology

Equilateral triangle: a grand trine as seen on the dial, where three planets are positioned at any multitude of 30° in a chart.

8th harmonic aspects: these are the conjunction, opposition, square, semisquare, and sesquisquare, all related to the square and the division of the 360° circle into 8 pieces, each 45° of arc. The semisquare is an aspect of 45°, the square has 2 pieces or 90°, the sesquisquare has 3 pieces, or 135°, the opposition has 4 pieces, or 180°.

Minor 8th harmonic aspects: the semisquare and sesquisquare are called minor aspects, but Ebertin found they were as powerful as the major 8th harmonic aspects of the conjunction, opposition, and square.

Nodal bendings: the degrees that square the lunar nodes. The south bending is the square earlier in the zodiac than the North Node and acts like a super Saturn. The north bending is the square that follows the North Node in the zodiac and acts like a super Jupiter.

Points: a catch-all word that includes the planets (including Sun and Moon), angles, and nodes.

Arc of Activation: a measurement of half the distance between the planets in a midpoint pair. To determine this, take the number of degrees between the pair of planets that make the midpoint, and divide by two.

45° Graphic Ephemeris: displays the transits over time in graphic form in 45° notation.

Annual Diagram: Ebertin's term for the 45° graphic ephemeris with the transits drawn for a year.

45° Ruler: gives the corresponding cardinal, fixed, and mutable modes in 45° notation.

Midpoint Shorthand

X = Y/Z: This is the notion for a midpoint. The forward slash (/) is used to indicate the midpoint pair. The equal sign (=) indicates that the midpoint is complete, with all three points occupied by a planet.

n/n: a midpoint pair formed by a natal planet/natal planet. In practice, using the natal chart as the basis, there will be no designated letter "n" before the two planets, as in Su/Mo.

d/d: midpoint pair formed by a directed planet/directed planet. In practice, because I do not use mixed midpoints, a "d" will only be used in front of the first planet, as in dSu/Mo, with the presumption the "d" pertains to both planets, as in dSu/dMo.

t/t: midpoint pair formed by a transiting planet/transiting planet. In practice, because I do not use mixed midpoints, a "t" will only be used in front of the first planet, as in tSu/Mo, with the presumption the "t" pertains to both (tSu/tMo).

d: in prefix (such as dSu) means a solar arc direction.

t: in prefix (such as tSu) means a transit.

Diurnal chart: a timed transiting chart that uses the time and place of birth and is cast for any given day.

Planetary Picture: these are two or more midpoint pairs that share an axis.

Type 1 axis: in Uranian astrology, has a planet at the focal point of a midpoint pair on an axis. These are identical to a completed midpoint, or a midpoint tree.

Type 2 axis: in Uranian, has no planet at the focal point of an axis, contains at least two midpoint pairs, and one of the points is a personal point. The personal points are the Sun, Moon, Ascendant, Midheaven, Node, and the Aries Point.

TNPs: trans-Neptunian planets (8 in total) recognized by Uranian astrologers.

Cosmogram: Ebertin's term for a superimposition of the 360° chart onto the 90° dial.

Planet and Point Abbreviations

Su: Sun
SO: abbreviation for the Sun sometimes used by Ebertin
Mo: Moon
Me: Mercury
Ve: Venus
Ma: Mars
Ju: Jupiter
Sa: Saturn
Ur: Uranus
Ne: Neptune
Pl: Pluto
No: True Node (unless otherwise specified, in which case, the Mean Node)
DR: Mean Node abbreviation sometimes used by Ebertin
As: Ascendant
Mc: Midheaven
P of F: Part of Fortune
AP: Aries Point (0° of any cardinal sign)

PART 1

MIDPOINT DELINEATION

The midpoints are almost equal in value to the aspects ...

REINHOLD EBERTIN

Chapter 1

Midpoints, Planets, and Points

hy use midpoints? Traditionally, to understand how a planet is working in a chart we look at a planet's sign, house, and aspects. We typically ignore midpoints, but these too add influence. Midpoints help define how a planet operates. Ebertin considered them to be almost as powerful as aspects in a chart.

What is a midpoint? It's the average of two numbers. The midpoint of four and ten is seven. We arrive at the answer by adding the two numbers together and dividing by two. In astrology, a midpoint contains three planets with one planet equidistant from the other two. It is written in the form X = Y/Z.

Before we look at midpoints, we need to consider the base factors that comprise them: the planets, angles, and nodes. Ebertin lumped these together and called them "points." There are thirteen of them. For ease of narration, my use of the word "planets" includes the angles and the nodes. Ebertin tweaked the meaning of planets, as described below (and in Appendix 1).

The lights are the Sun and the Moon. For the sake of convenience, they are called planets, although the Sun is a star, and the Moon is a satellite of the Earth. The planets are Mercury, Venus, Mars, Jupiter, Saturn, Uranus, Neptune, and Pluto. This group is subdivided into the inner planets (also called the personal planets): Mercury, Venus, and Mars; the social planets, Jupiter and Saturn; and the collective planets, Uranus, Neptune, and Pluto.

As in traditional astrology, the Sun and Moon are the most significant planets in a chart and in a midpoint. Whenever the Sun is in a midpoint, life's purpose and goals are highlighted. The Sun also has to do with health, vitality, and the physical body. It shows the type of activities that turn us on and make us shine. The Sun symbolizes men, the father, or husband.

The Moon represents nurturing, caretaking, mothering, the public, the need for safety, memory, the past, and emotional makeup. In a midpoint, it shows an emotional attachment, or an emotional response connected to the other two planets. In general, it symbolizes women, the mother, or the wife.

Mercury, Venus, and Mars are personal planets in the sense they denote preferences whose dictates come from within. Mercury represents the mind, thinking, communication, speaking, and writing. Mercury is also travel and young people. Venus shows what we love and value. It explains our relationships, what we find attractive, and what makes us happy. It symbolizes art and creative artistic pursuits. Although Ebertin did not consider it a money planet (that would be Jupiter), Venus is related to money because it is necessary for comfort and pleasure. Venus represents girls and women, peace, harmony, friendship, art, beauty, and grace. Mars is the planet of assertion, anger, and action. It shows how we fight, where we put our energy, the strength of our will, and work in general. Ebertin did not consider it to be malefic.

Jupiter and Saturn are the social planets. As such, they describe our place in society and how we fit in with society and contribute to it. These planets impose their energy from the outside through culture and upbringing. Jupiter shows our philosophy, higher education, religious inclination, and how we see the world and expand our borders, both interior and external. Jupiter is growth, expansion, optimism, law, and wealth. It is the royal planet of power and authority. In counterbalance is Saturn, which is restrictive, limiting, inhibiting, and separative. Saturn is also practical, realistic, and grounding. Saturn has to do with social standing, professional authority, ambition, and conscience—a need to do or not do the right thing. Saturn is conserving, pessimistic, and depressive. Ebertin viewed Saturn as a malefic influence.

As outer planets, Uranus, Neptune, and Pluto symbolize forces outside of our control. They add depth and difficulty to planets in midpoints. Each brings change. Uranus is the lightning bolt that comes from nowhere and shakes the world. As a higher octave of Mercury, it depicts inspiration and lofty thought. Neptune symbolizes the collective unconscious and the world of mythology and symbology. Ebertin took a dim view of Neptune and believed it ruined any planet it contacted. Keywords for Neptune are confusion, delusion, and illusion. Neptune also dissolves. However, it is spiritual, creative, and imaginative. It symbolizes the invisible otherworld. Pluto represents the underworld—the personal unconscious and heavy emotional issues that send us to therapy. Pluto is also the planet of power and control. It rules things many in number. Ebertin's view of Pluto was mixed, but he often saw it in a positive light.

THE THREE ANGLES

The three angles are the Ascendant, Midheaven, and Moon's Node. The Ascendant is the intersection between the ecliptic and the local horizon. In traditional astrology, it is the most personal point in the chart and represents the physical body—the vehicle in which we drive, and the persona—the part of our self we present to others. In Cosmobiology, the Ascendant also symbolizes the place (environment) and others in our immediate environment.

The Midheaven is the intersection of the ecliptic and the local meridian. It marks the highest point in the sky that the Sun reached on the day of birth. In traditional astrology, it shows our visibility in the world and the professions we choose. It is the public work face we are known for. In Cosmobiology, the Midheaven is more important than the Ascendant. It governs traits that overlap with those of the Sun—it also shows goals and purpose in life; the direction in which we are headed. The Midheaven shows the nature of our life's work and the types of activities that give us standing or infamy in the world.

The North and South Nodes of the Moon are the two points where the Moon's orbit intersects the ecliptic. When the Moon is traveling from the south to the north, moving from below the ecliptic to above it, it crosses the North Node. When the Moon cuts the ecliptic in the other direction, going below the ecliptic, it crosses the South Node. Ebertin lumped the nodes together and viewed them as similar. He used the Mean Node (an average point), whereas I use the True Node (a more exact spot). His keywords for the nodes are: union association, alliance, group, family.

There is a fourth angle that Uranian astrologers pay attention to and Ebertin ignored, and that is the Aries Point. This position is the intersection between the ecliptic and the earth's equator extended into space. This is similar to the Moon's node and can be considered the Earth's node. The Aries Point is 0° Aries—where the Sun is found on the first day of spring. In Cosmobiology, all 0° cardinal are considered equal in strength. This means that 0° Aries (onset of spring), 0° Cancer (onset of summer), 0° Libra (onset of autumn), and 0° Capricorn (onset of winter) are equivalent. Any cardinal point connects us to the greater world; one that is outside or beyond our typical environment. Breaking with Ebertin, I pay attention to planets that are conjunct the Aries Point. I do not use it in midpoints or by direction.

Of the thirteen points (3 angles and ten planets), the most important are the Sun, Moon, Ascendant, and Midheaven. When these are activated by transit or directions, stuff happens. If a personal point is not involved, the event may not be personal—perhaps something heard on the news, or something happening to someone else. Bottom line? These four points make things personal.

In this book, in the interest of brevity, I have abbreviated the points by the first two letters of their name, so that in midpoint notation, the Sun is written Su, Moon is written Mo, etc. The exception is the Midheaven which is abbreviated Mc. By convention, planets are listed before angles with the fastest-moving planet listed first. An exception is the Sun, which is listed first, then the Moon, and next the remaining planets in order from Mercury to Pluto. The angles are listed last in the order of Node, Ascendant, Midheaven. Thus, in Ebertin's book, the order of the points is Su, Mo, Me, Ve, Ma, Ju, Sa, Ur, Ne, Pl, No, As, Mc. It's the same for midpoints. The Su/Mo is the first midpoint pair listed, then Su/Me, then Su/Ve, and so on, with the last midpoint pair As/Mc the last pair in the book. The completed midpoints are given in the same order so that Me = Su/Mo is the first midpoint listed for Su/Mo, then Ve = Su/Mo, then Ma = Su/Mo, etc. The "/" is the symbol used to denote a midpoint. If two planets are together, as in a New Moon, for example, I write the combination as SuMo to show their connection. In the next chapter, we'll look at how to find midpoints.

HOMEWORK: Start a notebook where you can list the keywords of planets and midpoints. Look over the list of keywords in Appendix 1 and add your favorites.

Chapter 2

Finding Midpoints

E very two planets in the chart make a midpoint. That means that somewhere in the chart there is a degree that is equidistant to both planets. However, for a midpoint to be active, there has to be a planet at (or in aspect to) that equidistant degree. When a planet occupies that degree, we have a completed midpoint. If the degree is unoccupied, the midpoint is incomplete and inactive.

Look at the example natal chart in Figure 1 on page 8. Visually we can see that Mercury is near the midpoint of the Sun and Jupiter. If we add 11° to the Sun, we get 0° Pisces. Add 11° to Mercury and that brings us near Jupiter. Since Mercury occupies the equidistant degree between the Sun and Jupiter, we have a completed midpoint. This is written in the form: Me ♂ Su/Ju, or Me = Su/Ju, where the "=" sign symbolizes an aspect.

Look at Venus and Jupiter in Figure 1. Their midpoint is around 17° Pisces. There is no third planet at or near that degree. They form an incomplete midpoint.

For terminology's sake, it's important to distinguish between the midpoint itself, and the planetary pairs that "make" the midpoint. In the first example, the Sun and Jupiter "make" the midpoint. They are a midpoint pair. Mercury is conjunct their midpoint degree, so Mercury is "at" or "on" the midpoint. Another way of saying this is that Mercury is the focal planet of the midpoint, or Mercury completes the midpoint, or Mercury occupies the midpoint.

The midpoint pair of Venus and Jupiter do not form a completed midpoint. We can say the Venus/Jupiter midpoint is incomplete, unoccupied, or has no focal planet.

The term "midpoint" on its own refers to a completed midpoint, comprised of at least three planets.

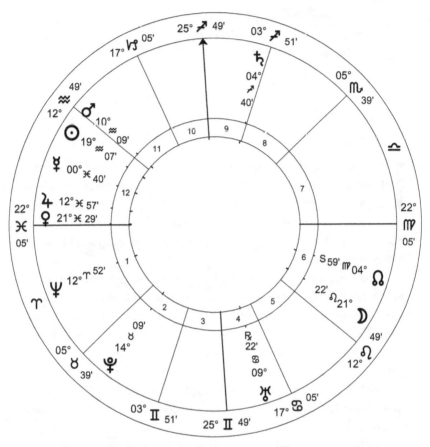

Figure 1. Example natal chart

MATH

What is the precise midpoint of the Sun and Jupiter shown in Figure 1? We can use simple math to precisely determine the midpoint degree. We need to first determine the absolute longitude of the planets from 0°Aries. The handy table shown in Figure 2 enables a simple conversion. All Aries planets fall from 0 to 30° of absolute longitude, while all Taurus planets are found in the range of 30 to 60°, etc. The Sun at 19°Aqu7′ has an absolute longitude of 319°7′. Jupiter at 12°Pis57′ has an absolute longitude of 342°57′. To find the midpoint of Sun and Jupiter we add their absolute longitude and divide by two:

Su + Ju = 319°7′ + 342°57′ = 661°64′
661°64 / 2 = 331°2′

This converts back to 01°Pisces2′. Mercury, at 00°Pis40, occupies the midpoint degree within 22′.

ABSOLUTE LONGITUDE	
Ari:	0–30
Tau:	30–60
Gem:	60–90
Can:	90–120
Leo:	120–150
Vir:	150–180
Lib:	180–210
Sco:	210–240
Sag:	240–270
Cap:	270 –300
Aqu:	300 –330
Pis:	330–360

Figure 2. Longitude equivalent

ORB

How close does a focal planet have to be to complete a midpoint? In midpoint work, orbs are kept small. Ebertin and Cosmobiologists typically use an orb of 1 1/2°. I set my orb for 2° so I can see the midpoints that are just over 1½ degrees, and I cross out the ones that are too wide. As always, use your judgment in determining whether or not to include a midpoint with a wider orb than recommended. Generally, as a rule, I look at them, but ignore them, even when they're close to the limit and really nice.

SHORT AND LONG ARC MIDPOINTS

Let's take another example from Chart 1 and find the midpoint of Mercury and Neptune. We can eyeball the pair and see that their midpoint will fall around Venus and the Ascendant. We determine the precise midpoint:

Neptune at 12°52 Aries gives an absolute longitude of 12°52

Mercury at 00°40 Pisces gives an absolute longitude of 330°42

12°52 + 330°42 = 342°92.

Now divide by 2:

342°92 / 2 = 171°46, which converts to 21°46 Virgo.

But wait! The Ascendant is Pisces, and 21° Virgo is near the Descendant. What is going on? The fact is, that in a circle, every pair of planets has a near midpoint and a far midpoint. Thus, every planetary pair has two midpoints in the 360° chart. (Figure 3 on page 10).

We can see from Figure 3 that the arc distance between Mercury and the Ascendant is the same as the arc distance between Neptune and the Ascendant. Similarly, the arc distance between Mercury and the Descendant is the same as the arc distance between Neptune and the Descendant. The software program Solar Fire always calculates the short arc midpoint

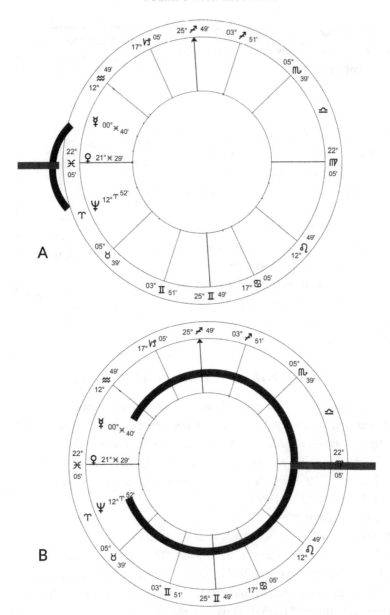

Figure 3. The near and far midpoint: (A) the arc distance between Mercury and the Ascendant is the same as the arc distance between the Ascendant and Neptune. This puts the Ascendant at the midpoint of Mercury and Neptune. (B) the arc distance between Mercury and the Descendant is the same as the arc distance between the Descendant and Neptune, which puts the Descendant at the midpoint of Mercury and Neptune. In this example, the near midpoint of the planets is the Ascendant and the far midpoint is the Descendant.

(21°Pisces), while old-fashioned math always gives the shortest distance from 0°Aries (21° Virgo). In practice, both midpoints are equivalent. In the 360° chart, the short and long midpoints are always opposite each other.

Let's take another example. The midpoint of the Moon and Saturn in Figure 1 appears to fall in mid-Libra, which is unoccupied. But look across the chart and there is Neptune at 12°Aries52 standing on the far midpoint. When looking visually for midpoints, it's necessary to scan the opposite point to see if there are any planets/points in that vicinity (Figure 4). Any focal planet that completes a midpoint by conjunction or opposition gives a direct midpoint. (We'll look at indirect midpoints later in chapter 8.)

In the 360° chart, since the long and short arc degrees are opposite each other, they form an axis. For this reason, Ebertin often referred to midpoint

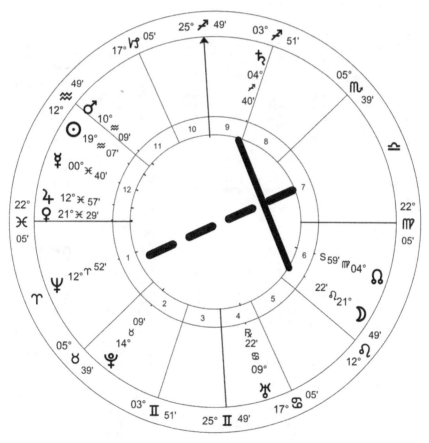

Figure 4. Midpoint axis

pairs as a "midpoint axis." In his terminology, every pair of planets forms an axis in the chart, whether completed or not. In Chart 1, Moon/Saturn makes an axis completed by Neptune. The Sun/Jupiter axis is completed by Mercury. The Venus/Jupiter axis is unoccupied—that is, there is no planet in the third point. We will discuss midpoint axes in more detail in chapter 5.

MIDPOINT LISTINGS AND TREES

While we can mathematically figure out the midpoint degree of each planetary pair in a chart, astrology software makes this easy. I use Solar Fire (see *www.solarfire.info*). In this program to find the midpoint listing, open a chart, go to Reports, then Midpoint Listing, and set the modulus for 360°.

In Planetary Sequence - Modulus 360°00'

☽	21°♌22	☉/♅	29°♈15	♀/♃	17°♓13	♃/♅	11°♉10	*♆*	12°♈52
☽/☉	20°♏15	☉/♆	16°♓00	♀/♄	28°♑05	♃/♆	27°♓55	♆/♇	28°♈31
☽/☿	26°♉01	☉/♇	01°♈38	♀/♅	15°♉26	♃/♇	13°♈33	♆/☊	23°♊56
☽/♀	06°♊26	☉/☊	27°♏03	♀/♆	02°♈11	♃/☊	08°♊58	♆/As	02°♈29
☽/♂	15°♏46	☉/As	05°♓36	♀/♇	17°♈49	♃/As	17°♓31	♆/Mc	19°♒21
☽/♃	02°♊10	☉/Mc	22°♑28	♀/☊	13°♊14	♃/Mc	04°♒23	*♇*	14°♉09
☽/♄	13°♎01	*☿*	00°♓40	♀/As	21°♓47	*♄*	04°♐40	♇/☊	09°♋34
☽/♅	00°♌22	☿/♀	11°♓05	♀/Mc	08°♒39	♄/♅	22°♍01	♇/As	18°♈07
☽/♆	17°♊07	☿/♂	20°♒25	*♂*	10°♒09	♄/♆	08°♒46	♇/Mc	04°♓59
☽/♇	02°♋46	☿/♃	06°♓49	♂/♃	26°♒33	♄/♇	24°♒25	*☊*	04°♍59
☽/☊	28°♌11	☿/♄	17°♑40	♂/♄	07°♑25	♄/☊	19°♎49	☊/As	13°♊32
☽/As	06°♊44	☿/♅	05°♉01	♂/♅	24°♈46	♄/As	28°♑23	☊/Mc	00°♏24
☽/Mc	23°♎36	☿/♆	21°♓46	♂/♆	11°♓31	♄/Mc	15°♐14	*As*	22°♓05
☉	19°♒07	☿/♇	07°♈25	♂/♇	27°♓09	*♅*	09°♋22	As/Mc	08°♒57
☉/☿	24°♒53	☿/☊	02°♐49	♂/☊	22°♏34	♅/♆	26°♉07	*Mc*	25°♐49
☉/♀	05°♓18	☿/As	11°♓23	♂/As	01°♓07	♅/♇	11°♊46		
☉/♂	14°♒38	☿/Mc	28°♑14	♂/Mc	17°♑59	♅/☊	07°♌11		
☉/♃	01°♓02	*♀*	21°♓29	*♃*	12°♓57	♅/As	15°♉44		
☉/♄	11°♑53	♀/♂	00°♓49	♃/♄	23°♑49	♅/Mc	02°♎36		

Sorted by Angle - Modulus 360°00'

☉/♇	01°♈38	☽/♀	06°♊26	♄/☊	19°♎49	♄/As	28°♑23	☉/As	05°♓36
♀/♆	02°♈11	☽/As	06°♊44	☽/Mc	23°♎36	♃/Mc	04°♒23	☿/♃	06°♓49
♆/As	02°♈29	♃/☊	08°♊58	☊/Mc	00°♏24	♀/Mc	08°♒39	☿/♀	11°♓05
☿/♇	07°♈25	♅/♇	11°♊46	☽/♂	15°♏46	♄/♆	08°♒46	☿/As	11°♓23
♆	12°♈52	♀/☊	13°♊14	☽/☉	20°♏15	As/Mc	08°♒57	♂/♆	11°♓31
♃/♇	13°♈33	☊/As	13°♊32	♂/☊	22°♏34	*♂*	10°♒09	*♃*	12°♓57
♀/♇	17°♈49	☽/♆	17°♊07	☉/☊	27°♏03	☉/♂	14°♒38	☉/♆	16°♓00
♇/As	18°♈07	♆/☊	23°♊56	☿/☊	02°♐49	*☉*	19°♒07	♀/♃	17°♓13
♂/♅	24°♈46	☽/♇	02°♋46	*♄*	04°♐40	♆/Mc	19°♒21	♃/As	17°♓31
♆/♇	28°♈31	*♅*	09°♋22	♄/Mc	15°♐14	☿/♂	20°♒25	*♀*	21°♓29
☉/♅	29°♈15	♇/☊	09°♋34	*Mc*	25°♐49	♄/♇	24°♒25	☿/♆	21°♓46
☿/♅	05°♉01	☽/♅	00°♌22	♂/♄	07°♑25	☉/☿	24°♒53	♀/As	21°♓47
♃/♅	11°♉10	♅/☊	07°♌11	☉/♄	11°♑53	♂/♃	26°♒33	*As*	22°♓05
♇	14°♉09	*☽*	21°♌22	☿/♄	17°♑40	*☿*	00°♓40	♂/♇	27°♓09
♀/♅	15°♉26	☽/☊	28°♌11	♂/Mc	17°♑59	♀/♂	00°♓49	♃/♆	27°♓55
♅/As	15°♉44	*☊*	04°♍59	☉/Mc	22°♑28	☉/♃	01°♓02		
☽/☿	26°♉01	♄/♅	22°♍01	♃/♄	23°♑49	♂/As	01°♓07		
♅/♆	26°♉07	♅/Mc	02°♎36	♀/♄	28°♑05	♇/Mc	04°♓59		
☽/♃	02°♊10	☽/♄	13°♎01	☿/Mc	28°♑14	☉/♀	05°♓18		

Figure 5. Example 1 corresponding midpoint list 360°

You'll get a list showing the midpoint degree of every planetary pair. An example of the midpoints of Chart 1 is shown in Figure 5. The top half of the page shows the midpoint degrees in order of the planets, starting from the Moon, while the bottom half of the page shows the midpoint degrees in order from 0° Aries.

The bottom half of the page can be used to find planets that complete midpoint pairs. Look at Venus at 21°Pisces29 in the last column. If we subtract 1½° from this we get 19°01, and if we add 1½° to this we get 22°59. This is the midpoint orb range for Venus. From the listing, we can see that Ve = Me/Ne = As. (We omit the midpoint pair of Ve/As because the same planet can't be simultaneously at the focal point and in a midpoint. To find all the midpoints, we can scan the list, search for a stand-alone planet, and see which midpoint pairs lie above it and below it.

A quicker method is to construct midpoint trees. Solar Fire does this in the Report section under the Midpoint trees listing. Figure 6 shows the completed midpoints as planetary trees set at a modulus of 360°. Again, I set the orb for 2° and cross out the midpoints at an orb greater than 1½°. As we just saw, Venus is on the midpoint of Mercury and Neptune. The +0°17d notation means it is a direct midpoint (the "d") and the exact midpoint of the planetary pair falls 17′ later in longitude than Venus (the +).

The trees show us, in a snapshot, all the midpoints associated with any planet. Note that some planets and points are missing from the list. There is no tree for the Moon, Node, or Midheaven. That is because these have no direct midpoints.

We saw earlier that Neptune was on the far midpoint of Moon/Saturn. If we look at Figure 6, we find Neptune configured with the midpoint

Modulus 360°00' – Max Orb 2°00'

♆	(Orb)	*♇*	(Orb)	*♅*	(Orb)	*♄*	(Orb)
♃/♇	+0°40' d	♀/♅	+1°16' d	♇/☊	+0°11' d	☿/☊	−1°50' d
		♅/As	+1°34' d				
♂	(Orb)	*☉*	(Orb)	*☿*	(Orb)	*♃*	(Orb)
As/Mc	−1°12' d	♆/Mc	+0°13' d	♀/♂	+0°09' d	♂/♆	−1°26' d
♄/♆	−1°23' d	☿/♂	+1°18' d	☉/♃	+0°21' d	☿/As	−1°34' d
♀/Mc	−1°30' d			♂/As	+0°27' d	☿/♀	−1°52' d
♀	(Orb)	*As*	(Orb)				
☿/♆	+0°17' d	☿/♆	−0°18' d				
As	+0°35' d	*♀*	−0°35' d				

Figure 6. Example 1 corresponding midpoint trees 360°

Modulus 180°00' – Max Orb 2°00'

Ψ	(Orb)	*♀*	(Orb)	*♄*	(Orb)	*Mc*	(Orb)
☽/♄	+0°08' d	♀/♅	+1°16' d	☽/♀	+1°45' d	Ψ/☊	−1°53' d
♃/♇	+0°40' d	♅/As	+1°34' d	☿/☊	−1°50' d		
		☽/♂	+1°36' d				

♅	(Orb)	*♂*	(Orb)	*☉*	(Orb)	*☽*	(Orb)
Ψ/☊	+0°11' d	As/Mc	−1°12' d	Ψ/Mc	+0°13' d	☿/♂	−0°57' d
♂/♄	−1°57' d	♄/Ψ	−1°23' d	☿/♂	+1°18' d		
		♀/Mc	−1°30' d				

☿	(Orb)	*☊*	(Orb)	*♃*	(Orb)	*♀*	(Orb)
♀/♂	+0°09' d	Ψ/Mc	+0°00' d	♂/Ψ	−1°26' d	☿/Ψ	+0°17' d
☉/♃	+0°21' d	☉/♀	+0°19' d	☿/As	−1°34' d	♄/♅	+0°32' d
♂/As	+0°27' d	☉/As	+0°37' d	☿/♀	−1°52' d	*As*	+0°35' d
		☿/♃	+1°50' d				

As	(Orb)
♄/♅	−0°03' d
☿/Ψ	−0°18' d
♀	−0°35' d

Figure 7. Example 1 corresponding midpoint trees 180°

of Jupiter/Pluto only. The reason for this is that the 360° modulus is only giving us midpoints that have a planet on the degree with the shortest arc (which Solar Fire sees as a conjunction). The listing is not showing us those planets on the midpoint at the longer arc (which Solar Fire sees as an opposition). To find the longer arc midpoints, we need to look at the 180° modulus. This is done in Solar Fire by changing the modulus from 360° to 180°.

The midpoint trees recalculated using a modulus of 180° are shown in Figure 7. Now, if you look at the Neptune tree, there is the Moon/Saturn midpoint. It has a "d" designation, as does every midpoint listing on the page. Since the short and long arc midpoints are equivalent, both are considered direct. Given they are equally powerful, a 180°modulus should always be made when looking for direct midpoints, as a 360° modulus misses about half of them.

At the most basic level, we now have a list of the midpoints configured with each planet. Our next task is to interpret completed midpoints—that is to figure out what they mean, by looking at how the energies might combine.

HOMEWORK: Print out your natal chart as a reference. Then, print out a listing of your 360°-module midpoints, a listing of your 360°-module midpoint trees, and your 180°-module midpoint trees. Compare the 2 midpoint tree pages. The difference is the addition of the long arc midpoints.

If you don't have midpoint software, you can download Planetdance software for free from the website: *www.jcremers.com*. You will find the midpoint option in the drop-down menu under Horoscopes. For the 360°midpoint and tree lists, check the conjunction box. For the 180° midpoint and tree lists, check both the conjunction and the opposition.

Chapter 3

Midpoint Delineation

To delineate a midpoint, we start by combining the symbolism of the pair that makes the midpoint. This involves considering keywords for each planet/point and envisioning how they affect each other. Then we add the symbolism of the focal point and consider how the three might work together. It helps to keep in mind the similarities and differences between the planets. Are they compatible? Do they conflict with or complement each other? Planets that are similar share a common ground and have an easier time combining than dissimilar planets.

The outer planets when combined are generational unless they are associated with an inner or social planet. Inner planets combined with outer planets are often difficult and problematic. These planets may also be projected and viewed as external rather than internal or act as blind spots. However, these combinations can also produce spectacular effects.

Planetary combinations can be analyzed according to element. The energetic and active Fire planets are the Sun, Mars, and Jupiter. The practical, grounded, and hard-working Earth planets are Saturn, Venus, and Mercury. The thinking and speaking Air planets are Mercury, Venus, and Uranus. The emotional Water planets are the Moon, Pluto, and Neptune.

In general, same-element planets get along with each other, although problems can arise from excess—there's too much of something. Fire planets and Air planets get along because both are outgoing. Earth and Water planets get along because both are introverted and reserved. A mix of a Fire planet with either Earth or Water is problematic because the latter can dampen the former, and the former can scorch the latter.

Similarly, an Air planet mixed with Earth or Water can result in over-thinking that impairs action. Whenever there is a problematic astrological combination, expect the combination will translate into problems in life.

Let's take for example the pair of Mercury and Uranus. Mercury keywords are: the mind, talking, thinking, writing ability, communication, intellect, critical analysis, short-term travel. Uranus keywords are: awakening, freeing, releasing, revolution, independence, rhythm, erratic, sudden intervention, surprise, upsets, sky, technology (see Appendix 1 for a complete list). Since both planets are concerned with thinking, we can expect them to be compatible. When combined, we get independent thinking, revolutionary communication, surprise criticism, upsets in short-term travel, sudden intervention in flying, upsetting conversation, analyzing rhythm, technical ability, and a critical analysis of the sky.

We can also look up what the pair means in Ebertin's *The Combination of Stellar Influences* (hereafter referred to as COSI). In the 1972 edition of COSI, the meaning of the Mercury/Uranus pair is given on the left-hand side on page 124, in the following form:

Principle: Astuteness, intuition.

Psychological Correspondence: +A revolutionary spirit and mind, shrewdness, inventive thinking, a talent for speaking, intuition, interest in or the ability for technical science or engineering, physics, mathematics, rhythm, etc. The desire to be independent, intellectual flexibility. −"Too many irons in the fire, also the inclination to scatter one's energies in too many directions at once, nervous haste, temporary or occasional confusion, tactlessness, a brutal frankness, over-estimation of self, a contradicting disposition. C. Self-will, moodiness, a good intellect.

Biological Correspondence: The statics of Man, depth-sensibility, the spinal cord as defined by Burdach and Goll, disturbances of equilibrium (facial pains and migraine).

Sociological Correspondence: Mathematician, technician, physicist, a person engaged professionally in the study and application of rhythmics, cosmobiologist

Probable Manifestations: +A good intellect, a person who learns and comprehends easily. The power to influence other people, the establishment of innovations and inventions, the stage of sudden cognition or perception in the mind. Rapid realization of plans. -Failures caused by scattering one's energies or through doing everything in too great a hurry, nervousness, eccentric actions, upset, and excitement.

To determine how the midpoint pair is affected by a third planet at the focal point, we look at the right side page of the COSI. For Mercury/Uranus, on page 125, we have:

Me/Ur:

Su: A good orator. Readiness for action, over-zealous character, a premature action or hastiness, the ability to grasp a situation quickly, the inclination to do one's work in haste; the ingenious or inventive man; sudden incidents, a quick adjustment to new circumstances, a surprise.

Mo: An excitable soul or disposition, a quick change of thoughts and moods, an instinctive and correct grasp of a subject, logical thinking, and a practical disposition.

Ve: An artistic feeling or perception, an eye for artistic creation and work, the ability to think in plastic forms or shapes, the ability to resonate and to tune in to rhythms such as occur in dancing, gymnastics, and song, a sudden awareness of a personal love-relationship, a sudden act of love.

Ma: Summing up a situation quickly and acting accordingly, courage, determination, sudden success, and advancement in life. A sudden realization of ideas, assaults, nervousness.

Ju: Fortunate ideas, the gift of repartee, optimism, and confidence, a good general view, a far-seeing mind coupled with the ability for long-term planning, a clear grasp or comprehension of a matter, a fortunate turn, success in the solution of a technical or mathematical task.

Sa: The desire to liberate oneself from tensions, a sudden overcoming of inhibitions through acting quickly, the correct grasp of a difficult situation and the attainment of success and advancement in life, the act of separating oneself from others, the attainment of safety for oneself.

Ne: Painful or tormenting emotional inhibitions, undermining circumstances also leading to a state of illness, neuroses, or diseases with causes difficult to ascertain.

Pl: A good mathematician, indefatigability in one's work or creative activity, a hasty realization of plans. Over-strained or over-stimulated nerves.

No: The ability to give and also receive stimulating sugges-
tions, the desire to work on the realization of new ideas together
with others (by cooperative effort); surprising news, turn or
changes.

A: The application of practical principles in the creation of
one's environment, circumspection, shrewdness, or deliberation,
organizing ability; a sudden contact of thoughts with other people,
accidents, motor damage.

M: A person with the ability to grasp all connective links and
relationships correctly and to draw logical conclusions from such
knowledge, an inventor, a mathematician, a physicist or cosmobiologist, the ability to think about a particular matter acutely and
keenly and to act swiftly.

From the definitions, we glimpse a sense of what the pair means and how
the completed midpoint may be expressed. We can also look to see how
people who have these midpoints in their charts express them in their lives.

Astrologer Evangeline Adams has natal Venus = Mercury/Uranus.
For her, Me/Ur was astrology, channeled through Venus, and outwardly
expressed as a labor of love and in her client relationships. She made money
through a mail-order astrology business. Single for many years, she married late in life to a man who helped her with her business. Her chart is the
one shown in Figure 1 on page 8.

Actress and activist Mia Farrow has the same midpoint. As the UNICEF
Good Will Ambassador, she raised awareness of child poverty in Africa: a
goodwill agent (Venus) speaking (Mercury) about a need for change (Uranus). She also got polio (sudden intervention in the nervous system) at
age 9 and made the most of it (Venus). A shocking upset (Uranus) in love
(Venus) also made news (Mercury).

Another activist actress and UNICEF Good Will Ambassador with
this midpoint is Susan Sarandon. As a political spokeswoman, she (Venus)
regularly speaks (Mercury) about promoting social equality (Uranus). Not
surprising for a country based on the fundamental value of free speech,
this midpoint is also found in the United States' Sibly chart. The midpoint
describes the value of independent thinking, higher education, and technological innovation.

Bobby Fischer, the great chess player, also has Ve = Me/Ur. According to Wikipedia, he played with "brilliance and dramatic flair." He "made the world recognize" that chess was "as esthetically satisfying as a fine work of art." Dr. Phil, who made a fortune helping folks on TV find happiness by talking about their problems (upsets) has this midpoint, as does Beatles' drummer, Ringo Starr, who expressed the midpoint through music—song and rhythm.

Let's look at focal planets other than Venus to see how this impacts the expression of the midpoint pair. Dr. Margaret Millard, author of *Casenotes of a Medical Astrologer*, has the Sun at the focal point: Sun = Mercury/Uranus. A practicing physician, Millard was also an outstanding astrologer. Her last book on astrology was published when she was eighty-eight. Jeanne Dixon, astrologer to Nancy Reagan, had the same midpoint. According to Wikipedia, Dixon was "one of the best-known American self-proclaimed psychics and astrologers of the 20th century." Scientist and researcher Louis Pasteur, who worked in medical microbiology in the pioneering days of the late 1800s, had this midpoint. He was partially paralyzed after suffering a cerebral stroke (Mercury-Uranus affecting his Sun, symbolizing his health), but he continued with research for twenty-seven more years.

What about Moon = Mercury/Uranus? Actor Michael J. Fox has this midpoint. He was afflicted with Parkinson's Disease but continued acting despite this debilitating neurological dysfunction. Musician Peter Gabriel, known for electronic music, has this midpoint as well, as does the off-beat brilliant writer Oscar Wilde.

The midpoint configured with Mars (Ma=Me/Ur) is found in the chart of Tonight Show host Johnny Carson, and also in the chart of gun advocate Charleston Heston who spent years speaking about the second amendment rights. Assassinated politician Robert Kennedy has the midpoint, which also describes a brother (Mercury) suddenly (Uranus) killed with a gun (Mars).

Singer Anita Bryant has the midpoint pair focused through Jupiter (Ju=Me/Ur). She was an outspoken critic of Jim Morrison of the Doors and was the force behind "Save the Children," a reactionary movement against gay rights. Leonardo da Vinci also has this midpoint. Leonardo was an Italian Renaissance polymath whose areas of interest included invention, painting, sculpting, architecture, science, music, mathematics, engineering, literature, anatomy, geology, astronomy, botany, writing, history, and cartography. Leonardo is regarded by history as the prime exemplar of the Universal Genius or Renaissance Man, an individual of "unquenchable curiosity and feverishly inventive imagination." In this description, the magnanimous, far-reaching vision of Ju=Me/Ur comes pouring through.

The environmental artist Ansel Adams had Mercury/Uranus configured with Saturn. According to his biography, he may have been dyslexic and struggled in school, obtaining only the equivalent of an eighth-grade education. He had to choose between being a concert pianist or a photographer. He chose the latter and became a technical master. He worked tirelessly, 18-hour days, working through weekends and holidays. While this midpoint does not pertain specifically to photography (we would expect Neptune to be involved), Saturn = Mercury/Uranus reflects difficulty in learning, as well as hard work.

The midpoint Neptune = Mercury/Uranus is found in the charts of O.J. Simpson, Nancy Reagan, author Henry Miller, actor Mel Gibson, and musician Michael Hutchence. While not an astrologer herself, Nancy publicized astrology and was derided for it. O.J. Simpson played a wide range of roles: football star, broadcaster, actor, advertising spokesman, armed robber, kidnapper, prisoner, and possible murderer. Neptune describes OJ's fame and notoriety. He was an endless source of unusual and surprising news.

Pluto configured with the midpoint is found in the chart of Christa McAuliffe who was killed when the Challenger spaceship blew up soon after take-off. The midpoint Pluto = Mercury/Uranus describes a death in flight. Troubled painter Vincent Van Gogh has the same midpoint. He suffered psychotic episodes and delusions, and though he may have questioned his mental stability, he wasn't known to take good care of his health. Others considered him something of a madman. In his lifetime, he was considered a failure as a painter. Today he considered one of the art world's quintessential geniuses. For Van Gogh, his brilliance (Me/Ur) came with a dark side (Pl).

Singer-songwriter Neil Diamond has Node = Mercury/Uranus. Before becoming famous for performing, he toiled as a songwriter for other people. Sigmund Freud has the midpoint Midheaven = Mercury/Uranus. He spent his life researching the mind. Carl Jung had the midpoint Ascendant = Mercury/Uranus. He developed the technique of word association to glean insight into the unconscious. Jung also knew astrology and used it with his patients.

So far, we have looked at just one midpoint pair, Mercury/Uranus, and how the energy of the pair is expressed through various focal planets and points. Throughout the above descriptions, the combined essence of intelligence and mental innovation is clear.

HELP WITH DELINEATION

Ebertin's COSI is my primary source for midpoint delineation. I find his symbolism insightful, at times surprising, and often right on the mark. Two things combined with a third frequently produce an unexpected effect.

However, his language is at times abstruse. Noel Tyl updated midpoint meanings, and these are found in the appendix of his book *Solar Arcs and Prediction in Astrology*. His midpoint meanings help clarify and explain some of Ebertin's perplexing definitions.

Michael Munkasey's book *Midpoints: Unleashing the Power of the Planets* is also helpful and goes into great detail about the meaning of the midpoints and provides examples of people who have them. His companion book, *The Concept Dictionary*, lists themes in alphabetical order along with the midpoints that symbolize those themes.

In the rare case where the definition didn't appear to apply, I took the definition given in the midpoint pair. When that failed, I delineated my own meaning using the symbolism of the three planets. When we consider everything in this world cannot only be described by the planets but must be described by them, we can get creative.

THE ANGLES

As in the natal chart, the angles of the Ascendant and Midheaven are powerful in midpoints. Michael Munkasey offers a method for envisioning how they work in combination. For example, the Mo/As pair can be thought of as the Moon conjunct the Ascendant, or a Cancer Ascendant. The Ve/Mc pair can be thought of as a Taurus or Libra Mc, or as Venus conjunct the Mc. When an angle is at the focal point of a midpoint, the midpoint pair has an outlet and will likely be highly visible. Since the angles move quickly, on average about 1° every four minutes, angles in midpoints or at a focal point are uniquely personal. These midpoints form quickly and dissolve quickly. For this reason, they can be used to distinguish the charts of twins and to rectify or confirm birth times. They highlight the most personal traits in a natal chart.

VARIATIONS OF A THEME

In theory, two planets form a midpoint pair and produce an effect that is transmitted through a focal point. However, in practice, it appears the energy of the three planets co-mingle, and whichever player acts as the focal point is fluid not fixed. Take the midpoint of Venus = Mercury/Uranus, for example. Its expression is not necessarily always Me/Ur working through Venus. There is a similar theme seen with Me = Ve/Ur or Ur = Me/Ve. In essence, the three midpoints, generated from the same three planets, appear equivalent, such that:

Ve = Me/Ur ~ Me = Ve/Ur ~ Ur = Me/Ve

I call midpoints comprised of the same three planets, midpoint variants, in recognition of the fact that they are variations of a single theme.

Given this, in cases where we can't find an appropriate delineation for a midpoint pair or midpoint, we can look up the other two variant combinations to see if another definition is more relevant. For example, Ebertin found:

Ve = Me/Ur: an artistic feeling or perception, resonating with rhythm, or suddenly falling in love.

Me= Ve/Ur: artistic ideas, the ability to give stimulating ideas to other people, or the sudden emergence of love thoughts.

Ur = Me/Ve: inventive ability, the gift of getting ideas, an appreciation of the necessity of reform, rhythms, periods, numbers, and symbols. A mathematician, a public speaker full of ideas, and quick at repartee.

From these three definitions, we can see that these three planets together in any combination point to unusual brilliance, largesse thinking, humanitarianism, love, and an understanding of rhythm.

In summary, completed midpoints in a chart translate into behaviors and activities in life. Astrology symbolism needs to be connected to relevant events. The best teacher is experience. Working with midpoints in your own chart helps you equate them with the experiences of your life. You will be amazed to see the book you're reading, the politician you just heard, the movie you saw, or the idea you had, or the work you do, being shown in a midpoint—but this is how it works. Midpoints manifest with an uncanny distinctiveness throughout our daily experiences. With practice, you will notice the literal expression of midpoints leap off the page and into real life. As Charles Harvey and Michael Harding wrote, "If we listen, we can start to hear the midpoints making themselves heard." In the next chapter, we'll look at special midpoints that should be looked for in every chart.

 HOMEWORK: Delineate ten of your midpoints. Find examples of how they have been expressed in your life.

Chapter 4

Special Midpoints

S ome midpoint pairs are extra-special and should be looked for in every chart to see if they are completed. The most important pair is the Sun/Moon. While Sun/Moon externally symbolizes the union of a man and woman, or husband and wife, they also symbolize the inner marriage. According to Charles Harvey (*Working with Midpoints*, p. 57), "the midpoint (pair) is, as it were, the point of conjunctio of the alchemists, the point of inner marriage, where the inner masculine and feminine can potentially join in creative union. This is that point in the chart where the individual can relate to the world wholeheartedly, 'body and soul,' 'heart and mind,' where they can get themselves together and give themselves to their life with abundant creative energy and joyous self-surrender to their larger purpose." When this point is occupied, Charles says, "This additional (third) factor appears to act as a catalyst or focal point for this process of inner fusion. When this happens the whole of life will tend to become concentrated and at the same time suffused with the qualities of this third factor, or factors."

The Sun/Moon midpoint with Saturn (Sa = Su/Mo) was found in the charts of John F. Kennedy and his son, John F. Kennedy Jr., and manifested as ambition and focus. It is also found in the charts of Nancy Kerrigan, Mao Zedong, and Vincent Van Gogh.

Ebertin had the midpoint with Venus, as do singers Peter Gabriel, Paul Simon, and Lady Gaga. Hitler had the midpoint with Pluto, which depicts a dark use of power. Hillary Clinton and George Lucas had the pair configured with Neptune. Bob Dylan and David Koresh had the pair with Uranus, while Willie Nelson, Janis Joplin, and Jim Morrison had it with Jupiter.

In a precisely timed chart, the Ascendant/Midheaven midpoint pair is the second most important. According to Witte, this midpoint pair describes the place (As) and time (Mc). Charles Harvey wrote this is "how an event is brought into being at its own precise moment. The Ascendant refers to our persona, our place, or our response to the world; the Mc depicts our aims, goals, and life direction. Brought together, we get an idea of how we may orientate ourselves in life and the way in which we might actualize our conscious or professional ambitions. ... It is the way we self-actualize moment by moment. A planet on the As/Mc midpoint is something like a direct hit. The individual will almost certainly use that energy constantly in life, generally thriving on it."

Roy Orbison and David Koresh had Uranus on the As/Mc pair. Astrologers Christeen Skinner, Ivy Goldstein-Jacobson, and Dr. Margaret Millard have the pair completed with the Moon. Astrologers Marcia Moore and Terri McCartney have it with the Sun, as did John F. Kennedy. Teacher/astronaut Christa McAuliffe had the pair with her Mercury, as did Isaac Newton. The transgender Olympian Caitlyn (né Bruce) Jenner, musician Quincy Jones, and billionaires Bill Gates and Rupert Murdoch, have the pair completed with Venus.

Ebertin considered the weakest pair in the chart to be Saturn/Neptune. For him, it was a point of sickness. He routinely viewed Neptune in a negative light, and when combined with Saturn, the planet of structure, the dissolving nature of the outer planet Neptune added detrimental chaos. He called the principle of the pair, "Suffering, renunciation, asceticism. The chronic and unhampered progress of malady. Organic decomposition. Undermining circumstances leading to illness, diseases with causes difficult to ascertain. A struggle between the lower and higher nature. The readiness for sacrifice."

There are other ways to interpret the pair though, and they can also mean making dreams real, practical spirituality, or grounding inspiration. The completed pair often appears in the charts of doctors, healers, and chemists. Nonetheless, Ebertin is correct that this midpoint is often active in times of sickness.

Actor Michael J. Fox, who fought a public battle against Parkinson's, has Sa/Ne configured with the Sun. Former CNN host Larry King had the same midpoint and he battled heart disease, suffering a heart attack at fifty-three. Robert Downey Jr. has Sa/Ne = Su and his weakness was drugs. After multiple public offenses, he went to prison for a year. Neptune (drugs) derailed his professional standing (Saturn), but true to the nature of redemptive Neptune, he rebounded and found new honor in a role as a superhero.

Ebertin called Mars/Saturn the death axis. For those with the completed midpoint, the axis is nearly always active at the time of physical death. However, the pair is also associated with figurative death and persistent hard work. Nonetheless, when the traditional malefics are together, Ebertin considered them to produce "Harmful or destructive energy, inhibited or destroyed vitality. Concentrated energy (is) either outwardly expressed as violence or inwardly shown as destructive power, hardness, harshness, or bitterness. There is also the tendency to get hurt or injured. Periods of impotence and weakness alternate with periods of brutal or ruthless progress." On a positive note, there is energy to overcome difficulties. Alternatively, a lack of energy to overcome them.

The midpoint Mars/Saturn = Sun is found in Jacqueline Kennedy's chart. After the assassination of her husband, the life she knew ended. Given the symbolism of the Sun as the husband, this midpoint also describes his death. Harvey Milk, the gay Californian politician also had Su = Ma/Sa. He did much to advance gay rights—an effort ascribed to Mars (sex) and Saturn (government), and he too was murdered. Freud had this midpoint, and the basis of his psychological theory was sexual repression and the unconscious motivation of an inherent death wish. Actress Natasha Richardson, of the famous Redgrave family, died in Montreal at 45 after a head injury from a skiing accident. She too had Sun = Mars/Saturn.

Mars/Neptune is a midpoint associated with infectious disease, alcoholism, and, in the case of the US chart, military battles at sea. For Ebertin, it is another point of weakness. He considered it to represent a lack of energy, paralysis of the muscles, sick people, a craving for drugs, the misfortune to suffer harm or exploitation, a dislike of work, but also inspiration, lots of plans, and help at the right time. To this, I would add high creativity, active imagination, and spiritual work. It also frequently shows up in charts of hurricanes.

Configured with the Sun, this midpoint appears in the chart of Robert Downey, Jr. and represents his battle with drugs. Oprah Winfrey has this midpoint, and among other things, she is a self-help guru and an advocate of spirituality. The politician Ted Kennedy had the midpoint, which expressed as alcoholism (active escapism) but also recovery (active spiritual work). Katie Holmes, former wife of Tom Cruise, has Su = Ma/Ne and she fought the influence of his religion Scientology.

The Jupiter/Uranus combination is a lucky midpoint that Ebertin called "Thank the Lord." He found the midpoint's manner of expression hard to pin down but found that it symbolized fortune. It represents "the principle of optimism, a lucky chance, blissful realizations." US President Barack Obama has this midpoint completed with the Sun, as did serial killer Ted Bundy, which may explain how he got away with murder. Princess Margaret had the same midpoint and she benefited from the monarchy without having to shoulder its responsibility. The completed midpoint is frequently found in the charts of lottery winners.

Sports figures often have the completed midpoint of Sun/Mars. O.J. Simpson and tennis great Steffi Graf had this midpoint completed with the Moon. Olympic sprinter Carl Lewis had it configured with Jupiter.

The Saturn/Pluto pair is difficult. Noel Tyl called the completed midpoint "alarming." Ebertin considered the principle of the pair to be hard labor and cruelty. On the positive side, it contributes "tenacity and toughness, endurance, the capacity to make record efforts of the highest possible order, the ability to perform the most difficult work with extreme self-discipline, self-denial, and renunciation." On a negative note, he found the pair associated with "a hard and unfeeling disposition, also cold-heartedness, severity, a tendency to violence, and a fanatical adherence to one's principle's once they have been adopted." Princess Diana had this midpoint pair completed by the Moon, as did Robin Williams and conservative political activist David Koch. Jim Jones and Ferdinand Marcos had the midpoint with Venus. Madonna, F. Scott Fitzgerald, and Hitler had it with Jupiter.

The completed Jupiter/Pluto midpoint is the millionaire's midpoint. Ebertin calls it the desire for power. Also, it describes a desire to lead the masses, exploit the masses (plutocracy), or the pursuit of fanatical aims. It shows the quality of leadership, and also the leading of uprisings, as well as the misfortune of losing everything. Michael Crichton, Harrison Ford, Elton John, and Janis Joplin had this midpoint configured with the Sun. Princess Diana and Neil DeGrasse Tyson had it with the Moon. Gann, the financial wizard, had it completed with Saturn.

A few other special midpoint pairs to be aware of is the "prone to accident" pair of Mars/Uranus, which can also mean surgery or childbirth. Venus/Uranus also shows childbirth. Mercury/Venus is the writer's pair and, as we saw, Mercury/Uranus is the astrology pair. Jupiter/Neptune is the speculation pair and is often seen in the chart of investors and lottery winners. Sun/Jupiter is the success pair.

In general, Ebertin wrote that success corresponds to combinations of the Sun, Mars, Jupiter, and Pluto. These combine in the form of Su/Ma, Su/Ju, Su/Pl, Ma/Ju, Ma/Pl, and Ju/Pl.

For vocation information, look to the midpoints of Mercury and Mars, which symbolize thought and action. Creative artists including writers have combinations of Sun, Mercury, Venus, Jupiter, and Uranus. If Pluto is a third factor, there is extraordinary success. The Venus/Mars pair is highly creative.

Midpoints that are comprised of a planet and angle are particularly potent. According to Charles Harvey, "When the angles lock into the picture, the planetary energy they trigger is far more likely to be expressed in life than a three-planet combination by itself." This is amplified when there are two angles in a midpoint—the lone planet tends to be highly energized and visible.

In summary, there are a handful of special midpoints that are easy to memorize. They are listed in Appendix 2. To find them in a chart, it's a simple process of scanning the midpoint trees (which we'll address in the next chapter) and looking for them. Also, be sure to note the midpoints comprised of one or two angles.

HOMEWORK: Examine your 180° midpoint tree list and circle your special midpoints. Double circle or star the Su/Mo and As/Mc midpoint if they are completed. Underline all natal midpoints that contain an angle, and double underline the midpoints that contain two angles. Delineate these midpoints if you haven't already done so.

Chapter 5

Interpreting Midpoint Trees

A midpoint axis is a line drawn from a focal planet to its opposite degree. Also called a midpoint tree, it is a handy way of showing all the midpoint pairs configured with a planet or point. We can see at a glance the number of pairs associated with any planet and its orb. The closest midpoints are likely the strongest. We can scan the axes to find the special midpoints, including their variants. To interpret an axis we break it down into its individual midpoints and determine the meaning of each. On average, a typical timed chart contains around 15 to 20 direct completed midpoints.

As we have seen, some planets are configured with several midpoint pairs, and some planets are not. Look at the trees shown in Figure 8 on page 32. We can see there is no tree listed for either Uranus or the Ascendant because these are not configured with a midpoint pair using our orb of 1 ½ °. Saturn and Neptune are listed because they are in tight opposition and share the same axis. However, neither is configured with any midpoint pairs. The remaining planets have one to three midpoint pairs.

Look at the axis of the Moon. It is at the midpoints of Me/Ve and Sa/Ne. To interpret this axis, we break it down into its individual midpoints, Mo = Me/Ve, and Mo = Su/Ne, and consider the meaning of each.

The Midheaven has two midpoint pairs and Jupiter on the axis. We break down the tree and get the midpoints: Mc = Ur/No and Mc = Ju/No. Do we combine Jupiter with these midpoint pairs? No. For Jupiter's midpoints, we look to the Jupiter axis. There we find Ju = Ur/Mc = Mc. These two axes have different midpoint pairs, unique to each focal point. However, on both axes, there is Mc = Ju. This is telling us there is an aspect (either conjunction or opposition) between Jupiter and the Midheaven. In this case, it is a conjunction.

The number of midpoints on a tree adds complexity to the meaning and expression of the focal point. The nature of the pairs lends insight into whether the focal point is likely to have problems, be successful, or of mixed nature. Look at Evangeline Adams's Mercury tree in Figure 7 on page 14. It is at the midpoint of Ve/Ma (creativity), Su/Ju (success), and Ma/As (hard working, disputes). These are nice midpoints and bode well for the function of her Mercury. Also, if someone is going to pick a fight with her, they will likely lose, thanks to Su/Ju.

The Mars axis is not so benign. We can see Mars is important because it is at the midpoint of As/Mc. But, Mars is also aligned with the sickness pair Sa/Ne, giving lack of energy, listlessness and lack of creative energy, as well as weak procreative powers, and inactivity through emotional depression or sickness. However, this midpoint could apply to her clients. The Ve/Mc is helpful because, at the end of the day, the intent of her work (Ma) was to make her clients happy (Ve/Mc).

Looking at individual midpoints on an axis with multiple midpoints makes midpoint variants easier to see. Evangeline Adams has the millionaire midpoint of Ne = Ju/Pl, which includes the occult variant Ju = Ne/Pl, and the speculation midpoint Pl = Ju/Ne. She has the illness variant Ne = Mo/Sa along with Ma = Sa/Ne.

CHART CONFIGURATIONS

One feature that Ebertin seems to have neglected, as did Charles Harvey and Michael Harding in *Working With Astrology,* is the fact that any tight three-planet configuration in the chart—such as a yod, t-square, or grand trine—forms a midpoint. Uranian astrologers pay attention to this fact. Look at the chart shown in Figure 9 (on page 32). It is the chart from which the trees in Figure 8 were generated. I'm not going to go into detail about this man who was an agronomist and studied soil and crop production at university; he went on to become Hitler's Chief of Police and Minister of the Interior who established Germany's concentration camps. Heinrich Himmler's chart shows multiple configurations. He had a t-square comprised of the Moon square an opposition of Saturn and Neptune, which gives the midpoint Mo = Sa/Ne. He had a yod formed with a quincunx of the Moon to Mercury, and Moon to Venus, which gives Mo = Me/Ve. He had a mini-trine configuration of Mercury sextile Venus and sextile Saturn: Me = Ve/Sa.

Modulus 180°00' – Max Orb 1°30'

* ☽ *	(Orb)	* ☉ *	(Orb)	* ☿ *	(Orb)
☿/♀	−0°35' d	♆/As	+1°05' d	♀/♄	−1°12' d
♄/♆	−0°55' d				

Mc	(Orb)	* ♃ *	(Orb)	* ♆ *	(Orb)
♅/☊	−0°28' d	♅/Mc	+0°20' d	♄/Mc	+0°25' d
* ♃ *	+1°04' d	*Mc*	−1°04' d	♃/♄	+0°57' d
♃/☊	−1°21' d			♄/☊	−1°28' d

* ♄ *	(Orb)	* ♂ *	(Orb)	* ♀ *	(Orb)
* ♆ *	−0°09' d	☽/♅	−1°24' d	☿/♆	+0°52' d

Figure 8. Example 2 180° trees

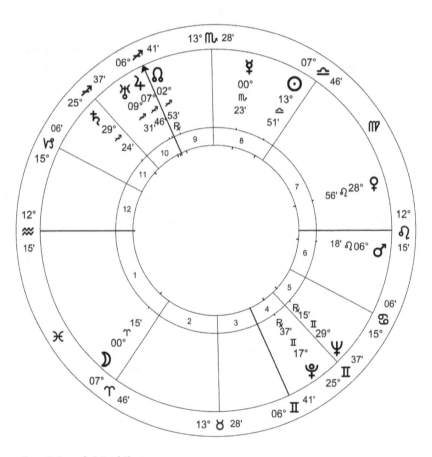

Figure 9. Example 2 Natal Chart

We can see the planets in these configurations in the midpoint trees, and grasp what the configurations mean by looking up the midpoints in the COSI:

Mo = Sa/Ne: Emotional depression, pessimism, the inability to develop or mature emotionally, a low character. Illness through emotional suffering, women's diseases; the methodical execution of plans, the slow attainment of success through intense activity and great painstaking effort. Painful or tormenting emotional inhibitions, and undermining circumstances also leading to a state of illness, neuroses, or diseases.

Mo = Me/Ve: The ability to shape plain surfaces, a talent for painting or drawing, a perception and feeling of beauty.

Me = Ve/Sa: Sober thinking, the visualization of stark reality, narrow-mindedness, or selfishness in love.

Note also that the Moon is the focal planet of two of these midpoints. It would appear the artistic Me/Ve was tainted by Sa/Ne, both to the detriment of his Moon—feelings, family, and women in general.

In summary, if you can delineate a midpoint, you can use the same skill to delineate a midpoint axis. To best understand how an axis works, look at them in your own chart to see how they are expressed.

 HOMEWORK: Examine your 180° Midpoint Tree List and delineate planetary axes of interest. Interpret the meaning of any configurations in your chart using midpoints.

Chapter 6

Natal Delineation Using Midpoints

Now that you know how to find and interpret midpoints, you can add these to natal chart delineation. In addition to looking at a planet's sign, house, dignity, and rulership, you can look at each planet's midpoints. In her book, *The Life Blueprint*, Jane Reynolds explained how to delineate a chart using Ebertin's COSI. I have not seen Ebertin use this method, but I assume that Jane learned the technique from cosmobiologists working in the late sixties. While this is not the method I use (in the chart I pay attention to dignity and house rulership) I'll go through it here for those who are interested. I'll use the traditional aspects of the conjunction, sextile, square, trine, and opposition, which most people use. Ebertin did not use the sextile or trine. I will use his orb, which is 5° for the Su, Mo, As, Mc (the personal points); 4° for Me, Ve, Ma; and 3° for Ju, Sa, Ur, Ne, Pl, No. The midpoint orb remains 1½°.

Ebertin's COSI simplifies chart interpretation. The beginning of the book is a cookbook in which he delineates planets in signs and houses. The midpoint pair delineations, given on the left side pages can be used to delineate aspects—the combination of two planets. The midpoints are delineated using the right-side pages—the combination of three planets.

As an example, we'll look at Evangeline Adams's chart and midpoints, which we have examined briefly in earlier chapters. The chart and 180° midpoint trees for the astrologer are shown in Figure 10. Before we look at the chart, here is a brief history taken verbatim from my book on the nodes:

> Working at the turn of the 20th Century when astrology was considered fortune-telling, Evangeline Adams elevated the practice of astrology to a science. Her family, distantly related to two presidents (John Adams and John Quincy Adams), was against

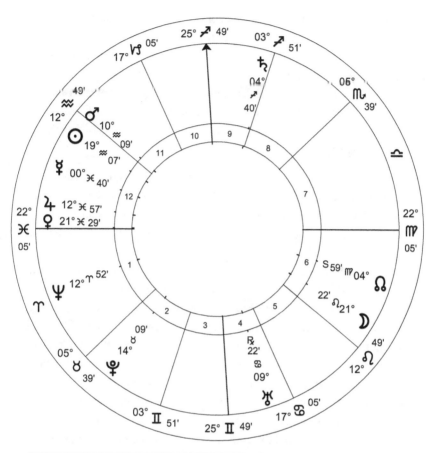

Midpoint Trees: Modulus 180°00' Max Orb 1°30'				
♆ Orb	♇ Orb	♅ Orb	♂ Orb	☉ Orb
☽ + ♄ 0°08' ☍	♀ ⊥ ♅ 1°16' ♂	♅ ⊥ ☋ 0°11' ♂	As + Mc 1°12' ♂	♆ + Mc 0°13' ♂
♃ ⊥ ♇ 0°40' ♂			♄ ⊥ ♆ 1°23' ♂	☿ ⊥ ♂ 1°18' ♂
☽ Orb	☿ Orb	☋ Orb	♃ Orb	♀ Orb
☿ ⊥ ♂ 0°57' ☍	♀ + ♂ 0°09' ♂	♅ + Mc 0°00' ☍	♂ ⊥ ♆ 1°26' ♂	☿ + ♆ 0°17' ♂
	☉ + ♃ 0°21' ♂	☉ + ♀ 0°19' ☍		♄ + ♅ 0°32' ☍
	♂ ⊥ As 0°27' ♂	☉ ⊥ As 0°37' ☍		As ⊥ As 0°35' ♂
As Orb				
♄ + ♅ 0°03' ☍				
☿ + ♆ 0°18' ♂				
♀ ⊥ ♀ 0°35' ♂				

Figure 10. Evangeline chart/midpoints

astrology, believing it to be heathenism. According to her, "Sometimes, as I look back, I smile to think how much easier it was to overcome the persecution of the law than the persecution of my own family. Naturally, I regarded the legalization of astrology as the finest thing an Adams had done since the signing of the Declaration of Independence. But the Adamses didn't think so! In fact, from the very beginning, they opposed my connection with astrology by every means within their power."

Nonetheless, after studying for ten years and recognizing auspicious progressions, Evangeline moved to New York and started her practice. On the day she moved, she gave a reading for her new landlord and predicted calamity. The next day his hotel burned to the ground, and she made headlines.

During the course of her career, she counseled over one hundred thousand clients, collaborated with Aleister Crowley, and read for Edgar Cayce, Joseph Campbell, and J.P. Morgan. She predicted the future of countries, monarchies, economies, and presidential elections. In forecasting, she used horary, progressions, and transits to the natal chart (without Pluto, which had not yet been discovered). She was arrested for practicing astrology and went to trial. She admitted using palmistry in astrology readings, but claimed she stayed true to her "science" and read the indications of the planets, "never claiming to know the future nor inform with certitude what would or would not come to pass." She was exonerated and brought legitimacy to the practice of astrology in the U.S.

While many today consider her clairvoyant and psychic, Evangeline believed she adhered to strict astrological rules. In a brochure she sold for ten cents she wrote, "The lesson of astrology is to teach you nature's intention as indicated by the planets; to deviate from it tends to failure, to know it gives power, to pursue it success." She strove to send her clients off with hope, and to never leave them "depressed or discouraged ... for inspiration to others is, in my philosophy, the soul of astrology." It was her whole life, and according to Aleister Crowley, "She talks astrology day and night. She dreams of it. She sets a horoscope for her vast family of cats and dogs, and is scared out of her life when some planet threatens her horoscope." When she died at the age of sixty-four, she had studied astrology for nearly forty-five years and had been a professional astrologer for thirty-five years.

NATAL DELINEATION USING THE COSI

For natal delineation, we'll go through the thirteen planets and points in turn. The following interpretations are based on and adapted from Ebertin's COSI. Following this, I'll give a summary of the planet. Note that Evangeline was born four hours after a Lunar Eclipse. She has 4 planets in the 12th house (Mars, Sun, Mercury, Jupiter), and an exalted Venus rising. She has the generational Uranus sextile Neptune.

Sun

Sun in Aquarius, in the 12th house, opposite Moon, square Pluto, at the midpoint Ne/Mc = Me/Ma:

Sun in Aquarius: observant, attention to detail, socially intuitive, understands human nature, rebels against authority or restriction; also shows help from others.

Sun in 12th house: reserved nature, receptive, quick to absorb information, patient, negligent, comfort loving.

Sun opposite Moon: A harmonious personality, internal balance, single-mindedness, either good or difficult personal partnerships, joint successes; represents the public life.

Sun square Pluto: power-hungry, a desire that craves to rule; the power to achieve goals, conscious aims, innovations, leadership. Can indicate sudden advancements in life or realization of new ideas. Also martyrdom.

Su = Ne/Mc: physical disguise, putting on an act, hiding one's character, pretentious.

Su = Me/Ma: assertive thinking and acting, bravery, a positive or firm demeanor, determination, the drive to succeed in life, easily excitable, quarrelsome; rash decisions.

We put this information together to get a sense of her Sun. Here, use all your astrological and life knowledge to understand her life force and mission. She was an astute woman with knowledge of human nature. The 12th house influence added compassion, intuition, and psychic perception. A Full Moon person needs other people, though others may cause problems. (Being born on a lunar eclipse reinforced this likelihood.) Connected to Pluto, the Sun had power and potential for leadership. But power could also be used against her. The Su = Ne/Mc indicated a career or public face based on spiritual or psychic matters. The Su = Me/Ma gave courage and energy she poured into writing and communication.

Moon

Moon in Leo in the 6th opposite the Sun, trine the Mc at the midpoint of Me/Ma.

Moon in Leo: Intuitive, instinctively creative, self-confident, generous, ambitious, social, passionate, loving luxury, pleasure, and amusement. Also indicates arrogance, snobbishness, and vanity. Affairs of the heart. Positions of responsibility.

Moon in the 6th house: head ruling the heart, practical, methodical, diligent and careful, tidy, proper behavior, simple, pedantic, and practical.

Moon opposite Sun: see above for Sun opposite Moon.

Moon trine Mc: deep emotion, a rich inner (soul) life, great aspirations, desire to care for others, appreciation of home and family.

Mo = Me/Ma: thinking and acting governed by emotion; a desire to clear the air either through argument or conversation, quarrelsome, a nagging or quarreling female.

This was a woman who needed to be noticed. She was intuitive, instinctive, ambitious, diligent, and practical. She needed other people to interact with and who recognized her talent. She talked a lot. She also had great spiritual depth.

Mercury

Mercury in Pisces in the 12th house at the midpoint of Ve/Ma, Su/Ju, and Ma/As.

Mercury in Pisces is a person who is easily influenced in thought by others, receptive to the thoughts of others, fanciful and imaginative, puts plans into action, philosophical.

Mercury in the 12th house: reiteration of the above.

Mercury square Saturn gives the 12th house Pisces Mercury much-needed grounding and practicality.

Me = Ve/Ma: thinking influenced by love, a tendency to delve into sexual problems in the relationship, a focus on love, marriage, and progeny; also actors and romance writers.

Me = Su/Ju: healthy body and healthy thought processes, productive thinking, effective modes of expression, reflecting on or studying health (medical doctor), a healthy outlook on life; success through thought, speech, and action; indicates good news, the conclusion of a contract or an agreement, recognition.

Me = Ma/As: argumentative, a sharp tongue, the desire for discussion. Disputes.

Summarizing these ideas, Evangeline had an intuitive, psychic mind that was attuned to others. She was creative and successful in writing. She spoke about love and health and had a positive outlook on life that she conveyed to others through counseling. She said what was on her mind.

Venus

Venus in Pisces on the cusp of the 1st house conjunct the Ascendant at the midpoint of Me/Ne and Sa/Ur.

Venus in Pisces: longing for love, driven by the emotional and sexual life, occasional lack of self-control, impressionable, easily seduced, carefree, a love of music and the arts.

Venus conjunct Ascendant gave a harmonious personality, sociableness, an appreciation of a beautiful and artfully furnished environment, artistic inclinations. Good vibes with others, a sense of beauty, good taste. Indicates working with women, and associations with people who lack good taste.

Ve = Me/Ne: rapturous imaginings, expecting too much of love, short-lived attraction and infatuation.

Ve = Sa/Ur: tensions in love life often leading to separation.

Here we see the strength of a powerful Venus (in exaltation) influencing self-expression and beautifying the environment. She would exhibit a charming personality. Her interactions would primarily be with women. Ve = Me/Ne can also mean speaking and thinking idealistically and artfully. She would see the beauty and best outcome of difficult situations. Rather than relating to sex, this Venus was used in her astrology practice where she tried to be upbeat with clients facing serious problems.

Mars

Mars in Aquarius on the cusp of the 12th house, square Pluto, sextile Neptune at the midpoint of As/Mc, Sa/Ne, Ve/Mc.

Mars in Aquarius: deliberative action, love of freedom, employing cutting-edge working methods, the desire to reform, teamwork, organization, independence.

Mars in the 12th house: hopefulness, a "wait and see" attitude, working silently, struggling for recognition, social activity, Interest in the occult; the inclination to join secret societies, craving alcohol, nicotine, etc.

Mars square Pluto: superhuman power, force, brutality, great self-confidence, obsessive work habits, working without break, ambitious, driven to succeed; also brutality and cruelty (given or received).

Mars sextile Neptune: control of feelings—mind over matter, inspirations, a lot of plans, help received at the right time.

Ma = As/Mc: the individual in action, a positive attitude toward family and colleagues, successful teamwork.

Ma = Sa/Ne: lack of energy, listlessness, lack of creative energy, weak procreative powers, inactivity through depression or mental illness.

Ma = Ve/Mc: an impulsive expression of sexuality (creativity), strong desire.

This 12th house Mars was hard at work behind the scenes trying to improve the human condition. Most of her consulting and writing work was done in private. The square to Pluto gave great ambition and obsession, and the input from Neptune gave inspiration. At the As/Mc degree where the four angles of the chart combine, this Mars had high energy and worked tirelessly. The pair of Sa/Ne seems more related to working practically with the other-world, counseling, and healing, as opposed to a chronic health problem. She was creative professionally, especially with her mail-order astrology business.

Jupiter

Jupiter, traditional ruler of the chart, in Pisces in the 12th house, sextile Pluto, at the midpoint of Ma/Ne.

Jupiter in Pisces: altruistic, kind-hearted, content, capacity for enjoyment, impressionable, enjoyment of alcohol, nicotine, etc.

Jupiter in the 12th, reiteration of Jupiter in Pisces.

Jupiter sextile Pluto: a desire for power and to lead the masses, a brilliant gift for organization, a spiritual and intellectual leader. Also indicates conflict with authority (arrest).

Ju = Ma/Ne: a rich imagination, sensitivity, inspiration, spiritual, a fortunate turn of events after disappointment (or disappointment under otherwise fortunate circumstances), unhappiness or ill luck in the midst of wealth, pulmonary diseases.

The great benefic in this chart was intuitive and humane. There was a softness to it that was magnified by the midpoint. Contained therein was the variant of Ma = Ju/Ne, which can mean work related to an expansive spiritual philosophy. Ju/Ne is the speculation pair, which when combined with Mars denoted predictive work. It can also show problems in court, as did Jupiter sextile to Pluto, where power can be used against you. The sextile spoke to Evangeline's organizational ability and vision to deliver quality information to the masses.

Saturn

Saturn in Sagittarius on the cusp of the 9th house square the nodes at the North Bending. No direct midpoints.

Saturn in Sagittarius: a strong sense of justice, religious aspirations, asceticism, philosophical research, prudence and discretion, a talent for the legal profession.

Saturn in the 9th: a reiteration of Saturn in Sagittarius.

Saturn square Node: isolation, separation, association with elderly (or experienced) persons, patronage from elders or experts, termination of blood relationships, cooperation or teamwork becoming increasingly difficult.

Traditionally the 9th house is the house of higher learning, which includes astrology. Saturn is also helpful in establishing a good reputation, growing a business, and lasting hard work. The problems she had with her family are shown by the square.

Uranus

Uranus in Cancer in the 4th square Neptune at the midpoint of Pl/No.

Uranus in Cancer: intuition, a quick exchange of ideas, association with peculiar or strange people, wanderlust, longing for faraway places (or the urge to break away from one's native country or parental home), rebellious.

Uranus in 4th: reiteration of Uranus in Cancer.

Uranus square Neptune bestowed development and growth of subconscious powers, inner vision and illumination, enlightenment, inspiration, idealism, an interest in spiritual subjects, and extraordinary and unusual inclinations. It describes mystics, mediums, and people involved in psychical research.

Ur = Pl/No: turmoil within a community, emotional suffering caused by separations. Noel Tyl adds to this the intense need for recognition and publicity; a need to crush the opposition.

Uranus described Evangeline's business and its operation from a hotel, as well as the nature of her clients and her estrangement from her family. The contact with Neptune depicts psychic ability. Pluto with Uranus gave brilliance, and the Node gave a desire to be the best in the group.

Neptune

Neptune in Aries in the 1st house square Uranus at the midpoint of Mo/Sa and Ju/Pl.

Neptune in Aries: the realization of inspiration, unselfish, a love of humanity, a delicate and sensitive nervous system, expanse of feeling, a longing to see distant countries; also community spirit.

Neptune in the 1st: reiteration of the above.

Neptune square Uranus we just looked at, which added enlightenment, idealism, and psychic ability.

Ne = Mo/Sa: feelings of inferiority, depression, a sad nature, lack of self-confidence, joylessness, anxiety, feeling sick in your soul.

Ne = Ju/Pl: deception, cheating and seduction; general disappointment, unknowingly suffering loss or damage caused by others.

Neptune in the 1st was another indicator of psychic ability. The midpoints were mostly difficult, but these likely described her emotionally distraught clients (Mo/Sa). Some were millionaires (Ju/Pl).

Pluto

Pluto in Taurus in the 2nd house, sextile Jupiter at the midpoint of Ve/Ur.

Pluto in Taurus: the urge to acquire, striving for possessions, over-dependence on material wealth, great gain or loss influenced by circumstance.

Pluto in the 2nd: reiteration of the above.

Pluto sextile Jupiter: need for power and organization, possible conflicts with authorities, including arrest.

Pl = Ve/Ur: highly excitable; blind love. Tyl adds fated attraction; the enormous thrust of love needs and activity; potential notoriety; possible exhibitionism.

This Pluto was busy making money and dealing with the masses, including millionaires. Exhibitionism manifested as the willingness to promote herself and her abilities. She had a problem with authority, and power was used against her. American astrologers are indebted to her for her fight to legitimize astrology and raise its stature to a science rather than a parlor game.

Node

The North Node in Virgo in the 6th house, square Saturn, at the midpoint of Pl/Mc, Su/Ve, and Su/As.

Node in Virgo: work and scientific associations, connection with teaching or research institutes.

Node in 6th house: reiteration of the above.

Node square Saturn: older associates, separation, increasingly difficult teamwork.

No = Pl/Mc: acquiring leadership by force over a community or group of people; power and influence over others.

No = Su/Ve: social contact with loving and kind-hearted people, association with art lovers and artistic events.

No = Su/As: a helpful nature, seeking contacts, one's attitude to others, acquaintances or contacts, and associations.

The Node described her consulting business and the influence she obtained in society as an astrologer. Face-to-face contact with other people was important—a behind-the-scenes mail-order business would never have been enough.

Ascendant

The Ascendant in Pisces conjunct Venus at the midpoint of Sa/Ur and Me/Ne.

A Pisces Ascendant gives a peculiar, lonely, and simple person; reserve, inhibition, timidity; a passive and inactive nature; abundance of feeling;-tendency to become depressed.

Ascendant conjunct Venus imparts a harmonious personality, sociableness, a sense of a beautiful environment, and affectionate behavior toward others.

As = Sa/Ur: being placed in difficult circumstances, the fate of standing alone in the world. Also suffering difficulties caused by others, experiencing emotional suffering with others, mourning, and bereavement.

As = Me/Ne: easily influenced by others, being exploited, deceived, or harmed by others.

The Pisces energy described by Ebertin does not fit her personality, and more likely describes those in her environment (her clients). A Pisces Ascendant with Venus rising denotes humanity, empathy, and idealism, and desire to improve the status quo. The midpoints show the deceit she experienced from the police, who set up a sham counseling session and used it as the basis for her arrest.

Midheaven

Midheaven in Sagittarius trine the Moon, aligned with no direct midpoints.

Sagittarius Mc: the need for material security and respect, great planning power, expansive mind, spiritual or inner growth, adventurous aspirations, conservative attitude, the need to be seen as a person of importance, craving the limelight.

Mc trine the Moon: deep feeling and a rich inner life, great aspirations, caring for others.

This is an ambitious Midheaven in need of a career or life direction that employed and developed the inner world and the mind, and was put in service to the profession in a manner that helped others.

In summary, Ebertin's delineations captured and reflected Evangeline's life. By paying attention to what was being repeated, we see dominant themes. She was psychic, ambitious, had a need to work with people and be influential and financially powerful. She was sympathetic, empathetic, and motivated to improve the human condition. Note that none of this pointed to astrology as the central thread that would pull the chart together and give meaning to her life.

Adding direct midpoints to a chart adds detail and repetition which echo important themes. In a natal chart, anything of importance is repeated. This is amplified with midpoints. When you use midpoints, the repeating themes become obvious and reveal a planet's modus operandi and motivation. A midpoint axis helps answer the question: What type of planet is this and what effects might it produce?

 HOMEWORK: Use Ebertin's method to delineate your chart and its midpoints.

Chapter 7

Introducing the Dial and 8th Harmonic Aspects

U p until now, we have been looking at direct midpoints in the 360° chart. However, midpoints (and minor hard aspects) are much easier to find in the 90° dial. An example chart is shown in Figure 11, with the corresponding dial in Figure 12 on page 48. (This is the dial generated by the software Nova Chartwheels.) Note the dial has no houses and no signs—just an array of planets situated around a circle.

To transform a chart into a dial, imagine cutting the 360°chart at 0° Aries. For this chart, the cut would take place around the middle of the 9th house. Making a single cut in a circle gives a straight line. This is shown in the top modulus strip in Figure 13 on page 49. In this format, the signs are shown in absolute longitude degree notation so that Aries encompasses 0-30°, Taurus 30-60°, Gemini 60-90° and so on up to Pisces 330-360°. We can see from the strip that this chart has no planets in Capricorn, Aquarius, or Pisces.

If we cut the 360° strip in half by making a cut at 180° and move the second piece to line it up with the first, we get the 180° modulus shown in Figure 13b. In the chart (Figure 11), the opposition of Jupiter and the North Node stand together in the 180°modulus format.

If we now cut the 180° modulus in half and line up these two pieces, we get a 90° modulus (Figure 13c). In this format, all the cardinal planets are found from 0-30°; all the fixed planets are found between 30-60°; and all the mutable planets are found from 60-90°. In this chart, the first planet after the Aries Point is Venus at 2°Libra. In order, the remaining cardinal points are Neptune at 10°Libra, Midheaven at 12°Aries, Mercury at 15°Libra, Mars at 24°Cancer, and the Ascendant at 29°Cancer. Thus, all the points in cardinal signs fall in this 30° swath. Using this method, we don't know what

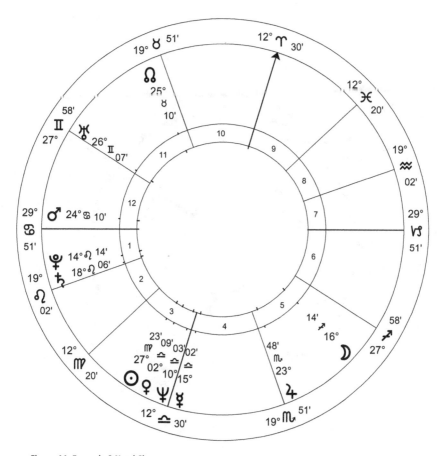

Figure 11. Example 3 Natal Chart

precise cardinal sign these planets are in, but since we aren't concerned with the signs, it doesn't matter. The fixed points fall in the next 30° swath and include Pluto at 14°Leo, Saturn at 18°Leo, Jupiter at 23°Scorpio and the North Node at 25°Taurus. The final swath has the 30° of mutable points: Moon at 16°Sagittarius, Uranus at 26° Gemini, and the Sun at 27° Virgo.

By this method, we have divided the wheel into quarters and wrapped the quarters around themselves four times, and superimposed the planets where they fall. We then recreate the circle by joining 0° Aries and 0° Cancer, which gives the 90° dial shown in Figure 12. If you compare the 90°strip (Figure 13C) with the dial, you will see the order of the planets in both is the same.

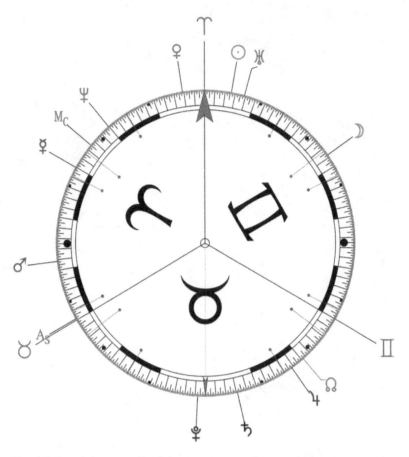

Figure 12. Example 3 corresponding dial

WORKING WITH THE DIAL

In standard dial format, the Aries Point is always placed at the top and represents 0° degrees of the four cardinal signs. There are two large dots halfway down each side of the dial and these denote 22½ degree points. The smaller dots on the dial mark the 11¼° and 5¾°—aspects Uranian astrologers use.

The markings on the dial's outer ring serve as useful counters (Figure 14). The alternating black and white bands on the inside of the dial mark 5° of arc. Each degree itself is marked by a long line. The degree is further divided in half by a short line in the middle that shows half a degree or 30'.

360° Modulus Strip **(A)**

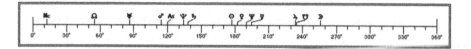

180° Modulus Strip **(B)**

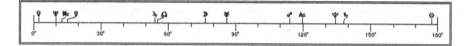

90° Modulus Strip **(C)**

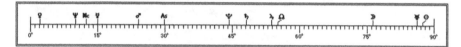

45° Modulus Strip **(D)**

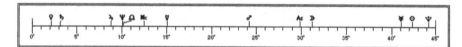

Figure 13. Example 3 Corresponding Modulus Strips

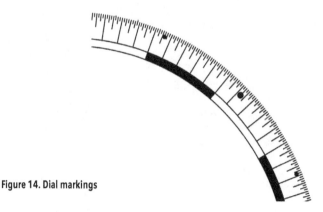

Figure 14. Dial markings

49

The smallest line shows a quarter of a degree or 15'. With the arrow on Aries (Figure 12), we can see Venus just past 2°. The Sun is about 2°½ degrees clockwise the other way, which puts it at 27°½ mutable. We can see Neptune at around 10° cardinal, and Saturn at about 18° fixed.

When the pointer is placed on the Aries Point, it resembles a tripod that divides the dial into three equal parts of 30°. These three parts denote the cardinal, fixed, and mutable sectors. When the axis is moved off the Aries Point, these baselines continue to show an arc distance of 30°.

A dial can also be drawn from a chart in Solar Fire (Figure 15). Open the View Chart option and on the top right side under the list of viewed charts a drop-down menu toggles between a wheel and a dial. In the Solar

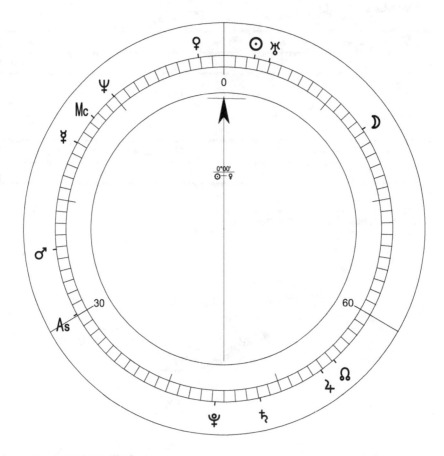

Figure 15. Solar Fire's Dial

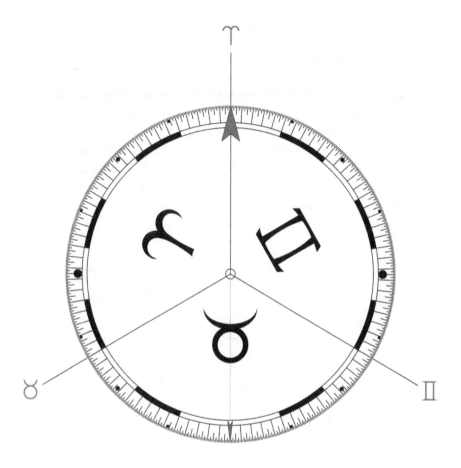

Figure 16. Blank dial. This dial and those used in the text are made using Nova Chartwheels.

Fire dial, the degree lines are shown, with a longer mark at every 10th degree. The 30 and 60 indicate the beginning of the fixed and mutable sections respectively. You can also construct a dial using the Ebertin-style chart at *www.astro.com*. Dials can also be purchased through *www.urani-anastrologybooks.com*. A blank dial that can be copied and laminated is shown in Figure 16.

ASPECTS ON THE DIAL

In Cosmobiology, only the hard aspects are used. These include the conjunction, square, and opposition, as well as the semisquare (45°) and sesquisquare (135°). These are the 8th harmonic aspects that are derived by dividing the circle into eight pieces (Figure 17). While traditionally, the 45° and 135° angles were considered "minor" aspects, in practice this is not the case. According to Ebertin, the derivatives of the square are all aspects of action. These five aspects are considered equivalent, as denoted by the equal sign (=). While these minor aspects are hard to see in a chart, they are obvious in a dial where they appear as an opposition. The 8th harmonic

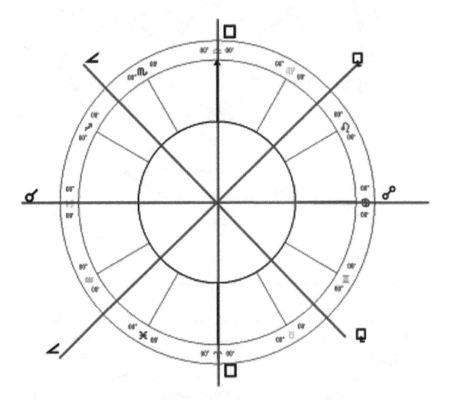

Hard aspects: ♂ ☍ ◻ ∠ ⋤ – 8th harmonic

∠: 45° semi–square
⋤: 135° sesquisquare

Figure 17. Hard aspects in a chart

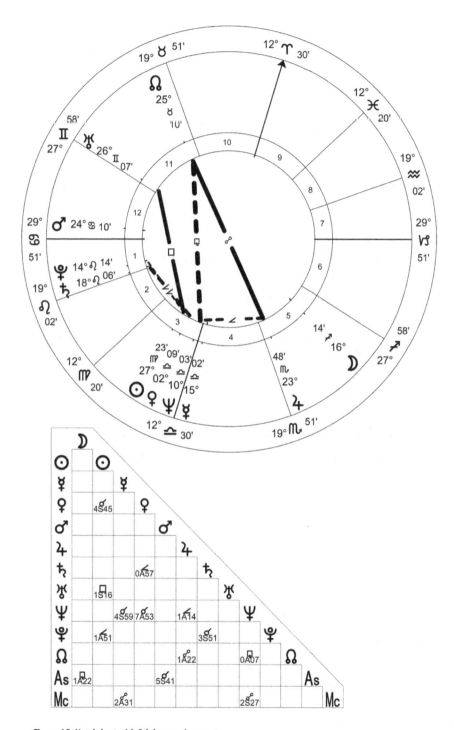

Figure 18. Natal chart with 8th harmonic aspects

53

aspects can also be generated in the aspectarian, using the aspect type set to this harmonic (Figure 18).

In the dial, the major aspects—the conjunction, square, and opposition—overlap and stand together. This is because they are all multiples of 90° (so when they are wrapped, they end up on top of each other). The minor aspects of the sesquisquare and semisquare, which are multiples of 45, share the same axis and are found on the opposite end of the pointer (90 divided by 2). In the dial shown in Figure 12 (page 48), we can see Jupiter on the axis with Neptune, which tells us they form an aspect of either 45° or 135°. A glance at the chart in Figure 11 (page 47) shows it to be the semisquare. There is also a cluster of Neptune, Midheaven, and Mercury as seen on the dial. The chart shows Mercury conjunct Neptune in opposition to the Midheaven.

By moving the arrow around the dial (the so-called movable dial) from planet to planet, the major and minor aspects stand out. Ebertin used the same aspect orb on the dial that he used in the chart. The orb for the personal points of the Sun, Moon, Ascendant, and Midheaven is 5°. The orb for the inner planets of Mercury, Venus, and Mars is 4°. The orb for Jupiter, Saturn, Uranus, Neptune, Pluto, and the Node is 3°.

 HOMEWORK: Look at your chart on a dial. Find all your 8th harmonic aspects. Do the minor hard aspects add pertinent information that was previously overlooked?

Chapter 8

Midpoints on the Dial

N ot only is the dial uniquely suited to showing minor 8th harmonic aspects, but it is also an excellent tool for finding midpoints. Up until now, we have ignored aspects to midpoints, and only looked at direct midpoints—those that had a planet on the degree of a midpoint pair, at the short (conjunction) or long (opposition) arc degree. However, Witte and Ebertin found that aspects to midpoint degrees are also valid. Not only that, but they also found that a hard 8th harmonic aspect to a midpoint is as powerful as a direct midpoint. Midpoints completed by an aspect other than the conjunction are indirect midpoints. (Even though the midpoints formed by a conjunction and opposition are equivalent, when considering aspects, only a pair completed by a conjunction is called direct.)

If we look at the chart shown in Figure 19 (pages 56–57), we can see that Venus forms a direct midpoint with Su/Ne, because Venus is sitting directly on their midpoint (Figure 19a). Look at Ma/Ur. Their midpoint is around 10° Cancer. There is nothing on that degree or opposite to it, but Neptune at 10° Libra makes a partile square to the midpoint (Figure 19b). This gives the indirect midpoint Ne = Ma/Ur. Look at Mercury and Pluto and envision their midpoint at about 14° Virgo. The Ascendant at 29° Cancer forms a semi-square to this degree (Figure 19c), giving the midpoint As = Me/Pl. All these midpoints are valid and similar in strength. Again, for this reason, we use the equal sign. The exact type of aspect doesn't matter.

Are some midpoints more important than others? We looked at special midpoint pairs earlier and they are equally strong when a planet casts a hard aspect to the midpoint degree. Any midpoints formed with the personal points of the Sun, Moon, Ascendant, or Midheaven are important. In Solar Fire, there is a feature in the "Reports" section named MWA (for Munkasey Midpoint Weighted Analysis) which ranks the importance of midpoint pairs. On the top left side of the page, there is a list of pairs numbered from 1 to 78. The highest ranked are those that his analysis found the most significant.

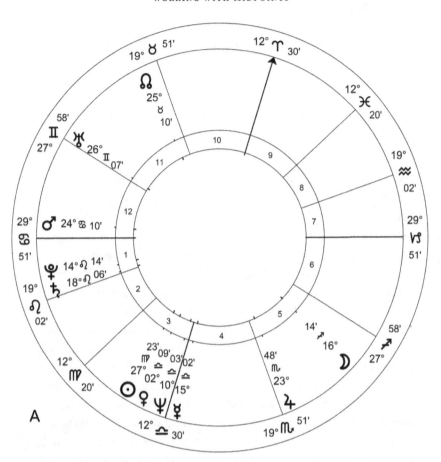

A

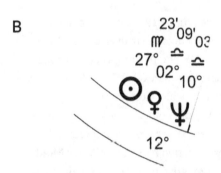

B

Figure 19 (A through D). Direct and Indirect midpoints

C

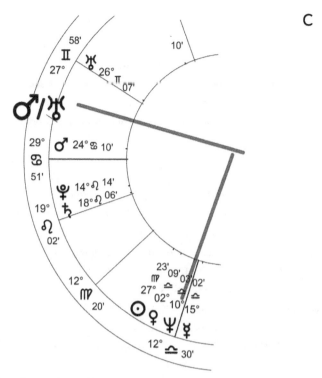

Figure 19C. Indirect midpoint of Neptune square Ma/Ur.

D

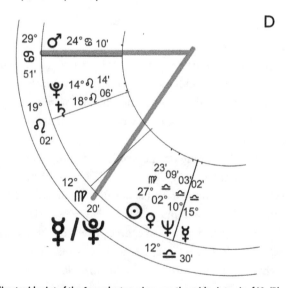

Figure 19D. The indirect midpoint of the Ascendant semi-square the midpoint pair of Me/Pl.

FINDING MIDPOINTS ON THE DIAL

Indirect midpoints are easy to find on the dial. I start with the pointer on the Aries Point and move the pointer counterclockwise around the dial (in the order of natural movement), examining the axis of each planet and point in turn. The orb used on the dial is 1½°, the same as used in the chart. With the pointer set on a planet, I move the pointer 1½° turn to the right and then to the left. This picks up midpoints that are off the axis but within orb. If a midpoint pair is 1 ½° before the planet, that midpoint pair is hit first by a transit or solar arc. If a midpoint pair is 1½° after a planet, it will be hit later. I jot down the midpoints and delineate each one separately.

I'll go through the method using the dial we first saw in Figure 12, now represented as Figures 20A through 20M with the pointers now turned 1½° to the right. (I delineate the axes in the next chapter). Here, I will outline how to find the midpoints and minor 8th harmonic aspects, and how to break down an axis into its component pieces that can be delineated. Since there are thirteen planets and points, we'll look at thirteen axes.

In Figure 20a, the pointer is set on Venus. We can see that Saturn is on the axis as well as three midpoint pairs. In sum, the Venus axis has Ve = Ur/Ne = Sa/Pl = Mo/Me = Sa. We expand this into its component parts and get:

Ve = Sa

Ve = Ur/Ne

Ve = Sa/Pl

Ve = Mo/Me

Even though Saturn is on the axis, I don't combine its midpoints here, because these will be addressed when we look at the Saturn axis. Here the focus is on Venus and the midpoints and 8th harmonic aspects associated solely with her. For delineation, we can look up the meaning of these in the COSI.

The axis of Neptune on the dial is shown in Figure 20b. Here we can see it is at the accident midpoint of Ma/Ur. If we shift the pointer a bit to the left, we pick up Su/Ma. On the far side of the pointer, we find the Node and Jupiter. In total, on the Neptune axis, we have: Ne = Ma/Ur = Su/Ma = No = Ju and Ne = Me/Ve. Here we have three planets on the axis in hard aspect to each other. To deal with them, we can look up all three variants of Ne = Ju = No, which would include: Ne = Ju/No; Ju = Ne/No; and No = Ju/Ne. Otherwise, we could look up Ne = Ju/No which is also a midpoint on the axis.

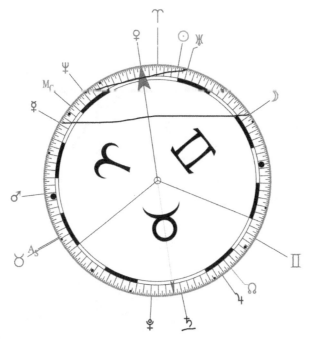

Figure 20A. Venus axis on the dial

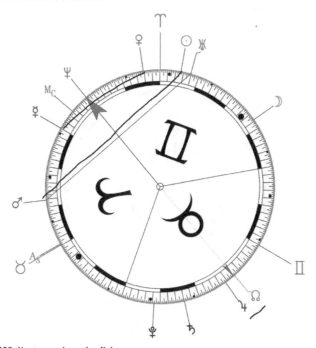

Figure 20B. Neptune axis on the dial

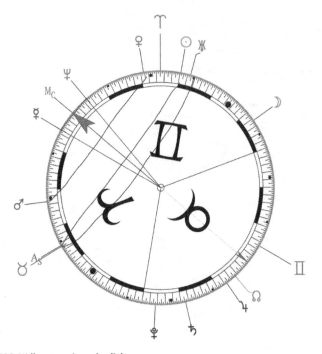

Figure 20C. Midheaven axis on the dial

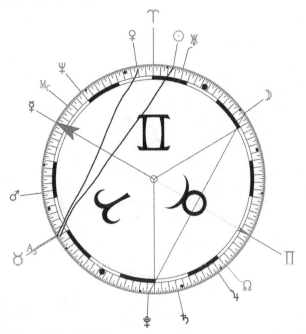

Figure 20D. Mercury axis on the dial

In short, we break the axis into the component pieces and delineate:

Ne = No = Ju

Ne = Ma/Ur

Ne = Su/Ma

Ne = Me/Ve

Since we are looking only at the Neptune axis, we ignore the midpoints formed using Jupiter and the Node. We will look at the midpoints associated with Jupiter and the Node when we come to them.

The axis of the Midheaven is shown in Figure 20c. On this axis we have: Mc = Me/Ne = Ur/As = Ve/Ma = Su/As. Breaking this into midpoints give:

Mc = Me/Ne

Mc = Ur/As

Mc = Ve/Ma

Mc = Su/As

The axis of Mercury is shown in Figure 20d. This axis has three midpoints: Me = Mo/Pl = Ve/As = Su/As. The midpoints are:

Me = Mo/Pl

Me = Ve/As

Me = Su/As

The Mars axis is shown in Figure 20e (page 62). There are six midpoints on this axis: Ma = Ju/Ur = Ve/Sa = Ve/Pl = Su/Ju = Su/Sa = Ur/No. This breaks down to:

Ma = Ju/Ur

Ma = Ve/Sa

Ma = Ve/Pl

Ma = Su/Ju

Ma = Su/Sa

Ma = Ur/No

The axis of the Ascendant has five midpoints and is in aspect to the Moon at the far end of the pointer (Figure 20f). This gives: As = Me/Pl = Sa/Mc = Sa/Ne = Ve/No = Pl/Mc = Mo. Expanding this into the component pieces we get:

As = Mo

As = Me/Pl

As = Sa/Mc

As = Sa/Ne

As = Ve/No

As = Pl/Mc

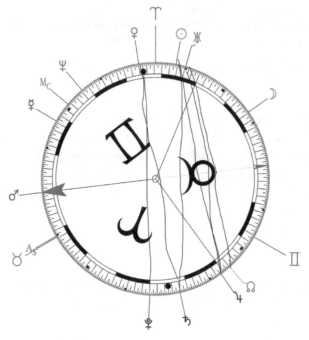

Figure 20E. Mars axis on the dial

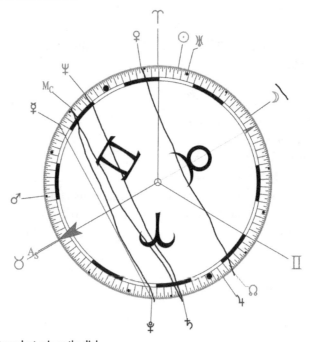

Figure 20F. Ascendant axis on the dial

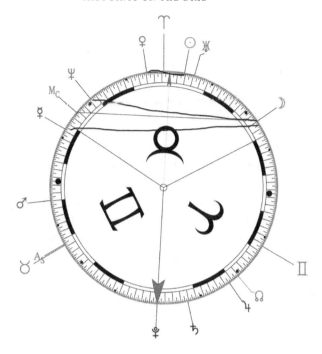

Figure 20G. Pluto axis on the dial

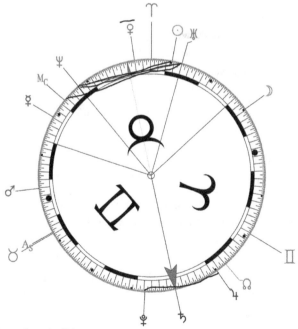

Figure 20H. Saturn axis on the dial

The Pluto axis is shown in Figure 20g. It has five midpoints: Pl = Ve/Ur = Mo/Mc = Su/Ve = Mo/Ne = Mo/Ve. This breaks down to:

Pl = Ve/Ur

Pl = Mo/Mc

Pl = Su/Ve

Pl = Mo/Ne

Pl = Mo/Ve

The Saturn axis is shown in Figure 20h. Venus is on the far end of the axis and there are 4 midpoints: Sa = Ur/Ne = Su/Ne = Ju/Pl = Ur/Mc = Ve. We have already looked at the Ve = Sa combination when we were examining the Venus axis, so we don't have to repeat it here, but for the sake of being comprehensive, I will. But there is no difference between Ve = Sa and Sa = Ve. Nor is this a repeated aspect. The main point is that Venus and Saturn are on the same axis and affect each other. When we break down this axis we get:

Sa = Ve

Sa = Ur/Ne

Sa = Su/Ne

Sa = Ju/Pl

Sa = Ur/Mc

The Jupiter axis is shown in Figure 20i. The Node is within orb to Jupiter and Neptune is on the far end of the axis. There are four midpoints. In total we have: Ju = No = Me/Ve = Mo/As = Ma/Ur = Ve/Mc = Ne. Expanding this gives:

Ju = No = Ne (or Ju = No/Ne or No = Ju/Ne or Ne = Ju/No)

Ju = Me/Ve

Ju = Mo/As

Ju = Ma/Ur

Ju = Ve/Mc

Given its proximity, not surprisingly, the axis of the Node shares some of Jupiter's midpoints and some of Neptune's. However, the nodal axis is unique (Figure 20j). On the axis we have: No = Ju = Ma/Ur = Su/Ma = Ne/Mc = Ne. Breaking this apart gives:

No = Ju = Ne (or the three midpoint variants of these)

No = Ma/Ur

No = Su/Ma

No = Ne/Mc

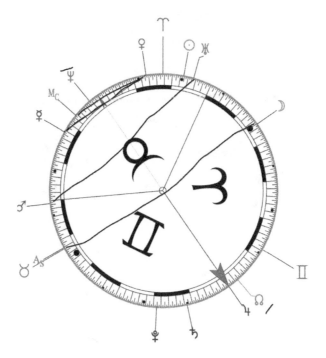

Figure 20I. Jupiter axis on the dial

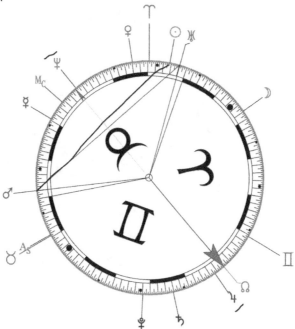

Figure 20J. Nodal axis on the dial

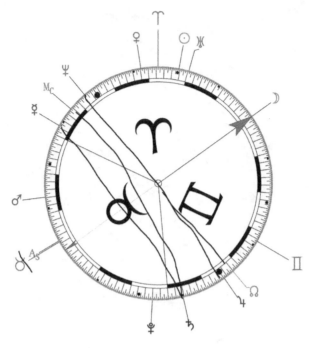

Figure 20K. Moon axis on the dial

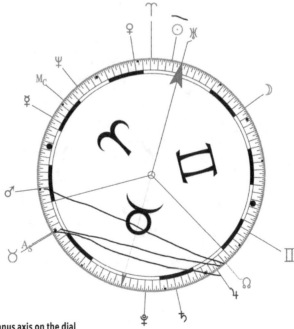

Figure 20L. Uranus axis on the dial

The axis of the Moon is shown in Figure 20k. The Ascendant is on the far end of the axis and there are four midpoints: Mo = Me/Sa = Ju/Ne = Sa/Mc = Ne/No = As. This gives:

Mo = As

Mo = Me/Sa

Mo = Ju/Ne

Mo = Sa/Mc

Mo = Ne/No

The Uranus axis is shown in Figure 20l. It is with the Sun and three midpoints: Ur = Su = Ju/As = No/As = Ma/No. This gives:

Ur = Su

Ur = Ju/As

Ur = No/As

Ur = Ma/No

The final axis is that of the Sun shown in Figure 20m. It also is connected to Uranus and has three midpoints. It is similar to the axis of Uranus, but one midpoint pair is different. On the axis, there is: Su = Ur = No/As = Ju/As = Mo/Ne. Breaking this apart gives:

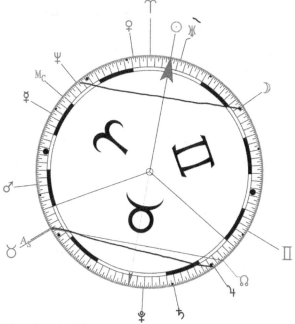

Figure 20M. Sun axis on the dial

Su = Ur
Su = No/As
Su = Ju/As
Su = Mo/Ne

Because the Sun and Uranus are within a degree (by square in the chart) on the dial, in practice they act as a unit. You may have noticed that when each is an arm of a midpoint pair, the other is well. For this reason, on paper, I typically take them together. For example, on the Neptune axis, there is Ne = Ma/Ur = Su/Ma, etc. On paper, I write this in a shortcut notation: Ne = Ma/SuUr. Then, looking up midpoints, I expand it as Ne = Ma/Ur and Ne = Su/Ma.

In this book, if you encounter a notation like SuUr, it means the planets on the dial stand together and should be read as Su = Ur.

EQUILATERAL TRIANGLES

We saw earlier that tight configurations in the chart form direct midpoints. This is also the case on the dial. Any three points in the chart that are a multiple of 30° apart will form a triangle on the dial. To distinguish it from a grand trine which it resembles, I call it an equilateral triangle, or an equilateral. These equilaterals are important because each planet in the triangle is at the midpoint of the other two. Automatically, this gives a triplicate repeat of the midpoint variants.

Look at the dial shown in Figure 20 on page 59. There are two equilaterals, one formed by Ur = Ma/No and the other by Me = Mo/Pl. These points are shown in the chart in Figure 18 on page 53. Here we can see that Uranus is semi-sextile both Mars and the Node. A semi-sextile is 30°. Mercury is sextile both the Moon and Pluto. A sextile is a multiple of 30°.

In the dial, the equilaterals give the three midpoint variants:

Ur = Ma/No   Ma = Ur/No   No = Ma/Ur; and
Me = Mo/Pl   Mo = Me/Pl   Pl = Mo/Me

The repetition of the three midpoints adds to their weight in expression. A person most certainly will prominently live out the theme indicated by an equilateral.

MIDPOINT TREES AND LIST: 45°-Modulus

Indirect midpoints can also be found using the Midpoint Tree list with the modulus set for 45°. Why 45°? For the same reason we used a modulus of 180° in the 360° chart: We want the midpoint pairs that are on the far side of the axis. In the chart, the far side was an opposition. In the dial, the far side is a semisquare or sesquisquare.

As usual, I set an orb of 2° and cross out the midpoint pairs that are wider than 1 ½°. The 45° trees corresponding to the dial we just looked at are shown in Figure 21. Note that the order of the planets on the page is given according to the longitude of the focal planet as it occurs in the 45°-modulus. Here, Venus at 2° Cardinal is first, then Saturn at 3° Cardinal. Why does Saturn go here? Because on the dial, if we put the pointer at 3° Cardinal, we find Saturn on the far side of the pointer. Next, there is Jupiter

Modulus 45°00' – Max Orb 2°00'

♀	(Orb)
♅/♆	+0°55'
♄	+0°57'
♄/♇	−0°58'
☽/☿	−1°30'
~~☉/♆~~	~~+1°34' d~~
~~♃/♇~~	~~+1°52' d~~

♄	(Orb)
♅/♆	−0°01' d
☉/♆	+0°36'
♃/♇	+0°54'
♀	−0°57'
♅/Mc	+1°11'
~~♇/☊~~	~~+1°35'~~
~~☉/Mc~~	~~+1°50'~~

♃	(Orb)
☿/♀	−0°12'
☽/As	−0°45'
♆	+1°14'
♂/♅	+1°20'
☊	+1°22' d
♀/Mc	−1°28'
~~☉/♂~~	~~+1°58'~~

♆	(Orb)
♂/♅	+0°05'
☊	+0°07'
♃/☊	−0°33'
☉/♂	+0°43'
♃	−1°14'
☿/♀	−1°27' d
~~☽/As~~	~~−1°59' d~~

☊	(Orb)
♂/♅	−0°01'
♆	−0°07'
☉/♂	+0°36'
♆/Mc	+1°06'
♃	−1°22' d
~~☿/♀~~	~~−1°34'~~

Mc	(Orb)
☿/♆	+0°02' d
♅/As	+0°29'
♀/♂	+0°39'
☉/As	+1°07'
~~☉/♂~~	~~−1°43'~~

☿	(Orb)
☽/♇	+0°12' d
♀/As	+0°58'
☉/As	−1°24'
~~♀/♂~~	~~−1°52'~~

♂	(Orb)
♃/♅	+0°47'
♀/♄	+0°57'
♀/♇	−0°58'
☉/♃	+1°25'
☉/♄	−1°25'
♅/☊	+1°28'
~~☿/As~~	~~1°43'~~

As	(Orb)
☿/♇	−0°13'
♄/Mc	+0°26'
♄/♆	−0°46'
♀/☊	−1°11' d
☽	+1°22'
♇/Mc	−1°29'
~~☿/♄~~	~~+1°42'~~
~~♀/♃~~	~~−1°53'~~

☽	(Orb)
☿/♄	+0°19'
♃/♆	+0°41'
♄/Mc	−0°55' d
♆/☊	+1°22'
As	−1°22'
~~☿/♇~~	~~−1°35'~~
~~♃/Mc~~	~~+1°54'~~

♅	(Orb)
♃/As	+0°43'
☉	+1°16'
☊/As	+1°24' d
♂/☊	−1°26' d
~~☽/♀~~	~~−1°55'~~

☉	(Orb)
☊/As	+0°07'
♃/As	−0°33' d
☽/♆	+0°45'
♅	−1°16'
~~♀/♅~~	~~+1°44'~~
~~*♇*~~	~~+1°51'~~
~~☽/Mc~~	~~+1°58'~~

♇	(Orb)
♀/♅	−0°06' d
☽/Mc	+0°07' d
☉/♀	+0°31'
☽/♆	−1°06'
☽/☿	+1°23'
☊/As	−1°43'
~~*☉*~~	~~−1°51'~~

Figure 21. 45° Trees

In Planetary Sequence – Modulus 45°00'

☽	31°14'	☉/♅	41°45'	♀/♃	27°58'	♃/♅	24°57'	*♆*	10°03'
☽/☉	36°49'	☉/♆	03°43'	♀/♄	25°07'	♃/♆	31°55'	♆/♇	27°09'
☽/☿	00°38'	☉/♇	20°49'	♀/♅	44°08'	♃/♇	04°01'	♆/☊	32°36'
☽/♀	39°11'	☉/☊	26°17'	♀/♆	06°06'	♃/☊	09°29'	♆/As	19°57'
☽/♂	05°12'	☉/As	13°37'	♀/♇	23°12'	♃/As	41°50'	♆/Mc	11°16'
☽/♃	20°01'	☉/Mc	04°56'	♀/☊	28°39'	♃/Mc	33°09'	*♇*	44°14'
☽/♄	17°10'	*☿*	15°02'	♀/As	16°00'	*♄*	03°06'	♇/☊	04°42'
☽/♅	36°10'	☿/♀	08°35'	♀/Mc	07°19'	♄/♅	22°06'	♇/As	37°03'
☽/♆	43°08'	☿/♂	19°36'	*♂*	24°10'	♄/♆	29°04'	♇/Mc	28°22'
☽/♇	15°14'	☿/♃	34°25'	♂/♃	38°59'	♄/♇	01°10'	*☊*	10°10'
☽/☊	20°42'	☿/♄	31°34'	♂/♄	36°08'	♄/☊	06°38'	☊/As	42°31'
☽/As	08°03'	☿/♅	05°34'	♂/♅	10°08'	♄/As	38°59'	☊/Mc	33°50'
☽/Mc	44°22'	☿/♆	12°32'	♂/♆	17°06'	♄/Mc	30°18'	*As*	29°51'
☉	42°23'	☿/♇	29°38'	♂/♇	34°12'	*♅*	41°07'	As/Mc	21°11'
☉/☿	06°12'	☿/☊	35°06'	♂/☊	39°40'	♅/♆	03°05'	*Mc*	12°30'
☉/♀	44°46'	☿/As	22°26'	♂/As	27°01'	♅/♇	20°10'		
☉/♂	10°47'	☿/Mc	13°46'	♂/Mc	18°20'	♅/☊	25°38'		
☉/♃	25°35'	*♀*	02°09'	*♃*	08°48'	♅/As	12°59'		
☉/♄	22°45'	♀/♂	13°09'	♃/♄	05°57'	♅/Mc	04°18'		

Sorted by Angle – Modulus 45°00'

☽/☿	00°38'	*♃*	08°48'	☿/♂	19°36'	♀/♃	27°58'	♇/As	37°03'
♄/♇	01°10'	♃/☊	09°29'	♆/As	19°57'	♇/Mc	28°22'	♄/As	38°59'
♀	02°09'	*♆*	10°03'	☽/♃	20°01'	♀/☊	28°39'	♂/♃	38°59'
♅/♆	03°05'	♂/♅	10°08'	♅/♇	20°10'	♄/♆	29°04'	☽/♀	39°11'
♄	03°06'	*☊*	10°10'	☽/☊	20°42'	☿/♇	29°38'	♂/☊	39°40'
☉/♆	03°43'	☉/♂	10°47'	☉/♇	20°49'	*As*	29°51'	*♅*	41°07'
♃/♇	04°01'	♆/Mc	11°16'	As/Mc	21°11'	♄/Mc	30°18'	☉/♅	41°45'
♅/Mc	04°18'	*Mc*	12°30'	♄/♅	22°06'	*☽*	31°14'	♃/As	41°50'
♇/☊	04°42'	☿/♆	12°32'	☿/As	22°26'	☿/♄	31°34'	*☉*	42°23'
☉/Mc	04°56'	♅/As	12°59'	☉/♄	22°45'	♃/♆	31°55'	☊/As	42°31'
☽/♂	05°12'	♀/♂	13°09'	♀/♇	23°12'	♆/☊	32°36'	☽/♆	43°08'
☿/♅	05°34'	☉/As	13°37'	*♂*	24°10'	♃/Mc	33°09'	♀/♅	44°08'
♃/♄	05°57'	☿/Mc	13°46'	♃/♅	24°57'	☊/Mc	33°50'	*♇*	44°14'
♀/♆	06°06'	*☿*	15°02'	♀/♄	25°07'	♂/♇	34°12'	☽/Mc	44°22'
☉/☿	06°12'	☽/♇	15°14'	☉/♃	25°35'	☿/♃	34°25'	☉/♀	44°46'
♄/☊	06°38'	♀/As	16°00'	♅/☊	25°38'	☿/☊	35°06'		
♀/Mc	07°19'	♂/♆	17°06'	☉/☊	26°17'	♂/♄	36°08'		
☽/As	08°03'	☽/♄	17°10'	♂/As	27°01'	☽/♅	36°10'		
☿/♀	08°35'	♂/Mc	18°20'	♆/♇	27°09'	☽/☉	36°49'		

Figure 22. Midpoint listing with 45° sort

on the far side, then Neptune on the near side, then the Node on the far side, etc. (Note that this is order given by the trees, and not the order I follow on the dial where I go planet by planet, not axis by axis.)

We can see from Figure 21 there are many midpoint pairs on most axes. This is because we are looking at aspects to midpoints. Typically, every planet will be configured with midpoint pairs, with some planets configured with more pairs than others. In the Solar Fire format, the closest midpoints are listed in order of proximity to the focal planet. The - and + indicate if a midpoint pair comes before or after the focal planet respectively. Direct midpoints (by conjunction, not opposition) are denoted with a "d." Indirect midpoints have no designation. The drawback to the trees is that the order of the midpoints by degree is lost. However, we can turn to the 45°-modulus midpoint list for this information.

This midpoint listing is shown in Figure 22. The bottom portion of the list can be used to find the midpoints associated with each planet. For example, the Sun at 27° Virgo is listed in the 5th column at 42°23. Using an orb of 1½ ° we look for midpoints that fall between 40°53 and 43°53 mutable. The listing shows these midpoint pairs (and planet) in order: Ur, Ju/As, Su, No/As, Mo/Ne. (Note that we did not include midpoints that contained the Sun, because the Sun cannot be both in a midpoint and at the focal point.) This was the axis that we looked at in Figure 20m (page 67). Here, we have the added information of order. The beauty of the list is that it shows the sequence that midpoints will be hit by a transit or direction.

INTERPRETING MIDPOINT AXES

Looking at individual midpoints is simpler than analyzing a whole tree configured with multiple midpoints and trying to come up with a coherent narrative that ties them all together. However, this is precisely what Charles Harvey and Michael Harding did in Chapter 6 of Working With Astrology. They analyzed each tree according to seven different criteria to find the most important trees. Ebertin did not do this, and neither do I. This process adds a whole extra level of complexity that to me is a lot of work for little return. It's too much information for my mind to hold at one time. If you can do it, that is fantastic. Charles and Michael's delineation of trees is nothing short of spectacular and a wonder to behold. If you're interested, here is a summary of their method.

1. Print out a list of the midpoint trees (45° sort) with an orb of 2° and scan the axes. Delete the pairs that are out of orb and mark the closest midpoints.

2. Note any trees that contain the Su/Mo or As/Mc midpoints, as these energize the focal planet and bring it to the forefront.

3. Note the axes which contain multiple planets. We saw this earlier where Jupiter, Neptune, and the Node were on the same axis. This setup repeats and thus emphasizes the midpoint pairs on the axis.

4. Note combinations of the lights and main angles—such as Su/As, Su/Mc, Mo/As, Mo/Mc—as these add energy to their axes. Any planet configured with an angle has a boost. In practice, I find there are too

many to note, but if I see them, I'm aware that a planet joined with an angle carries more weight than usual.

5.   Look for the axes that contain midpoints that are comprised of two angle midpoint pairs: As/No, Mc/No, As/Mc, as any axis containing these pairs will likely stand out.

6.   Check for special midpoints (see Appendix 2 for the list).

7.   Note the midpoints associated with configurations in the chart. Any planets 30° apart will form a triangle on the dial.

I'll go through these seven points using the chart shown in Figure 11 on page 47 and the corresponding dial in Figure 12 (page 48), the 45°-midpoint trees (Figure 21, page 69), and the midpoint listing (Figure 22, page 70).

MIDPOINT SUMMARY

1.   Closest midpoints: Sa=Ur/Ne, No=Ma/Ur, Mc=Me/Ne, Ne=Ma/Ur, Su=No/As, Pl=Ve/Ur=Mo/Mc (Note that these are exact <10′ orb.).

2.   Su/Mo or As/Mc: not completed.

3.   Multiple planets on axis: Ve=Sa; Ju=Ne=No; As=Mo.

4.   Combinations of Lights and Main Angles: Mc=Su/As, Pl=Mo/Mc, Su=No/As.

5.   Angle/Angle midpoints: Ur=No/As; Su=No/As, Pl=No/As.

6.   Special midpoints: Ve=Sa/Pl=Ju/Pl; Sa=Ju/Pl; Ju=Me/Ve; Ne=Ma/Ur; Ne=Me/Ve; No=Ma/Ur; No=Me/Ve; Ma=Ju/Ur; Ma=Su/Ju; As=Sa/Ne.

7.   Chart configuration midpoints: Ma = Ur/No; Me=Mo/Pl.

The summary shows the closest midpoints and the important axes as denoted by the combinations of the personal points and special midpoints. Michael Harding and Charles Harvey interpreted the axis in pieces and then put the pieces together in a narrative that included them all. I don't take that extra step. I take the meaning of the individual midpoints and string them together. I find the midpoints on an axis often conflict with each other. In only one instance did Ebertin look at the influence one pair had on another pair when they were on the same axis.

Keep in mind an axis answers the question: What type of planet is this and what kind of effects may it elicit? We expect the focal planet to be influenced by each midpoint pair that is on the axis, but some midpoint pairs stand out more than others. Sometimes the midpoint pair closest to the focal planet is dominant, or sometimes it's a midpoint pair configured with the Sun, Moon, or an angle. If a single planet appears in multiple midpoints on an axis, (as in Mo/Ve and Ve/Sa), the repetition of Venus points to its important influence on the focal planet. When there is an outer planet-outer planet combination, this pair can be a blind spot—unless the focal planet is an inner planet, in which case, the outer planet midpoint pair impacts the focal planet according to its meaning. In the case of an inner planet-outer planet combination, these add strife and power and typically the focal planet (person) struggles to find a way to combine them. Any midpoint may strike a dumb note and may not be in evidence, which points to a blind spot in the psyche. Other midpoints may be projected and seen to be coming from outside the native from others, such as a spouse, child, friend, or business partner. Midpoints can also show what we're thinking and what's in the news.

OCCUPIED VS UNOCCUPIED MIDPOINTS

Just as everyone has a Jupiter and a Uranus in their chart, they only bring luck to a native that has them connected. So it is with the midpoints: I have found that only completed midpoints consistently work. It is regarding this issue that I am most at odds with previously published work. In Michael Munkasey's Midpoint Weighting Analysis, some natal charts show pairs (incomplete midpoints) that are highly ranked, but I have not found in practice they are significant. In the natal chart/dial, to my knowledge, Ebertin never used unoccupied midpoints. In natal delineation, he looked at complete midpoints, period.

INDIRECT VS UNOCCUPIED MIDPOINTS

It's important to keep in mind the distinction between an indirect midpoint and an unoccupied midpoint. An indirect midpoint is a completed midpoint in which the midpoint pair is in hard aspect to the focal planet by either a square, semisquare, or sesquisquare. That is, an aspect other than the conjunction or opposition, which makes a direct midpoint. An indirect or direct midpoint is comprised of at least three planets. An unoccupied midpoint is a midpoint pair or a midpoint axis that has no third planet at the focal point, or in aspect to it. That is, an unoccupied midpoint is comprised of two planets. There is no third planet at the focal point.

LOST IN SPACE

As Michael Harding and Charles Harvey noted in *Working With Astrology*, there is a vast number of midpoint pairs that occupy a 45 degree swath in every chart. We saw the chart in Figure 17 divided into eight pieces with each piece comprising 45° of longitude. In Figure 23, a 45° swath is shown that occupies 0° Aries to 15° Taurus. The accompanying list shows the degrees of the 78 midpoint pairs contained in the swath. Since there are eight sections of 45°, this midpoint list is repeated eight times in the chart.

In total then, in every 360° chart, there are eight sections of 45°, each containing 78 midpoint pairs, which generates 624 (8 x 78) midpoint pairs. Look at the chart in Figure 23. It appears only the Moon and the Midheaven occupy the 106° section that lies between 16° Sagittarius and 12° Aries. But what we have just seen tells us that this is not the case. This area of the chart contains all the midpoint pairs shown in the list, times two and then some.

Most of these midpoints are not active since they are not completed. How many are there? Everyone has a different number. If you've made a 45° tree list you can count them. The chart in Figure 23 has 51 midpoints, which is about average using an orb <1°30.

As we have seen, indirect midpoints are not readily visible in the chart (see Figures 19b & 19c). This does not mean they are not effective. They are. Working with midpoints helps explain and clarify what is unfolding in the chart when nothing seems to be active or manifesting as expected during a life experience.

 HOMEWORK: Find and delineate your direct and indirect midpoints and any chart configurations.

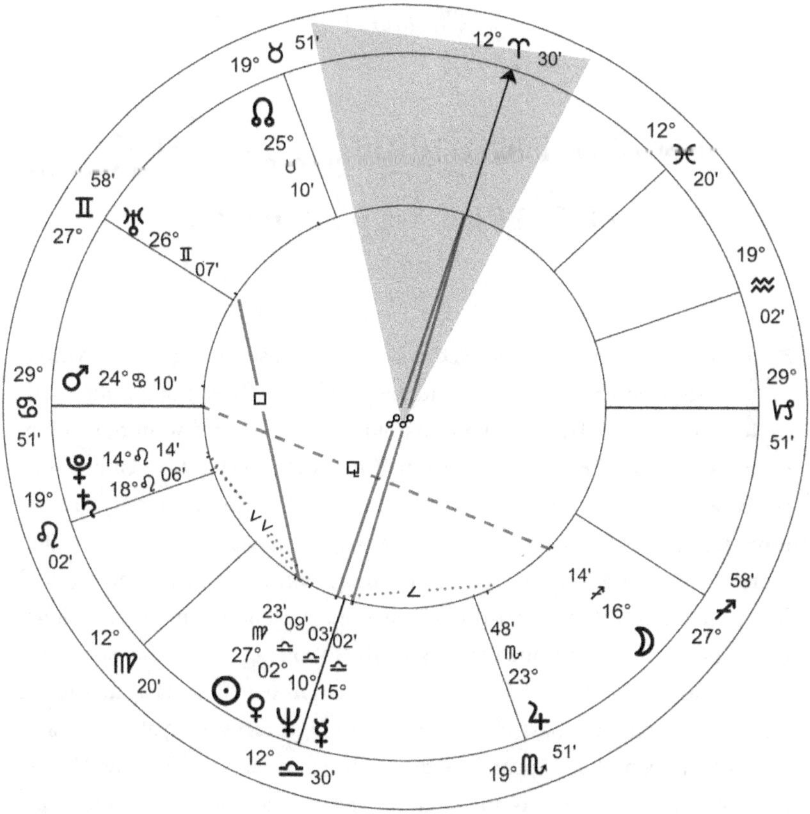

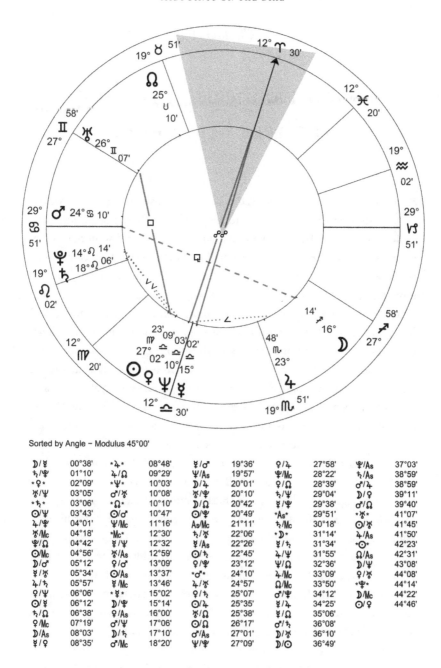

Sorted by Angle – Modulus 45°00'

☽/☿	00°38'	*♃*	08°48'	☿/♂	19°36'	♀/♃	27°58'	♇/As	37°03'
♄/♇	01°10'	♃/☊	09°29'	♆/As	19°57'	♇/Mc	28°22'	♄/As	38°59'
♀	02°09'	*♆*	10°03'	☽/♃	20°01'	♀/☊	28°39'	♂/♃	38°59'
♅/♆	03°05'	♂/♅	10°08'	♅/♇	20°10'	♄/♆	29°04'	☽/♀	39°11'
♄	03°06'	*☊*	10°10'	☽/☊	20°42'	☿/♇	29°38'	♂/☊	39°40'
☉/♆	03°43'	☉/♂	10°47'	☉/♇	20°49'	*As*	29°51'	*♅*	41°07'
♃/♇	04°01'	♆/Mc	11°16'	As/Mc	21°11'	♄/Mc	30°18'	☉/♅	41°45'
♅/Mc	04°18'	*Mc*	12°30'	♄/♅	22°06'	*☽*	31°14'	♃/As	41°50'
♇/☊	04°42'	☿/♆	12°32'	☿/As	22°26'	☿/♄	31°34'	*☉*	42°23'
☉/Mc	04°56'	♅/As	12°59'	☉/♄	22°45'	♃/♆	31°55'	☊/As	42°31'
☽/♂	05°12'	♀/♂	13°09'	♀/♇	23°12'	♆/☊	32°36'	☽/♆	43°08'
☿/♅	05°34'	☉/As	13°37'	*♂*	24°10'	♃/Mc	33°09'	♀/♅	44°08'
♃/♄	05°57'	☿/Mc	13°46'	♃/♅	24°57'	☊/Mc	33°50'	*♇*	44°14'
♀/♆	06°06'	*☿*	15°02'	♀/♄	25°07'	♂/♇	34°12'	☽/Mc	44°22'
☉/☿	06°12'	☽/♇	15°14'	☉/♃	25°35'	☿/♃	34°25'	☉/♀	44°46'
♄/☊	06°38'	♀/As	16°00'	♅/☊	25°38'	☿/☊	35°06'		
♀/Mc	07°19'	♂/♆	17°06'	☉/☊	26°17'	♂/♄	36°08'		
☽/As	08°03'	☽/♄	17°10'	♂/As	27°01'	☽/♅	36°10'		
☿/♀	08°35'	♂/Mc	18°20'	♆/♇	27°09'	☽/☉	36°49'		

Figure 23. Natal chart with 45° midpoint list. The 45° swath shown in the dark triangle from 0 Aries to 15 Taurus *appears* empty, but in fact there are 78 midpoint pairs.

Chapter 9

Natal Delineation Adding Indirect Midpoints

T he dial we have just looked at is that of the successful horror writer, Stephen King. Here is a brief biography for those not familiar with the author. He was two years old when his father went out to buy cigarettes and never came back. He had his first novel published at twenty-six, a story he thought was so bad he threw it in the trash, only to have it rescued by his wife. At the time he was a schoolteacher living in a trailer, unable to afford a telephone, with an infant son and a wife who worked nights at a donut shop. After thirty rejections, he sold the hardcover rights to a publisher for an advance of $2,500. The following month the paperback rights sold for $400,000. Soon after that, he quit teaching. That first novel was the international bestseller, *Carrie*. King is a recovering alcoholic and drug addict, who had a near-fatal accident when he was fifty-one. He has currently written 62 novels and sold over 350 million books. We'll look for these features in the midpoints and aspects as we delineate his chart.

In the last chapter, we went through his dial and found his midpoints and 8th harmonic aspects. Now we'll delineate them. For ease of reference, a one-page copy of Stephen King's chart is shown in Figure 24, along with the closest aspects and 45° midpoint trees. (Refer to Figure 20 for his dial, Figure 21 for his full midpoint tree listing, and Figure 22 for his midpoint listing.) Note that in Solar Fire, the 45°-modulus midpoint trees shown in Figure 24 gives the type of aspect that forms a midpoint. If there are too many pairs to fit in the space, two vertical dots at the bottom of a tree indicate there are additional midpoints not shown. These can be found by looking on the page with the stand-alone 45° trees (Figure 21).

I'll go through Ebertin's method, as outlined by Jane Reynolds, which was the method we used previously in delineating Evangeline's chart. The difference is that we'll add indirect midpoints and use 8th harmonic aspects (no sextiles or trines). I use a natal worksheet to analyze the chart (Figure

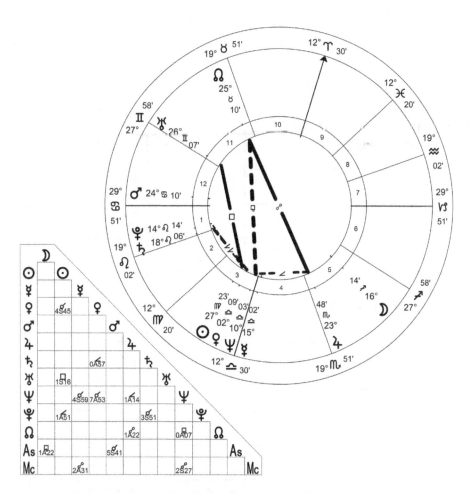

Figure 24. Stephen King's natal chart with aspectarian and 45° midpoint trees

Natal Worksheet

Name __Stephen King_____

Planet	Sign	House	Dignity	Aspects	Midpoints
☉	♍	3		♂♀, □♅, ∠♇	No/As Ju/As Mo/Ne
☽	♐	5		⊡Asc	Me/Sa Ju/Ne Sa/Me Ne/No
☿	♎	4		☍MC	Mo/Pl Ve/As Su/As
♀	♎	3	Ruler	∠♄	Ur/Ne Sa/Pl Mo/Mc
♂	♋	12/1	Fall		Ju/Ur Ve/Sa Ve/Pl Su/Ju Su/Sa Ur/No
♃	♏	5		∠♆, ☍☊	Me/Ve Mo/As Ma/Ur Ve/Mc
♄	♌	1	Detri	∠♀	Ur/Ne Su/Ne Ju/Pl Ur/Mc
♅	♊	12		□☉	Ju/As No/As Ma/No
♆	♎	3		∠♃, ⊡☊, ♂IC	Ma/Ur Ju/No Su/Ma Me/Ve
♇	♌	1		∠☉	Ve/Ur Mo/Mc Su/Ve Mo/Ne Mo/Me
☊	♉	11		☍♃, ⊡♆	Ma/Ur Su/Ma Ne/Mc
Asc	♋			⊡☽	Me/Pl Sa/Mc Sa/Ne Ve/No Pl/Mc
MC	♈			☍☿, ☍♆	Me/Ne Ur/As Ve/Ma Su/As

Standout Features

29° Cancer rising   Two Dial triangles: Mo, Me, Pl;   Ma, Ur, No
Moon and Jupiter in the 5th
Sun and Venus in the writer's third

Note: Mercury in 7 midpoints

Figure 25. Example natal worksheet for Stephen King

25). There is a blank copy in Appendix 3. The meanings of the midpoints are adapted from Ebertin's COSI. Any outside delineation is added in parenthesis. We'll analyze each planet and point in turn, working from the Sun, Moon, out to the Midheaven, looking at the sign, house, aspects, and midpoints of each. Instead of naming the aspect type, I use the equal sign. The orbs remain the same, with 5° for Su, Mo, As, Mc; 4° for Me, Ve, Ma; 3° for the rest; and 1½° for midpoints. In delineating an axis, I always start with the aspects first and then move on to the midpoints.

NATAL CHART DELINEATION

Sun

Sun in Virgo in the 3rd house, in aspect to Venus, Uranus, and Pluto, at the midpoint of No/As, Ju/As, and Mo/Ne.

Sun in Virgo: careful, diligent, attention to detail, orderly, correct, critical, a methodical and analytical mind; strives for simplicity,

Sun in the 3rd house: vivacious, the joy of life, versatile, adaptable, restless, superficial, eager to learn or study, the ability to grasp a subject, love of change.

Sun = Venus: physical love, harmony, beauty, art, the ideal. The feeling of love, the power of attraction, popularity, artistic leaning, a sense of beauty, music, nature. Potentially expressive in the realms of soul and love. The love of social life. Popularity, love relationships, potential for artistic development. Overindulgence or too rich living can be detrimental to health.

Sun = Uranus: a revolutionary spirit, a progressive mind (interest in reform and technology). Excitable and easily upset. Original, concentrated focus on objectives or goals, foresight, love of freedom, mobile, strives for reforms. Also speaks to sudden changes in life, improved living conditions, a change of job or vocation, carrying out innovations. Tension, sudden setbacks in life, upsetting experiences, sudden adjustments to changing life circumstances (found repeatedly in cases of military call-up and of imprisonment), connection with accidents or catastrophes.

Su = Pl: power hungry, craving for rulership, attaining power, physical strength or mental energy, creative power, focused aims or goal, an appreciation of innovation, qualities of leadership, fanatical aspirations, over-estimation of self, arrogance. Also speaks to a sudden advancement in life, the ability to establish leadership and consolidate power, and manifest new ideas into reality. Physical suffering, martyrdom; danger to life, separation by fated events(force majeure).

Su = No/As: cultivating of social contacts, entertainment, the desire to meet new people.

Su = Ju/As: taking joy in pleasant and congenial company, a preference to socialize with generous or rich people, the desire to create a beautiful home; a lucky or influential association.

Su = Mo/Ne: sensitivity, receptive power, a delicate and sensitive body or physique. A sensitive wife. Illusions and deceptions.

To sum up the axis of the Sun, this man has an analytical mind and an artistic bent. He thinks outside the box and his life may change dramatically, suddenly. He craves leadership and seeks to be the best in some capacity. He likes other people and has influential associates. A 3rd house Sun is interested in writing and communication.

Moon

Moon in Sagittarius, in the 5th house, in aspect to the Ascendant, at the midpoint of Me/Sa, Ju/Ne, Sa/Mc, Ne/No.

Moon in Sagittarius: a vivid inner life, moody, striving for wisdom, idealistic in thought and action, alternating periods of optimism and pessimism, a life full of changes.

Moon in 5th: intuitive and instinctive creativity, confident, generous, ambitious, passionate, love of luxury, amusement.

Mo = As: The personal relationship to other people.

Mo = Me/Sa: underdeveloped mind and soul, inconsistent, a love of variety, desire to gain experience and absorb and digest diverse input, a woman thinking of separation. (Also, serious thought or communication with feeling.)

Mo = Ju/Ne: unrealistic, dreamy, the tendency to get lost in planning, becoming involved in speculation.

Mo = Sa/Mc: sad impressionable, inclined toward depression or psychoses; suffering from women. (Also emotional need to realize professional ambitions.)

Mo = Ne/No: nonadaptable, lacking community spirit; disappointments, unsatisfactory relationships with women, losing understanding between people. (Also, an emotional connection to spiritual or imaginative groups.)

This is a creative Moon that can lean toward depression if the energy is not properly channeled. He needs other people and a creative association with them would benefit his inner self. He has problems relating to women and suffers because of it.

Mercury

Mercury in Libra on the cusp of the 4th, in aspect with the Midheaven, at the midpoint of Ur/Ne, Sa/Pl, Mo/Me.

Mercury in Libra: creative thinking within existing frameworks, teamwork, adaptable, discerning, a sense of justice, form, and beauty, good manners, tactful.

Mercury in 4th: perception, the interrelationship between thinking and feeling, a good memory, a tendency to become deeply immersed in something, positive or constructive criticism, a solid work ethic and method, a sense of harmony, artistic interests.

Me = Mc: one's individual outlook, self-knowledge, opinionated. Also the pursuit of life goals and objectives, advancement in career, vocational changes.

Me = Mo/Pl: Far-reaching plans, the zealous pursuit of ideas, the ability to wield powerful influence through speeches or writings.

Me = Ve/As: a sociable and entertaining, conversational about beauty, love, and art.

Me = Su/As: seeking intellectual stimuli, critical attitude; also contact with young people, scientists, or business people.

This is a powerful angular Mercury; a thinking planet in a thinking sign. He would spend much time thinking, speaking, and socializing. He can see two sides of everything.

Venus

Venus in Libra in the 3rd in aspect to Saturn at the midpoints of Ur/Ne, Sa/Pl, Mo/Me.

81

Venus in Libra: living the good life, helpful and quick to form friendships, enjoying social interactions, good taste, artistic skill.

Venus in 3rd: all-embracing sympathy, charm, courtesy, the desire to discuss ideas.

Ve = Sa: sense of reality, soberness, sense of duty, thrift and economy, reservation, loyalty and faithfulness, self-control. (Also serious about art.)

Ve = Ur/Ne: extreme or highly sensitive, drawn to peculiar art, one-sided rapture in love relationships. A peculiar kind of love.

Ve = Sa/Pl: self-discipline, a love of solitude and seclusion, asceticism; feelings of estrangement and alienation. (Also poverty, hard, hard work in an artistic field.)

Ve = Mo/Me: thinking influenced by feeling, emotionally perceptive (expressed through art). Exposure to criticism, gossip, slander. Appreciation of beauty and art.

Venus, among other things, refers to art and creativity. This is a dignified Venus, in her air sign, placed in the 3rd house of communication. With these midpoints, Venus is neither superficial nor frivolous and has the ability to turn hardship into art.

Mars

Mars in Cancer on the 12th side of the 1st house, ruling the 10th house, unaspected, at the midpoint of Ju/Ur, Ve/Sa, Ve/Pl, Su/Ju, Ur/No.

Mars in Cancer: an intense emotional life, moody, impulsive, lacks perseverance and self-control, actions governed by instinct.

Mars in the 1st: a fighting spirit, the urge to do something, ambition, independent.

Mars in the 12th: working silently, struggling for recognition, interest in the occult, craving for alcohol, nicotine, etc.

Ma = Ju/Ur: eager to make one's fortune in life, speculative, makes fortunate decisions. (Great luck in work.)

Ma = Ve/Sa: jealousy, violence, impotent, acting out; sobriety, , discussion or dispute, separation.

Ma = Ve/Pl: strongly sensual, the desire for many children (rape), a coarse expression.

Ma = Su/Ju: a healthy demonstration of will-power, urges, or desires; achievements in life, zealous and eager, courageous, successful activity.

Ma = Ur/No: easily excited in social situations, quarrelsome, exercises self-control only with great difficulty. Disputes can be accompanied by violence.

This is an ambitious Mars who wants recognition and thanks to great luck, will likely achieve his aspirations. Despite significant struggle and upsetting interference from others, he will obtain his professional goals.

Jupiter

Jupiter in Scorpio in the 5th house in aspect to Neptune and the Node at the midpoint of Me/Ve, Mo/As, Ma/Ur, Ve/Mc.

Jupiter in Scorpio: an optimistic attitude. Ruthless striving for wealth and pleasure; materialistic.

Jupiter in 5th: great self-confidence, large-scale planning, and a conscious desire to lead are combined with popularity.

Ju = Ne: apparent happiness, speculation, abundant feeling or emotional expression, active imagination, idealism, joy of shaping things, art, music, interest in metaphysics and religion, love of humanity, impressionability, easily seducible, dreamy, a conflict between visualized idealism and reality. Dreamers, mystics, hypocrites, speculators.

Ju = No: good relationships and connections, agreeable or pleasant contacts. Also, advantageous associations and business gain through other people, luck in finding a good partner.

Ju = Me/Ve: wealth of artistic design, artistic successes, acting upon thoughts of love, an advantageous union.

Ju = Mo/As: community and society, entertainment, social activity, harmonious relationships with others, adaptable, happy and fortunate contacts.

Ju = Ma/Ur: grasp of a situation and timely action, contests of strength, good fortune, luck in unusual actions, good luck with injuries, accidents, or operations.

Ju = Ve/Mc: rich emotional expression, the need to give love, healthy and confident attitude, easily gains the affection of others, popularity and happiness.

The greater benefic always tries to help and this Jupiter is optimistic and materialistic, creative and imaginative. He has luck with associates and with love.

Saturn

Saturn in Leo in the 1st house conjunct the 2nd house, in aspect with Venus, at the midpoint of Ur/Ne, Su/Ne, Ju/Pl, Ur/Mc.

Saturn in Leo: reliable, loyal, simplistic, shy, cautionary.

Saturn in the 1st: ambitious, diligent, industrious, endurance, obstinate, modest, serious worker.

Saturn in the 2nd: perseverance, enduring energy, applying oneself to the task at hand, economically minded, acquisitive of possessions and property.

Sa = Ve: a sense of reality, soberness, duty, thrift and economy, reserve, loyalty and faithfulness, self-control, impeded emotional expression.

Sa = Ur/Ne: depression, instability, pessimism. Also painful loss, mourning, or bereavement. (Tyl adds: A clash among ambitions; the need for recognition.)

Sa = Su/Ne: held back by illness or physical debility, emotional affliction or mental illness; mental and emotional suffering, impeded or poor vascular circulation, health issues with the blood.

Sa = Ju/Pl: ambitious, successful in real estate, hindered self-development, unable to progress, difficulties, separation.

Sa = Ur/Mc: frigid, narrow-minded, egotistic; regaining sobriety and coming down to earth, quick departures, quick goodbyes, loss of work position or termination notice.

Saturn is always difficult, but with hard work Saturn is not without reward. Saturn in Leo will work hard to be the best. Self-worth and confidence issues may drive ambition—for example, by doing something great, one will become someone great. Health issues may cause problems. In this chart, both malefics are debilitated, indicating trouble in the extreme, some of which was channeled into his stories.

Uranus

Uranus in Gemini on the 12th house cusp in aspect with the Sun at the midpoint of Ju/As, No/As, Ma/No.

Uranus in Gemini: quick comprehension, organization, convincing speaker, scientific aspirations, original thinker, methodical.

Uranus in 12th: inclined to mysticism, mysterious aspirations, subconscious forces.

Ur = Su: revolutionary spirit, a progressive mind, originality, conscious focus on objectives and goals, foresight. Also speaks to a sudden change in life circumstances, improvement of living conditions, a change of place or vocation, carrying out innovations and reforms; periods of tension, sudden setbacks, upsetting experiences, sudden new conditions or circumstances, accidents or catastrophes.

Ur = Ju/As: optimistic attitude toward others, luck guiding others in new ventures. Also a fortunate turn of conditions and circumstances.

Ur = No/As: perpetual need for company, the sudden seeking out of contacts, sudden experiences with associates.

Ur = Ma/No: active cooperation, activity or occupation focused on an organization, sudden unions and associations, sudden shared experiences, unexpected upset in an organization or community.

This Uranus is a quick thinker and an accomplished communicator. He is open to messages from the unconscious. There will likely be a turn or turns in life, for better or worse. Again, luck with associates is highlighted.

Neptune

Neptune in Libra in the 4th in aspect to Jupiter, Node, Midheaven, at the midpoint of Ma/Ur, Ju/No, Su/Ma, Me/Ve.

Neptune in Libra: receptive, the expression of feeling, high ideals. Also indicates active and integral participation in the community.

Neptune in the 4th: sensitivity, growth of spiritual perception, deep feelings, affectionate, an inner connection with others, soul-suffering disappointments.

Ne = Ju: seeming happiness, speculation, richness of feeling or emotional expression, actively and intensely imaginative, idealistic, joy through the shaping of things, art, music, interest in metaphysics and religious issues, a great love of humanity. Also, impressionable, easily seduced, dreamy, idealism conflicting with reality. Visionaries, dreamers, mystics, hypocrites, speculators.

Ne = No: peculiar or strange personal conduct, occasionally unreliable; expects more than is possible from people or society; disappointment, or the tendency to be deceptive.

Ne = Mc: long-term objectives, peculiar ideas, interest in the unconscious and supernatural realms. Undefined life objectives, insecurity, lack of self-confidence, a tendency to succumb to strange and unusual influences, and a devotion to peculiar objectives; inclined to feign, pose, or put on an act.

Ne = Ma/Ur: cunning and deceitful, a low and mean way of acting, harming others, a person with bad intentions. Prone to fainting when strength is overtaxed and to fits of rage or frenzy. Also indicates raving madness, a car accident.

Ne = Ju/No: emotionally held back in relationships, indecisive or vacillating, unstable, unreliable; getting sober again, disappointment.

Ne = Su/Ma: disinclined to work, lack of energy, dishonest activity; the undermining of one's vocation, being let go from a job, disappointment, fraud; lack of vitality, illness; being deceived or defrauded.

Ne = Me/Ve: ability to see everything pictured clearly, fantasy and imagination, inspiration, sympathetic understanding of others, an appreciation of poetry, fairy tales, and fantastic stories.

The planet of the imagination is strengthened by angularity. There is a need to have significant relationships with others, but this may bring disappointment. This Neptune can dream and fantasize. He can be cunning and deceitful, or write about these things,and is in danger of having a car accident. This is a very active axis in King's chart.

Pluto

Pluto in Leo in the 1st at the midpoint of Ve/Ur, Mo/Mc, Su/Ve, Mo/Ne, Mo/Me.

Pluto in Leo: strong dynamic emotional urges or forces, the tendency to speculate (ask, WHAT IF?) the need for power, great achievements in a specialized field.

Pluto in the 1st: subconscious forces try to come to light to assist in the recognition of new and entirely novel ideas. Extraordinary energy, power of self assertion, leadership qualities, craving for power.

Pl = Ve/Ur: highly excitable, "blind love."

Pl = Mo/Mc: a peculiar or strange soul-life, great emotional depression, inner or spiritual evolution hampered by a female (mother or wife), emotional shock and upheaval.

Pl = Su/Ve: highly excitable love life can easily lead to excesses, a fateful love union. (Venus is also related to art.)

Pl = Mo/Ne: high sensitivity coupled with being easily influenced by others, an emotional shock or upheaval.

Pl = Mo/Me: adjusting one's thinking to new conditions, transformed thinking caused by tragic events or experiences.

The Dark Lord in the 1st in Leo depicts a desire for power and leadership. There is deep emotional sensitivity that can be channeled into love or art.

Node

The Node in Taurus in the 11th in aspect to Jupiter and Neptune, at the midpoint of Ma/Ur, Su/Ma, Ne/Mc.

Node in Taurus: permanent unions, consolidation of alliances, using others for personal advantage.

Node in 11th: stimulating and friendly associations with many-faceted interests and reformatory objectives, love of social contacts.

No = Ju: good relationships and connections, agreeable or pleasant contacts; entering into advantageous associations and advantageous gains in business with others, the good luck in finding a good partner.

No = Ne: peculiar or strange conduct, occasional unreliability. Also, expecting more than is possible from others and society. Disappointment or the tendency to deceive others.

No = Ma/Ur: excitement in the presence of others, sharing the experience of sudden events with others, undertaking extraordinary and unusual enterprises.

No = Su/Ma: the cultivation of goodwill, successful teamwork, joint plans or undertakings, unity and alliance in working toward objectives.

No = Ne/Mc: unpleasant associations, bad company, bad intentions shared with others.

Unsurprisingly, the Node describes his associations. He seeks them and is excited by them. He may also encounter unpleasant associates and does so in his books.

Ascendant

Ascendant in Cancer in aspect to the Moon at the midpoint of Me/Pl, Sa/Mc, Sa/Ne, Ve/No, Pl/Mc.

Ascendant in Cancer: moodiness; a rich home and family life; living simply and humbly; caring, sympathetic, and dedicated nature, impressionable, and industrious.

As = Me/Pl: intellectual domination, also the ability to exercise influence upon others.

As = Sa/Mc: inhibited growth or development, suffering caused by others, being placed in bad circumstances; sharing anxiety with others, loneliness, parting from others, sadness.

As = Sa/Ne: being placed in an unusual or restless environment; applications of force, an accident.

As = Ve/No: affectionate, an obliging and cordial manner, harmonious relationships.

As = Pl/Mc: procuring an important position and recognition by any means; a person of fame.

The Ascendant repeats messages we have already heard. He is intellectually ambitious and will likely want and achieve fame. He likes and needs other people. He is in danger of having an accident.

Midheaven

Midheaven in Aries in aspect with Mercury and Neptune at the midpoint of Me/Ne, Ur/As, Ve/Ma, Su/As.

Midheaven in Aries: individuation coupled with awareness of life goals, ambitious, optimistic, confident, the desire to lead.

Mc = Me: having a personal outlook, self-knowledge, expression of opinions, pursuing and attaining life goals and objectives, career advancement, vocational changes.

Mc = Ne: devotion to far-reaching objectives, peculiar ideas, interest in the unconscious and supernatural realms. Also undefined objectives, insecurity, lack of self-confidence, succumbing to strange or unusual influences, peculiar objectives, an inclination to feign, pose or put on an act.

Mc = Me/Ne: rich inner life, imaginative, sweeping ideas and plans, intuitive thinking, sympathetic understanding of others, self-deception, going the wrong way, lying.

Mc = Ur/As: restlessness, changes in life objectives, a constant search for new stimuli; excitement, making changes.

Mc = Ve/Ma: the drive for love. Passion. (Creativity).

Mc = Su/As: the desire for soul connections, seeking of mental or intellectual contact, attaining esteem and respect.

The Midheaven reiterates the themes of a need for others, high creativity and imagination, and a desire for recognition. The type of associations he forms involves mental contact.

In summary, knowing these midpoints and aspects astrologically describe Stephen King, we can see how the vignettes capture the context of his life. While I ignored some statements in the COSI I didn't think applied to King's life, some of Ebertin's more negative attributes refer to Stephen King's novels and describe his characters, who experience conflict, deceit, and enjoy bad company. Keep in mind, a fiction writer is essentially a liar, living in a fantasy world comprised of imagination.

We can't overlook the importance of Stephen King's two equilateral triangles. The first is Mercury = Moon/Pluto and the variants of Pluto = Moon/Mercury and Moon = Mercury/Pluto. In a nutshell, this speaks to writing about dark emotions: for example, horror. The Mercury/Pluto pair bestows the ability to influence the thoughts of others.

King, the creative writer, also has an equilateral composed of the Node, Mars, and Uranus. Translated simply, these three can mean an association with unusual work, or interruptions in work, or excitement with others. This triangle shows the nature and impact of his work. When we read a book, we are actively cooperating with the writer, even if it is at a distance in time. We put the book down and pick it up later—suggesting sudden unions and associations. With this writer, most of his work is both exciting and shocking.

In the dial, as we've seen, there are many more midpoints than are apparent in the chart—mainly because now we are adding two aspects and indirect midpoints. All this information gives more than a thumbnail sketch of a person. The repetition is telling as the major themes are reiterated over and over in varying ways and guises, but always pointing to the main issues of the individual's life.

As you might expect, this is an excellent technique to use where there is no birth time. If you set the chart or dial at noon and ignore the aspects and midpoints involving the Moon, Ascendant, and Midheaven, there is still much to work with.

HOMEWORK: Use this method of delineation to examine another person's life. Analyze an untimed chart.

PART 2

SOLAR ARC DIRECTIONS

... the solar arc directions are of great value ...
these can be quickly and simply applied for the year of life under
consideration and nearly always prove effective.

REINHOLD EBERTIN

Chapter 10

Solar Arc Directions in the Chart

Solar arcs time the manifestation of the promise and potential shown in the natal chart and show the manner (good or bad) by which it is likely to be expressed. Solar arcs are also known as "solar arc directions" and abbreviated either as "directions" or "solar arcs." Solar arc is a method of forecasting that advances the entire chart forward at the rate of the natal Sun, approximately 1° per year. This holds true for retrograde planets, which are also moved forward. Thus, at age five, every planet would advance roughly five degrees; at age ten, every planet has advanced about ten degrees, and so on. This is in contrast to secondary progressions in which each planet is advanced according to its own rate of speed. In solar arc, every planet is advanced at the Sun's speed. Since the Sun in secondary progressions is advanced at a rate of its solar arc, the position of the Sun in both techniques is identical. Directions are located at the place of birth.

Adding one degree to planets is easy math and enables us to estimate solar arcs in our heads. For example, at age five, Stephen King experienced a traumatic life event. Look at his natal chart shown in Figure 26a on page 94. If we add 5° to Mars' position, we get 29° Cancer, the natal Ascendant. We add 5° to the Sun and get 2° Libra, and Venus. Add 5° to Saturn and get 23° Leo, which is square Jupiter. Add 5° to the Midheaven and get 17° Aries, trine Saturn. Add 5° to Neptune and we come to Mercury. What happened when Stephen King was five? He went out to play with a friend and that friend got hit by a train and was killed. King went home and never mentioned it. Barbara Kingsolver, a friend and colleague of King, told him he'd been writing about the tragedy ever since. A look at the directions confirms the impact of the event: Mars at the Ascendant is an act of violence that affects you personally. Neptune with Mercury is something that blows your mind. Saturn square Jupiter is a hard reality that steals your hope. The Midheaven trine Saturn is a difficult encounter with reality with no escape. The Sun with Venus is art.

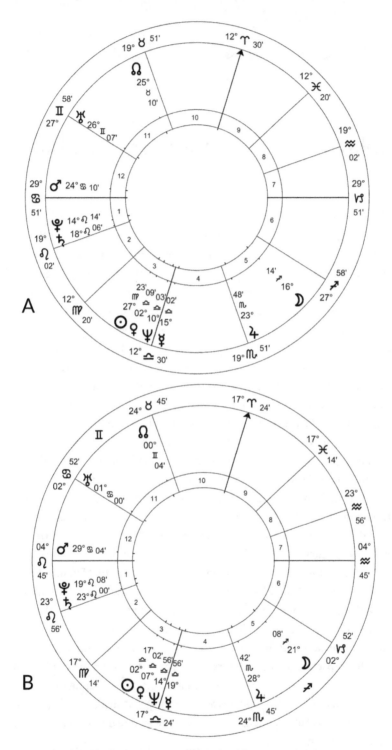

Figure 26. Dual wheels: Stephen King's natal chart (A) and directions age 5 (B).

Solar arc directions enable us to anticipate the year of an upcoming event. We can look at the natal chart, count the distance in degree between two planets, and determine when a directed aspect will be completed. There is 2° between Neptune and the IC, Moon trine Saturn, and Jupiter conjunct the South Node. What happened when Stephen King was two years old? His father went out to buy cigarettes and never came home.

With solar arcs, one thing to be aware of is that the Sun moves at a variable speed during the year. In the summer, the Sun appears to slow down, and in the winter, the Sun speeds up. Because its motion is not uniform, its daily motion ranges from about 57′ of travel around the summer solstice to around 1.01° of travel around the winter solstice. For this reason, the solar arc of a summer birth is usually less than 1° per year, and the solar arc of a winter birth is usually a bit more.

The most precise solar arc movement (which is the exact arc each planet should be directed) is determined for each chart by taking the position of the Sun one day after birth and subtracting the degree of the Sun on the day of birth. In the ephemeris, the Sun on September 22 at midnight, the day after Stephen King's birthday, was 28°56′38″ Virgo. The previous day, on his birthday at midnight on September 21, the Sun was at 27°57′59″. The subtraction gives an arc of 00°58′39″, a bit less than 1° a year.

This "bit less" adds up over time, accumulating through the years. What this means is that by age 30, equating directed arc degree and age will be slightly off. For winter births, at age 30, events will happen a bit sooner than expected. For summer births, events will happen a bit later. To correct for this, it's best to use a computer to run a solar arc-directed chart for the year of interest.

Solar Fire will create a directed chart for any age, any date. Figure 26b shows Stephen King's natal chart directed to age 5 on his birthday. From a distance, the two charts look identical. The order and position of the planets in both charts are the same. The only difference is the degree of longitude of all the points.

This is the significance of advancing the chart at a uniform rate—the layout of the natal chart stays the same. That means that the relationship between the natal planets doesn't change over time. Essentially the method works by taking a copy of the natal chart and using it as the outer wheel in a biwheel. The outer wheel advances counter-clockwise about one degree per year.

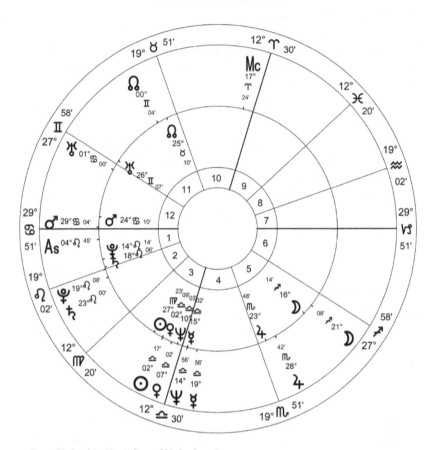

Figure 27. Stephen King's directed biwheel age 5

The two charts are shown in a biwheel in Figure 27, with the natal chart on the inner wheel and the age 5-directed chart on the outer wheel. From this, we can see the directions that we figured out in our heads.

DIFFERENCE LISTING

A quick way to see when planets will become conjunct by solar arc is to look at the difference listing, which is a feature in Solar Fire that is accessed from the Reports menu. The modulus is set for 180° to pick up the oppositions. Stephen King's difference listing is shown in Figures 28A (planetary sequence) and 28B on pages 97–98; this second list shows the two planets sorted by orb. Note the "/" in this listing does not symbolize a midpoint, but the solar arc direction of the first planet listed coming to the second planet.

In Planetary Sequence – Modulus 180°00'

Pair	°	Pair	°	Pair	°	Pair	°	Pair	°
☽/⊙	101°08'	☿/♇	119°12'	♃/♂	060°22'	♆/☽	066°11'	☊/♆	134°52'
☽/☿	118°47'	☿/☊	040°08'	♃/♄	084°18'	♆/⊙	167°20'	☊/♇	079°04'
☽/♀	105°54'	☿/As	104°49'	♃/♅	032°18'	♆/☿	004°59'	☊/As	064°41'
☽/♂	037°56'	☿/Mc	177°28'	♃/♆	136°14'	♆/♀	172°06'	☊/Mc	137°19'
☽/♃	157°33'	♀/☽	074°05'	♃/♇	080°26'	♆/♂	104°07'	As/☽	136°22'
☽/♄	061°52'	♀/⊙	175°14'	♃/☊	001°22'	♆/♃	043°45'	As/⊙	057°31'
☽/♅	009°52'	♀/☿	012°53'	♃/As	066°03'	♆/♄	128°03'	As/☿	075°10'
☽/♆	113°48'	♀/♂	112°01'	♃/Mc	138°41'	♆/♅	076°03'	As/♀	062°17'
☽/♇	058°00'	♀/♃	051°39'	♄/☽	118°07'	♆/♇	124°11'	As/♂	174°18'
☽/☊	158°56'	♀/♄	135°57'	♄/⊙	039°16'	♆/☊	045°07'	As/♃	113°56'
☽/As	043°37'	♀/♅	083°57'	♄/☿	056°55'	♆/As	109°48'	As/♄	018°15'
☽/Mc	116°15'	♀/♆	007°53'	♄/♀	044°02'	♆/Mc	002°27'	As/♅	146°15'
⊙/☽	078°51'	♀/♇	132°05'	♄/♂	156°03'	♇/☽	121°59'	As/♆	070°11'
⊙/☿	017°38'	♀/☊	053°01'	♄/♃	095°41'	♇/⊙	043°08'	As/♇	014°23'
⊙/♀	004°45'	♀/As	117°42'	♄/♅	128°00'	♇/☿	060°47'	As/☊	115°18'
⊙/♂	116°47'	♀/Mc	010°21'	♄/♆	051°56'	♇/♀	047°54'	As/Mc	072°38'
⊙/♃	056°24'	♂/☽	142°03'	♄/♇	176°08'	♇/♂	159°55'	Mc/☽	063°44'
⊙/♄	140°43'	♂/⊙	063°12'	♄/☊	097°03'	♇/♃	099°33'	Mc/⊙	164°53'
⊙/♅	088°43'	♂/☿	080°51'	♄/As	161°44'	♇/♄	003°51'	Mc/☿	002°31'
⊙/♆	012°39'	♂/♀	067°58'	♄/Mc	054°23'	♇/♅	131°52'	Mc/♀	169°38'
⊙/♇	136°51'	♂/♃	119°37'	♅/☽	170°07'	♇/♆	055°48'	Mc/♂	101°40'
⊙/☊	057°47'	♂/♄	023°56'	♅/⊙	091°16'	♇/☊	100°55'	Mc/♃	041°18'
⊙/As	122°28'	♂/♅	151°56'	♅/☿	108°55'	♇/As	165°36'	Mc/♄	125°36'
⊙/Mc	015°06'	♂/♆	075°52'	♅/♀	096°02'	♇/Mc	058°15'	Mc/♅	073°36'
☿/☽	061°12'	♂/♇	020°04'	♅/♂	028°03'	☊/☽	021°03'	Mc/♆	177°32'
☿/⊙	162°21'	♂/☊	120°59'	♅/♃	147°41'	☊/⊙	122°12'	Mc/♇	121°44'
☿/♀	167°06'	♂/As	005°41'	♅/♄	051°59'	☊/☿	139°51'	Mc/☊	042°40'
☿/♂	099°08'	♂/Mc	078°19'	♅/♆	103°56'	☊/♀	126°58'	Mc/As	107°21'
☿/♃	038°46'	♃/☽	022°26'	♅/♇	048°07'	☊/♂	059°00'		
☿/♄	123°04'	♃/⊙	123°35'	♅/☊	149°03'	☊/♃	178°37'		
☿/♅	071°04'	♃/☿	141°13'	♅/As	033°44'	☊/♄	082°56'		
☿/♆	175°00'	♃/♀	128°20'	♅/Mc	106°23'	☊/♅	030°56'		

Figure 28A. Stephen King's Difference Listing 180°

97

Sorted by Angle – Modulus 180°00'

♃/☊	001°22'	♆/♃	043°45'	Mc/♅	073°36'	☽/♆	113°48'	☊/☿	139°51'
♆/Mc	002°27'	♄/♀	044°02'	♀/☽	074°05'	As/♃	113°56'	☉/♄	140°43'
Mc/☿	002°31'	♆/☊	045°07'	As/☿	075°10'	As/☊	115°18'	♃/☿	141°13'
♇/♄	003°51'	♇/♀	047°54'	♂/♆	075°52'	☽/Mc	116°15'	♂/☽	142°03'
☉/♀	004°45'	♅/♇	048°07'	♆/♅	076°03'	☉/♂	116°47'	As/♅	146°15'
♆/☿	004°59'	♀/♃	051°39'	♂/Mc	078°19'	♀/As	117°42'	♅/♃	147°41'
♂/As	005°41'	♄/♆	051°56'	☉/☽	078°51'	♄/☽	118°07'	♅/☊	149°03'
♀/♆	007°53'	♅/♄	051°59'	☊/♇	079°04'	☽/☿	118°47'	♂/♅	151°56'
☽/♅	009°52'	♀/☊	053°01'	♃/♇	080°26'	☿/♇	119°12'	♄/♂	156°03'
♀/Mc	010°21'	♄/Mc	054°23'	♂/☿	080°51'	♂/♃	119°37'	☽/♃	157°33'
☉/♆	012°39'	♇/♆	055°48'	☊/♄	082°56'	♂/☊	120°59'	☽/☊	158°56'
♀/☿	012°53'	☉/♃	056°24'	♀/♅	083°57'	Mc/♇	121°44'	♇/♂	159°55'
As/♇	014°23'	♄/☿	056°55'	♃/♄	084°18'	♇/☽	121°59'	♄/As	161°44'
☉/Mc	015°06'	As/☉	057°31'	☉/♅	088°43'	☊/☉	122°12'	☿/☉	162°21'
☉/☿	017°38'	☉/☊	057°47'	♅/☉	091°16'	☉/As	122°28'	Mc/☉	164°53'
As/♄	018°15'	☽/♇	058°00'	♄/♃	095°41'	☿/♄	123°04'	♇/As	165°36'
♂/♇	020°04'	♇/Mc	058°15'	♅/♀	096°02'	♃/☉	123°35'	☿/♀	167°06'
☊/☽	021°03'	☊/♂	059°00'	♄/☊	097°03'	♆/♇	124°11'	♆/☉	167°20'
♃/☽	022°26'	♃/♂	060°22'	☿/♂	099°08'	Mc/♄	125°36'	Mc/♀	169°38'
♂/♄	023°56'	♇/☿	060°47'	♇/♃	099°33'	☊/♀	126°58'	♅/☽	170°07'
♅/♂	028°03'	☿/☽	061°12'	♇/☊	100°55'	♄/♅	128°00'	♆/♀	172°06'
☊/♅	030°56'	☽/♄	061°52'	☽/☉	101°08'	♆/♄	128°03'	As/♂	174°18'
♃/♅	032°18'	As/♀	062°17'	Mc/♂	101°40'	♃/♀	128°20'	☿/♆	175°00'
♅/As	033°44'	♂/☉	063°12'	♅/♆	103°56'	♇/♅	131°52'	♀/☉	175°14'
☽/♂	037°56'	Mc/☽	063°44'	♆/♂	104°07'	♀/♇	132°05'	♄/♇	176°08'
☿/♃	038°46'	☊/As	064°41'	☿/As	104°49'	☊/♆	134°52'	☿/Mc	177°28'
♄/☉	039°16'	♃/As	066°03'	☽/♀	105°54'	♀/♄	135°57'	Mc/♆	177°32'
☿/☊	040°08'	♆/☽	066°11'	♅/Mc	106°23'	♃/♆	136°14'	☊/♃	178°37'
Mc/♃	041°18'	♂/♀	067°58'	Mc/As	107°21'	As/☽	136°22'		
Mc/☊	042°40'	As/♆	070°11'	♅/☿	108°55'	☉/♇	136°51'		
♇/☉	043°08'	☿/♅	071°04'	♆/As	109°48'	☊/Mc	137°19'		
☽/As	043°37'	As/Mc	072°38'	♀/♂	112°01'	♃/Mc	138°41'		

Figure 28B. Stephen King's Difference Listing 180°

For example, the first direction of his life occurred at a solar arc of 1°22, which was around age one year and three months, when Jupiter came to the nodal axis and met the South Node. It could not have been a nice time in his life. The alarming association of Pluto to Saturn occurred approximately two months before his 4th birthday (the orb of separation is 3°51).

The list is especially useful in quickly pinpointing the years of multiple directions and their type. For example, in his 12th year (solar arc 12°), two directions occurred: Sun came to Neptune, and Venus came to Mercury. From this, we might suspect that around this time he started writing.

Note that the order of the pairs of planets in the list is uni-directional. Two months before he turned four, Pluto directed to Saturn. Saturn did not direct to Pluto, and will not direct there during his lifetime unless he lives to be 176. (You can find the age by looking for the pair Sa/Pl in the top half of the list).

ADDING MIDPOINTS

One outstanding feature of solar arc directions is that the midpoints associated with each natal planet remain the same throughout life. The entire planetary axis moves forward as a unit. This means that each directed planet carries its midpoints as it advances.

We saw for Stephen King that at age five, Neptune directed to Mercury. However, he actually had Ne = Me/Ve, the writer of fantasy, advance to hit Me = Mo/Pl, thinking dark thoughts. We write this direction as:

dNe = dMe/Ve = Me = Mo/Pl

Here the "d" denotes solar arc-directed planets and directed midpoint pairs. (The "d" in front of Me/Ve refers to both planets, i.e., dMe/dVe.) The midpoint Me = Mo/Pl is the natal midpoint and has no "d." The axis is composed of the natal midpoint Ne = Me/Ve that has directed to the natal midpoint Me = Mo/Pl. To interpret the direction, we first look at the direction itself (dNe = Me) and then add the meaning of the directed midpoint (dNe = dMe/Ve) to the meaning of the natal midpoint (Me = Mo/Pl):

Me = Mo/Pl (natal midpoint)

dNe = dMe/Ve (directed midpoint)

dNe = Me (directed aspect)

We interpret each in turn, starting with the aspect dNe = Me: disturbances that originate in the psyche, self-deception, and the imaginative faculty. The aspect tells us the main thrust of the direction is the activation of imagination and creative thinking. The midpoints are qualifying and show the manner the creativity is expressed.

The midpoints add the following:

dNe = dMe/Ve: the power of picturing everything clearly, fantasy and imagination, inspiration, sympathetic understanding of others, an appreciation of fairy tales, and fantastic stories.

Me = Mo/Pl: extreme emotions or extreme emotional expression, sweeping plans, the ability to powerfully influence the larger public through speech or writing.

Putting this together, the direction describes an activation of the mind (Mercury) by the imagination (Neptune) that is used to write stories. He employed fantasy to handle dark emotions.

Ebertin had one rule for solar arc directions—you can't mix levels. What does this mean? We can't use midpoints formed between a natal planet and a directed planet. (In Uranian astrology you can.) In Cosmobiology, the pairs have to be formed within one chart. We ignore any midpoint combinations such as n/d = n (natal/directed = natal) or n/d = d (natal/directed = directed). For this reason, the notation of dMe/Ve indicates the direction of the midpoint pair itself. However, there is an exception we'll look at it later.

As usual in astrology, the more directed aspects in a given year, the more significant the year. Directions predict themes and trends, but their onset is approximate rather than exact. They are typically triggered by a transit. For this reason, solar arc directions are not accurate timers. Still, we know that, on average, everything in the directed chart will move about 1° degree a year. This means the planets and angles advance about 5′ per month. In three months, a directed planet will move about 15′. In six months, the directed planet will move about 30′ or ½° forward, and in nine months, the directed planet will advance 45′ (¾°). In a year, on the next birthday, the planet will have moved about 1° forward.

SOLAR ARCS DIRECTIONS IN A CHART

To identify solar arc directions, use a bi-wheel with the directed chart placed on the outer wheel of the natal chart. Because the directed planets carry the same midpoints as their natal counterpart, we can use the natal midpoint list to find both natal and directed midpoints. In the chart, I only add midpoints to directed conjunctions and oppositions. In my view, these are the strongest directions, and there is direct activation of the midpoints on the planetary axis. This is not the case when looking at sextiles, trines, or squares. With these, I only take the directed aspect.

In solar arc, when using the 360° chart, I use the traditional aspects, conjunction, sextile, square, trine, and opposition. I use the same orb for solar arc directions that I use for secondary progressions. Typically, about a year before the direction is exact its influence can be felt. As the direction separates, its influence is abating and when the direction has separated by 1° it's over.

We looked at Evangeline's natal chart in Chapter 6 and delineated her natal trees. We'll now look at how these trees were activated by solar arc at seminal times of her life. To generate the solar arc chart, I use the birth location and noon if no event time is available. Since directions in the chart advance slowly, the difference in solar arc over the course of a single day is negligible.

MOVE

Evangeline moved to New York City on March 16, 1899. Her solar arc was 31°15′59″. The previous month she turned 31. She wrote in her biography that she saw propitious transits coming up and on that basis planned her move. She did not use solar arc directions, so she would not have seen those shown in Figure 29 on page 102.

She was experiencing three directions: dMoon opposite Ascendant, dUranus opposite Mars, and dNeptune conjunct Pluto. Also apparent are three approaching directions that will perfect in the next two years: dMars conjunct Jupiter; dSun conjunct Venus, and dSun conjunct the Ascendant. Taken together, the six directions point to a very auspicious time in the near future.

Let's look at the three current directions. A move is shown by the opposition of the directed Moon to the Ascendant. She is leaving her family (Moon) and going far away (Moon opposite the Ascendant). The Moon is on the midpoint of Me/Ma. Given Mercury is the ruler of the 4th house, this midpoint can mean moving on account of work. She likely also had an argument and angry words (Me/Ma) with her family. The Ascendant

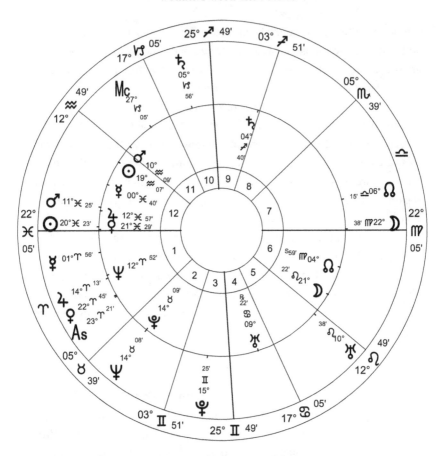

Figure 29. Evangeline Adams biwheel with directions at time of move

is on the midpoint of Sa/Ur, a pair that denote a break from the past and a major change in the status quo. In this context, the change is brought about by the directed Moon: leaving her family and going to work. The midpoint pair of Me/Ne is also on the Ascendant, activated by the directed Moon, bringing, according to Ebertin: pictures and ideas emerging from the subconscious mind, receptiveness, a sympathetic understanding of other souls, an impressionable mind. She was operating with high intuitive power when she moved.

The combination of Mars with dUranus describes an accident. The day she moved from New Jersey and into a hotel, she predicted the hotel owner would have a tragedy and the next day his hotel caught fire. Because of her prediction, Evangeline made news and became famous. Mars in her chart is at the midpoint of As/Mc, Ve/Mc, and Sa/Ne. Directed Uranus hitting these showed a major change in life and life direction, happiness in an unusual career, and an exciting spiritual profession.

Noel Tyl wrote the combination of Neptune and Pluto by direction can cause miraculous effects. Due to her prediction, Evangeline's new practice started with a bang of high publicity and a long list of new clients. Neptune is at the midpoint of Mo/Sa and Ju/Pl, while Pluto is at the midpoint of Ve/Ur. The Mo/Sa shows a separation from family, while Ju/Pl is the success pair, and Ve/Ur symbolizes birth. She left her family and birthed a new venture that was successful beyond measure.

A COURT CASE

On December 11, 1914, Evangeline was tried in court on a charge of fortune-telling. Her solar arc was 46°54. She was forty-six years old and would turn forty-seven in less than two months. The biwheel with her directions is shown in Figure 30. There are several directed sextiles and trines at the time, pointers of a successful outcome. Notable is the absence of conjunctions and oppositions which take directed midpoints out of the equation. There is:

dSa sextile Ve: a sense of reality, soberness, a sense of duty.

dMc sextile Ne: insecurity, uncertainty, crooks, swindlers, prone to deception.

dPl trine Me: persuasive, successes as a speaker or a writer (mostly in specialized fields), public recognition.

dAs sextile Ur: quick responses to one's surroundings (Tyl: showcase opportunity for individuality; "show off" time").

dUr trine Mc: assertive; the energetic pursuit of objectives, emotional tension or stress, ambition, ready for action, shrewdness and vision, originality, organizing ability; making career advancements, good fortune.

dSa sextile As: gaining experience; feeling inhibited or frustrated; occupants and inmates of a secluded institution.

dJu sextile Me: sound common sense, the intellect, a wealth of ideas, the gift of gab, an active mind, optimism; success as a businessperson, scientist; failure due to dishonesty, negligence or clumsiness, fraud, slander.

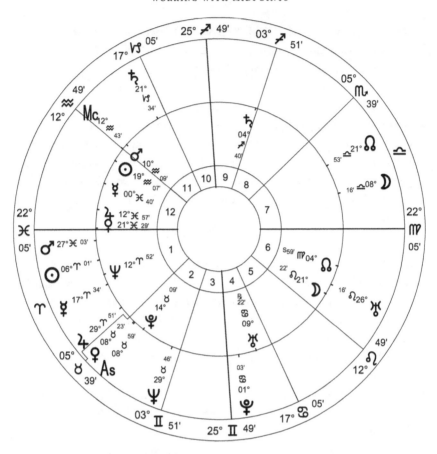

Figure 30. Evangeline Adams biwheel with directions at time of trial

dNe square Me: sympathy and compassion for others, intuitive thinking, perception and depth of vision, a grasp of subtle correlations or relationships, idealism; deceitful people, liars.

At the conclusion of the trial, Evangeline was exonerated. She had been set up by a policewoman who pretended to be a client in need of counseling. The judge ruled Evangeline was no fortune-teller, and that she raised "astrology to the dignity of an exact science."

DEATH

Evangeline died unexpectedly on the afternoon of November 10, 1932. Her solar arc was 64°31 (Figure 31). She died three months before her sixty-fifth birthday. In the year of her death, there were six active solar arc directions.

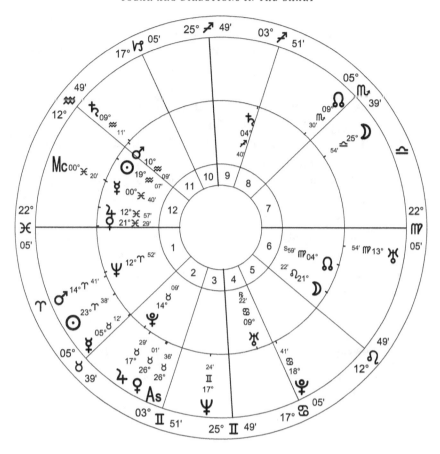

Figure 31. Evangeline death biwheel with directions at time of death

dMo sextile Mc: great aspirations, caring for others, motherliness.

dUr trine Pl: transformation; collapse of the old order, the construction of the new; changes in biological rhythms; the relationship between pulse and breathing; grand objectives achieved through great effort, acts of violence, upsets, subversive activities, an accident.

dMc conjunct Me: clear aims and life goals. The Midheaven has no direct midpoints, and Mercury is at the midpoint of Ve/Ma, Su/Ju, and Ma/As. This whole direction appears to be related to a successful period of work, which would have presumably continued had she not passed away.

dUr opposite Ju: Jupiter is often active at the time of death, and its suddenness is symbolized by Uranus. Ebertin considered Jupiter-Uranus constellations as inner tensions or strains which are suddenly released. He

105

called this midpoint "Thank the Lord" due to the release of tension. Jupiter is at the difficult midpoint of Ma/Ne, which depicts bodily weakness. Uranus is at the midpoint Pl/No, which means great upsets within a community, and emotional suffering through separations. This direction likely refers to those left behind, shocked by her sudden exit.

dSa conjunct Ma: Most telling for this event was the combination of Mars and Saturn, the death pair. In this case, they were at the North Bending of the directed node, suggesting a literal, not figurative death. Saturn has no direct midpoints, but as we saw earlier, Mars sits on two special midpoints: As/Mc and Sa/Ne. Because of the latter, Mars would always be related to illness in her chart.

To conclude, in all honesty, I don't use directions or midpoints in the chart. Here I use secondary progressions with transits and no midpoints. I look at solar arc directions and midpoints on the dial. We'll see the method at work in the next chapter.

 HOMEWORK: Find a significant event in your life and look at the solar arc directions. Do the directions and midpoints help define what happened?

Chapter 11

Solar Arc on the Dial

S olar arc on the dial works the same way as in the chart. Just as we counted degrees in a counter-clockwise motion in the chart, we can do the same on the dial. Since the Sun moves approximately one degree by solar arc in a year, in six months it moves 30′ of arc; in three months (one season), 15′ of arc; and in one month, 5′ of arc. This is a handy guide to estimate when a direction will come due, and whether a direction is in orb to be considered active. In the dial, I use a little wider orb for directions than Ebertin. Since we are looking at an orb of midpoints of 1°½, that is the orb I use for directions, both approaching and separating.

Ebertin thought that when the direction perfected, it was over. I'm not convinced. Certainly, in the year leading up to the partile contact with the natal planet, the direction is in play. But, when there are midpoints that fall after the natal planet, these will still be stimulated by the direction as it separates from the natal planet. These late falling midpoints can also be active.

In regard to timing, Ebertin said repeatedly that solar arcs were not timers. They give a general time frame when an event is due, but transits are the trigger. (We'll look at this in a later chapter.)

The same rule for directions in the chart holds on the dial—there is no mixing of levels. The midpoints have to be contained within one dial, either the natal dial or the directed dial (n/n = n or d/d = d). We ignore mixed-level midpoint combinations such as n/d = n and n/d = d (where n is a natal planet and d is a directed planet).

Ebertin noted two exceptions. On page 27 of his book *Directions*, he wrote: "there are exceptions such as, for example, the midpoint nSu/tSu or nSu/dSu. Nevertheless, it would be better to leave these particularities aside until all other configurations have been brought into clear focus." I have found these particularities to be most informative! The duplication of a planet doubles the influence of that planet on the axis, and I pay attention to these mixed pairs.

Ebertin thought the most significant solar arcs are those that involve the personal points of the Sun, Moon, Ascendant, or Midheaven. That is, when these points direct to a natal planet, or, when a direction comes to them, we can expect a noteworthy event. This is all the more so when a directed personal point connects with a natal personal point. Ebertin only considered directions that made 8th harmonic aspects. In the dial, these are the directions that come to a natal axis and activate the focal planet from either end of the axis.

In directions, I only use completed midpoints, both natally and directed. This means I don't use a natal pair that is completed by a direction (d = n/n), or a directed pair that is completed by a natal point (n = d/d). This may be controversial, but it works. Ebertin wrote incomplete midpoints should be used with caution. On page 22 of his book *Directions*, while investigating the axis: dUr = dAs = Su/Sa, he wrote, "In this case, there is in the natal chart itself no factor located at the midpoint Su/Sa. In such cases, caution is necessary, and conclusions should only be drawn when similar statements are yielded up by the other directions."

What he is saying is that Su/Sa is an incomplete midpoint. It's just a midpoint pair. He is warning that a direction to a natal midpoint pair on its own—that has no planet at the focal point— may not be as effective as a direction coming to an occupied natal midpoint. This bears repeating and emphasizing as it is of enormous importance. In a roundabout way, he is saying to focus on directions to completed midpoints. In practice, he didn't always do this, but I do.

In his many books, Ebertin often mentioned there were too many midpoints to list, and so he described those pertinent to the subject under investigation. But he never explained why he ignored the midpoints that he did, some of which seemed apropos to the event. I agree with him that looking at natal and directed (and transiting) midpoints, is too much. The trick is to find the activated axes that matter the most. In my view, these involve using only completed midpoints, both natal and directed (and transiting).

DIFFERENCE LISTING

The Difference Listing set at a modulus of 45° will highlight the approximate age that a direction will occur by an 8th harmonic aspect. Stephen King's Difference Listing for the 45°-modulus is shown in Figure 32. You

In Planetary Sequence – Modulus 45°00'

☽/☉	11°08'	☿/♇	29°12'	♃/♂	15°22'	♆/☽	21°11'	☊/♆	44°52'
☽/☿	28°47'	☿/☊	40°08'	♃/♄	39°18'	♆/☉	32°20'	☊/♇	34°04'
☽/♀	15°54'	☿/As	14°49'	♃/♅	32°18'	♆/☿	04°59'	☊/As	19°41'
☽/♂	37°56'	☿/Mc	42°28'	♃/♆	01°14'	♆/♀	37°06'	☊/Mc	02°19'
☽/♃	22°33'	♀/☽	29°05'	♃/♇	35°26'	♆/♂	14°07'	As/☽	01°22'
☽/♄	16°52'	♀/☉	40°14'	♃/☊	01°22'	♆/♃	43°45'	As/☉	12°31'
☽/♅	09°52'	♀/☿	12°53'	♃/As	21°03'	♆/♄	38°03'	As/☿	30°10'
☽/♆	23°48'	♀/♂	22°01'	♃/Mc	03°41'	♆/♅	31°03'	As/♀	17°17'
☽/♇	13°00'	♀/♃	06°39'	♄/☽	28°07'	♆/♇	34°11'	As/♂	39°18'
☽/☊	23°56'	♀/♄	00°57'	♄/☉	39°16'	♆/☊	00°07'	As/♃	23°56'
☽/As	43°37'	♀/♅	38°57'	♄/☿	11°55'	♆/As	19°48'	As/♄	18°15'
☽/Mc	26°15'	♀/♆	07°53'	♄/♀	44°02'	♆/Mc	02°27'	As/♅	11°15'
☉/☽	33°51'	♀/♇	42°05'	♄/♂	21°03'	♇/☽	31°59'	As/♆	25°11'
☉/☿	17°38'	♀/☊	08°01'	♄/♃	05°41'	♇/☉	43°08'	As/♇	14°23'
☉/♀	04°45'	♀/As	27°42'	♄/♅	38°00'	♇/☿	15°47'	As/☊	25°18'
☉/♂	26°47'	♀/Mc	10°21'	♄/♆	06°56'	♇/♀	02°54'	As/Mc	27°38'
☉/♃	11°24'	♂/☽	07°03'	♄/♇	41°08'	♇/♂	24°55'	Mc/☽	18°44'
☉/♄	05°43'	♂/☉	18°12'	♄/☊	07°03'	♇/♃	09°33'	Mc/☉	29°53'
☉/♅	43°43'	♂/☿	35°51'	♄/As	26°44'	♇/♄	03°51'	Mc/☿	02°31'
☉/♆	12°39'	♂/♀	22°58'	♄/Mc	09°23'	♇/♅	41°52'	Mc/♀	34°38'
☉/♇	01°51'	♂/♃	29°37'	♅/☽	35°07'	♇/♆	10°48'	Mc/♂	11°40'
☉/☊	12°47'	♂/♄	23°56'	♅/☉	01°16'	♇/☊	10°55'	Mc/♃	41°18'
☉/As	32°28'	♂/♅	16°56'	♅/☿	18°55'	♇/As	30°36'	Mc/♄	35°36'
☉/Mc	15°06'	♂/♆	30°52'	♅/♀	06°02'	♇/Mc	13°15'	Mc/♅	28°36'
☿/☽	16°12'	♂/♇	20°04'	♅/♂	28°03'	☊/☽	21°03'	Mc/♆	42°32'
☿/☉	27°21'	♂/☊	30°59'	♅/♃	12°41'	☊/☉	32°12'	Mc/♇	31°44'
☿/♀	32°06'	♂/As	05°41'	♅/♄	06°59'	☊/☿	04°51'	Mc/☊	42°40'
☿/♂	09°08'	♂/Mc	33°19'	♅/♆	13°56'	☊/♀	36°58'	Mc/As	17°21'
☿/♃	38°46'	♃/☽	22°26'	♅/♇	03°07'	☊/♂	14°00'		
☿/♄	33°04'	♃/☉	33°35'	♅/☊	14°03'	☊/♃	43°37'		
☿/♅	26°04'	♃/☿	06°13'	♅/As	33°44'	☊/♄	37°56'		
☿/♆	40°00'	♃/♀	38°20'	♅/Mc	16°23'	☊/♅	30°56'		

Figure 32A. Stephen King's difference listing 45°, in planetary sequence

Sorted by Angle – Modulus 45°00'

♆/☊	00°07'	☽/♅	09°52'	☉/☿	17°38'	Mc/♅	28°36'	♆/♀	37°06'
♀/♄	00°57'	♀/Mc	10°21'	♂/☉	18°12'	☽/☿	28°47'	☽/♂	37°56'
♃/♆	01°14'	♇/♆	10°48'	As/♄	18°15'	♀/☽	29°05'	☊/♄	37°56'
♅/☉	01°16'	♇/☊	10°55'	Mc/☽	18°44'	☿/♇	29°12'	♄/♅	38°00'
♃/☊	01°22'	☽/☉	11°08'	♅/☿	18°55'	♂/♃	29°37'	♆/♄	38°03'
As/☽	01°22'	As/♅	11°15'	☊/As	19°41'	Mc/☉	29°53'	♃/♀	38°20'
☉/♇	01°51'	☉/♃	11°24'	♆/As	19°48'	As/☿	30°10'	☿/♃	38°46'
☊/Mc	02°19'	Mc/♂	11°40'	♂/♇	20°04'	♇/As	30°36'	♀/♅	38°57'
♆/Mc	02°27'	♄/☿	11°55'	♃/As	21°03'	♂/♆	30°52'	♄/☉	39°16'
Mc/☿	02°31'	As/☉	12°31'	♄/♂	21°03'	☊/♅	30°56'	♃/♄	39°18'
♇/♀	02°54'	☉/♆	12°39'	☊/☽	21°03'	♂/☊	30°59'	As/♂	39°18'
♅/♇	03°07'	♅/♃	12°41'	♆/☽	21°11'	♆/♅	31°03'	☿/♆	40°00'
♃/Mc	03°41'	☉/☊	12°47'	♀/♂	22°01'	Mc/♇	31°44'	☿/☊	40°08'
♇/♄	03°51'	♀/☿	12°53'	♃/☽	22°26'	♇/☽	31°59'	♀/☉	40°14'
☉/♀	04°45'	☽/♇	13°00'	☽/♃	22°33'	☿/♀	32°06'	♄/♇	41°08'
☊/☿	04°51'	♇/Mc	13°15'	♂/♀	22°58'	☊/☉	32°12'	Mc/♃	41°18'
♆/☿	04°59'	♅/♆	13°56'	☽/♆	23°48'	♃/♅	32°18'	♇/♅	41°52'
♂/As	05°41'	☊/♂	14°00'	☽/☊	23°56'	♆/☉	32°20'	♀/♇	42°05'
♄/♃	05°41'	♅/☊	14°03'	♂/♄	23°56'	☉/As	32°28'	☿/Mc	42°28'
☉/♄	05°43'	♆/♂	14°07'	As/♃	23°56'	☿/♄	33°04'	Mc/♆	42°32'
♅/♀	06°02'	As/♇	14°23'	♇/♂	24°55'	♂/Mc	33°19'	Mc/☊	42°40'
♃/☿	06°13'	☿/As	14°49'	As/♆	25°11'	♃/☉	33°35'	♇/☉	43°08'
♀/♃	06°39'	☉/Mc	15°06'	As/☊	25°18'	♅/As	33°44'	☽/As	43°37'
♄/♆	06°56'	♃/♂	15°22'	☿/♅	26°04'	☉/☽	33°51'	☊/♃	43°37'
♅/♄	06°59'	♇/☿	15°47'	☽/Mc	26°15'	☊/♇	34°04'	☉/♅	43°43'
♄/☊	07°03'	☽/♀	15°54'	♄/As	26°44'	♆/♇	34°11'	♆/♃	43°45'
♂/☽	07°03'	☿/☽	16°12'	☉/♂	26°47'	Mc/♀	34°38'	♄/♀	44°02'
♀/♆	07°53'	♅/Mc	16°23'	☿/☉	27°21'	♅/☽	35°07'	☊/♆	44°52'
♀/☊	08°01'	☽/♄	16°52'	As/Mc	27°38'	♃/♇	35°26'		
☿/♂	09°08'	♂/♅	16°56'	♀/As	27°42'	Mc/♄	35°36'		
♄/Mc	09°23'	As/♀	17°17'	♅/♂	28°03'	♂/☿	35°51'		
♇/♃	09°33'	Mc/As	17°21'	♄/☽	28°07'	☊/♀	36°58'		

Figure 32B: Stephen King's difference listing 45°, sorted by angle

can compare it to his 180-modulus shown in Figure 28 (refer to page 97). Again, the "/" in this list does not refer to a midpoint pair, but rather the direction of the first planet to the second planet, and the arc distance in degree between them. The list is an easy way to see which directions will occur at any approximate age.

In the next section, we'll look at Stephen King's directions at three pivotal times of his life. If you have Solar Fire or Nova Chartwheels, as we go through each example, print out the dial and follow along. Doing it yourself is always the best way to learn something. Be aware that in the Nova Chartwheels Software, the orb of a midpoint pair associated with the pointer is 15′ or less, so these are the midpoints that pop up. In an event timed to the minute or day, close midpoints help clarify what is of importance. However, not every midpoint pair that pops up is valid, so discrimination is necessary.

A HORROR STORY

When Stephen King was 26½ years old, his first novel, *Carrie*, hit the shelves. His solar arc was 26°08. His natal-directed dial set for this date is shown in Figure 33 on page 112. To find the directions that were active at this time, visually scan the dial, counterclockwise, starting at the Aries Point. There were four directions:

dMo = Mc
dSu = Ma
dMe = Ur
dSa = As

We'll look at each of these directions in turn, as well as their associated midpoints. Keep in mind, these four directions are aspects of the 8th harmonic. The natal planet responding to the directed planet will give the theme of the direction. Any associated midpoints of either the natal planet or directed planet, add ancillary information.

The first direction is dMo = Mc. The bidial with the axis set to this direction is shown in Figure 34 on page 113. This is a significant direction because it involves two personal points, the Midheaven (career and life goals) and the Moon (needs, emotions). From the diagram, we can see on the axis the natal pair Me/Ne, the directed pair dMe/Sa, and the exception pair Pl/dPl. This last mixed pair is valid because it combines the same planet, essentially adding a doubled influence of Pluto.

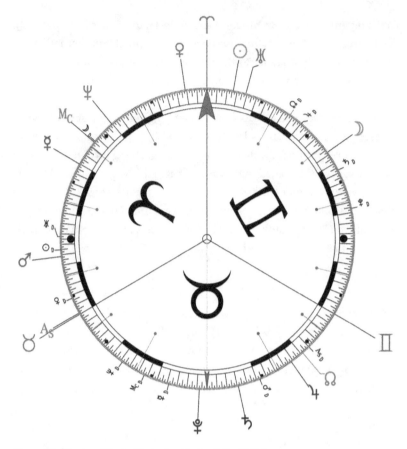

Figure 33: Stephen King's *Carrie* directions on the bidial

Note the mixed midpoint pair Mo/dMc is also on the axis. This mixed pair is a reiteration of the direction of dMo = Mc. This is always the case: In the dial, when a directed planet comes to the axis of a natal planet, such as dMo = Mc in this example, the same two planets always form a corresponding midpoint pair (Mo/dMc). This repeated mixed pair should be ignored. The other mixed midpoints should also be ignored: nUr/dVe and nVe/dUr..

In sum, the directed axis is dMo = Mc = Me/Ne = dMe/Sa = dPl/Pl. Here we have the directed Moon carrying the directed pair dMe/Sa to the axis of the Midheaven, which itself is on the midpoint of Me/Ne. At this particular time, natal Pluto and directed Pluto also form a midpoint on the axis. We'll break the axis apart and delineate each component in turn, starting with the main direction (the aspect):

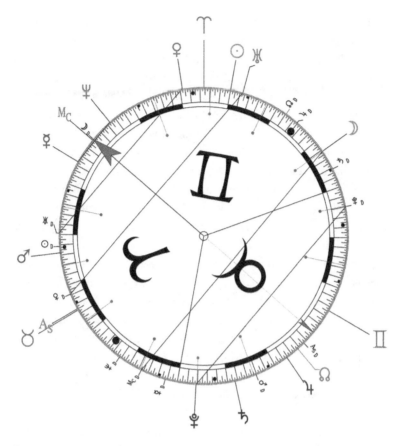

Figure 34: Stephen King's *Carrie* directed dMo = Mc axis

dMo = Mc: great aspirations, people with feeling and sentiment, changing life objectives that lead to many changes.

It was a time when life goals were highlighted and indicates a far-reaching change. What were these goals and what changed? For this we turn to the midpoints:

Mc = Me/Ne: a rich imagination, sweeping ideas and plans, intuitive thinking, sympathetic understanding of others, deception.

dMo = dMe/Sa: gaining wide experience, the ability to absorb and digest diverse impressions.

Pl/dPl: force majeure or providence, invisible forces or powers, the manifestation of unconscious powers, the urge to influence many others.

To summarize this axis, we see the success and recognition of a novelist. In interpreting the axis, we combined the meaning of the natal midpoint with the directed midpoint and added the exceptional midpoint. It's also possible to string the meaning of each planet together in a sentence. Here dMo = Mc = Me/Ne = dMe/Sa = dPl/Pl describes a feeling (Mo) related to the profession and life goals (Mc) of being a creative and imaginative (Ne) thinker (Me), but also a serious (Sa) thinker (Me), giving great power (Pl).

As an aid to interpretation only, we can look up the meaning of a directed planet with a natal pair in the COSI to gain a further understanding of what the combination may mean. In this instance, dMo = Me/Ne means thinking with the heart. Mc = dMe/Sa means serious thinking. If we weren't sure before what the axis means, we can see from this it is likely related to thinking.

The second directed axis involves the solar arc Sun, a personal planet, which is always significant, coming to Mars (Figure 35). Putting the pointer on dSun we get the pair dNo/As. Moving the pointer to Mars, we pick up the midpoint of dMo/Ne, which is a midpoint pair associated with the Sun in the nativity that is ahead of the Sun by 45′. The directed Mo/Ne falls squarely on natal Mars. Natally Mars is on the midpoints of Ju/Ur and Ve/Pl. Putting this together we get:

dSu = Ma = dNo/As = dMo/Ne = Ju/Ur = Ve/Pl. This breaks down into:

dSu = Ma: Vitality and vigor, activity. Advancing in life through hard work, positions of leadership, overcoming difficulties and dangers, vocational success, extraordinary achievements.

The midpoints shed insight into the nature of the leading position, vocational success, and type of extraordinary achievement.

dSu = dNo/As: cultivating social contacts and entertainment, making new contacts.

dSu = dMo/Ne: illusions and deceptions.

Ma = Ju/Ur: achieving good fortune in life.

Ma = Ve/Pl: brutal and coarse expression of feeling.

The midpoints show a leader in the social arena, extraordinary illusions and deceptions, connecting with others, making a fortune through expressing feelings. We know in hindsight this axis describes a successful author.

If we string together the keywords from dSu = Ma = dNo/As = dMo/Ne = Ju/Ur = Ve/Pl, we get revitalizing and illuminating (Su) work (Ma) for others (No) in a personal relationship (As) that is emotional (Mo) and

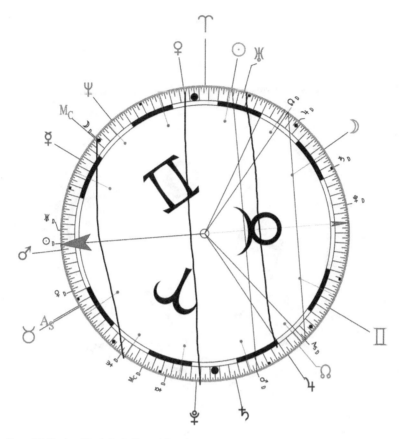

Figure 35. Stephen King's *Carrie* directed Su axis

imaginative and creative (Ne), and an unusual (Ur) publication (Ju) that is artistically (Ve) disturbing and dark (Pl).

The third direction is dMe = Ur (Figure 36). This is the pair that means astuteness and intuition. Because the direction is an opposition on the dial, it is an aspect of a semisquare or sesquisquare, not that it matters. However, with this setup, the corresponding mixed pair of Me = dUr is not present. On this axis, we have dMo/Pl. (Note the invalid mixed pair of Ve/dJu on the axis, along with the corresponding invalid dVe/Ju. There is also the invalid Mc/dPl and corresponding invalid Pl/dMc, all of which we ignore.)

On this axis, we pay attention to dMe = Ur = dMo/Pl = Ju/As. Simply, the axis of Me = Mo/Pl has directed to the natal axis of Ur = Ju/As. Delineating the axis, starting with the aspect, we have:

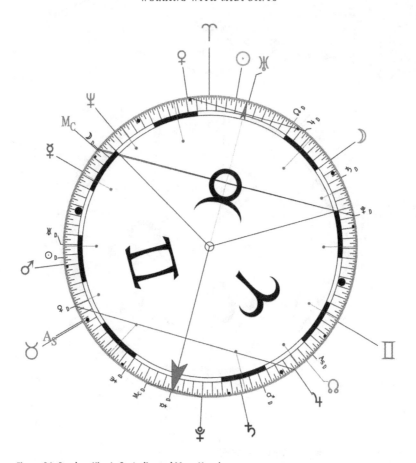

Figure 36. Stephen King's *Carrie* directed Me = Ur axis

dMe = Ur: a revolutionary spirit and mind, shrewd, inventive thinking, a talent for speaking (I would add writing), innovative, inventive.

Adding midpoints to flesh out what is revolutionary and inventive, we see:

Ur = Ju/As: optimistic attitude toward others, a lucky hand in the guidance of others as well as new ventures. Fortunate conditions and circumstances.

dMe = dMo/Pl: far-reaching plans, the zealous pursuit of comprehension, ability to powerfully influence the public through speech or writing.

The axis shows the nature of the book, a showcasing of his talent, his impending influence on readers, and a change in circumstance. However,

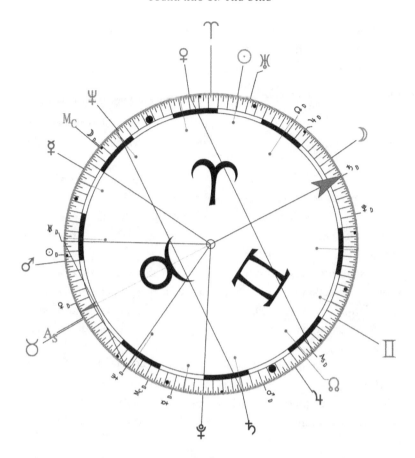

Figure 37. Stephen King's *Carrie* directed Sa = As axis

this axis is not without tension. Before publication, Stephen King had no idea how successful the novel would be.

Taking the shortcut and using keywords associated with dMe = Ur = dMo/PL = Ju/As gives an unusual (Ur) book (Me) that has dark (Pluto) emotions (Moon) read and enjoyed by many (Ju/As).

The 4th and final direction is dSa = As (Figure 37), with directed Saturn approaching the Ascendant from the opposite end of the pointer. On the axis we have dSa = As = Me/Pl = Ne/Sa = dSu/Ne = dUr/Ne. We start with the directed aspect:

dSa = As: early maturity and gained experience through outer events and occurrences.

117

To answer what event or occurrence provided experience leading to early maturity, we add the midpoints:

As = Me/Pl: intellectual domination of the environment, also influencing others in one's environment.

dSa = dSu/Ne: held back by illness or disability, an emotional affliction; mental and emotional illness. (Tyl adds concerns about blood. This midpoint describes the nature of the book, *Carrie*, which was published on this day.)

dSa = dUr/Ne: depression, instability, pessimism. A painful loss, mourning, or bereavement. (Seems related to the book.)

As = Sa/Ne: a depressing environment, oppressive family life, emotional suffering inflicted by others, limitation of freedom. (A description apropos of the main character, Carrie.)

In summary, this axis uncannily describes the theme of the book. We know the direction is important because it involves a personal point, the Ascendant. The Ascendant configured with the influential writing pair of Me/Pl tells us the axis is related to his writing. The midpoints describe what he was writing about.

Taking the shortcut to delineate dSa = As = Me/Pl = Ne/Sa = dSu/Ne = dUr/Ne, gives a sad (Saturn) situation (As) that is powerfully (Pl) written (Me) and brings otherworldly (Ne) elements into everyday reality (Sa). The book details shocking (Ur) otherworldly (Ne) intrusions affecting the book's star (Su).

In summary, the directions at the time of publication of a first novel are shown in the dial delineation. I have not included every meaning given in the COSI. Since publication is a successful event, I cherry-picked the positive statements and ignored the negative options. In prediction, such cherry-picking would be ill-advised.

AN INTERVENTION

Stephen King's directions on September 22, 1987, are shown on the bidial in Figure 38, the day his wife staged an intervention to force him to stop drinking. There were five active solar arc directions: dJu = Sa; dAs = Ma; dVe = Ur = Su; dMe = No = Ne; dSa = Su. Since this was likely an unsettling and unpleasant experience, I'll weigh the meanings toward the negative. We'll delineate each direction in turn.

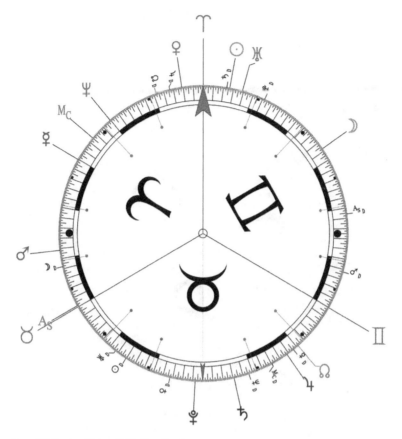

Figure 38. Stephen King quit drinking directions

The direction of Jupiter to Saturn is shown in Figure 39 on page 120. Directed Jupiter is opposite natal Saturn and separating. The pairs Ur/Ne and dMe/Ve stand on the axis. Given directed Jupiter is leaving, it would appear the party's over. In sum we have: dJu = Sa = Ur/Ne = dMe/Ve. Starting with the aspect, we get:

dJu = Sa: patience, perseverance, hard work, clear objectives, a sense of duty, the desire for possessions. An unsettled life, a change of residence or employed staff, an angry upset, vexation, or annoyance.

We see in this direction someone with their back against the wall. There was a choice to make. The midpoints add:

dJu = dMe/Ve: great wealth of artistic design, love of luxury, artistic success, an advantageous union.

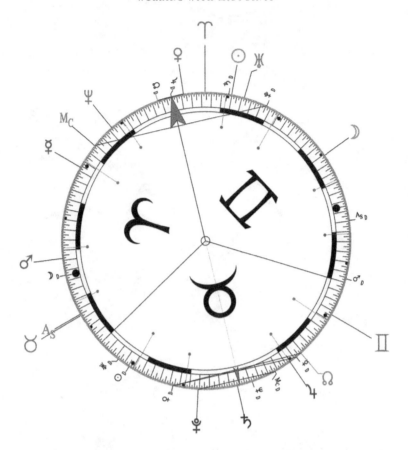

Figure 39. Stephen King sober Sa = dJu axis

Sa = Ur/Ne: depression, instability, pessimism. A painful loss, mourning, or bereavement.

The axis shows seriousness, depression, but also hope. King would not have realized his good fortune at the time.

If we take a shortcut, the string of keywords from dJu = Sa = Ur/Ne = dMe/Ve, give optimism (Ju) that depression and melancholy (Sa) can be helped by changed (Ur) drinking habits (Ne), resulting in happy (Ve) thoughts (Me).

I don't know if he went to rehab, but the change of residence and staff shown by dJu = Sa suggests it.

The second direction was directed Ascendant = natal Mars, found on opposite ends of the pointer, as illustrated in Figure 40. This is an important

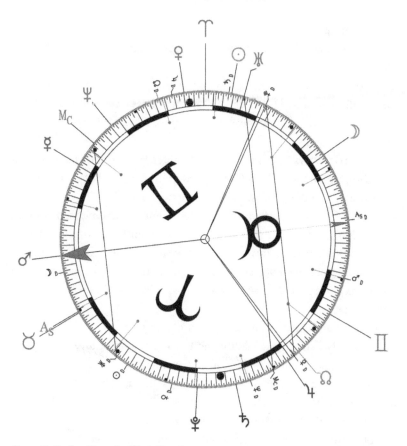

Figure 40. Stephen King sober Ma = dAs axis

direction because of the involvement of the Ascendant, a personal point. The Ascendant is at the midpoints of Me/Pl and Sa/Ne. Mars is at the midpoint of Ju/Ur. In sum, there is on the axis:

dAs = Ma = dMe/Pl = dSa/Ne = Ju/Ur

The aspect gives:

dAs = Ma: fighting spirit. The tendency to force one's own will upon others, the ability to lead or guide others resolutely, and active teamwork. A fighting and aggressive attitude toward others. The tendency to drive and push others to work, successful creative activity in teamwork, and the forceful attainment of successes. Quarrels, conflicts, disputes. Presumably, this axis is symbolizing his wife who was the driving force behind the scene pushing for the intervention.

The midpoints add:

dAs = dMe/Pl: intellectually dominating, exercising influence over others.

dAs = dSa/Ne: depressing environment, oppressive family life, emotional suffering caused by others, limitation of freedom.

Ma = Ju/Ur: bringing ideas to realization, a love of freedom, making fortunate decisions.

The axis shows how antagonistic the intervention must have been. It would appear he fought back and lobbied in his defense, but in the end, he lost the battle with his wife who had the upper hand.

The third direction involved directed Venus separating from Uranus and applying to the Sun from across the axis (Figure 41). This is a significant direction due to the involvement of the Sun, as well as the simultaneous activation of two natal planets. (We will ignore dSa = Su for the moment.) On the axis, we have dVe = Su = Ur = Ju/As = No/As. We take the aspects first and get:

dVe = Su: feelings of love, the power of attraction.

dVe = Ur: strong excitability and overexpression of love, strong and barely controllable emotions, willful and obstinate.

With this direction, love life is in focus and affected by a change or upset. Adding the midpoints we see:

Su = Ju/As: a fortunate or influential meeting.

Su = No/As: meeting other people personally; a new contact.

Ur = Ju/As: optimistic attitude, a lucky hand in the guidance of others as well as new ventures; a fortunate change of one's environment.

Ur = No/As: suddenly seeking out new contacts; sudden experiences with associates.

On this axis, the feeling of love and affection in Stephen King's family comes across loud and clear. It appears they brought in outside help for the intervention. Everything seems upbeat as he takes the difficult step (not shown here) to stop drinking.

If we use keywords for this axis: dVe = Su = Ur= Ju/As = No/As, we see love (Ve) for a man (Su) who must change (Ur) by associating (No) with others (As) who have a positive philosophy (Ju) on life (Su).

The fourth direction is dMe = No = Ne. The axis is shown in Figure 42 on page 124. Should Jupiter be included in the axis? For this, we look to the

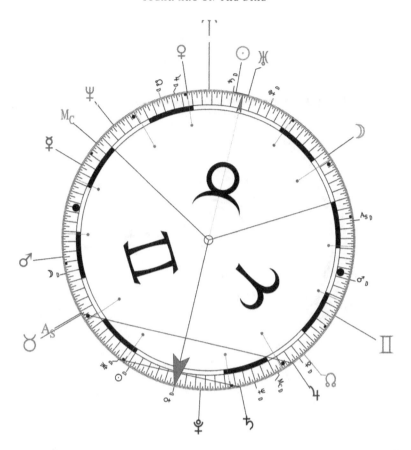

Figure 41. Stephen King sober dVe = Su axis

degrees of dMe and Jupiter. The latter is 23°48 fixed, and dMe is at 24°35, so technically they will separate in 43'. Since dMercury is now advancing upon the Node and Neptune, to keep things simple, I will focus on these. It doesn't seem like a Jupiter moment to me. (As always, we use judgment, rather than hard, fixed rules when considering whether to include a factor or not.)

The axis we will examine has dMe = No = Ne = Ma/Ur = dMo/Pl. Natally, both the Node and Neptune are at the explosive midpoint of Ma/Ur. Natal Mercury is on the Mo/Pl midpoint and they have come together by direction. The aspects give:

dMe = No: the exchange of ideas, joint plans.

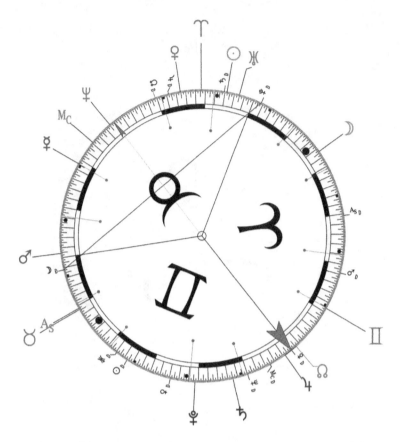

Figure 42 Stephen King sober dVe = No axis

dMe = Ne: wrong thinking, faulty judgment, confused ideas, nervous sensitivity, insincerity, a lack of clarity, self-deception. Also, subconscious, failures due to improper behavior.

The aspects show a discussion of the need for sobriety. The process was likely laid out in precise detail. From the midpoints we get:

No = Ma/Ur: excitement in the presence of others, sudden events shared with others, extraordinary and unusual enterprises.

Ne = Ma/Ur: cunning and deceitfulness, a low and mean way of acting, harming others, someone with bad intentions; a fainting fit, a fit of rage or frenzy, also raving madness.

dMe = dMo/Pl: grand plans, the zealous pursuit of ideas.

This axis shows the crux of the problem. Here is Stephen King confronted by his family—and likely addiction specialists as well— trying to

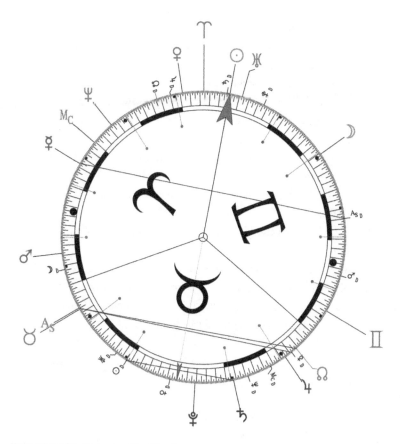

Figure 43 Stephen King sober dSa = Su axis

convince him he has a problem that he has to address, This axis also indicates his refusal to recognize or accept his problem, and the probability that
he throws an angry fit only to eventually capitulate.

The keywords of the axis of dMe = No = Ne = Ma/Ur = dMo/Pl give
sudden (Ur) explosive (Ma/Ur) words (Me) with others (No) about dark
(Pluto) emotions (Mo) erupting while drinking (Ne). He is hearing how he
behaved when drunk.

The final, depressing direction is that of Saturn coming to the Sun,
shown on the axis in Figure 43. On the axis, we have dSa = Su = dVe = No/
As = dUr/Ne. The aspects give:

dSa = Su: struggling to advance in life. Delicate health, a secluded or
solitary life, being suppressed by others, separations.

dVe = Su: love, harmony, art, happiness.

Love is on the line, separation is in the air, and life cannot continue as usual. The midpoints add:

dVe = Su = Sa: suppressed feelings, reserve; inhibited love life, the separation of lovers (to which I would add unhappiness).

Su = No/As: cultivating social contacts, the desire to meet others ; a new contact.

dSa = dUr/Ne: depressed, unstable, pessimistic; a painful loss, mourning or bereavement.

dVe = dUr/Ne: highly sensitive, peculiar art, unrequited love; a peculiar kind of love.

The axis describes the problem and a plan for sobriety that was ultimately successful.

A look at the keywords from the axis dSa = Su = dVe = No/As = Ur/Ne gives a reality check (Sa) that health (Su) and happiness (Ve) require a separation (Sa) and making a relationship (Ve) with associates (No) in another place (As) that will change (Ur) drinking habits (Ne).

In summary, the directions at the time of the intervention point to varying perspectives of an unpleasant event.

AN ACCIDENT

We'll look at one last event in this writer's life. At age 51, Stephen King had a near-death experience that he wrote about in his biography, *On Writing*. On June 19, 1999, he left his house around four o'clock for his daily 4-mile walk. He had just returned from taking his younger son to the airport and his other two kids were still visiting; the family planned on going to a 7.00 p.m. movie and he wanted to fit in a walk beforehand.

A portion of his walk took him on the highway. He was walking north on a gravel shoulder up a steep hill, facing oncoming traffic, when a van came over the top. The driver had his face turned to the back seat where a rottweiler was trying to take a cover off a cooler. Stephen King had less than a second to react and thought, My god, I'm going to be hit by a school bus. He turned to his left.

The next thing he knew he was on the ground; the van was off the road and tilted to one side. He lost consciousness and when he came to, the

42-year-old van driver (who had a dozen vehicle infractions) was sitting next to him on a rock. The driver thought he'd hit a small deer until he saw glasses lying on his passenger seat.

Stephen King lost consciousness again and when he came to, an ambulance had arrived. An EMT made him wiggle his toes and Stephen King made him promise that he was telling the truth that his toes had moved. Later, the EMT told him: "When I saw the way you were lying in the ditch, plus the extent of impact injuries, I didn't think you'd make it to the hospital. You're a lucky camper to still be with the program."

Stephen King was taken to a nearby hospital, then flown by helicopter to a larger trauma hospital. His left leg was shattered, broken in nine pieces; the bones looked like marbles. His right hip was broken. His spine was chipped in eight places. He had four broken ribs. A cut on his scalp needed twenty stitches. His lung collapsed in the helicopter.

The gash on his scalp came when he hit the windshield. He landed two inches from a steel support post on the driver's side. Had he struck that, he would have been impaled—killed or permanently comatose, "a vegetable with legs." Had he struck the rocks jutting out of the ground, he also would likely have been killed or paralyzed. He was thrown over the van fourteen feet in the air, landing just shy of the rocks. His surgeon told him that he must have pivoted to the left at the last second. If that hadn't happened, he would have died. It took eight surgeries to fix his broken bones.

In the helicopter, King was thinking that he didn't want to die. He loved his wife, his kids, writing, and his afternoon walks by the lake. As he was looking at the blue summer sky, he realized he was on death's doorstep, and thought: *Someone is going to pull me one way or the other pretty soon. It's mostly out of my hands.*

A bidial set for the time he left his house is shown in Figure 44. The solar arc was 51° 20. By now, finding the natal midpoints and directed midpoints on an axis should be clear. I'll leave it to you to move the pointer around the directed bidial to view the activated axes for yourself. Find these before reading on.

There are six directions. The first is dUr = Ve. Do we include natal Saturn and directed Sun? Because the dSun is well past Venus, I would not. I would take dUr = Sa = dSu as a separate axis, which is the second direction. The third is dSa = Ne = No. Do we include dVe = Ju? I would not, because directed Venus is approaching Jupiter; I put them on their own axis, as the

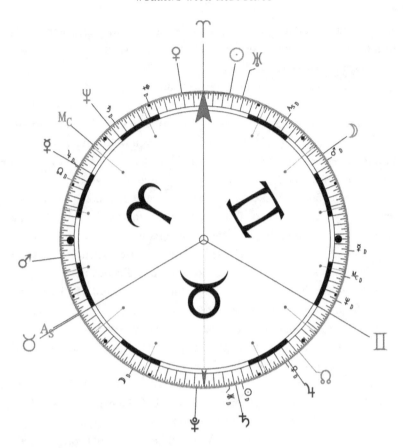

Figure 44. Stephen King directions when hit by a car

fourth direction. The fifth direction is dJu = Me. The sixth direction is dMa = Mo = As. We'll look at each axis in turn. Before you read on, list all the midpoint pairs, both natal and directed, that are associated with each axis.

The first axis of dUr = Ve has no immediate midpoints. We can just look at the aspect.

dUr = Ve: This is a sudden upset in happiness.

The second axis is dUr = Sa = dSu, with Saturn on the midpoint of dJu/As, Su/Ne, and Ur/Ne, and dSu on the midpoint of dNo/As and Ju/Pl. Do we include the obvious Sa = dSu/Ur? Answer: No. We only look at midpoint pairs that are completed. The axis has dUr = Sa = dSu = dJu/As = Ur/Ne = Su/Ne = dAs/No = Ju/Pl. From the aspects we get:

dSu = Sa: inhibition, karma, reparation; testing if one is on the right track; awareness of responsibility; difficulty, depletion, confinement, discipline; fear of loss; being alone; grief. Delicate health, forced by events to lead a modest and simple life, suppression by others, and separations.

dUr = Sa: unusual emotional tension, irritable emotional conflicts, rebellious, the urge to be free, provocative conduct, an act of violence. The ability to cope with every situation, to persevere and endure, indefatigable, willpower, and determination.

The hard aspects to Saturn show a difficult time, possibly impacting health. The keywords for the three planets give something sudden, unexpected (Ur), and sad or restrictive (Sa) impacting vitality or the physical body (Su).

Next, we add midpoints:

Sa = Ur/Ne: depression, instability, pessimism; a painful loss, mourning or bereavement.

Sa = Ju/Pl: blocked self-development; the inability to progress, difficulties, separation.

Sa = Su/Ne: inhibited by illness or disability, impeded blood circulation, bad or unhealthy blood.

dUr = dJu/As:; luck from others, a fortunate rearrangement of circumstances.

dSu = dJu/As: fortunate or influential connections.

dUr = dNo/As: suddenly seeking contacts.

dSu = dNo/As: the desire to meet others.

The theme is separation, illness, and lots of luck (also finding good doctors). If we string keywords from the axis: dUr = Sa = dSu = dJu/As = Ur/Ne = Su/Ne = dAs/No = Ju/Pl, we get sudden (Ur) limits (Sa) for the physical body (Su) and unconsciousness (Ne) due to an associate (No) in the place (As) causing major (Ju) destruction (Pl).

The third axis is dSa = Ne = No. We note dVe = Ju nearby. Do we include them? We could, but I won't because dSa is separating from Jupiter (though it is within orb.) It's a tough call and I depend on transits to show me what is active. Here we are just looking at directions and one axis (Ve = Ju) coming to another axis (Ne = Ju = No). Since the aspects are not exact, the alignment is staggered. I tend to break them up into those that are exact. The important thing is to see them and note they are occurring together. However, I interpret them separately.

So, on the axis, we have dSa = Ne = No = Ma/Ur = dSu/Ne = dUr/Ne. The aspects are dSa = Ne and dSa = No:

dSa = No: isolation, social inhibition; a group of elderly or needy people (such as a nursing home/retirement home); disadvantages through others.

dSa = Ne: (the sickness axis) suffering, renunciation, asceticism, illness; wanting to give up under stress; denial; loss of focus or ambition; depression; a sense of being wronged.

The three points together give an association (Node) of the sick (Sa/Ne). The midpoints add:

Ne = Ma/Ur: a fainting fit, a fit of rage or frenzy, raving madness, a car accident.

No = Ma/Ur: excitability in the presence of others, experiencing sudden events with others, the undertaking of extraordinary and unusual enterprises.

dSa = dSu/Ne: held back by illness or physical debility, blocked blood circulation, bad or unhealthy blood.

dSa = dUr/Ne: depression, instability, pessimism; a painful loss, mourning or bereavement.

This axis points to illness and an accident with a grievous injury and hospitalization.

The fourth axis is dVe = Ju = Me/Ve. One reason I preferred to separate this axis from the third axis is because I think this axis saved his life. Here are the two benefics in aspect on the Me/Ve midpoint, which represent not only the mind but also the limbs. From the aspect we get:

dVe = Ju: the joy of love, success.

This is a positive aspect to see amid the difficult directions. The midpoint adds:

Ju = Me/Ve: the realization of love thoughts, an advantageous union; (also luck in regard to limbs).

Given the previous problematic axes we looked at, this one gives hope for a good outcome.

The fifth axis is dJu = Me = Mo/Pl = dMe/Ve. In the last direction, we had the midpoint of Ju = Me/Ve active and here it is the direction (dJu = dMe/Ve) configured with Mercury. This is doubly fortunate. The aspect, which is the theme of the axis is:

dJu = Me: common sense, the intellect, scientists.

We add the midpoints:

Me = Mo/Pl: far-reaching plans, the zealous pursuit of ideas.

dJu = dMe/Ve: an advantageous union.

Here is another axis pointing to a successful outcome. Stephen King likely had the best doctors and excellent medical care. You can't also overlook the healing power of love and an optimistic desire to live.

The sixth axis is dMa = Mo = As = dVe/Sa = dJu/Ur = Me/Sa = Me/Pl. This is a significant direction because the activation of the axis comprises two personal points—the Moon and Ascendant. This direction brings dVenus and dSaturn together (the pair we examined separately in axes three and four). Also on the axis is the directed "thank the lord" pair of dJu/Ur.

The aspects are: dMa = Mo and dMa = As:

dMa = Mo: excitability, impulsive, intense emotion. (Actions which are directed by the unconscious). Industrious. Strong inner tensions, willpower, a fighting spirit, hasty, or premature action.

dMa = As: a fighting spirit, robust; accident prone, surgery.

The aspects show an operation and an emotional upset. From the midpoints:

dMa = dVe/Sa: the inclination to act on the dictates of emotional inhibition or of regained soberness, discussion or dispute, separation (note the death pair Ma/Sa).

dMa = dJu/Ur: a quick determination, making fortunate decisions (as in jumping at the absolutely right angle).

Mo = Me/Sa: assimilating many different impressions.

As = Me/Sa: preoccupied with ideas, a busy mind, a short journey, separation.

Mo = Me/Pl: evolving and changing thinking, a woman who can speak with conviction.

As = Me/Pl: an intellectual environment, also the ability to influence others in the environment. Good fortune is colored with emotional upset. The midpoints coat the tension of the aspect with luck. An important author was critically injured and received the best treatment possible.

In summary, these six directions together describe the incident with clarity, as well as the outcome. Only one midpoint states outright the possibility of an accident. The remaining midpoints define the situation without clearly naming the event that created the harrowing circumstance described. This seems to be the rule, rather than an exception—the directions show a situation and the response to it, but not its cause.

EXAMPLE EBERTIN

Let's look at how Ebertin studied directions using an example from his book, *Directions*. On page 134 he analyzed the dial of Brigitte Bardot at the time of one of her attempted suicides (Figure 45). The Mean Node is used, and the natal dial is set for 1.15 p.m. in Paris on September 29, 1960. In the text, Ebertin states a time of 1.20 pm, but the dial shown in his text is set five minutes prior. It seems Ebertin is using the diurnal time of 1.15 pm. Her solar arc at the time is 25°44.

In directions, Ebertin typically looked for "the main configurations that first strike us." The first thing to catch Ebertin's eye is dSu = Ur = As = Ma/Mc. He wrote "this means the desire to assert oneself, hindered plans, and acting without thinking." He pointed out that the natal axis of the Sun carried the Ma/Sa midpoint, which he notes is "the tendency to often be unable to handle life demands and crises." Although directed Mars had passed natal Neptune, it is on the midpoint of Me/Ur, to which he attributes "the rapid realization of plans which have resulted in an emotional and mental crisis through dMa = Su/Sa." This is a completed natal midpoint because natally Ne = Su/Sa. Here directed Mars is activating natal Neptune and its midpoints. Curiously, Ebertin doesn't mention the lucky midpoint of Ne = Ju/Ur, which directed Mars is also activating, and may have saved her life.

He notes that directed Pluto is approaching Saturn on the axis of Sa = dMe/Pl = dJu/Pl = Ur/Ne = Mo/Ur, which he describes as "extreme nervous irritation, separation, checks in personal development, difficulties, pessimism, thoughts of separation." He remarks that directed Moon and Neptune on the far side of the axis have recently separated from Saturn, "designating a preceding period of a depressed state of mind."

We can see from the dial that what is going on is that the natal complex of Pl = Me = Ju = Mo = Ne has directed to Saturn. While it appears as if Ebertin is delineating two directed midpoint pairs (dMe/Pl and dJu/Pl), these are in fact aligned with dNe and dMo and are occupied midpoints. He went on to look at the transits at the time, which we'll look at later.

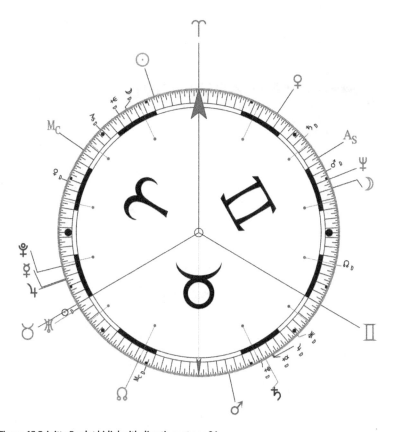

Figure 45 Brigitte Bardot bidial with directions at age 26

This case led him to look at the dials of other individuals who attempted suicide and he found one with Mc = Su = dMa/Sa, another with Ur = dSu = dMa/Sa, and Bardot with Ur = dSu = dMa/Sa. Here he went cherry-picking—seeking the activation of the death pair Ma/Sa.

In summary, we can see from this that our methods are similar. In this example, Ebertin used only completed solar arc midpoints, although this was not always the case. He also searched for specific midpoints that described the event, which I do not do. I let the chart/dial show me what is significant.

Directions and midpoints provide great detail into discrete periods of time. The directed aspect shows the theme, and the attending midpoints add qualifying information. Directions are not timers. They indicate a general time frame when an event may occur, and they describe the nature of the impending event. Sticking to complete midpoints narrows the scope of detail, without sacrificing necessary information.

 HOMEWORK: Chose a significant event in your life and find the directions active at the time. Delineate the axes.

Chapter 12

Features of Dial Solar Arcs

An approximation of when a natal axis will be activated can be estimated by determining when a planet in a pair on the axis, directs to the axis. Ebertin was clear that this would manifest an event. In *Applied Cosmobiology,* he wrote, "important planetary pictures (axes) stimulate themselves as one factor reaches another and vice-versa (p.154)." In practice, these are reliable directions and shed light on the meaning of the natal midpoint, which is useful in prediction.

In her book *The Life Blueprint, Cosmobiology II,* Jane Reynolds gives her method of finding and recording all solar arcs associated with midpoints pairs, which she calls the arc of activation. This depends on the distance between two planets in a midpoint pair. This is not a measure of the distance the pair are from the focal planet (orb), but rather the distance the pair are from each other, i.e., the length of the arms. This distance can be found in the 45° difference listing or taken from the dial.

Let's use Stephen King again as an example. His 45°-modulus tree list is shown in Figure 46 on page 136. Look at the axis of the Midheaven that has four midpoint pairs. In the dial (Figure 47a), the pointer is set on the natal Mc, showing the natal midpoint Me/Ne. The midpoint tree tells us the actual midpoint is 2′ off the Mc. However, what we are interested in is the distance of Neptune to Mercury. If we count the degrees on the dial we get an arc difference of 5°. If we look up Ne/Me in the 45°-modulus Difference Listing shown in Figure 32 on page 109, we get 4°59′, which rounds up to 5°. To get the arc of activation of this pair, we divide 5° by 2, which gives 2°30′. The bidial of his solar arc at age 2½ is shown in Figure 47b. At an age equivalent to an arc of 2°30′, directed Neptune reached the Midheaven. Simultaneously, the Midheaven directed to Mercury. This was around the time King's father disappeared.

The Midheaven will again be activated at a solar arc of 42½° (Figure 48, page 138). Here, directed Mercury is at the far end of the pointer. The

Modulus 45°00' – Max Orb 1°30'

♀	(Orb)	*♄*	(Orb)	*♃*	(Orb)	*♆*	(Orb)
♅/♆	+0°55'	♅/♆	-0°01' d	☿/♀	-0°12'	♂/♅	+0°05'
♄	+0°57'	☉/♆	+0°36'	☽/As	-0°45'	*☊*	+0°07'
♄/♇	-0°58'	♃/♇	+0°54'	*♆*	+1°14'	♃/☊	-0°33'
		♀	-0°57'	♂/♅	+1°20'	☉/♂	+0°43'
		♅/Mc	+1°11'	*☊*	+1°22' d	*♃*	-1°14'
				♀/Mc	-1°28'	☿/♀	-1°27' d

☊	(Orb)	*Mc*	(Orb)	*☿*	(Orb)	*♂*	(Orb)
♂/♅	-0°01'	☿/♆	+0°02' d	☽/♇	+0°12' d	♃/♅	+0°47'
♆	-0°07'	♅/As	+0°29'	♀/As	+0°58'	♀/♄	+0°57'
☉/♂	+0°36'	♀/♂	+0°39'	☉/As	-1°24'	♀/♇	-0°58'
♆/Mc	+1°06'	☉/As	+1°07'			☉/♃	+1°25'
♃	-1°22' d					☉/♄	-1°25'
						♅/☊	+1°28'

As	(Orb)	*☽*	(Orb)	*♅*	(Orb)	*☉*	(Orb)
☿/♇	-0°13'	☿/♄	+0°19'	♃/As	+0°43'	☊/As	+0°07'
♄/Mc	+0°26'	♃/♆	+0°41'	*☉*	+1°16'	♃/As	-0°33' d
♄/♆	-0°46'	♄/Mc	-0°55' d	☊/As	+1°24' d	☽/♆	+0°45'
♀/☊	-1°11' d	♆/☊	+1°22'	♂/☊	-1°26' d	*♅*	-1°16'
☽	+1°22'	*As*	-1°22'				
♇/Mc	-1°29'						

♇	(Orb)
♀/♅	-0°06' d
☽/Mc	+0°07' d
☉/♀	+0°31'
☽/♆	-1°06'
☽/☿	+1°23'

Figure 46. Stephen King's 45° trees

directed Midheaven at this time is on the far side of the axis on Neptune (at the near side of the Node).

The axis is predictably activated again at a solar arc of 47.5. Now, directed Neptune has come to the far side of the Midheaven (Figure 49, page 138). At this time, the directed Midheaven is on the far side of the axis of Mercury.

The axis is activated again at a solar arc of 87.5 when directed Mercury reaches the Midheaven (Figure 50, page 139). At this time, the directed Midheaven has reached Neptune.

Where do these solar arcs (and ages) come from? As Jane Reynolds pointed out, they are obtained by subtracting and adding the smallest number from 45 and 90. In this example, the smallest arc was 2½°. This solar arc is the first time the midpoint Mc = Me/Ne will be self-activated. Subtract 2½ from 45 and we get 42½, which is the second time the midpoint is activated. Add 2½ to 45 and we get 47½ which is the third time the midpoint

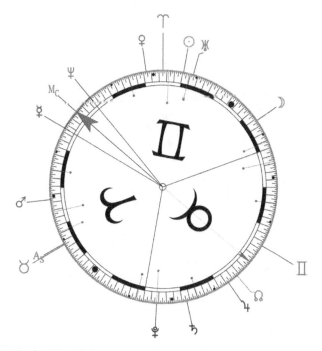

Figure 47a. Stephen King's dial set on Mc

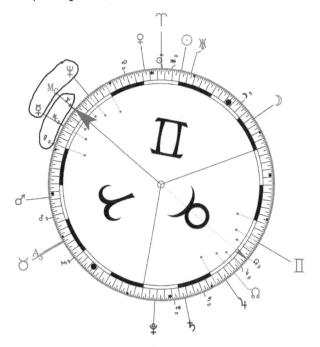

Figure 47b. Stephen King's bidial set on Mc at solar arc 2½°

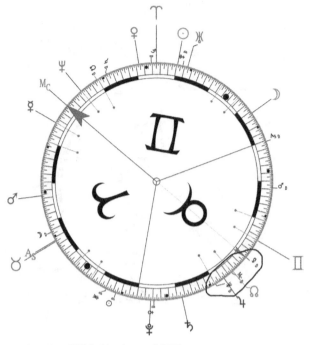

Figure 48. Stephen King's bidial with solar arc of 42½°

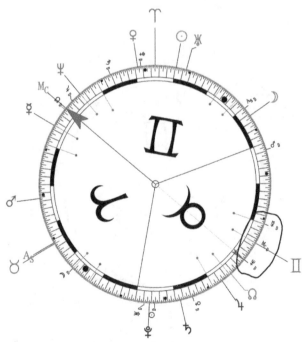

Figure 49. Stephen King's bidial with solar arc of 47½°

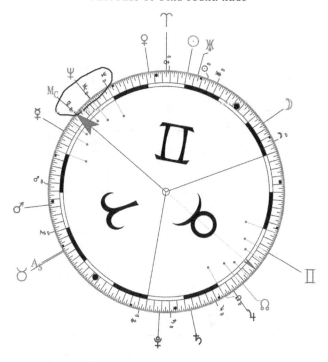

Figure 50. Stephen King's bidial with solar arc of 87½°

is activated. Finally, subtract 2½ from 90 which gives 87½, the fourth time the midpoint is activated.

In a long life, each midpoint will be activated four times—at dates that can be estimated in advance. The four time periods will have a similar theme. Reynolds recommended writing down the two smallest solar arcs next to each midpoint pair on the 45° Tree list. Then, use easy math to figure out the remaining two arcs. It's even simpler to write down the smallest solar arc on the 45° Tree list and use the table shown in Figure 51 to find the other three arcs.

In the table, the four columns correspond to the four solar arcs of activation. The rows show the degree of separation (divided by two) of the midpoint pairs. In the above example, with the first arc of activation occurring at 2½°, we look at the row of 2° and find the three approximate corresponding arcs.

Let's take another example and find the arc of activation of another midpoint on the axis of the Midheaven. The Mc axis shown in Figure 46 indicates the midpoint pair Ur/As, is almost ½° past the Midheaven. The

1st	2nd	3rd	4th
0°	45°	45°	90°
1°	44°	46°	89°
2°	43°	47°	88°
3°	42°	48°	87°
4°	41°	49°	86°
5°	40°	50°	85°
6°	39°	51°	84°
7°	38°	52°	83°
8°	37°	53°	82°
9°	36°	54°	81°
10°	35°	55°	80°
11°	34°	56°	79°
12°	33°	57°	78°
13°	32°	58°	77°
14°	31°	59°	76°
15°	30°	60°	75°
16°	29°	61°	74°
17°	28°	62°	73°
18°	27°	63°	72°
19°	26°	64°	71°
20°	25°	65°	70°
21°	24°	66°	69°
22°	23°	67°	68°

Figure 51. Table of Solar Arc Activation

arc distance between Uranus and the Ascendant is 33°34, rounded up to 34, divided by 2, giving an arc of activation of around 17° (Figure 52). From this, we know the can expect the midpoint Mc = Ur/As to self-activate at a solar arc of 17°, 28°, 62°, and 73°.

At a solar arc of 17°, dUr is just past the Mc, while the dMc is just before the As. The precision is now less because the orb of the pair to the midpoint is not as exact as it was in the previous example. Due to the imprecision, it is easy to overlook directions that are related to natal midpoints. This would

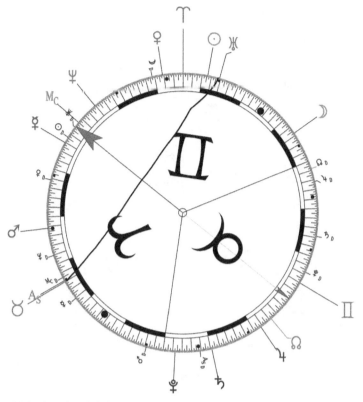

Figure 52. Stephen King's bidial with solar arc 17° on axis of Mc = Ur/As

be a mistake. If the directed planet is a component of the natal midpoint, the direction is self-activating the natal midpoint, giving a significant direction. Alternatively, if the directed planet is not in the natal midpoint being stimulated, the direction may be of lesser importance.

A CRITICAL DIRECTION

In life, the age of 45 usually stands out. Yes, it coincides with the ending of the second Saturn opposition and the third reversal of the nodes, but in addition, significantly, at this time all planets have directed by semisquare to aspect themselves. In the dial, at a solar arc of 45°, every planet and point is on the opposite end of their own natal axis. Thus, at this arc, every planet is stimulating itself by direction.

Stephen King's solar arcs set for 45° are shown in Figure 53 on page 142. He was 45 years and 5 months old at this solar arc. At this time, the axis

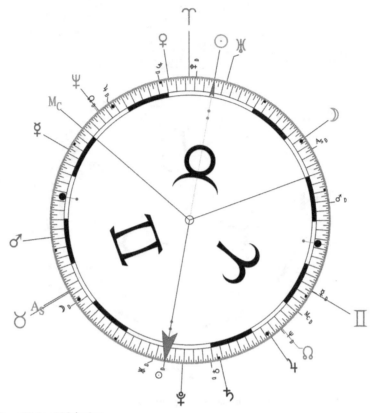

Figure 53. Age 45 Solar Arcs

of every natal planet and point is aligned with its directed self. This means the directed Sun is on the axis of the natal Sun, directed Jupiter is on the axis of natal Jupiter, directed Node is on the axis of natal Node, and so forth. For this reason, this age equates to a mid-life awakening that is generally under-appreciated.

For anyone with dial triangles, the ages of 30 and 60 also stand out. While these years are well-known for the Saturn Return, at these ages, planets in a dial triangle are mutually activated by direction. We looked at Stephen King's dial equilateral triangle comprised of Mercury-Moon-Pluto, which gives the midpoints: Me = Mo/Pl; Mo = Me/Pl, and Pl = Mo/Me. (Figure 54) At a solar arc of 29°, directed Moon came to Mercury and directed Mercury reached Pluto, activating two sides of the equilateral. As these directions separated, the third involving dPl = Mo came into orb, producing a protracted stretch of

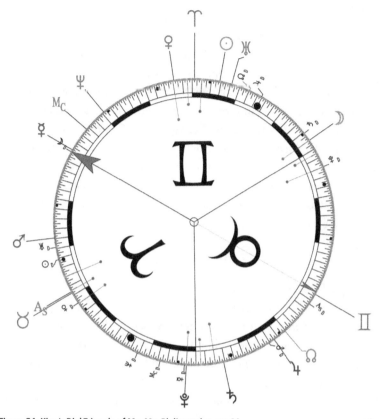

Figure 54. King's Dial Triangle of Mo, Me, Pl directed at age 30

years when the whole configuration was active. This was likely a productive and professionally successful period for the writer.

For the major events that occur before the solar arc of 45, look at the corresponding arcs that transpire at the same arc after 45. For example, if you went to university at 19, moved away from home, and had a major relationship, the corresponding solar arc at 64 may be as significant.

PLANETARY CLUSTERS

In a related topic, look for clusters of natal planets on the dial. These are several planets that are close in degree. Stephen King has no close cluster, but he does have a 7° range (from 26° mutable to 3° cardinal) that includes five planets: Uranus, Sun, Pluto, Saturn, Venus (yes, include the planets on the opposite end of the axis). When this cluster directs, it will lead with

143

Saturn, followed by Venus, Pluto, Sun, and finish with Uranus. This will be a busy 7-year period, especially if there is a transiting outer planet in the span of these degrees. The reverse is true for directions moving into this 7° range. The direction will first come to Uranus, then the Sun, Pluto, Venus, and finish with Saturn. A transit moving retrograde near these degrees will also hit the natal planets in reverse order. Stephen King has a second cluster that falls in a 6° range (from 9° cardinal to 15° cardinal) that includes in order Jupiter, Neptune, Node, Midheaven, and Mercury. Watch out for years when two clusters meet by direction, as this will be a prolonged busy and significant time. When Stephen King was five, the cluster with Saturn first directed to the cluster of Jupiter, corresponding with the time his friend was hit by a train.

LIST OF LIFE EVENTS

Jane Reynolds used a handy form for organizing life events according to year, age, and solar arc (*Cosmobiology II*; p.145). She called it a List of Life Events. It is a convenient reference for correlating the year, age, and arc of major events. I added two columns to her form: one with the four arcs of activation and the second noting midpoints. After age twenty-two, the solar arcs repeat, so the first twenty-two years can be used as a guide to the midpoints activated at later times. The blank form she used is shown in Appendix 5.

I have filled out the form for Stephen King as best I can (Figure 55). While a personal list will have detail for every year, I've only included some of Stephen King's years to illustrate the process. In your own list, be as comprehensive as possible. Add the years you started kindergarten, high school, and college. You can list every move, every job, every joy, and every crisis. Update the list every year to stay current as it will serve as a useful reference.

REVIEW OF STEPHEN KING'S SOLAR ARCS

In the last chapter, we went through Stephen King's solar arcs that were active when he published Carrie. In 1974, Stephen King's solar arc was 26°09 and he was 26½ years old. Did any of these directions self-activate their own natal midpoints? As we saw earlier, there were four active directions: dMo = Mc, dSu = Ma, dMe = Ur, dSa = As. To determine if a directed planet

Year	Age	SA	Mdpts	Event
1947	0	0 45 45 90	Ne – Ju/No Mo = Ju/Ne	
1948	1	1 44 46 89	No = Ne/Mc	
1949	2	2 43 47 88	Mc = Me/Ne Pl= Su/Ve	Father leaves
1950	3	3 42 48 87	Pl = Ve/Ur	
1951	4	4 41 49 86		
1952	5	5 40 50 85	Sa = Ju/Pl Sa = Ur/Mc Ju = Ve/Mc	Friend hit by train
1953	6	6 39 51 84	Ju = Me/Ve Ne = Me/Ve	
1954	7	7 38 52 83	Ve =Ur/Ne Sa = Ur/Ne Sa = Su/Ve Ma = Ur/No	Began writing stories?
1955	8	8 37 53 82		
1956	9	9 36 54 81		
1957	10	10 35 55 80	No = Ma/Ur	
1958	11	11 34 56 79	Mc = Ve/Ma	
1959	12	12 33 57 78	Ur = Ju/As Su = No/As Su = Ju/As Su = Mo/Ne Pl = Mo/Ne	
1960	13	13 32 58 77	Ne = Su/Ma No = Su/Ma Ur = No/As Pl = Mo/Mc	
1961	14	14 31 59 76	Ju = Ma/Ur Ne = Ma/Ur Me = Ve/As Pl = Mo/Me	
1962	15	15 30 60 75	As = Me/Pl Ur = Ma/No	
1963	16	16 29 61 74	Mc = Su/As Me = Mo/Pl Me = Su/As Ma = Ju/Ur Mo = Me/Sa	
1964	17	17 28 62 73	Ma = Ur/As Ma = Su/Ju	
1965	18	18 27 63 72	As = Sa/Mc As = Ve/No As = Pl/Mc Mo = Sa/Mc	
1966	19	19 26 64 71	As = Sa/Ne	Graduated high school, go to university
1967	20	20 25 65 70	Ve = Sa/Pl Ma = Su/Sa	
1968	21	21 24 66 69	Ma = Ve/Pl	
1969	22	22 23 67 68	Ju = Mo/As Ma = Ve/Sa Mo = Ne/No	
1970	23	23 67 68		Graduated university, daughter born, arrested
1971	24	24 66 69		Married, started teaching
1972	25	25 65 70		Son born
1973	26	26 64 71		Carrie accepted for publication, mom died, began drinking
1974	27	27 63 72		Move to Colorado, Carrie published
1975	28	28 62 73		Salem's Lot published, move to Maine
1976	29	29 61 74		Movie of Carrie out
1977	30	30 60 75		3rd child born, brief trip UK, start teaching U. of Maine
1987	40	40 50 85		sober
1999	52	52 83		Hit by car

Figure 55. Life Events Table for Stephen King

is a component of the natal axis it has reached, we look at the midpoints in the 45°-module Tree list (Figure 46, page 136) and take each direction in turn. Is the Moon in a midpoint pair configured with the Mc? Answer: No. This is not a self-activating direction. Same for the direction of dMe = Ur. Mercury is not contained in any of Uranus's midpoints. The direction of dSa = As is related to the natal midpoints of As = Sa/Ne and As = Sa/Mc, so it is self-activating at this time. Finally, the direction of the Sun to Mars (dSu = Ma) is an activation of the natal midpoint Ma = Su/Sa and Ma = Su/Ju since the Sun is involved in two midpoint pairs.

In summary, we know Ebertin found that directions involving the four personal points were of primary significance. To this, we can add a second distinguishing criterion—those directions which self-activate a natal axis are also important.

HOMEWORK: Figure out the arcs of activation for your midpoints. Start a Life Event Table and write in your arcs of activation for as many years as you have lived. If you've experienced repeated arcs, are the events with the same arc of activation occurring at two different times, similar?

PART 3

TRANSITS

... examples ... taken from real life show to what extent prognostications based on the transits do indeed agree with fact.

REINHOLD EBERTIN

Chapter 13

Transits in the Chart with Midpoints

A transiting chart is similar to a natal chart in that it symbolizes a captured moment in time. The active transits and their midpoints change daily as the planets advance or regress, change signs, and form aspects and separate from them. Since the inner planets move fast, they create more midpoints of shorter duration than outer planet combinations. The transiting angles move the fastest of all, and because of this, their positions as focal points and in midpoint pairs are unique characteristics in any chart.

The method of writing the midpoints is the same as that for directions. The notation tJu/Pl means that we are considering the midpoint pair of transiting Jupiter and transiting Pluto. (The "t" pertains to both.)

In examining stand-alone event charts, if there is no time for an event, and if we are assessing the impact of the event chart on a natal chart, we can use a sunrise time, a noon time, or a diurnal chart. The diurnal chart uses the place and time of birth to generate the angles of the transiting chart. The correct diurnal chart has the diurnal Sun in the same house as the natal Sun.

In delineating stand-alone event charts, I read them briefly as a thumbnail sketch. If I don't have a precise time, I don't pay attention to the angles, chart ruler, or the houses. (In this case, I often jump straight to the bidial.) Otherwise, I follow the Worksheet given in Appendix 3 and look at: planets in signs, dignity, close aspects, and direct midpoints. I use the major aspects. I am quite loose with my orbs in a stand-alone chart and use around 3° to 5°. For midpoints, I stick to less than 1½ °. Once I understand and get a feeling for the energy in the event chart, I look at it in combination with the natal chart through a biwheel, paying attention to the angular planets and active houses. I use the house rulership of the natal chart and the stand-alone chart.

For example, if there is a Sun-Jupiter conjunction in the event chart, I look to see which houses they rule in the natal chart, and vice versa.

When a timed event of significance occurs, the transits and transiting midpoints highlight the potential in the natal chart. For this reason, studying timed events sheds light on how a natal chart is working, and what the natal factors (planets in their signs, houses, aspects, and midpoints)) mean specifically for that chart.

In a biwheel, the same rule holds for transits as for solar arc directions: midpoint pairs must be formed within one chart; there is no mixing of levels. This means we ignore any midpoint pairs formed between a transit and a natal point. The midpoints used are transit/transit = transit, or natal/natal = natal, with the exception of a repeated planet comprising a midpoint pair, as in natal Sun/transiting Sun. In a transiting chart, I only use occupied midpoints that are direct (conjunction or opposition). In a previous chapter, we looked at directions during three events in Evangeline Adam's life. Here we will look at the transits for the three events.

A MOVE

Evangeline moved to New York on March 16, 1899. According to Noel Tyl in *Prediction in Astrology* (p.31), she checked into the hotel "around 8.00 p.m." Presumably, that morning she left her family in New Jersey. She had tried to rent a room at the Fifth Avenue Hotel and was turned down (Tyl p.30). She arrived at the Windsor Hotel and booked a room. She could have had a cheaper room on a higher floor but opted for a more expensive room on a lower floor. That night the hotel owner came for a reading. Evangeline was alarmed at what she saw in his chart: "the very depths of disaster." The next day the hotel caught fire and guests on the higher floors were killed, including the hotel owner's wife and daughter.

The transiting chart set for 8.00 p.m. is shown in Figure 56. Notably, Mars in fall is on the Midheaven. (In this chart, Mars rules the 7th house, the client, and he received a prediction of impending doom, which turned out to be the destruction of his hotel.) There are two dominating aspects. The first is a close opposition of Saturn and Neptune, the sickness/spirituality pair. There is a wider opposition between the revolutionary pair of Uranus and Pluto. This opposition is bridged by Mercury in Aries, and Venus in Aquarius.

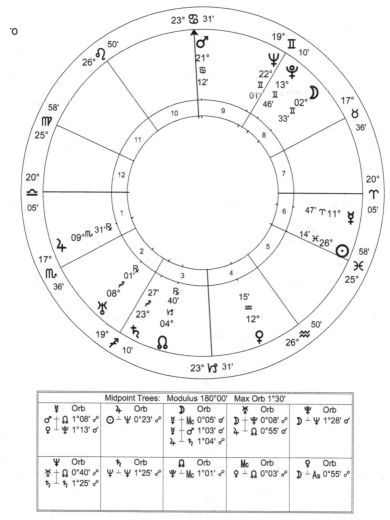

Midpoint Trees:	Modulus 180°00'	Max Orb 1°30'		
☿ Orb	♃ Orb	☽ Orb	♅ Orb	♆ Orb
♂ + ☊ 1°08' ⚼	☉ ⊥ ♆ 0°23' ⚼	☿ + Mc 0°05' ♂	☽ + ♆ 0°08' ⚼	☽ ⊥ ♆ 1°28' ♂
♀ ⊥ ♆ 1°13' ♂		☿ + ♂ 1°03' ♂	♃ ⊥ ☊ 0°55' ♂	
		♃ ⊥ ♄ 1°04' ⚼		

♆ Orb	♄ Orb	☊ Orb	Mc Orb	♀ Orb
♅ + ☊ 0°40' ⚼	♄ ⊥ ♆ 1°25' ⚼	♆ ⊥ Mc 1°01' ⚼	♀ ⊥ ☊ 0°03' ⚼	☽ ⊥ As 0°55' ⚼
♄ ⊥ ♄ 1°25' ♂				

Figure 56. Transiting chart of Evangeline Adam's move to New York

There are four close midpoints:

Ju = Su/Ne: achieving success with little effort; success through inspiration or imagination (note the speculation variant).

Mo = Me/Mc: life purpose driven by feelings; expressing one's opinions.

Ur = Mo/Pl: intensity that can get out of hand (note the Moon involved by midpoint in the opposition).

Mc = Ve/No: being known for one's art (I would add, pleasant, professional associations).

BiWheel

The question is, how did this energy impact Evangeline's chart? The biwheel is shown in Figure 57. The natal chart has brought the transiting opposition of Saturn and Neptune to the natal Mc-Ic providing an outlet of practical spiritual energy. The transiting Sun in the natal first house is brought into play through the square to the Mc/Ic. The transiting opposition hit the natal Sun-Moon opposition by sextile/trine. I imagine her intuition was on the mark that night.

The wider opposition of transiting Uranus-Pluto interacted with her natal Saturn. Natal Mars and Neptune were each stimulated by transiting Venus and transiting Mercury respectively. The natal Mars-Neptune sextile means working with intuition. She gave it a voice (transiting Mercury) in a manner that would ultimately give power to astrology on a grand scale.

No direct transiting midpoints aligned with her horoscope. The triggering of natal Neptune at the midpoints of Mo/Sa and Ju/Pl describes an awareness of ambition, strategy, direction (Ma/Sa), and great successes (Ju/Pl). It was an auspicious beginning to a long and successful career.

THE TRIAL

Fifteen years later, Evangeline went on trial for the offense of "fortune telling." She would lose her career if she was found guilty. Her defense was that astrology was not a parlor game aimed at deceiving people and taking their money, but instead a science. The trial began on December 11, 1914. I assume it started in the morning, but since I don't have a time, I'll erect a diurnal chart and use the natal time of 8.30 a.m. set for New Jersey, even though the trial was held in New York. The stand-alone chart is shown in Figure 58 on page 154.

In the diurnal, the last 5′ of Libra, the sign of fairness, is on the Midheaven. The ruler, Venus, in detriment in Scorpio and retrograde, is in terrible condition. Helping out is a sextile between the Sun in Sagittarius, the sign of law, and Jupiter in Aquarius, the sign of astrology. The Moon was just past the Aries Point in Libra, sextile Neptune in Leo, square Pluto, trine Uranus in Aquarius, and sextile a debilitated Mercury in Sagittarius. This configuration symbolizes the trial and the forces aligned against Evangeline. She was set up on dubious charges that were based on nefarious grounds that compelled her to argue against the notion of astrology being a deceptive game.

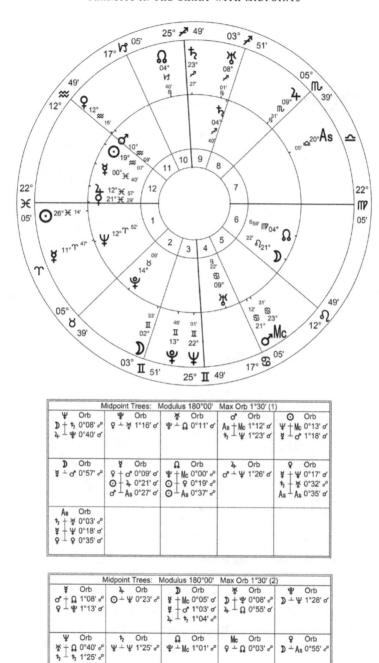

Midpoint Trees: Modulus 180°00' Max Orb 1°30' (1)				
Ψ Orb	♇ Orb	♅ Orb	♂ Orb	☉ Orb
☽ + ♄ 0°08' ☍	♀ ⊥ ♅ 1°16' ☌	♇ ⊥ ☊ 0°11' ☌	As + Mc 1°12' ♂	Ψ + Mc 0°13' ♂
♃ ⊥ Ψ 0°40' ♂			♄ ⊥ Ψ 1°23' ♂	☿ ⊥ ♂ 1°18' ♂
☽ Orb	☿ Orb	☊ Orb	♃ Orb	♀ Orb
☿ ⊥ ♂ 0°57' ♂	♀ + ♂ 0°09' ♂	♇ + Mc 0°00' ☍	♂ ⊥ Ψ 1°26' ♂	☿ + Ψ 0°17' ♂
	☉ + ♃ 0°21' ♂	☉ ⊥ ♀ 0°19' ♂		♄ + ♅ 0°32' ☍
	♂ ⊥ As 0°27' ♂	☉ ⊥ As 0°37' ☍		As ⊥ As 0°35' ♂
As Orb				
♄ + ♅ 0°03' ☍				
☿ + Ψ 0°18' ♂				
♀ ⊥ ♀ 0°35' ♂				

Midpoint Trees: Modulus 180°00' Max Orb 1°30' (2)				
☿ Orb	♃ Orb	☽ Orb	♅ Orb	Ψ Orb
♂ + ☊ 1°08' ☍	☉ ⊥ Ψ 0°23' ☍	☿ + Mc 0°05' ♂	☽ + Ψ 0°08' ☍	☽ ⊥ Ψ 1°28' ♂
♀ ⊥ Ψ 1°13' ☍		☿ + ♂ 1°03' ♂	♃ ⊥ ☊ 0°55' ♂	
		♃ ⊥ ♄ 1°04' ☍		
Ψ Orb	♄ Orb	☊ Orb	Mc Orb	♀ Orb
♅ + ☊ 0°40' ☍	Ψ ⊥ Ψ 1°25' ☍	♇ ⊥ Mc 1°01' ☍	♀ ⊥ ☊ 0°03' ☍	☽ ⊥ As 0°55' ☍
♄ ⊥ ♄ 1°25' ☍				

Figure 57. Evangeline Adam's biwheel with transits at time of move

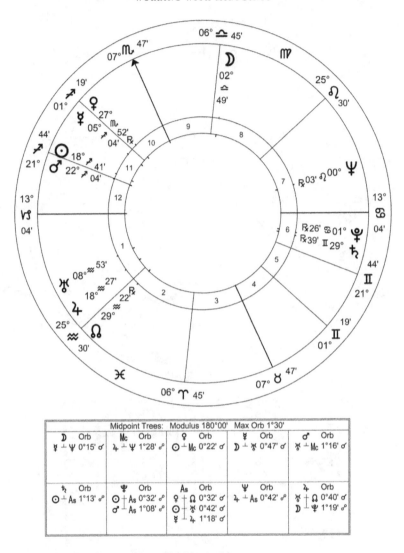

Midpoint Trees: Modulus 180°00' Max Orb 1°30'				
☽ Orb ☿ ⊥ ♆ 0°15' ♂	Mc Orb ♃ ⊥ ♆ 1°28' ⚹	♀ Orb ☉ ⊥ Mc 0°22' ♂	☿ Orb ☽ ⊥ ⚸ 0°47' ♂	♂ Orb ⚸ ⊥ Mc 1°16' ♂
♄ Orb ☉ ⊥ As 1°13' ⚹	♇ Orb ☉ ⊥ As 0°32' ♂ ♂ ⊥ As 1°08' ♂	As Orb ♀ ⊥ ☊ 0°32' ♂ ☉ ⊥ ⚸ 0°42' ♂ ☿ ⊥ ♃ 1°18' ♂	♆ Orb ♃ ⊥ As 0°42' ⚹	♃ Orb ⚸ ⊥ ☊ 0°40' ♂ ☽ ⊥ ♆ 1°19' ⚹

Figure 58. Transits at the start of Evangeline Adam's trial

Saturn and Pluto were conjunct but out-of-sign. The conjunction coincided with the beginning of World War 1. Here both planets were retrograde and would meet three times. The two previous conjunctions took place in early Cancer, as would the third. The Moon was square the October and November 1914 conjunction degree, suggesting a societal transformation, of which this Moon and this event were a part. The North Node had just entered Aquarius, indicating another recent shift—leaving mysticism for science.

154

There are fifteen direct midpoints in the diurnal:

Mo = Me/Ne: a sympathetic understanding of other souls, a deceived or a deceptive woman.

Mo = Sa/As: inhibited around others, ill humor and disagreeable moods, a person easily influenced by their surroundings.

Mc = Mo/Ve: (I love making people happy and feeling better.)

Mc = Sa/No: feeling depressed, standing alone in life.

Mc = Pl/No: having one's future depend on associations and contacts with others.

Me = Mo/Ur: intuition, great mental activity, a thinking woman, sudden understanding, a surprise, sudden news.

Su = Ur/Mc: emotional and physical unrest, easily angered, a nervous psyche (also, my purpose as an astrologer).

Sa = No/Mc: preferring to go one's own way (also, ending professional associations).

Sa = Ma/As: disputes, defeats, shared worries and anxieties with others.

As = Me/Ur: cautious or deliberate, organizational skill; a sudden mental connection with others (also, using astrology with others).

Ju = Ur/No: joy in social functions and entertainments, seeking advantages with the help of others; sharing happy life experiences.

Ju = Mo/Pl: great successes, lucky chances.

No = Sa/Mc: sympathy and compassion; being linked to others through bad circumstances.

No = Pl/Mc: becoming a leader; exerting a powerful influence over others.

In a nutshell, the diurnal describes the event in startling detail. What is missing, is the actual event itself that will elicit these reactions.

The biwheel of the diurnal outside her natal chart is shown in Figure 59. At this time, transiting Mars is conjunct her 10th cusp and square the Ascendant and natal Venus. The transiting conjunction of Saturn and Pluto are in her fourth house trine natal Mercury and square the diurnal Moon. The question at hand is whether she can continue her robust practice and publishing business.

There is a double whammy with Mercury and the nodes. The transiting North Node is conjunct natal Mercury. While the true Node is in Aquarius, the Mean Node is at 0° Pisces. The pair is square natal Saturn and transiting Mercury on the cusp of the 9th. Transiting Mercury, like natal Saturn,

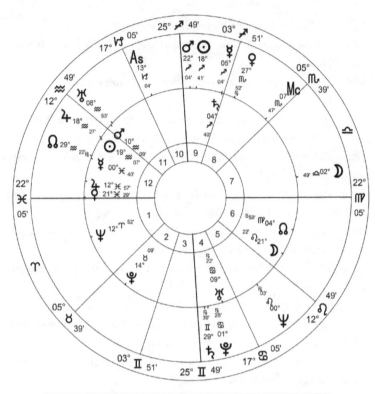

Midpoint Trees: Modulus 180°00' Max Orb 1°30' (1)				
♆ Orb	♀ Orb	♅ Orb	♂ Orb	☉ Orb
☽ + ♄ 0°08' ☌	♀ ⊥ ♅ 1°16' ♂	♆ ⊥ ☊ 0°11' ♂	As + Mc 1°12' ♂	♆ + Mc 0°13' ♂
♃ ⊥ ♆ 0°40' ☌			♄ ⊥ ♆ 1°23' ♂	☿ ⊥ ♆ 1°18' ♂
☽ Orb	☿ Orb	☊ Orb	♃ Orb	♀ Orb
☿ ⊥ ♂ 0°57' ☌	♀ + ♂ 0°09' ☌	♆ + Mc 0°00' ☌	♂ ⊥ ♆ 1°26' ☌	☿ + ♆ 0°17' ☌
	☉ + ♃ 0°21' ☌	☉ + ♀ 0°19' ☍		♄ ⊥ ♅ 0°32' ☍
	♂ ⊥ As 0°27' ☌	☉ ⊥ As 0°37' ☍		As ⊥ As 0°35' ☌
As Orb				
♄ + ♅ 0°03' ☍				
☿ + ♆ 0°18' ☌				
♀ ⊥ ♀ 0°35' ☌				

Midpoint Trees: Modulus 180°00' Max Orb 1°30' (2)				
☽ Orb	Mc Orb	♀ Orb	☿ Orb	♂ Orb
☿ ⊥ ♆ 0°15' ☌	♃ ⊥ ♆ 1°28' ☍	☉ + Mc 0°22' ☌	☽ ⊥ ♅ 0°47' ☌	♅ ⊥ Mc 1°16' ☌
♄ Orb	♆ Orb	As Orb	♆ Orb	♃ Orb
☉ ⊥ As 1°13' ☌	☉ + As 0°32' ☌	♀ + ☊ 0°32' ☌	♃ ⊥ As 0°42' ☍	♅ + ☊ 0°40' ☌
	♂ ⊥ As 1°08' ☌	☉ ⊥ ♅ 0°42' ☌		☽ ⊥ ♆ 1°19' ☍
		☿ ⊥ ♃ 1°18' ☌		

Figure 59. Evangeline Adam's biwheel with transits at the start of her trial

156

is square the natal North Node at the North Bending. In the natal chart, Mercury rules the 3rd, 4th, and 7th houses. She is called to defend herself against an open enemy. The nodal opposition marks a turning point.

Notably, transiting Jupiter is conjunct the natal Sun. In the natal chart, Jupiter rules the 1st, 9th, and 10th houses, and as such is integrally tied to the law, Evangeline herself, and her profession. Transiting Jupiter is sextile the transiting Sun-Mars, activating the natal t-square with the Sun, Moon, and Pluto.

Transiting Uranus is conjunct natal Mars and square natal Pluto. With natal Mars at the natal midpoints of As/Mc = Sa/Ne = Ve/Mc, she is in for a fight, which had some surprises, such as the judge asking her to interpret a mystery chart, which ended up belonging to his son.

Of the fifteen completed direct midpoints in the diurnal, only two aligned with the natal chart by conjunction or opposition. The transiting Mercury midpoint of Me = Mo/Ur is conjunct natal Saturn, giving: tMe = Sa = tMo/Ur. Here the thinking woman described by the transit is on trial, standing up against the authority of the law and a judge.

The conjunction of transiting Jupiter and the natal Sun is especially fortunate, as transiting Jupiter's midpoints (Ju = Ur/No = Mo/Pl) describe great successes. Jupiter aligned with the Sun made that success personal to her. Note that the defeat midpoint of Sa = Ma/As did not connect to her natal chart. She would not personally experience defeat, but no doubt, the possibility was in the courtroom air.

In summary, a timed transiting chart activates the natal chart by aspects. The transiting midpoints shed light on how the aspects will be expressed. However, because the 360° chart is not set up to deal with midpoints easily, I look at midpoints on the dial, as described in the next chapter.

 HOMEWORK: Look at the event chart for when Evangeline died and see if you can find her death in the natal chart. (Death: Nov 10, 1932, 4.00 pm, New York, NY.)

Chapter 14

Transits and Midpoints
on the Dial

Transits work the same on the dial as they do in the chart. There is one significant difference: Because the dial acts as a magnifying glass, blowing up the chart by a factor of four, we see on average four times the number of contacts compared to the chart.

The transiting angles move the fastest. We know that in the chart the Ascendant changes 1° for every 4 minutes of clock time. In the dial, the Ascendant moves halfway around every three hours, hitting every axis. It makes a complete circuit every 6 hours. Thus, in a single day, the Ascendant circles the dial four times. The same holds true for the transiting Midheaven. It, too, travels around the dial making four completed circuits a day. Together, the angles make a total of eight passes in twenty-four hours, continually forming and dissolving midpoints, making and breaking aspects as they go.

The Moon moves through a sign every 2½ days. It goes around the dial in a week. It hits every axis on the dial every 3½ days.

The Sun goes around the dial in 90 days, which is around three months, or a season. In 45 days, it goes halfway around the dial, illuminating every axis. In the ensuing 45 days, it hits each axis from the opposite end.

These fast-moving planets and angles and the midpoints they form are unique for any moment and are therefore important. In a timed event, I look at the transits in a stand-alone dial, noting the 8th harmonic aspects and close completed midpoints. Then I look at the synastry of the transits on the bidial.

With midpoints, the same rules we saw in the chart hold on the dial. In a bidial, I don't mix midpoint pairs across levels. We use completed pairs within a transiting dial, and completed pairs within a natal dial, but not midpoints formed between the two. The exception noted earlier holds—a midpoint pair formed with the same planet (e.g., Ma/tMa) is valid.

In practice, in examining a timed event, I start with the stand-alone 360° chart. I look at the planets' signs, distribution, major aspects, and contacts to the angles. Then I look at the synastry between the event and the natal chart as explained in the last chapter. Next, I view the stand-alone chart on the dial, adding minor 8th harmonic aspects and midpoints. I use only the close completed midpoints and delineate these. Finally, I look at the bidial. If the predictive chart shows me a landscape, the bidial points out the important features in the picture, and what is activated in the natal horoscope. In the bidial, I note the 8th house harmonic aspects of transits to natal planets and their associated midpoints. The following examples should make this clear. It's best if you print out the charts and dials in advance and find the aspects and midpoints for yourself.

CARRIE

Stephen King's first novel was published on April 5, 1974. There is no time, so I used a diurnal chart, set for his birthplace at 1.30 a.m. (Figure 60 on page 160). In the diurnal chart, the Ascendant had just changed to Capricorn, ruled by diurnal Saturn in Gemini, the sign of books. At 0°, something new is being birthed. Uranus is on the diurnal Mc, suggestive of a surprise or shock. In a grand trine with Venus and Saturn, the surprise looks professionally pleasant. Jupiter is square Neptune, an indication of speculation and excess; did a publisher take a chance, or does the author have high hopes? The Moon on the cusp of the diurnal 9th is opposite Mercury, showing a culmination and, in this context, the publication of a book. The opposition is square Mars in Gemini, which looks like blowback, which was the case. The book had its detractors and later was banned from some libraries, shown by Mars at the South Node in applying conjunction to Saturn.

In synastry (natal chart shown in Figure 24 on page 77), transiting Sun is conjunct the Midheaven and opposite natal Mercury and forming a grand trine with natal Pluto and natal Moon. The spotlight is shining on the author, empowering him inside and out. The transiting Midheaven-Uranus trine natal Uranus and transiting Saturn brings professional change. The diurnal transiting Moon is sextile natal Mars and sextile natal Jupiter, showing successful work. Transiting Neptune is sextile natal Neptune, adding fantasy and dreams that come true.

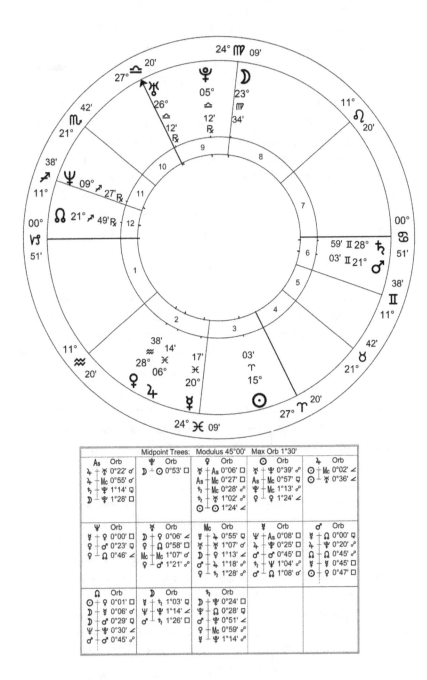

Figure 60. Stephen King's diurnal chart at the publication of *Carrie*

The stand-alone dial is shown in Figure 61 on page 162. The conjunction between Uranus and the Mc is evident, as is the Me-Ma-No-Mo complex. The Sun and Venus also share an axis. Here are the close midpoints:

As = Ju/Ur: molding one's environment to one's ideals, happiness shared with others.

Ur = Mc = Mo/Ve: a heart filled with love (Tyl: feeling valuable).

Ve = Ur/As: emotional response to events, the urge to quickly beautify one's environment.

Ju = Su/Mc: bright outlook, optimism, positive, clear-cut objectives, a happy disposition, attaining one's objective (in my view, the best midpoint of all).

Ne = Me/Ve: picturing everything clearly, fantasy and imagination, inspiration, an appreciation of fairy tales and fantastic stories.

Me = Ne/As: (Creative writing for others).

Ma = Me/No: intense teamwork, working with others to bring thoughts and plans to fruition.

No = Su/Ve = Mo/Me: connecting with lovable and kind-hearted people, affiliation with art lovers, artistic events; the exchange of thoughts or ideas with others.

There are only excellent midpoints in the diurnal chart, a testament to a favorable moment, which fell on the day a young writer's first novel was published.

The bidial with Stephen King's natal and diurnal event is shown in Figure 62 on page 163. There are three transiting aspects to natal planets:

tSu = Me

tNe = Ma

tSa = Pl

Mercury is the writer, so it's no surprise it is in the spotlight thanks to the transiting Sun, with an orb of 1 minute. It activated the natal midpoint pair, Mo/Pl, adding talent for powerfully impacting others through writing, zealously pursing and achieving life goals. The pair of Ju/tJu is also on the axis. Here we double the influence of Jupiter, the benefic, that always tries to help and expands whatever it touches.

Transiting Neptune is sesquisquare Mars, symbolic of a work of fiction. As we saw above, tNe = t/Me/Ve points to the nature of the work, which is artistic writing.

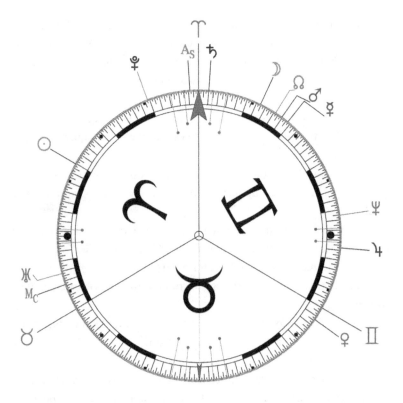

Figure 61. Diurnal dial of *Carrie* publication

The third aspect is transiting Saturn semisquare Pluto, which suggests sparing no pains in one's work. Also on the axis are Ve/Ur, Mo/Mc, and tMo/Mc. Note the double whammy of the Mo/Mc—it is active both natally and by transit. It is always significant when a natal midpoint is replicated by a transiting midpoint. Ebertin, too, took notice of an axis that contained a repeated midpoint pair.

Putting the axis together, we get:

tSa = Pl: struggling for success, participating in group achievements, difficult work, silent activity.

Pl = Ve/Ur: highly excitable.

Pl = Mo/Mc: emotional shocks.

tSa = tMo/Mc: professional shock.

This is a mixed axis that shows both the hard work to create the book and the criticism against it. While panned by some critics, most readers loved it.

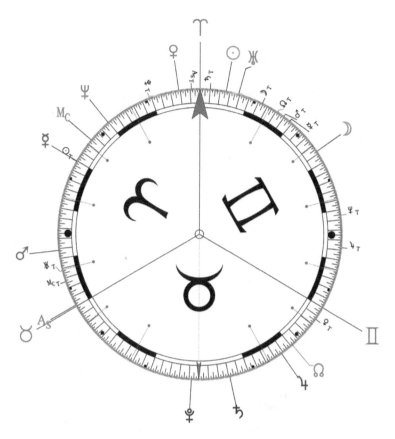

Figure 62. Stephen King's bidial of transits at time of *Carrie* publication

SOBRIETY

On that note, let's look at another event diurnal that is not so rosy. The day Stephen King's wife staged an intervention is shown in Figure 63. Because it is the day after his birthday, the diurnal angles are similar to the birth angles, plus 1°. This gives a diurnal Ascendant of early Leo. With all planets, except Jupiter, on the bottom half of the chart, it would be an introspective day. Jupiter was high in the sky, so hope may have been the only uplifting thing there was. Venus is conjunct the South Node, indicating a loss of happiness. Neptune is at the South Bending, showing harm from drinking and drugs—as well as their impending loss. The Moon and Mars are conjunct in Virgo, and health was likely an issue. The pair is square Saturn, denoting sadness and separation. Mercury in Libra, the sign of relationship, is

163

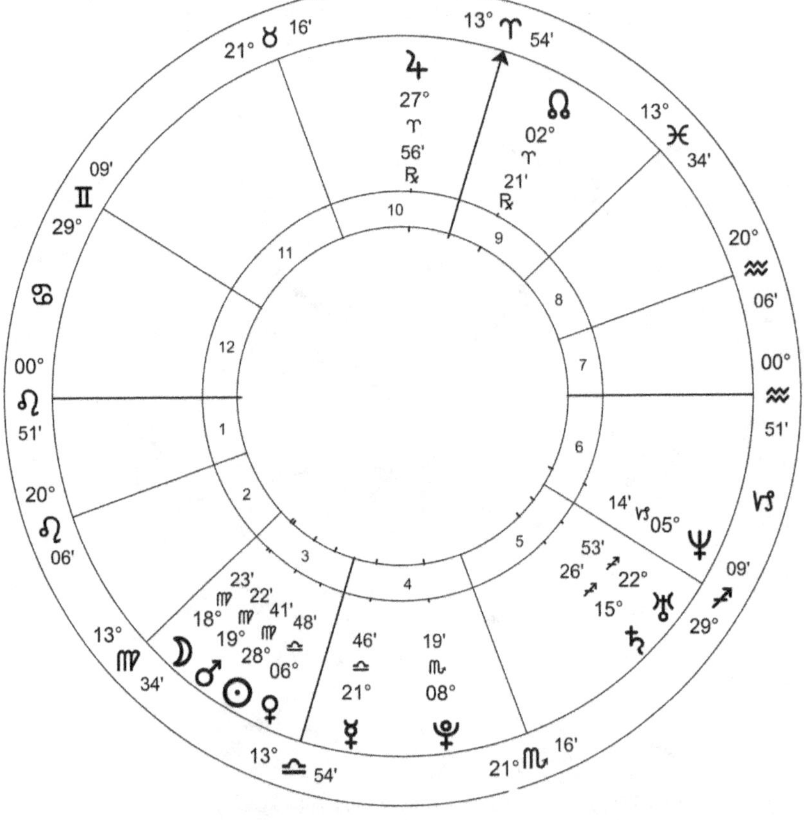

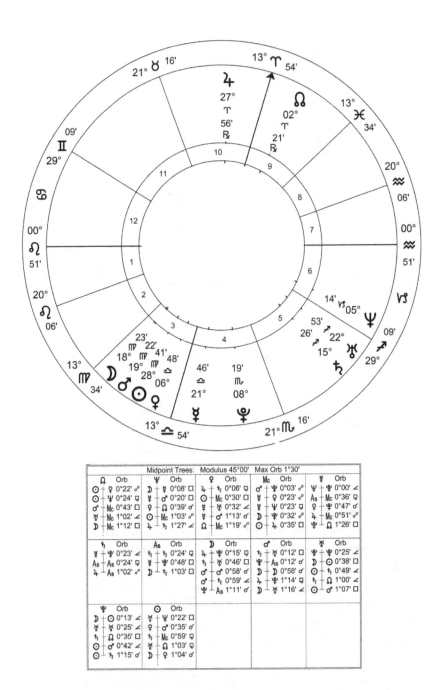

Midpoint Trees: Modulus 45°00' Max Orb 1°30'				
☊ Orb	♆ Orb	♀ Orb	Mc Orb	☿ Orb
☉/♀ 0°22' ☍	☽/☿ 0°08' □	♃/♄ 0°06' ⚼	♂/♇ 0°03' ☍	♆/♇ 0°00' ∠
☉/♆ 0°24' ⚼	☿/♂ 0°20' □	☉/Mc 0°30' □	☿/♀ 0°23' ☍	As/Mc 0°36' ⚼
♂/Mc 0°43' □	♀/☊ 0°39' ☌	☿/♅ 0°32' ∠	☿/♆ 0°23' ⚼	♀/♇ 0°47' ☌
♅/Mc 1°02' ∠	☉/Mc 1°03' ☍	☿/♂ 1°13' ☌	☽/♇ 0°32' ☍	♃/Mc 0°51' ☍
☽/Mc 1°12' □	♃/♄ 1°27' ∠	☊/Mc 1°19' ☍	☉/♃ 0°35' □	♇/☊ 1°26' □
♄ Orb	As Orb	☽ Orb	♂ Orb	♅ Orb
☿/♇ 0°23' ∠	♄/♄ 0°24' ⚼	♃/♇ 0°15' ⚼	♄/♅ 0°12' □	♇/♇ 0°25' ∠
As/As 0°24' ⚼	☿/♇ 0°48' □	♄/♅ 0°46' □	♇/As 0°12' ☌	☽/☉ 0°38' □
♃/As 1°02' ☍	☽/♄ 1°03' □	♂/♂ 0°58' ☌	☽/☽ 0°58' ☌	☉/♄ 0°49' ∠
		♂/♄ 0°59' ∠	♃/♇ 1°14' ⚼	♄/☊ 1°00' ∠
		♇/As 1°11' ☌	☽/♅ 1°16' ∠	☉/♂ 1°07' □
♇ Orb	☉ Orb			
☽/☉ 0°13' ∠	♅/♆ 0°22' □			
♅/♅ 0°25' ∠	♀/♂ 0°35' ☌			
♄/☊ 0°35' □	♄/Mc 0°59' ⚼			
☉/♂ 0°42' ∠	♅/☊ 1°03' ⚼			
☉/♄ 1°15' ☌	☽/♀ 1°04' ☌			

Figure 63. Transits on the day Stephen King quit drinking

sextile Uranus, describing what must have been a shock. Putting emphasis on upset and shock is the square between Mars and Uranus.

There is a triple conjunction of the transiting South Node and natal and transiting Venus. It would have been a sad, sad day. The transiting Midheaven is trine natal Pluto, and the theme is transformation and change. Notably, transiting Saturn is conjunct the natal Moon and sextile Mercury. In the chart, the Moon is the chart ruler and Saturn rules the 7th. It's never a good moment when a spouse wants to talk, especially when "Saturn is on the Moon." A very unhappy time indeed.

The stand-alone dial is shown in Figure 64. There are two minor 8th harmonic aspects:

Sa = As: feeling held back, depression, suffering from imposed limitations; occupants and inmates in a secluded place.

Pl = Ur: the process of transformation; the collapse of the old order, construction of the new.

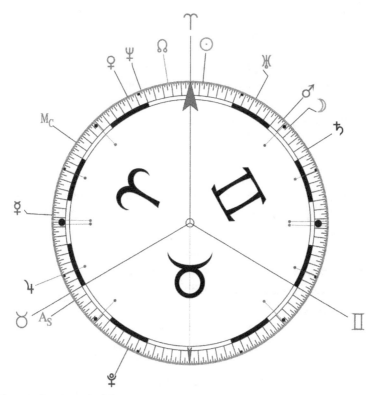

Figure 64. Transits on the dial day Stephen King quit drinking

These are the midpoints:

No = Su/Ve: to coming together with lovable and kind-hearted people

Ne =Mo/Me: (we need to talk about drinking and drugs).

Ve = Ju/Sa: discontent, changing fortunes in love.

Mc = Ma/Pl: misfortune to encounter crushing force without power.

Me = Ne/Pl: thinking and acting while under strange influences, sensitive nerves, plans incapable of being realized.

Pl = Ur = Su/Mo: a change of circumstances lead to crises in life or separation from others; the urge for freedom and independence, difficulty adapting to change, inner rebellion; sudden events in friendship, marriage, parental home, shared upsets, separation of partners.

Mo = Ju/Pl: losing everything, misfortune, (note the millionaire pair).

Ma = Pl/As = Sa/Ur: a tendency to expose oneself to danger; injury, accident; the occasional misuse of extraordinary energy; great effort and toil; a violent or forced release from tensions or strains; challenging others by decisive contest or fight; injury, accident, deprivation of freedom.

Su = Ur/Ne: unconsciousness, illness.

In summary, the midpoints of the stand-alone dial capture the intent of the intervention in a precise manner. The circumstances of the family meeting are clear, while the reason for the meeting itself is not shown.

How did the event diurnal impact the nativity? The bidial is shown in Figure 65. Three natal axes are activated:

tNo = Ve = Sa

tSa = As = tAs = Mo

tSu = Pl

First, the transiting Node came to the axis of natal Venus and Saturn at the midpoint of tSu/Ne and Ur/Ne. In sum, there is tNo = Ve = Sa = tSu/Ne = Ur/Ne. Breaking this apart, we get:

tNo = Ve = Sa: coolness in love unions.

tNo = tSu/Ne: a negative or weak attitude around others, association with sick, weak persons or with blood relations, a hospital stay.

Ve = Ur/Ne: hyper-sensitivity.

Sa = Ur/Ve: depression, instability, pessimism; a painful loss.

Here we see possible hospitalization (in rehab), emotionality, and depression.

The second axis has the transiting Ascendant with the Moon and transiting Saturn on the Ascendant. Natally, the Moon and Ascendant are on

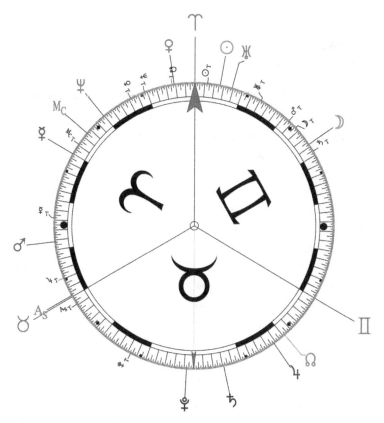

Figure 65. Stephen King's bidial with transits on the day he quit drinking

the same axis. This is an important axis because it contains two of the four personal natal points. On the axis we have tAs = Mo = tSa = As = Sa/Mc = Me/Pl = tMe/Pl. We break this apart and get:

tAs = Mo = tSa: meeting with sick or depressed people, mourning or bereavement.

tAs = tMe/Pl: intellectually dominating the room, also ability to influence others in the environment (this midpoint repeats the natal midpoint).

tSa = tMe/Pl: quarrelsome, nagging, irritable, skepticism, exposed to heavy and bitter attacks.

Mo = Sa/Mc: sadness, influenced by others, being easily depressed, a tendency to states of depression or psychoses; suffering caused by females.

As = Sa/Mc: suffering from others, put in unfortunate circumstances; sharing anxiety with others, a lonely person, parting from others, sadness.

Mo = Me/Pl: the power to speak with heart and soul and consequently to convince people.

As = Me/Pl: intellectual social domination, able to exercise an influence upon others.

Here again is a double-whammy, where a natal midpoint is replicated by a transiting midpoint. The repeated pair, Me/Pl, means persuasive communication. In this case, the persuasion is likely heavy-handed. Given the Ascendant symbolizes the environment and people in it, and the Moon symbolizes women, the persuasive individual is likely his wife.

The third axis is tSu = Pl = tUr/Ne = Mo/Mc = Ve/Ur. The aspect of tSu = Pl indicates a physical transformation. The midpoints add:

Pl = Mo/Mc: emotional shock and upheaval.

Pl = Ve/Ur: highly excitable.

tSu = tUr/Ne: lack of vitality, delicate physical make-up, impressionable; unconscious, illness, lifeless, or impassive.

In summary, the nature of the active axes on the day of the intervention and the day of a book publication was shockingly different. It's amazing how the same chart can be activated so differently at different times of life.

ACCIDENT

What was the ambient energy when Stephen King was hit by that car on June 19, 1999? He said in his autobiography that he left home at about 4 p.m. and I set the chart for that time (Figure 66). As a departure chart, it describes the trip—in this case what was supposed to be a routine walk around the lake. In the chart, Uranus is conjunct the IC and the South Node, opposite a conjunction of Venus, the North Node, and Midheaven, in a t-square with Saturn at the South Bending. His happiness is about to change radically and suddenly for the worse. Mars is in detriment in Libra opposite Jupiter in Aries, the sign of Mars. Jupiter is under the power of Mars and will expand what Mars instigates. He is going to fall. The opposition is eased by a sextile/trine to the Sun in late Gemini. Vitality and willpower lessen the impact of the fall.

In the biwheel, transiting Mars is trine natal Uranus, bringing the accident pair together in easy aspect. Transiting Uranus is sextile the natal Moon, the chart ruler, showing something unexpected. The transiting Venus-Node conjunction fell on his natal Pluto as he embarked on a

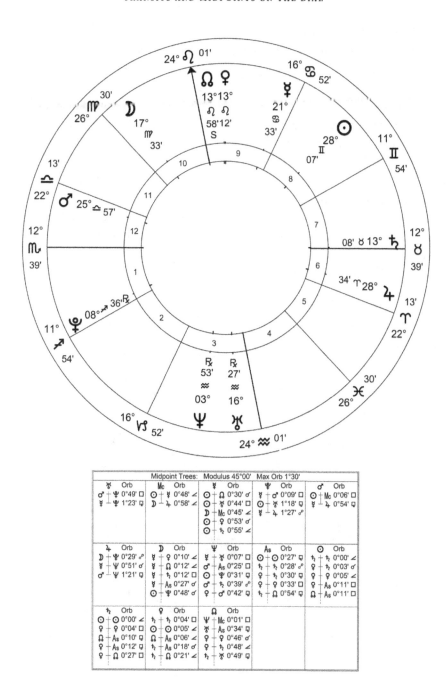

Midpoint Trees: Modulus 45°00' Max Orb 1°30'				
♅ Orb	Mc Orb	☿ Orb	♆ Orb	♂ Orb
♂ + ♆ 0°49' □	☉ + ☿ 0°48' ∠	☉ + ☊ 0°30' ♂	☿ + ♂ 0°09' □	☉ + Mc 0°06' □
☿ + ♆ 1°23' ⊓	☽ + ♃ 0°58' ∠	☉ + ♅ 0°44' □	☉ + ♅ 1°18' ⊓	☉ + ♃ 0°54' ⊓
		☽ + Mc 0°45' ∠	☿ + ♃ 1°27' ⚹	
		☉ + ♀ 0°53' ♂		
		☉ + ♄ 0°55' ∠		
♃ Orb	☽ Orb	♆ Orb	As Orb	☉ Orb
☽ + ♆ 0°29' ⚹	☿ + ♀ 0°10' ∠	☿ + ♅ 0°07' □	☉ + ☉ 0°27' ⊓	♄ + ♄ 0°00' ∠
☿ + ♆ 0°51' ♂	☿ + ☊ 0°12' ∠	♂ + As 0°25' □	♄ + ♄ 0°28' ⚹	♀ + ♄ 0°03' ⊓
♂ + ♆ 1°21' ⊓	☿ + ♄ 0°12' □	☉ + ♆ 0°31' ⊓	♀ + ♄ 0°30' ⊓	♀ + ♀ 0°05' ∠
	☿ + As 0°27' ♂	♂ + ♄ 0°39' ♂	♀ + ♀ 0°33' □	♀ + As 0°11' □
	☉ + ♆ 0°48' ♂	♀ + ♂ 0°42' ⊓	♄ + ☊ 0°54' ⊓	☊ + As 0°11' □
♄ Orb	♀ Orb	☊ Orb		
☉ + ☉ 0°00' ∠	♄ + ♄ 0°04' □	♆ + Mc 0°01' □		
♀ + ♀ 0°04' □	☉ + ☉ 0°05' ∠	♅ + As 0°34' ⊓		
☊ + As 0°10' ⊓	☊ + As 0°06' ∠	♀ + ♀ 0°46' ♂		
♀ + As 0°12' ⊓	♄ + As 0°18' ∠	♀ + ♄ 0°48' ∠		
♀ + ☊ 0°27' □	♄ + ☊ 0°21' ∠	♄ + ♅ 0°49' ⊓		

Figure 66. Transiting chart when Stephen King hit by a car

169

descent into the underworld. Interestingly, the transiting Moon is square the natal Moon, and the transiting Sun is square the natal Sun (and conjunct natal Uranus on the cusp of the hospitalization 12th).

The stand-alone dial is shown in Figure 67. The Sun is in minor 8th harmonic aspect to Venus and Saturn. This indicates separation in love or marriage, organic troubles. There are no close midpoints on this axis. Here are the other midpoints on the dial:

Me = Su/No: family ties.

Ju = Mo/Pl: great successes, luck (he came within a fraction of fatally hitting his head in the crash).

Ne = Me/UrMc: painful or tormenting emotions, circumstances triggering illness; affected by external influences, disappointments.

Pl = Me/Ma: suffering heavy attacks or assaults.

Mo = Me/VeSa: a perception and feeling of love (and its potential loss).

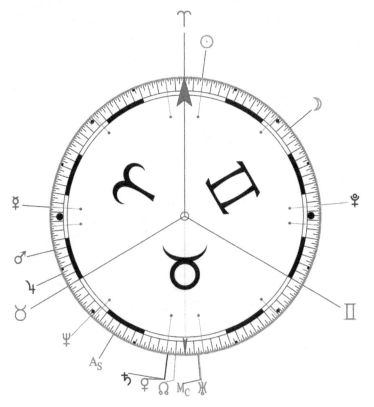

Figure 67. Transits on the dial at time of the accident

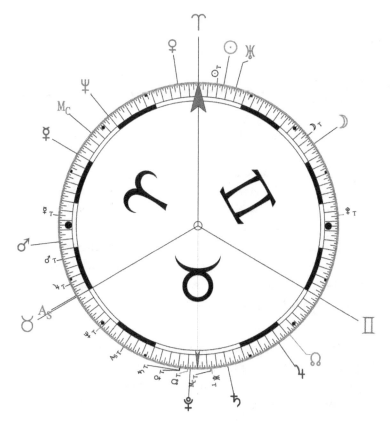

Figure 68. Stephen King's bidial with transits at time of the accident

How did this energy impact the chart? The bidial is shown in Figure 68. There are three transiting aspects:

tPl = Ma

tNoMc = Pl

tSu = Su

On the first axis there is tPl = Ma = tMe/Ma = Ve/Pl:

tPl = Ma: suffering violent assaults, injuries; misfortune.

tPl = tMe/Ma: suffering heavy attacks or assaults; misfortune.

Ma = Ve/Pl: a brutal and coarse expression of feeling.

This axis describes the brutality of the incident.

On the second axis, there is there is tMcUr = Ve = Sa = tMa/Pl. This gives:

171

tMc = tUr =Ve = Sa: tension in relationship, separation, emotional inhibitions.

tUr = tMa/Pl: cruelty, violence, brutality, calamities of great consequence, an attack.

This axis suggests a disastrous, ruinous event resulting in separation and emotional upset.

The last axis contained: tSu = Su = tVe = tSa = Mo/Ne = No/As. This means:

tSu = Su: the physical body, vitality.

tSu = tVe = tSa: weak powers, biological troubles, separation.

Su = Mo/Ne: sensitivity, receptive, a delicate and sensitive body.

Su = No/As: a new contact.

In summary, peril is shown throughout the event chart aspects and midpoints and is not confined to one axis. The natal planets hit by specific transits show the response to the event. It was life-threatening and horrific, but a will to live and luck pulled him through.

 HOMEWORK: Pick a significant timed event in your life and look at the stand-alone chart, biwheel, stand-alone dial, and bidial, and see how these charts describe what happened.

Chapter 15

Predictive Charts

While event charts bring insight to the natal chart and an astrological understanding as to why things happen and happen when they do, predictive charts are useful for identifying in advance which natal planets will be coming into the spotlight and what this might portend. Predictive charts, such as the diurnal, solar return, lunar return, lunations (New and Full Moons), eclipses (Solar and Lunar), and seasonal ingress charts (Aries, Cancer, Libra, Capricorn), afford us a glimpse of the near future. It helps to keep the time frame of these charts in perspective. An eclipse chart is active for six months. A New Moon chart is active for a month, possibly only 2 weeks when the Full Moon chart takes over. A solar return is in effect for a year, while a lunar return lasts a month. The seasonal ingress charts of the Sun's entry into a cardinal degree last for three months. The diurnal chart lasts for a day.

I differentiate the predictive charts into two types. The first type is based on the natal chart, such as the diurnal, and the solar and lunar return charts. I always cast these for the birth location. This stand-alone chart can be looked at on its own; whatever story it tells is a valid one. Looking at the synastry between the stand-alone and the natal chart adds information, but it's not necessary. The second type of predictive chart is a mundane chart, such as an eclipse, ingress, or lunation chart. These charts are based on the current location. While the stand-alone chart gives information, the information is general and applicable to the world or those in that place. Specificity comes from the synastry—how the energy of the mundane chart is channeled into a natal chart.

In a biwheel or bidial it's helpful to keep in mind what we are looking at—namely aspects. We know all aspects aren't created equal. A planet on an angle has more power to act and bring about effects than one that is not. We know an outer planet–outer planet aspect is in orb for a long time, and the inner planets form and dissolve aspects quickly. By keeping a tight orb, we focus on what is going on in the predictive chart at a precise moment.

The midpoints in the predictive chart show influences on a focal planet. The main energy is between the transiting planet and the natal planet. The midpoints of each add qualifying information.

I use the same procedure to analyze a predictive chart as I use for a transiting event chart. The only difference is that the predictive charts are cast in advance. We just looked at Stephen King's accident. We'll now look at some predictive charts leading up to this event. I am especially intrigued by accidents—something that happens unexpectedly, suddenly, and without warning. I am curious if predictive charts can see accidents in advance.

Note that the transiting midpoints in the stand-alone dial are the same transiting midpoints that appear on the bidial, and these can be copied from the delineation of the stand-alone axes to the synastry axes. Also, the natal axes remain the same through time and if they were previously delineated earlier, these can also be copied.

Stephen King's solar return for the year of the accident is shown in Figure 69. In the return, set for the place of birth, retrograde Saturn is on the Descendant and Uranus is on the IC. With both planets simultaneously on the angles, they form a mundane square. The aspect indicates an unpleasant change from the status quo during the solar year likely resulting from the actions of a partner or open enemy (Saturn ruling the natal 7th). Mars rules the chart from the 10th and is in Leo, unaspected. In the natal chart, Mars also rules the Midheaven and the 5th house, implying the year seems related to creativity and his profession.

There is a Virgo stellium consisting of Mercury in its sign in rulership and Venus in fall, featuring writing and a potential problem with creative endeavors. A dark Virgo Moon applying to conjunct the Sun suggests an ending and a new beginning. A strong Jupiter in Pisces opposes the stellium, adds imagination and creativity. In the natal chart, the opposition falls across the 3 to 9th houses, which alludes to writing and publishing.

Adding natal synastry, the transiting Sun-Moon is square natal Uranus (risk of upset or accident). This is especially significant since the Moon is the natal chart ruler. Transiting Neptune is on the natal Descendant, which depicts confusion in the relationship or an attack from an unsavory enemy. Transiting Uranus is trine Neptune, associated with a change in creativity or imagination, or the elimination of the waking consciousness. Transiting

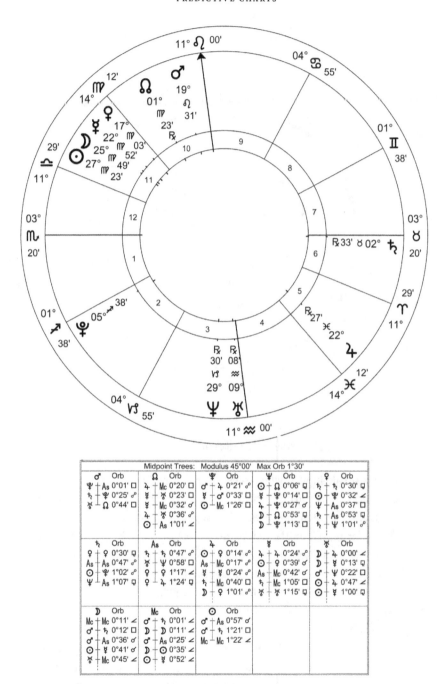

		Midpoint Trees:		Modulus 45°00'	Max Orb 1°30'				
♂	Orb	☊	Orb	♇	Orb	♆	Orb	♀	Orb
♇ + As	0°01' □	♃ + Mc	0°20' □	♂ + ♃	0°21' ☍	☉ + ☊	0°06' ⚼	♄ + ♄	0°30' ⚼
♄ + ♆	0°25' ☍	☿ + ♄	0°23' ☍	☿ + ♂	0°33' □	☿ + ♆	0°14' □	☉ + ♆	0°32' ∠
♓ + ☊	0°44' □	☿ + Mc	0°32' ♂	☉ + Mc	1°26' □	♃ + ♆	0°27' ♂	♀ + As	0°37' □
		♃ + ♓	0°36' ☍			☽ + ☊	0°53' ⚼	♄ + As	0°53' ⚼
		☉ + As	1°01' ∠			☽ + ♆	1°13' □	♄ + ♆	1°01' ☍
♄	Orb	As	Orb	♃	Orb	☿	Orb	♓	Orb
♀ + ♀	0°30' ⚼	♄ + ♄	0°47' ♂	☉ + ♀	0°14' ♂	♃ + ♃	0°24' ☍	☽ + ♓	0°00' ∠
As + As	0°47' ♂	♓ + ♆	0°58' □	As + Mc	0°17' ♂	☉ + ♀	0°39' ♂	☽ + ♓	0°13' ⚼
☉ + ♇	1°02' ♂	♀ + ♀	1°17' ∠	☿ + ♀	0°24' ♂	As + Mc	0°42' ♂	♂ + ♆	0°22' □
♆ + As	1°07' ⚼	♀ + ♃	1°24' ⚼	♄ + Mc	0°40' □	♄ + Mc	1°05' □	☉ + ♃	0°47' ∠
				☽ + ♀	1°01' ♂	♄ + ♓	1°15' ⚼	☉ + ☿	1°00' ⚼
☽	Orb	Mc	Orb	☉	Orb				
Mc + Mc	0°11' ∠	♂ + ♄	0°01' ∠	♂ + As	0°57' ♂				
♂ + ♄	0°12' □	☽ + ☽	0°11' ∠	♂ + ♄	1°21' □				
♂ + As	0°36' ♂	♂ + As	0°25' ∠	Mc + Mc	1°22' ∠				
☉ + ☿	0°41' ∠	☽ + ☉	0°35' ∠						
♓ + Mc	0°45' ∠	☉ + ☿	0°52' ∠						

Figure 69. Stephen King's 1998 solar return chart

175

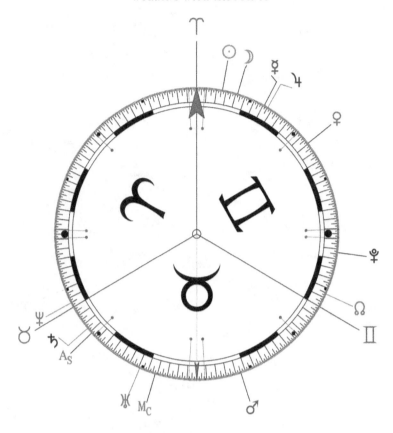

Figure 70. Stephen King's Solar Return 1998 on the dial

Mercury is sextile Jupiter, which seems like writing for publication, though it is combust (destroyed). Transiting Venus square the Moon points to happiness. Transiting Mercury sextile Mars suggests an effort to write.

The solar return on the dial is shown in Figure 70. In evidence is the Sun-Moon conjunction, the Mercury-Jupiter opposition, and the Saturn-Ascendant opposition. In addition, there are two minor aspects—the Moon is on the axis of the Midheaven (in the public eye), and Venus is on the axis of Saturn-Ascendant (separation from love). These are the following close midpoints:

Ne = Su/No = MeJu/Pl: inability to adapt, easily annoyed by others, disappointed by others, misfortune and losing everything, the pursuit of peculiar plans, cunning, falsehood, slander, and libel (or creative fiction).

Ur = MoMe/Ju = Ma/Ne: sudden assistance; changing energy levels, states of sudden weakness; a life crisis, an illness, or an accident; occasional outbursts of hilarity, confidence, optimism, the love of work; inquisitive and curious, quick witted, the ability to give a good answer when being challenged (an axis also dealing with writing).

Mc = Mo = Su/Me = Ma/Sa: the need to overcome difficulties, the ability to endure suffering (with dignity and without complaint); mourning and bereavement, death; illness, separation; speaking up for oneself.

Ma = SaAs/Pl: brutality, destructive rage or fury; the intervention of a Higher Power, bodily injury or harm (murder); obstacles or roadblocks caused by others, the need to economize, illness, separation, mourning, and bereavement.

No = VeJu/Mc: affection toward others, deep bonds of love; fortunate associations.

Pl = Ma/MeJu: people capable of tackling big projects, suffering heavy attacks or assaults.

MeJu = Su/Ve: thoughts of love; popularity.

The midpoints point to trouble, but also creative fiction. It would be difficult to know in advance if they describe an accident as opposed to a plot line. In any case, it's fascinating to see the midpoints in the stand-alone solar return describe with high accuracy an event that is nine months down the road.

The bidial is shown in Figure 71 on page 178. Three natal planets align with return planets:

tSu = Su (necessary for a solar return)

tMc = tMo = Ur

tNe = As

On the Su = tSu axis, there are no transiting midpoints on the axis, so although it is the Sun's chart, it is not a big player.

The axis of tMo = Ur = tMc symbolizes an unusual emotional state and an unusual degree of emotional excitability, irritability, and nervousness. On the axis is the midpoint tMa/SaAs and the exception midpoint of Ju/dJu. Breaking down the axis, we get:

tMo = tMa/Sa: weak-willed, a depressive episode, lack of courage; illness, separation, or death of a female.

tMc = tMa/Sa: endurance, resistance, indefatigable; the necessity to overcome difficulties.

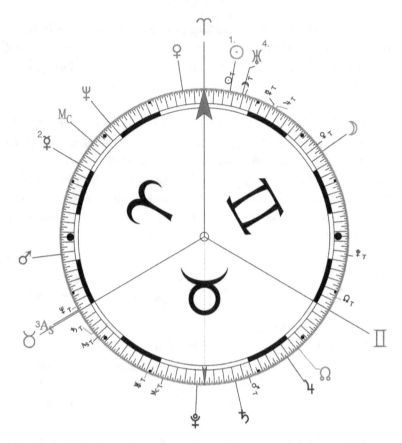

Figure 71. Stephen King's Solar Return 1998 on the bidial

tMo = tMa/As: anger and annoyance, provocative behavior; a quarrelsome woman.

tMc = tMa/As: a fighter, a joint task achieved with others.

Ju/dJu: a double dose of luck.

This is a difficult axis, helped by the exception pair of Ju/dJu.

The third axis is tNe = As = tMeJu/Pl = tSu/No = Me/Pl:

tNe = As: dominated by or under the influence of others, making strange or peculiar contacts with other people.

tNe = tMe/Pl: nervous sensitivity, the pursuit of peculiar plans, cunning, falsehood, slander, and libel, also defamation.

tNe = Ju/Pl: suffering damage or loss because of others; susceptible to infection.

tNe = tSu/No: inability to easily adapt, being easily annoyed with others, being quickly disappointed by others.

As = Me/Pl: the ability to influence others.

In this last axis, there is a double whammy with the repetition of tMe/Pl and Me/Pl, which point to the art of persuasion and powerful writing. However, it also symbolizes the destruction of limbs. It would appear others are exercising an influence on him, as opposed to King exerting an influence himself. It would be hard to tell if this was the subject of a novel or not.

In all, the solar return, with Saturn and Uranus on the return angles, and transiting Neptune on the natal Descendant, along with the activity of tMc = tMa/Sa, underscore a potentially difficult year and the possibility of an accident.

LUNAR ECLIPSE

Five months before being hit by a car, there was a Lunar Eclipse (LE) at 11° Leo on January 31, 1999 (Figure 72 on page 180). The chart was set for Bangor, the author's place of residence. Note, the eclipse degree landed on the Solar Return Midheaven. In the LE chart, Taurus is rising, which on the surface looks nice were it not for the malefic star Algol that is also rising, bringing a warning that someone could lose their head. The Ascendant is also square the North Node at the South Bending, suggesting physical, bodily loss. However, an exalted Venus in Pisces rules the chart, in trine to a dignified Mars in Scorpio, promising a period of heightened creativity. Neptune conjunct the Midheaven square Mars is not so nice and looks like a relapse in sobriety. It could also be an active imagination. The Sun is conjunct Uranus, as the Moon is opposite Uranus, all sextile/trine Pluto in the 7th. This looks like something happening suddenly, bringing change.

In summary, the Leo eclipse with the Sun in detriment in Aquarius, configured with Uranus and Pluto and Mercury, and with Algol rising at the South Bending, all point to a difficult eclipse.

Looking at the synastry, the eclipse was especially problematic because the eclipse Moon is conjunct the 1st house Pluto. The eclipse fell across the 1-7 axis, indicating a crisis of some kind in the physical body, marriage or a business relationship. Transiting Jupiter is opposite the natal Sun and square natal Uranus, giving an element of luck, or a sudden unexpected

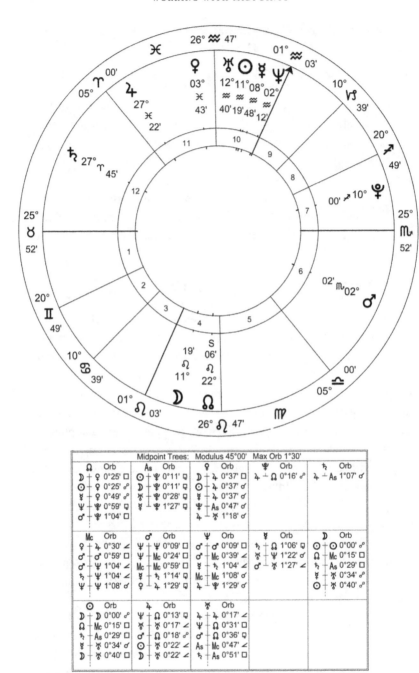

Figure 72. Lunar Eclipse chart before the accident

apocalypse. The transiting Ascendant is conjunct the natal North Node and opposite natal Jupiter, bringing Algol into the nativity.

The Lunar Eclipse on the dial is shown in Figure 73. The connection of Mars and Neptune (weakness, illness, or inspiration) is in evidence, as is that of Uranus and the lights (excitement, upset). Jupiter and Uranus (luck) are on the same axis. These were the following midpoints:

SuMo = No/Mc = Me/Ur: emotional and physical ties; sudden incidents, a quick adjustment to new circumstances.

No = SuMo/Ve: coming together with loving and kind-hearted people

As = SuMo/Pl: being victim of the ruthlessness of others, the crisis of self-preservation; a violent reaction to environmental influences, many upsets.

Pl = Ju/No: the desire for pleasant and happy contact with many people.

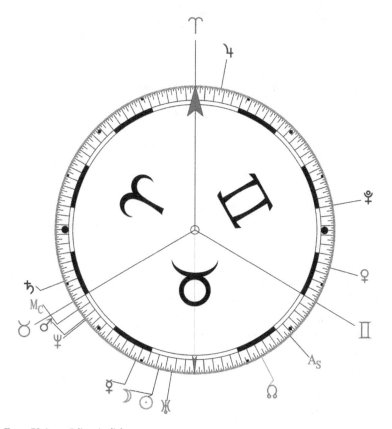

Figure 73. Lunar Eclipse in dial

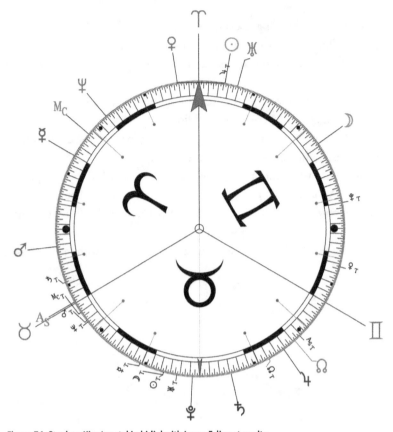

Figure 74. Stephen King's natal in bidial with Lunar Eclipse transits

Ju = Ur = MaNe/No: community upset or excitement; successful team-work; getting upset over the anti-social conduct of others; sudden under-mining or destruction of relationships; disappointments or disadvantages through others.

In the dial set for the location, the stand-alone midpoints indicate all is not well. However, this chart applies to all residents of Bangor, Maine. How this energy impacted the author is shown on the bidial in Figure 74. Five natal points are triggered by the eclipse:

tAs = Ne = No

tPl = Ma

tMc = Mo

tSuMo = Ur

tUr = Su = tJu

The first axis consists of: tAs = Ne = No = Su/Ma = tSuMo/Pl = Ma/Ur:

tAs = Ne = No: suffering caused by others.

Ne = Su/Ma: lack of energy, dishonest activity; the undermining of one's vocation; illness.

No = Su/Ma: success in teamwork, joint plans or undertakings; fighting for objectives.

Ne = Ma/Ur: fainting due to physical exertion, a fit of rage or frenzy, also raving madness, a car accident.

No = Ma/Ur: demonstrably excited in the presence of others, the experience of sudden events shared with others, the execution of extraordinary and unusual enterprises.

tAs = tSu/Pl: being victim to the ruthlessness of others, the crisis of self-preservation.

tAs = tMo/Pl: violent reaction to environmental influences; many upsets.

This axis indicates misfortune and upset. The possibility of a car accident, or in this case, an accident from a car, is clearly stated.

The second axis has: tPl = Ma = Ve/Sa = Ju/Ur = tJu/No. From this we get:

tPl = Ma: suffering violent assaults, injuries; misfortune.

Ma = Ve/Sa: regained sobriety; discussion or dispute; separation.

Ma = Ju/Ur: quick determination, quick realizations, a love of freedom; the drive to make one's fortune, speculations, making a fortunate decision.

tPl = tJu/No: antisocial contact.

This is a mixed axis that shows the brutal attack, as well as a life-saving decision.

The third axis has tMc = Mo = Me/Sa = tVe/Ju. This gives:

tMc = Mo: strong needs on display.

Mo = Me/Sa: retarded development, gaining experience.

tMc = tVe/Ju: wonderment, love, success.

The axis shows luck and recovery.

On the fourth axis there is: tSuMo = Ur = tSa/As = tMe/Ur = Ju/As:

tSu = tMo = Ur: shared upsets, sudden conflicts, separation of the partners.

tSu = tSa/As: keenly aware of the lack of freedom of movement, a strong desire to go one's own way; difficult circumstances, suffering from surrounding conditions, becoming ill.

tMo = tSa/As: depression due to situation. Inhibitions in the presence of others, ill humor and disagreeable moods, a person easily influenced by their surroundings.

tSu = tMe/Ur: able to quickly grasp a situation, sudden incidents, adjusting quickly to new circumstances, a surprise.

tMo = tMe/Ur: excitable, quickly changing thoughts and moods, instinctively correct grasp of a subject, logical thinking, practical.

Ur = Ju/As: optimistic, lucky, new ventures, rearrangement of conditions and circumstances.

Here is another mixed axis showing difficulty and also luck.

The fifth axis has tUr = Su = tJu = No/As = As/tAs:

tUr = Su = tJu: physical agility or mobility.

Su = No/As: cultivating new social and personal connections; a new contact.

As/tAs: the environment or people in the environment.

This axis shows the connection between King and the driver and the lucky jump that saved his life.

In summary, the stand-alone Lunar Eclipse in Bangor is difficult and points to unpleasantness. This is confirmed in the manner in which the eclipse planets hit the natal points and midpoints seen on the bidial. Still, months passed with no crisis, until the unexpected occurred, and then the meaning of the lunar eclipse became clear.

ARIES INGRESS:

The Aries Ingress occurred on March 20, 1999, at 8.46 p.m. in Bangor, Maine (Figure 75). Notably, the angles of the ingress mimic those of the Solar Return, an indication this is the season when the promise of the Solar Return will manifest. Uranus in Aquarius is conjunct the IC and in a tight square to the Moon and square retrograde Mars rising in Scorpio. Here is the accident pair aligned in tense configuration with the exalted Moon, the natal chart ruler. Did the exaltation help him survive? Venus and Saturn are also angular, conjunct the Descendant, in Taurus. Venus is in rulership giving strength, in this case, to the 7th house. The pair are square Neptune at the nadir. Saturn and Neptune are the sickness pair, and in the natal chart, Venus rules the 4th house of endings and Saturn rules the 7th house of partnership and open enemies, and the 8th house of

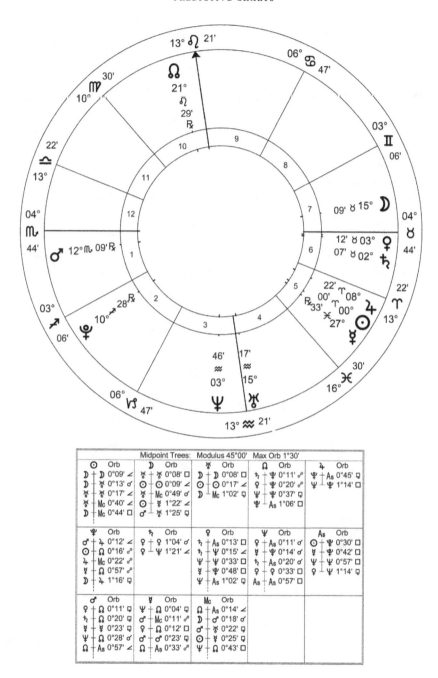

Figure 75. Aries Ingress chart before accident

death. The ingress Jupiter is trine Pluto, which may indicate making—or spending—a lot of money, but given Jupiter's natal rulership of the 6th house of health and the 9th house of doctors, in hindsight, it symbolizes the upcoming accident. Otherwise, it might be interpreted as high creativity and publishing power.

Viewed against the natal chart, ingress Mercury is opposite the natal Sun. In mundane rulership, Mercury rules travel and cars. The natal Sun is in the 3rd house, and Mercury rules the natal 3rd of cars and travel, as well as the 12th house of unknown enemies. Ingress Uranus is trine natal Mercury, on the cusp of the natal 4th House of endings. Significantly, the ingress Midheaven is conjunct natal Pluto, while the ingress Moon is square natal Pluto. This is a dangerous setup given the Moon is the natal chart ruler.

The Aries Ingress on the dial is shown in Figure 76. Here there is an echo of the lunar eclipse, with the Sun, Moon, and Uranus sharing an axis,

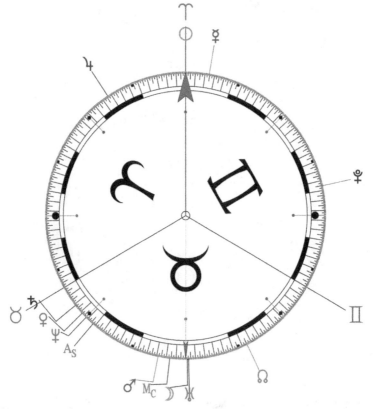

Figure 76. Aries Ingress in dial

signaling inner and outer excitement or upset. The tight complex of Saturn, Venus, Neptune, and Ascendant is indicative of illness, sadness, and separation. Mercury, Mars, and the Midheaven are on the same axis symbolizing a willingness to fight. These are the following midpoints:

Ve = Sa/Ne = Sa/As: sadness from sickness; separation.

Ne = Ve/As = Me/Pl: thinking about death and "I love my life and don't want to die."

Ma = Ve/No = Sa/No = Me = Ma/Mc: power of thought; passionate; suffering through others; unforced separation, family bereavement; a person giving orders.

Mc = No/As: striving for close cooperation with others.

No = Sa/Pl = Ve/Pl = Ne/Pl: the misery of the masses, common suffering shared with many; the ability to fascinate or attract many people; sharing peculiar experiences with others.

Pl = Ma/Ju: people capable of tackling big projects.

In the midpoints, we can see the event that is still three months away. While nothing is pointing directly to an accident, the circumstance of being injured, hospitalized, with a long road to recovery, is apparent.

The bidial is shown in Figure 77 on page 188. As expected for an ingress chart, the transiting Sun is on the Aries axis, near natal Pluto and aligned with transiting Moon-Uranus. Once again, as in the lunar eclipse, the Sun, Moon, and Uranus share an axis, only here with natal Pluto: shared upsets; changed circumstances lead to critical phases of development in life or to separation from others.

Stephen King was very lucky that he wasn't instantly killed. As the doctor told him, if he had landed a millimeter from where he did, he would have smashed his head into a rock and been dead or paralyzed. We expect that Jupiter would be in play, and it is. In the ingress, tJu = Ju = Me/Ve = No/tNo, we find a double dose of the greater benefic, and also the source of luck: he had a dynamite medical team (No/tNo), and a lot of love and positive thinking.

It would have been a depressing time though, with transiting Saturn crossing the axis of his Moon on the natal midpoint pair of Ju/Ne. The naturally optimistic writer would feel abandoned by luck and would experience the consequences of false hopes, plans which come to nothing, disappointments, and losses.

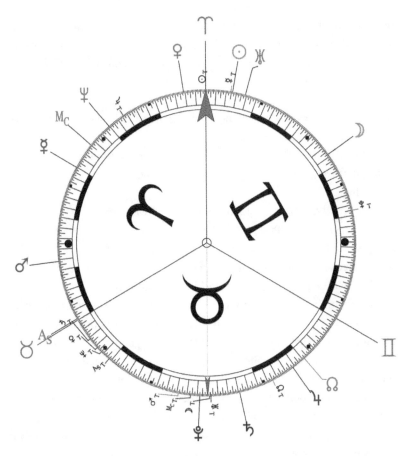

Figure 77. Stephen King's Aries Ingress in bidial

The axis of transiting Mars-Mercury landed on the natal Sun at the midpoints of tVeNe/No. Ma = Me = Su together gives the thinking fighter or the leader in a struggle. The midpoints add a personal effort to meet others halfway; obliging, a pleasant and engaging personality; the misfortune to be tormented or disappointed; the inability to adapt to circumstances or conditions; false expectations.

In sum, the information from the Aries Ingress confirms what we've learned from the earlier charts: the writer seems headed for a difficult crisis. The nature of this crisis is unclear but upset is in evidence.

LUNAR RETURN

Was there a clear warning in the lunar return before the accident? The stand-alone Lunar Return is shown in Figure 78. Scorpio is rising with ruler Mars retrograde and in its sign of detriment. It is in a t-square opposite Jupiter and square Venus. This looks like a creative configuration. The return has captured the partile opposition of the Sun and Pluto, which can mean an attack on life. Mercury is combust and opposite the Moon, suggesting a mind and heart at odds with each other. Uranus is conjunct the South Node and square the Ascendant. It seems as if King will fall suddenly into a hole.

How does this unsettled energy impact the natal chart? The transiting t-square is lined up with the compromised natal Mars, also in fall in Cancer, and in contact with transiting Venus. Is there a problem with creativity? Transiting Mars in Libra, retrograde, is square natal Mars, compounding the natal weakness. Significantly, the return is resonating with the Lunar Eclipse chart of January, five months prior. The Lunar Return Ascendant is conjunct eclipse Venus, ruler of that chart. Mars, Jupiter, and the Sun of the return chart are in aspect to Pluto in the eclipse chart. The return Saturn is in t-square to the lunar opposition of the eclipse. The synastry points to this return as the month the promise of the eclipse will manifest.

The Lunar Return on the dial is shown in Figure 79 on page 191. Most startling is the shared axis of Venus, Mars, Jupiter, Sun, and Pluto, which speaks to success, hope, happiness, and love, but also brutality, violent assaults, and injuries. Uranus and Node share an axis (experience of upsets with others), as do Moon and Mercury (the writer). The following mid-points are in play:

No = Sa/As: unpleasant family circumstances.

Sa = Ur/Ne: depression, instability, pessimism, a painful loss, mourning or bereavement, elimination of the waking consciousness.

Ve = Ma = Ju = Su = Pl: unscrupulous procedure, overtaxing one's strength, violence (war); successful action; intense expression of love; misfortune and losing everything; extraordinary physical or mental powers, creating magical effects; giving one's love to many; desire for achieving great things.

Ne = Ve/No: disappointment; unhappy relationship.

Mc = Me/As: frank discussions, cooperating in the scientific or commercial arena.

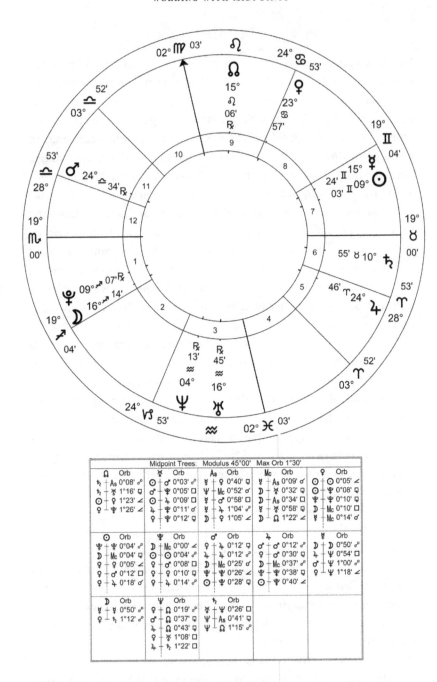

Figure 78. Stephen King's Lunar Return chart before accident

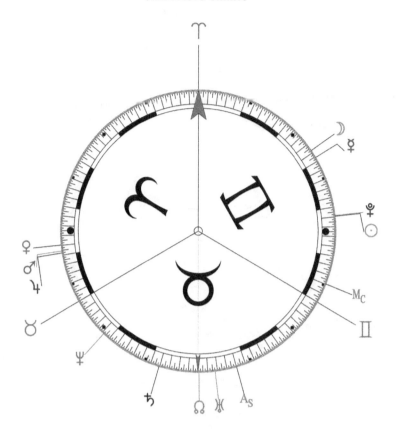

Figure 79. Stephen King's Lunar Return on the dial

Mo = Me: sympathy, kindness, protective care, thoughtfulness and discretion, good judgment.

Ur = VeMaJu/SuPl: cruelty, violence, brutality; sudden disasters or
great calamities; sudden success; unusual experiences in love; hasty or
premature action, impulsive behavior, sudden events, adjusting to new circumstances, change of vocation, compulsory change in daily life and work.

Here, in the stand-alone lunar return, we see an indication of an accident in the form of "sudden disasters or great calamities."

The bidial is shown in Figure 80. Notably, natal Venus is activated by
the complex axis of tUr = tVeMaJu/SuPl. The accident waiting to happen is
going to impact Venus—happiness, well-being, art, and relationships.

The axis of tVeMaJu = SuPl landed on his Mars, doubling the influence
of Mars: impulsiveness, energy, breakage, surgery, and cuts.

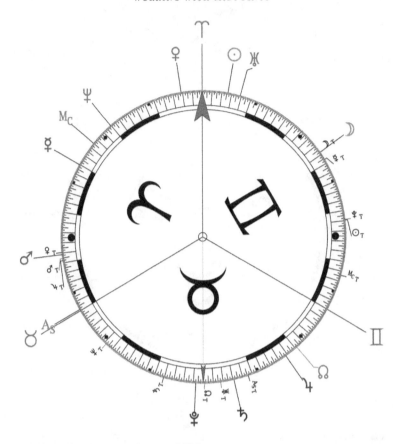

Figure 80. Stephen King's Lunar Return on bidial

Transiting Mercury was on the axis of the Ascendant along with the midpoints of Sa/Mc and Me/Pl: meeting other people, cultivating the exchange of ideas and thoughts; the ability to influence others; indulging melancholy thoughts, unhappy experiences, concentrating on oneself, an inclination to meditate or to brood; thoughts of separation, the moment of saying good-bye; suffering from others, being placed in unfortunate circumstances.

Since we are dealing with a lunar return, the transiting Moon was conjunct the natal Moon on the axis of Me/Sa and tMercury: the opportunity to gain abundant experience, the absorption and digestion of many different impressions.

In sum, the month of the Lunar Return as shown on the dial, and its ties to the prior Lunar Eclipse, marked this period as dangerous.

NEW MOON

The last predictive chart we'll look at is the New Moon before the accident that occurred on June 13, 1999, at 3.02.51 pm in Bangor, Maine (Figure 81). The natal Ascendant is now conjunct the lunation Midheaven, suggesting Stephen King will be in the public eye—not unusual for a famous writer. The lunation is trine the debilitated Mars, now direct and rising. Mars is opposite Jupiter indicative of a large expenditure of energy. Mars and Jupiter are square the lunation Mc-Ic, suggesting a public struggle or confrontation. Mercury sextile Saturn attests to serious writing, but as rulers of the natal 12th and 7th, and 8th houses, also a personal crisis potentially dealing with hospitalization.

Viewed in light of the natal chart, the lunation Midheaven is highlighting the natal Ascendant and debilitated Mars—which rules natal 5th and 10th—visibility and creativity. Furthermore, transiting Mars is square natal Mars from the 4th house, pointing to aggravation at home. Transiting Mars is trine Uranus, the accident pair coming together in easy aspect. This is the second chart that shows a potential accident. However, it may be a spark of creativity. Transiting Jupiter is sextile Uranus, bringing much-needed luck. Troubling is the transiting North Node conjunct natal Pluto, square transiting Saturn at the South Bending, signaling some kind of destructive loss associated with hardship and possible self-destruction. The lunation itself is conjunct Uranus near the cusp of the 12th house of self-undoing and harm. It could also be a writer in seclusion working hard on a shocking new book.

The dial of the lunation is shown in Figure 82 on page 195. The Sun-Moon shares an axis with Venus (love, happiness). Mars, Jupiter, and the Mc are on the same axis, pointing to success. The Node and Saturn are in close proximity and add an association with sickness, isolation, and difficulties. These are the midpoints:

Me = Ur/Pl: transformation, preoccupation with new things and plans.

Ma = Me/Ve: the writer at work.

Mc = Ma/Ju: the joy of living, the ability to make favorable arrangements.

Ju = Me/Sa: success with difficult work, separation, farewell, short journeys.

Ne = Ma/Sa = Ur/As: lack of vigor, unable to overcome obstacles; waning powers, self-torment, damaged vitality (through poison, gas, or an epidemic); a mysterious death, a grievous loss; suffering emotionally

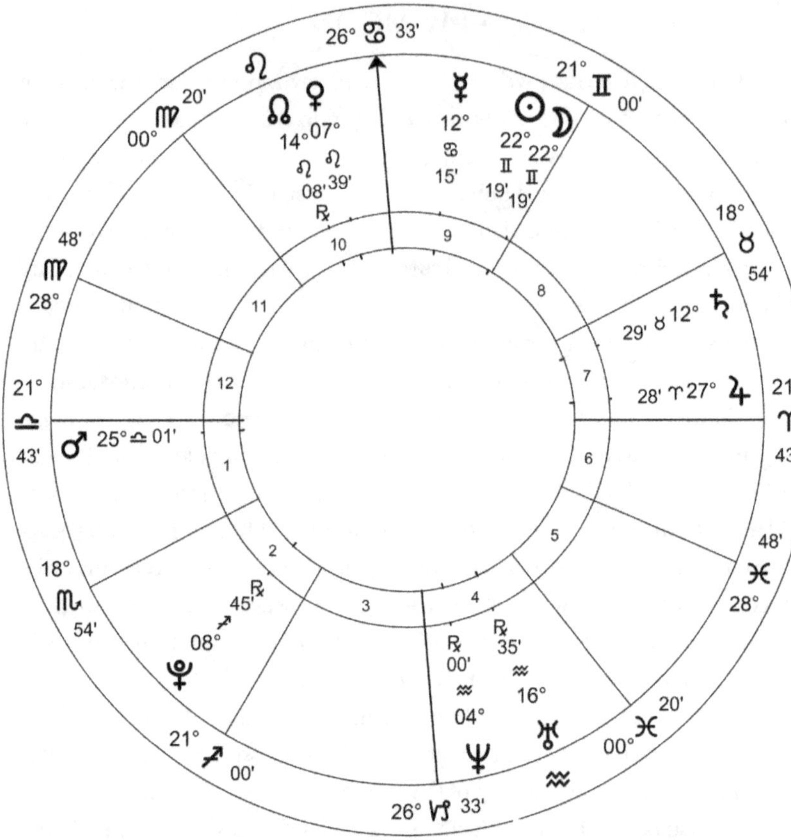

Midpoint Trees: Modulus 45°00' Max Orb 1°30'				
♅ Orb ♂ ♇ 0°18' □ ☽ ☿ 0°42' ⚼ ☉ ☿ 0°42' ⚼ ♇ Mc 1°04' ⚼ ♇ As 1°20' □	☿ Orb ♅ ♇ 0°25' ☍ ♇ ☊ 0°48' □ ☽ ♆ 0°54' □ ☉ ♆ 0°54' □	As Orb ☿ ♆ 1°24' ☍	♇ Orb As Mc 0°22' □ ♂ As 0°23' ∠ ☿ ♆ 0°37' ⚼ ♃ As 0°50' ⚼ ☿ ♀ 1°11' ⚼	♂ Orb ☿ ♀ 0°04' □ ♃ As 0°25' □ As Mc 0°53' ∠ ♇ ♇ 1°16' ∠
Mc Orb ♂ ♃ 0°18' ☌ ☿ ♄ 0°48' ∠ ♃ ♃ 0°55' □ ♆ As 1°18' ⚼	♃ Orb ☿ ♄ 0°06' ∠ ♆ As 0°22' ⚼ ☿ ☊ 0°42' □ Mc Mc 0°55' □	♆ Orb ♅ As 0°09' ∠ ♂ ♄ 0°14' ☍ ♄ Mc 0°31' ⚼ ♂ ☊ 0°34' ⚼ ♃ ♄ 0°59' □	☽ Orb ☉ ☉ 0°00' ☌ ♃ ♅ 0°17' □ ♀ ♀ 0°19' ∠ ♅ Mc 0°45' ∠ ♄ ♆ 0°55' □	☉ Orb ☽ ☽ 0°00' ☌ ♃ ♅ 0°17' □ ♀ ♀ 0°19' ∠ ♅ Mc 0°45' ∠ ♄ ♆ 0°55' □
♀ Orb ☉ ☉ 0°19' ∠ ☽ ☉ 0°19' ∠ ☽ ☽ 0°19' ∠ ♄ ♆ 0°35' ⚼ ♃ ♅ 0°37' ⚼	♄ Orb ♀ ♅ 0°22' ☌	☊ Orb ♄ ♅ 0°23' ⚼ ♇ As 1°06' □		

Figure 81. New Moon chart before accident

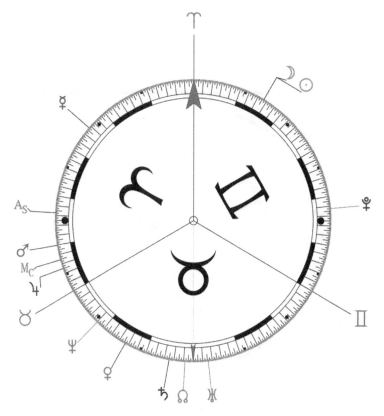

Figure 82. New Moon on the dial

from contact with restless people; disappointment or falsehood, the sudden weakening of associations, sudden, sad experiences.

Ve = Mo = Su = Ju/Ur = Sa/Ne: sickness that impacts the native's happiness, health, and emotional wellbeing, and luck.

Sa = Ve/Sa: sudden separation or sadness.

No = Sa/Ur: provocative conduct; joint resistance to an adversary, separation.

Ur = Ma/Pl: cruelty, violence, brutality; sudden disasters or great calamities.

Pl = As/Mc: an unusual person in unusual surroundings, a fascinating personality; able to place strong influence upon others.

In the stand-alone return, we hear the drumbeat of danger growing ever louder. The themes of illness, accident, transformation, brutality, and luck are all present.

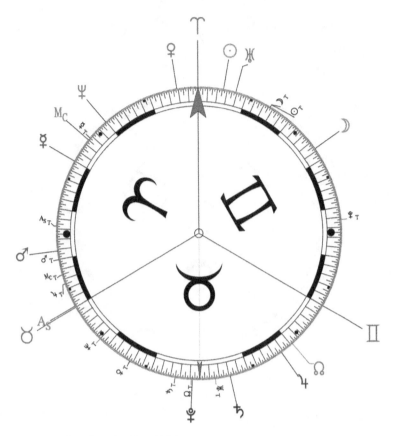

Figure 83. Stephen King's New Moon bidial

The bidial is shown in Figure 83. Transiting Uranus is on the axis of Venus at the midpoints of tSuMo/Me, which looks like a change to his work and writing schedule.

Transiting Mercury is on the axis of the Midheaven at the midpoint of Ur/Pl. The Ur/Pl pair can mean a major life-changing accident, though also creative power and endurance.

Notably, transiting Pluto is on the axis of Mars at the crucial midpoint of tAs/Mc. The involvement of the two angles tells us to pay attention. tPl = Ma gives the attainment of success through excessive effort, and/or the misfortune of having to suffer violent assaults or injuries. For the last few charts, transiting Pluto has been dancing around Mars, and is now staring it down. The moment of change has come.

Transiting Saturn on the axis of the Sun is another warning. tSa = Su means a difficult struggle to advance in life, little help from other people, and working silently or in solitude; delicate health, a secluded or solitary mode of life, a simple life compelled by circumstances, suppression through others, and separations. On the axis is No/As: feelings of oppression or suppression in the presence of others.

Finally, the transiting Node is on the axis of Pluto at the midpoints of Mo/Mc and Ve/Ur, giving the beginning of new associations, which may be important with regard to one's future; a common and tragic destiny shared with others; a peculiar or strange soul life, great emotional depression, emotional shock and upheaval; a sympathetic understanding of others; high degree of excitability.

Certainly, an astrologer could not be faulted for advising caution for the month.

Does the lunation unequivocally point to a life-threatening accident? It does not. Always, it is hard to separate what is going on in the writer's book and what is happening on the outside in real life. However, every chart in this series that we have looked at gave indications of danger, which eventually appeared as a physical assault caused by a motor vehicle and a brush with death.

In sum, the charts reflect Stephen King's life as an author as it was before the accident, and his rehabilitation afterward. In 1999, three books were published. Presumably, he was writing up to the day of the crash. When he got out of the hospital he began again: *On Writing: A Memoir of the Craft*. In life, on any given day, there can be a lot going on—multiple fires are burning. For this reason, looking at your own chart is the best way of seeing how simultaneous events are expressed.

In this chapter, we looked at several predictive charts. However, this was not Ebertin's preferred method of prediction. We'll see what he favored in the next chapter.

 HOMEWORK: Pick a significant event in your life and look at a predictive chart leading up to the event. Examine the stand-alone event chart, the stand-alone dial, and the bidial. Was the event visible in the predictive chart?

Chapter 16

Tools of Cosmobiology

We have been looking at frozen snapshots of time and precise midpoints captured in an event or predictive chart. But this does not tell the whole story, nor does it show the buildup and separation of the transiting planets. This is primarily how Ebertin worked with transits—he watched how transits and transiting midpoints moved over time. He devised an amazing tool to track this movement that he called the Graphic 45° Ephemeris or the Annual Diagram.

We saw in Chapter 7 (Figure 13 on page 49) how planets in a 360° layout can be transposed into a 90° format. If we cut the 90° strip in half again and line up the two pieces, we get the 45° modulus strip. We have been looking at 45° midpoint trees, 45° midpoint lists, and 45° distance arcs, recognizing that we are looking at both ends of an axis, considering both the pointer and the tail (Figure 13d).

45° RULER

If we rotate the 45° modulus strip—making a one-quarter turn to the right so that 0° is at the top and 45° is at the bottom—we end up with the strip shown in the left side of Figure 84. On the right is what I call a 45° ruler. Feel free to photocopy the ruler and laminate it, as it is a handy tool for finding the minor 8th harmonic aspects.

The ruler is easy to use. The first column is labeled 45 and has the numbers 1 through 45. This refers to a total of 45° of longitude—half a square or half the distance of the dial. The second column is labeled C for cardinal. It contains 30° of the cardinal signs of Aries, Cancer, Libra, and Capricorn. This section goes from numbers 1 to 30 as there are only 30° in any one sign or mode. The next column shows the superimposition of the fixed degrees—Taurus, Leo, Scorpio, and Aquarius. Note that 1° fixed corresponds to number 31 shown in the 1st column. The first 15° of the fixed signs follow in order and go from numbers 30 to 45. When we reach the bottom of the ruler or number 45, we jump to the top. The remaining 16 through 30° of fixed signs are listed from numbers 1 to 15. The last column shows the mutable degrees—Gemini, Virgo, Sagittarius, and Pisces, which begin at number 16 (column 1) and run down to number 45. The entire 30° of the mode runs in order to the bottom as seen in the last column.

We look across the rows to find the minor 45° and 135° aspects. The ruler tells us that a planet at 1° cardinal is in minor aspect to a planet at 16° of any fixed sign. Similarly, a planet at 29° fixed is in minor aspect to any planet at 14° cardinal. A planet at 7° mutable is in minor aspect to a planet at 22° cardinal. A planet at 9° fixed is in minor aspect to 24° mutable, and so on.

Stephen King's natal Venus is at 2° cardinal. From the ruler, we know that any planet at 2° cardinal is in minor aspect to 17° fixed. Where is his Saturn? At 18° Leo. Does he have any planets in minor aspect to his Neptune at 10° cardinal? Using the ruler, look across the row from 10° cardinal and there is 25° fixed. Where is the North Node? At 25° Taurus. The ruler is a handy tool to identify the minor 45° and 135° aspects and their corresponding degrees. The ruler is also the basis for the 45° ephemeris.

45°	C	F	M
1	1	16	
2	2	17	
3	3	18	♊
4	4	19	
5	5	20	
6	6	21	
7	7	22	♍
8	8	23	
9	9	24	
10	10	25	
11	11	26	♐
12	12	27	
13	13	28	
14	14	29	♓
15	15	30	
16	16		1
17	17		2
18	18	♉	3
19	19		4
20	20		5
31	21		6
22	22	♌	7
23	23		8
24	24		9
25	25		10
26	26	♏	11
27	27		12
28	28		13
29	29	♒	14
30	30		15
31		1	16
32		2	17
33	♈	3	18
34		4	19
35		5	20
36		6	21
37	♋	7	22
38		8	23
39		9	24
40	♎	10	25
41		11	26
42		12	27
43	♑	13	28
44		14	29
45		15	30

Figure 84. 45° Ruler.
At left is the 45° modulus strip

GRAPHIC 45° DEGREE EPHEMERIS

The graphic 45° ephemeris uses the 45° strip as the vertical axis in a graph that shows the transiting planets over time. Stephen King's 45° ephemeris of his natal planets is shown in Figure 85. The graph is from Solar Fire's "Dynamic" menu and is accessed through the second option on the list: graphic ephemeris. There are pre-set selections that are found by scrolling down the "saved selection" list. The figure shown here has only the radix planets. (Please note that this figure, and all following similar graphic ephemeri, has been turned counterclockwise to fit the length of the book page to make it easier to read. References to "vertical" and "horizontal"in the discussion that follows will refer to its presented book orientation.)

The horizontal axis on the bottom of the figure, the Y-axis, runs from 1° to 45°, which corresponds to the first column of the 45° ruler. The X-axis, running down the left side of this figure, shows time. The top horizontal side lists the planets and points in their 45° format. (You can verify the position of the planets on the graph match their position in the 45° strip shown in Figure 13d.) Since natal planets don't change position over time, they appear in the graph as a straight line.

We can add directions to the graph. Figure 86 on page 202 shows 80 years of solar arcs. The X-axis shows time in decades. The solar arc planets are shown as slanted lines on the graph. The natal planets are the vertical lines. Note the slope of the solar arc planets is identical and remain parallel. This is because they are based on the slope of the Sun. Everything moves in the same direction over time, going from the top of the graph (lower degree) toward the bottom of the graph (higher degree). In these graphs, what is important is the intersection of lines between the solar arc directions and the natal planet lines. Note the vertical line shown in late 1999 which corresponds to Stephen King's accident. Here we can see the directions at a glance: directed Uranus = natal Venus, directed Sun = natal Saturn, directed Venus = Jupiter, directed Saturn = Jupiter, directed Jupiter = Mercury, directed Mars = Moon.

To zoom in on a time in question, we change the time frame, using an increasingly smaller range. The solar arcs around 1999 are shown in a 2-year graph in Figure 87. Note the gradual slope of the directions, which in a year change only 1°. We can eyeball when the directions will come exact in this time frame.

Figure 85. Graphic ephemeris with Stephen King's natal points

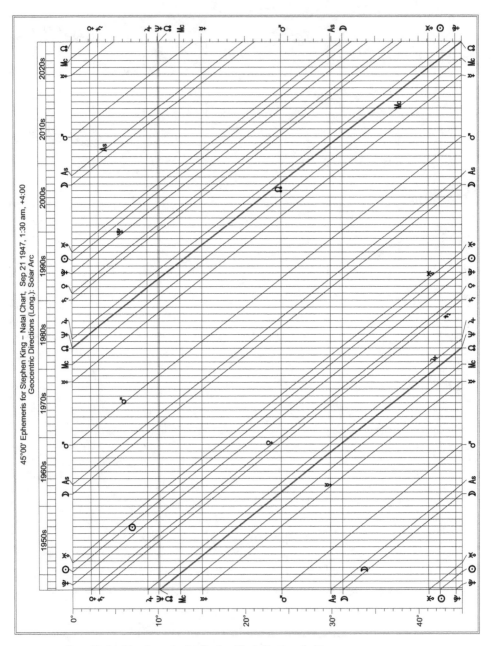

Figure 86. Graphic ephemeris with Stephen King's directions for 80 years

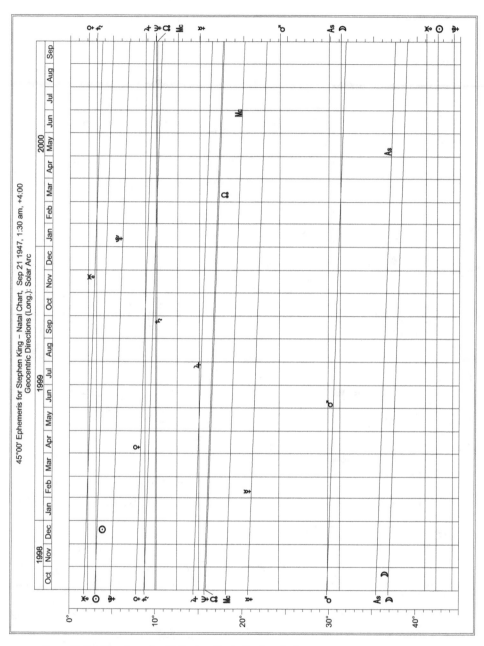

Figure 87. Graphic ephemeris with Stephen King's directions for 2 years

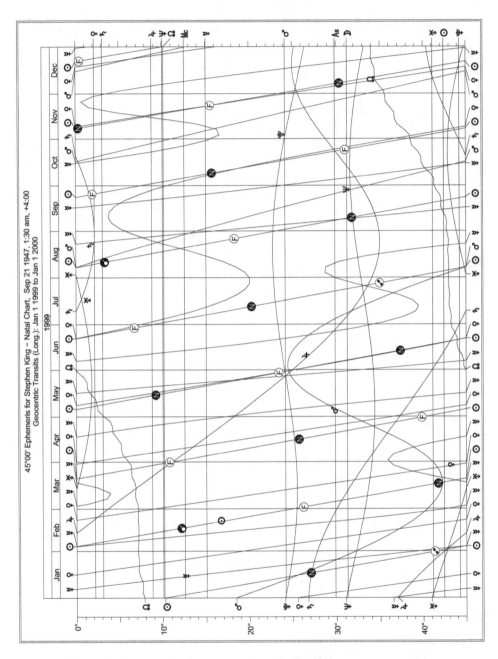

Figure 88. Stephen King's graphic ephemeris 1-year transiting 1999

The transits are more striking. Ebertin used the dial to find the directions, and the graphic 45° ephemeris to view the transits. Stephen King's graphic 45° ephemeris for the year of his accident is shown in Figure 88. Here, the slope of the transiting planets reflects their speed—the steeper the slope, the faster the movement. Direct movement is downward from 0° to 45° longitude. Once a planet reaches 45°, it jumps to the top and resumes its downward travel. This is equivalent to going from 15° fixed to 16° fixed, or 30° mutable to 1° cardinal. Retrograde planets move upward, backward in degree. Stations correspond to a flattening of slope, where no longitude is gained or lost over time. Lunations are marked with an "N" for New Moon and "F" for Full Moon. The eclipses are shown by their symbols. Note the late January lunar eclipse near natal Uranus, while the February solar eclipse falls on his Midheaven. The Moon is not shown on this time frame as it adds too much noise to the graph. In these graphs, the main thing to watch for is the intersection of lines, which denote 8th harmonic aspects.

Typically, to investigate a period of time, I start with an overview, beginning with the month of the solar return and looking at the main transits for the coming year, using only the outer planets (Jupiter to Pluto) and the Nodes, as shown in Figure 89 on page 206. Without the inner planets, the main transits are easier to see, along with the lunations and eclipses. The aspects formed to the natal planets are readily visible. For example, in mid-October, transiting Saturn will connect to the natal Moon and soon after transiting Neptune and the natal Ascendant. Transiting Saturn stations near the end of 1998 and begins forward motion toward the end of January. There is a second transiting Saturn-Neptune connection in April that doesn't hit his chart.

After scanning the transits for a year, I zoom in and look at a season. The graph for April, May, and June 1999, is shown in Figure 90 on page 207. In Spring, transiting Jupiter will cross the natal Midheaven and Mercury, then Mars, and finally the Ascendant. Transiting Saturn and transiting Neptune will meet in early April and separate. Transiting Saturn will go on to meet up with natal Uranus, Sun, and Pluto. This latter connection occurs with the transiting Node. Transiting Uranus is connecting to natal Venus, and in May, the transiting Node. After the initial meeting of transiting Neptune with transiting Saturn, transiting Neptune is out of the picture. Transiting Pluto's main connection is with

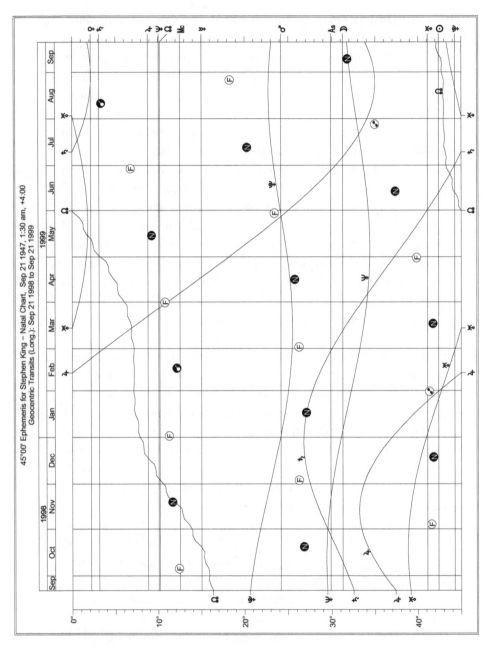

Figure 89. Stephen King's graphic ephemeris 1-year transiting outers

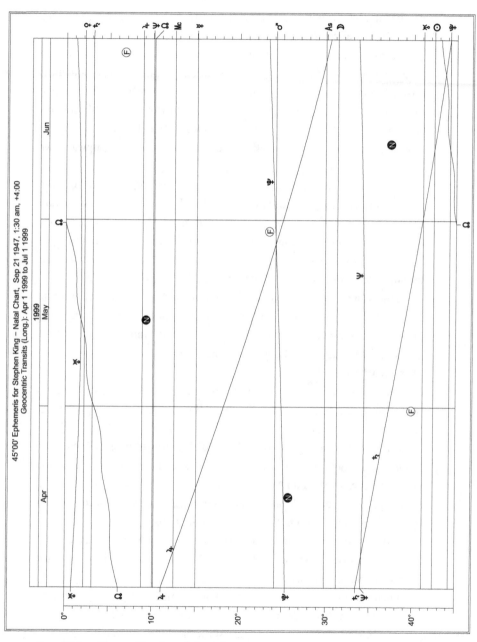

Figure 90. Transiting graphic ephemeris 3 months outers

natal Mars, which will coincide with transiting Jupiter coming to Mars, at the time of a Full Moon.

To zoom in further, we can look at a month, and add the Moon and the inner planets to find active days. The month of Stephen King's accident is shown in Figure 91. Since a day contains 24 hours, starting and ending at midnight, it is possible to approximate a given time on a monthly ephemeris. The month starts with transiting Uranus near natal Venus. During the month Uranus is slowly separating. Since Uranus is moving upward, we know it is retrograde.

Early in the month, transiting Mars and transiting Pluto are in hard aspect to natal Mars. Pluto will remain in orb to natal Mars all month. Transiting Mars is slowly moving away from natal Mars, and it must have been stationing direct because it is moving so slowly. (A check of the regular ephemeris shows it turned direct on June 4th.) Around the 12th of the month, it picks up speed, moving more rapidly in forward motion.

Transiting Jupiter is near transiting Mars and moving direct at a rate comparable to Mars until the end of the month. Jupiter will not hit any natal planets until June 25-26 when it reaches the natal Moon and Ascendant. Transiting Mercury and the Moon make contact around the same time. There may be some happy news.

The transiting Sun and Venus are traveling at the same rate of speed throughout the month. Towards the end of the month, the Sun is picking up speed. We can see their ingresses into Cancer on June 21st, when they jump to the top of the graph going from 29° to 0°. The transiting Sun line is easy to distinguish because the lunations always happen on this line. From the graph, we can see the Full Moon is within two degrees of a hard aspect to natal Jupiter. The New Moon on June 13 is hanging in space, accompanied by transiting Venus, and not hitting any natal points.

Down at the base of the graph, we can see the outer planet aspects we looked at previously. As we saw, transiting Neptune is not making any hard aspects to the natal chart and is stationary. Transiting Saturn is separating from natal Uranus and will cross the natal Sun and Pluto mid-month. The node for the first two-thirds of the month is traveling close to Pluto.

The horizontal lines in this figure show the day. We can tell in advance when the most important days of the month will be by the number of close aspects on any given day. Look at the vertical line of June 3rd. We have

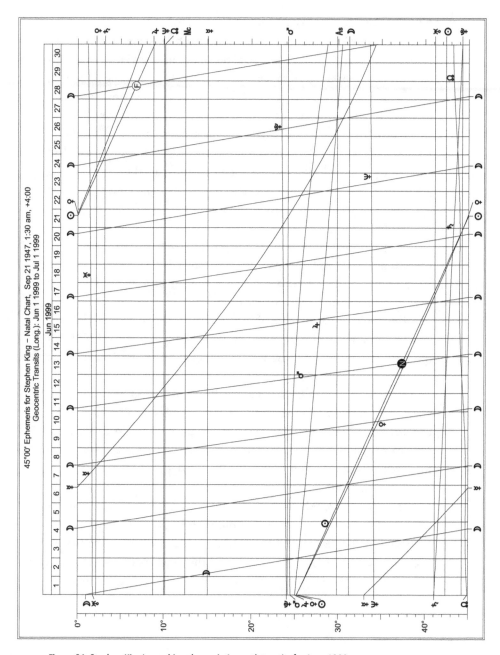

Figure 91. Stephen King's graphic ephemeris 1-month transits for June 1999

transiting Uranus near natal Venus. The transiting Moon is hitting natal Mars, transiting Pluto, transiting Mars, and transiting Jupiter in short order. A few hours later it will hit transiting Sun and transiting Venus. Transiting Saturn is just separating from natal Uranus, and the transiting Node is in close approach to natal Pluto. It would be interesting to know what happened in King's life that day. Of course, in your own life, you would know.

We can zoom in further and look at the transits on June 19, the day of the accident (Figure 92). In this short time frame, the transiting Ascendant and Midheaven can be added. As mentioned, these are the fastest moving points in the chart. They each traverse the 90° dial four times a day and often serve as triggers for events. The transiting Moon is the only other sloping line in the graph.

During the day, aside from the angles, the Moon will cross natal Mars, transiting Mars, transiting Jupiter, natal Ascendant, natal Moon, and transiting Neptune. The transiting Sun-Venus lines are crossing the line of the natal Sun and transiting Saturn. The transiting Node is with natal Pluto.

The accident occurred around 16.30 military time. At this time, the transiting Midheaven crossed natal Jupiter, natal Neptune, and natal Node. At the same time, the transiting Ascendant crossed the natal Sun, Uranus, Pluto complex that was hit by transiting Saturn, Node, Venus, and Sun, repeating the emphasis of Saturn and the Node. Could we tell in advance this hour was a dangerous time for him? No. A glance at the graph shows the natal points and directions being stimulated repeatedly by the transiting Ascendant and Midheaven (but not the Moon), during the day. We need to look elsewhere for the explanation of a near-fatal accident occurring at this time.

Transiting midpoint pairs can also be added to the graphic ephemeris. Figure 93 on page 212 shows the difficult transiting pairs on the day of the accident. From this it is evident that during the hour of the accident, the transiting Midheaven crossed Ma/Pl, then Sa/Pl, then Ur/Pl. The transiting Ascendant crossed Sa/Ne and Ur/Ne. The exact transiting midpoints formed were captured in the event dial that we looked at in Figure 67 on page 170.

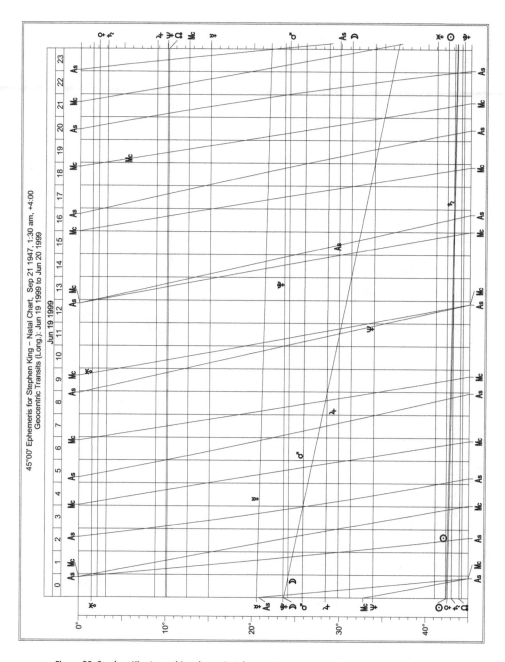

Figure 92. Stephen King's graphic ephemeris 1-day transits on June 19, 1999

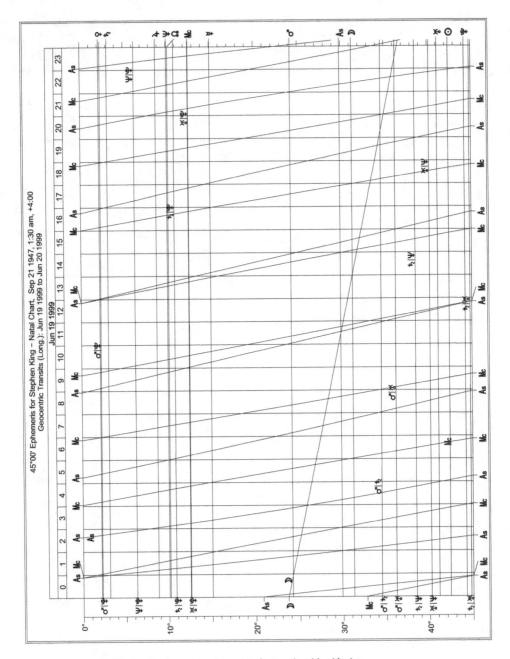

Figure 93. Stephen King's graphic ephemeris 1-day transits with midpoints

EXAMPLE EBERTIN

We saw how Ebertin interpreted Brigitte Bardot's dial and directions in Chapter 11 at the time of her attempted suicide, and in the same example (*Directions*, page 134) he examined the activating transits. The 45° Graphic Ephemeris of the event is shown in Figure 94 (page 214). Here he looked at Bardot's Su = Ma/Sa death axis in light of the transits from July through September 1960. He saw transiting Uranus coming to the line of the Sun, and then transiting Mars. He wrote that "transiting Uranus passed over natal Mars, Sun, and Saturn around this time." In addition, transiting Saturn, retrograde, passed over the Midheaven. Furthermore, transiting Neptune stationed on natal Node (and natal Venus which went unremarked). He concluded the point of looking at such examples was to identify possible times of depression, and that suicide attempts "are foreseeable and it is hence potentially possible to prevent the worst from happening."

As seen from this example, Ebertin's focus was on transiting aspects, which show up in the graph as the crossing of planetary lines. He did not look at any transiting midpoints. In his pre-computer age, creating dials for timed transiting charts would have been time-consuming. Drawing a transiting graph for a season that could be reprinted and used over and over would have been a time-saver. But we live in a different age where a transiting chart that shows transiting midpoint pairs can be created in an instant.

TRANSITING MIDPOINT PAIR LISTING

A list of the transiting midpoint pairs can be generated in Solar Fire using the Dynamic function's Ephemeris. Alternatively, Astrolabe publishes a list every year that can be accessed through their website. An example of the listing from Jupiter through Pluto is shown in Figure 95 on page 215. The list can be used to find the degrees of transiting midpoint pairs.

In Stephen King's case, for the year of his accident, the listing indicates that the transiting Jupiter/Saturn midpoint crossed his Midheaven in Feb 1999. Transiting Jupiter/Pluto opposed his natal Pluto and natal Saturn between May and August 1999. Transiting Saturn/Uranus opposed his natal Sun in May–June. The transiting Saturn/Pluto midpoint opposed his Saturn in February.

When we know these transiting contacts are coming, we can look at the 45° ephemeris to see when they will be triggered by fast-moving planets.

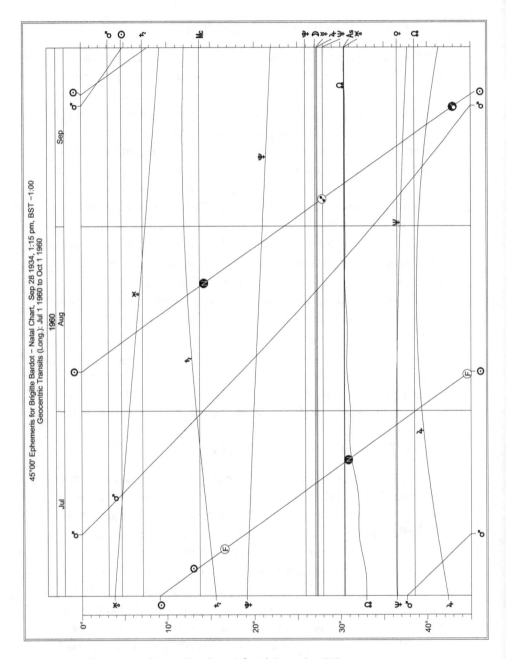

Figure 94. Brigette Bardot's graphic ephemeris for July-September 1960

Jan 6 2022 Solar Fire v9.0.16

GMT +0:00 Tropical Geocentric Long	Jup/Sat ♃/♄	Jup/Ura ♃/♅	Jup/Nep ♃/♆	Jup/Plu ♃/♇	Sat/Ura ♄/♅	Sat/Nep ♄/♆	Sat/Plu ♄/♇	Ura/Nep ♅/♆	Ura/Plu ♅/♇
Jan 1 1999	09°♈21'	01°♓26'	26°♒29'	00°♒31'	18°♓51'	13°♓54'	17°♒56'	06°♒00'	10°♑02'
Feb 1 1999	12°♈36'	05°♓04'	29°♒50'	03°♒44'	20°♓14'	14°♓59'	18°♒53'	07°♒27'	11°♑21'
Mar 1 1999	16°♈47'	08°♓56'	03°♓24'	07°♒01'	22°♓08'	16°♓36'	20°♒13'	08°♒45'	12°♑22'
Apr 1 1999	22°♈13'	13°♓23'	07°♓30'	10°♒42'	24°♓35'	18°♓43'	21°♒54'	09°♒53'	13°♑04'
May 1 1999	27°♈41'	17°♓23'	11°♓16'	14°♒02'	26°♓54'	20°♓46'	23°♒33'	10°♒29'	13°♑15' ℞
Jun 1 1999	03°♉01'	20°♓52'	14°♓35'	17°♒02'	28°♓54'	22°♓37'	25°♒04'	10°♒28' ℞	12°♑55'
Jul 1 1999	07°♉18'	23°♓17'	17°♓01'	19°♒22'	00°♈12'	23°♓55'	26°♒16'	09°♒54'	12°♑15'
Aug 1 1999	10°♉14'	24°♓33'	18°♓26'	20°♒56'	00°♈45'	24°♓38'	27°♒08'	08°♒57'	11°♑27'
Sep 1 1999	11°♉02' ℞	24°♓23' ℞	18°♓29' ℞	21°♒20' ℞	00°♈31' ℞	24°♓37' ℞	27°♒28'	07°♒58'	10°♑50'
Oct 1 1999	09°♉33'	22°♓56'	17°♓13'	20°♒31'	29°♓41'	23°♓58'	27°♒16' ℞	07°♒21'	10°♑39' D
Nov 1 1999	06°♉29'	20°♓51'	15°♓15'	18°♒58'	28°♓31'	22°♓54'	26°♒38'	07°♒17' D	11°♑01'
Dec 1 1999	03°♉45'	19°♓35'	13°♓56'	17°♒58'	27°♓39'	22°♓01'	26°♒03'	07°♒51'	11°♑52'

GMT +0:00 Tropical Geocentric Long	Nep/Plu ♆/♇
Jan 1 1999	05°♑05'
Feb 1 1999	06°♑07'
Mar 1 1999	06°♑49'
Apr 1 1999	07°♑12'
May 1 1999	07°♑07' ℞
Jun 1 1999	06°♑39'
Jul 1 1999	05°♑59'
Aug 1 1999	05°♑19'
Sep 1 1999	04°♑55'
Oct 1 1999	04°♑56' D
Nov 1 1999	05°♑24'
Dec 1 1999	06°♑14'

Figure 95. Solar Fire ephemeris with outer midpoint listing for 1999

Since the transiting outer pairs can be activated by the transiting angles, Moon, Sun, Mercury, Venus, or Mars, and since the transiting angles circle the dial eight times in a day, they are bound to trigger a transiting midpoint pair, sooner rather than later. For this reason, if an outer pair is near a natal planet, they can be considered active, because they will be triggered multiple times during the days and months they are in orb.

LINEAR DIAGRAM

Cosmobiologist Eleonora Kimmel introduced a tool for organizing solar arcs, transits, and natal points, and all of their midpoints. It is a table she called the Linear Diagram. The table uses the 45° ruler as its index. A blank form made in a word program is shown in Appendix 5. A table filled out for the transits in the predictive charts we looked at previously for Stephen King is shown in Figure 96. The diagram shows the placements of the planets and angles in the various charts as tabulated over time. While erecting this diagram is labor intensive, the natal points and midpoints can be used over and over in subsequent diagrams for any given person.

How is the table constructed? The first two columns resemble the 45° ruler. The next column lists the natal points in their 45° notation. In the next column, I list the in-orb natal midpoint pairs associated with the planets. This information can be lifted off the 45° midpoint listing. For Stephen King, this was shown in Figure 21. These two columns are enlightening as they illustrate the degree spans that are active and those which are not. In the next column, I list the solar arc degree of the planets as determined on that year's birthday. There is no need to add the directed midpoint degrees as these can be seen from the natal midpoint pair column. The remaining columns are for the transits in the predictive charts. As the year passes, I add these as they occur.

Typically, for each year, I track the planets in the Solar Return, the four ingresses, all lunar and solar eclipse charts, the lunar returns, and the New and Full Moon lunations. I recalculate the directions six months after the birth date. When the page is filled, I add a new page and tape the pages together.

I use a ruler to scan across the rows to find natal degrees which are repeatedly triggered. Especially significant are contacts with the angles across the various charts. For example, in Figure 96, on row 4 we can see

#	C F M	Natal	Natal mps	SR	LE	Aries Ing	LR	NM	Accident	#
0	0 15		Mo/Me			Su Mo Ur	No			0
1	1 16		Sa/Pl				Ur	Ur	Ur	1
2	2 17	Ve								2
3	3 18	Sa	Ur/Ne Su/Ne							3
4	4 19		Ju/Pl Ur/Mc	Ma			As			4
5	5 20									5
6	6 21					No				6
7	7 22				No					7
8	8 23	Ju	Me/Ve			Ju				8
9	9 24								Mc	9
10	10 25	Ne	Ma/Ur Su/Ma	As						10
11	11 26		Ne/Mc							11
12	12 27	Mc	Me/Ne Ur/As					Me		12
13	13 28		Ve/Ma Su/As Me/Mc							13
14	14 29									14
15	15 30 0	Me	Mo/Pl							15
16	16 1		Ve/As	No						16
17	17 2						Mc			17
18	18 3				Ve					18
19	19 4									19
20	20 5			Pl						20
21	21 6							As	Me	21
22	22 7		Su/Sa							22
23	23 8		Ve/Pl				Ve	Pl	Pl	23
24	24 9	Ma	Ju/Ur				Ma Ju Pl Su			24
25	25 10		Ve/Sa Su/Ju Ur/No		Pl	Pl		Ma	Ma	25
26	26 11							Mc		26
27	27 12				Sa			Ju		27
28	28 13		Pl/Mc Ve/No						Ju	28
29	29 14	As	Sa/Ne Me/Pl	Ne						29
30	30 0 15		Sa/Mc				Me			30
31	1 16	Mo	Me/Sa Ju/Ne		Mc		Mo			31
32	2 17		Ne/No	Sa Ve	Ma Ne	Sa			Mo	32
33	3 18			As		Ne Ve			Ne	33
34	4 19					As	Ne	Ne		34
35	5 20									35
36	6 21									36
37	7 22			Ju Me				Su Mo Ve		37
38	8 23				Me					38
39	9 24		Ma/Ur	Ur						39
40	10 25			Mo			Sa			40
41	11 26	Ur	Ju/As	Mc	Su Mo					41
42	12 27	Su	No/As	Su	Ur Ju	Ma Me		Sa	As	42
43	13 28		Mo/Ne			Mc			Su Ve Sa No	43
44	14 29	Pl	Ve/Ur Mo/Mc Su/Ve					No		44

Figure 96. Linear diagram for Stephen King's predictive charts for lead up to the accident

the Lunar Return Ascendant is in the degree of Solar Return Mars, which is within one degree of natal Saturn. Toward the month of the accident, natal Mars is in repeated contact with transiting Pluto and transiting Mars. The natal Sun is also experiencing many hits as the year proceeds.

Cosmobiology provides a number of tools that are helpful in prediction. When there is so much information, the linear diagram helps isolate specific planets and angles that are active at an event.

HOMEWORK: Take an event from your life and examine it using the 45° ephemeris tools.

PART 4

COMBINING TRANSITS AND SOLAR ARCS

In certain instances, one may not wish to go to the trouble of examining all configurations, but only investigate certain factors correlating to special objectives or events.

REINHOLD EBERTIN

Chapter 17

Combining Transits and Solar Arcs in the Chart

Transits typically trigger solar arc directions. While the directions show the nature of significant events, the timing is shown by a transit, which adds its own nature to the symbolism. Ebertin thought that directions were more significant than transits. However, he believed the transiting three outer planets and Saturn were almost as powerful. Ebertin opined that he didn't expect much from a simple transit to a natal contact if there was no associated solar arc. He wrote, "transiting Jupiter coming to natal Pluto will not likely be significant if natal Pluto is not active by solar arc."

When a timed event of significance occurs, the transits highlight the potential activated in the natal chart. For this reason, studying timed events sheds light on how a natal chart is working, and what the natal factors (planets and angles in their signs, houses, aspects, and midpoints) specifically mean in a given chart.

The easiest way to look at transiting triggers in a chart is to construct a triwheel with the natal, directed, and transits of an event. First, find the directions as we did in Chapter 10. These can be circled or starred. Second, look at the outer planet transits and note the ones that are conjunct or opposite natal planets. Third, in a timed event chart, find the fast-moving triggering transits that aspect the directed-natal combinations, and the outer transit-natal combinations. Fourth, add the remaining transits-to-natal combinations. Once all these are found, examine the midpoints associated with these to see what energy is in play. In the chart, I use an orb for transits of about 3 to 5°. The orb for midpoints remains about 1½°.

The same rule holds that there is no mixing of levels. This means we ignore any midpoint pairs formed between a transit and a natal point, between a transit and a direction, or a transit and a natal point. As always, we ignore a transit that aspects a direction that is not in contact with a natal planet or point—we need a natal planet to ground the incoming energy. The following example will make these points clear.

A FAIRY TALE WEDDING

For a change of pace, we'll look at the solar arcs, transits, and midpoints at the time of the marriage of the late Princess of Wales. The stand-alone marriage chart is shown in Figure 97. Is this an elected chart created by one of Diana's astrologers? Not likely—no astrologer would recommend this timing for her wedding. In the example chart, we can see a debilitated Mars in Cancer conjunct the Midheaven, a dark, though dignified Moon, a debilitated Venus ruling the event, and an impending total Solar Eclipse in two days. The conjunction of Jupiter on the Ascendant is nice, and its conjunction with Saturn, is epic, though not so nice. Mercury square Pluto is a problem. These are the direct midpoints as read from the trees:

Sa = Ju/As: hobbled personal development, inconsistent associations; estrangement and alienation, separation, departure.

Ju = Sa/As: indifference, ignoring or brushing off difficulties; joy over a separation, a change of place or residence.

As = Me/Ne: being too open to the influences of others; exploitation, deception, or harm from others.

Mc = Mo/Ma: getting married.

Me = Su/Mc: gaining experiences, achieving goals; thinking about one's social position.

Me = Mo/No: one's attitude toward others; the exchange of ideas; being critical of others, a relationship of convenience.

Me = Su/Mo: thoughts of marriage; the union of thoughts between husband and wife.

Su = Ve/Ma: a strongly physical love, artistic power of creation, the urge union, marriage, procreation.

Ve = Su/Sa: suppressed feelings, reserve; inhibited in love life, the separation of lovers, love-sickness; feeling victimized.

Ve = Su/Ju: a healthy love relationship, a harmonious sex life; a beautiful body, good art, success in love, the happy loving husband.

Ve = No/As: agreeable, affectionate, or tactful treatment of others. A union of two people who share the same interests and feelings. A love union

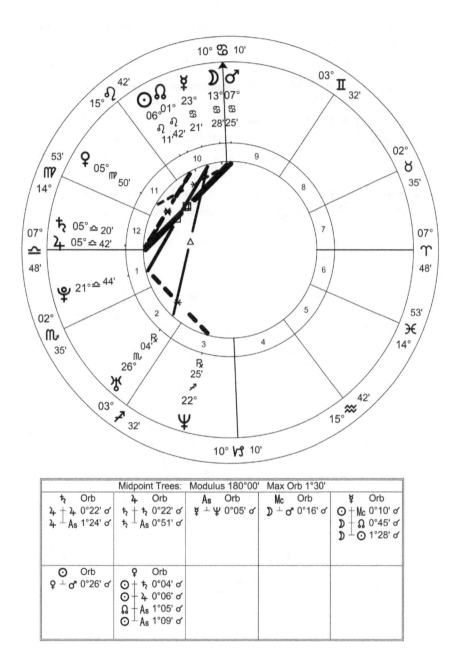

Midpoint Trees:		Modulus 180°00'	Max Orb 1°30'	
♄ Orb	♃ Orb	As Orb	Mc Orb	☿ Orb
♃ ⊤ ♃ 0°22' ♂	♄ ⊤ ♄ 0°22' ♂	☿ ⊥ ♆ 0°05' ♂	☽ ⊥ ♂ 0°16' ♂	☉ ⊤ Mc 0°10' ♂
♃ ⊥ As 1°24' ♂	♄ ⊥ As 0°51' ♂			☽ ⊤ ☊ 0°45' ♂
				☽ ⊥ ☉ 1°28' ♂
☉ Orb	♀ Orb			
♀ ⊥ ♂ 0°26' ♂	☉ ⊤ ♄ 0°04' ♂			
	☉ ⊤ ♃ 0°06' ♂			
	☊ ⊤ As 1°05' ♂			
	☉ ⊥ As 1°09' ♂			

Figure 97. Princess Diana's wedding chart

223

Ve = Su/As: the impersonal love of humanity, a harmonious relation-ship with one's environment; affections; love of others.

This chart captures the marriage of Prince Charles and Diana in a snapshot, showing both love and its demise.

The triwheel of the event is shown in Figure 98A (solar arc in the mid-dle wheel). The midpoint trees are shown in figure 98B. There are several solar arcs. Directed Jupiter is conjunct the natal Moon and opposite Ura-nus. Directed Jupiter conjunct the Moon gives great happiness, while Jupi-ter opposite Uranus indicates luck by association with another person. The directed Sun is opposite Saturn, showing an older man and wealth as well as inhibition, loneliness, and grief. The natal Moon is on the midpoint of

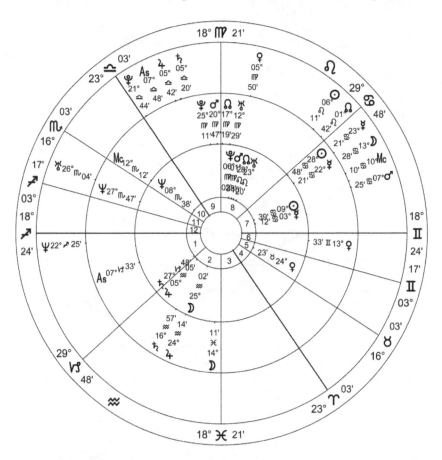

Figure 98A. Princess Diana's triwheel with solar arc and transits at wedding

Midpoint Trees: Modulus 45°00' Max Orb 1°30' (1)

☿ Orb	♅ Orb	♀ Orb	☉ Orb	☽ Orb
♂/♃ 0°10' ⚼	♄/As 0°13' ⚼	☽/♅ 0°12' ☌	☽/♀ 0°03' □	☉/☉ 0°22' ⚼
♆/☊ 0°12' □	♆/♇ 0°59' ∠	☉/☉ 0°15' ∠	♀/♀ 0°15' ∠	♀/♀ 0°38' □
♄/♇ 1°16' ⚼	♀/♀ 1°03' □	☽/☽ 0°38' □	☽/☽ 0°22' ⚼	♅/☊ 0°43' ☍
☽/♆ 1°21' ☍	☉/☉ 1°19' ∠	♅/♅ 1°03' □	☽/♅ 0°28' ∠	♀/♅ 1°10' ⚼
	☽/♀ 1°22' ⚼	♄/As 1°17' ⚼	♀/♅ 0°47' ☌	♀/☊ 1°14' ⚼
☊ Orb	**♂ Orb**	**♇ Orb**	**Mc Orb**	**♄ Orb**
☿/Mc 0°02' ☌	☉/Mc 0°17' ☌	☿/♆ 0°07' ☌	☊/As 0°14' ☌	☿/♅ 0°27' ☍
♀/♂ 0°09' ∠	♇/☊ 0°27' ☌	♅/As 0°10' ∠	☉/♃ 0°40' ☍	♇/As 0°35' □
☽/♂ 0°10' □	☽/♇ 1°06' □	♀/As 0°21' ☍	☉/♆ 1°05' ∠	☿/♀ 0°59' ⚼
♆/As 0°20' □	☿/♄ 1°08' ⚼	☽/As 0°40' ⚼	☽/As 1°19' □	♃/Mc 1°15' ∠
♂/♅ 0°41' ☌	♀/♇ 1°25' ∠	☉/♃ 1°20' ⚼		☽/☿ 1°18' □
As Orb	**♃ Orb**	**♆ Orb**		
♄/♆ 0°10' ☌	☿/♇ 0°28' ☍	♀/Mc 0°05' □		
☉/☊ 0°30' ⚼	☉/♂ 0°33' ☍	☽/Mc 0°24' ∠		
☿/♂ 0°58' ⚼	☉/☊ 1°10' ☍	♅/Mc 0°26' ∠		
☽/☉ 1°03' ⚼		☉/♇ 0°46' □		
☿/♇ 1°12' ⚼				

Midpoint Trees: Modulus 45°00' Max Orb 1°30' (2)

☿ Orb	♇ Orb	♄ Orb	♆ Orb	♀ Orb
☽/♇ 0°09' ⚼	☿/♄ 0°17' ☍	♀/♂ 0°05' ⚼	♄/♅ 0°26' ∠	♅/♆ 0°08' ☍
♆/Mc 0°35' □	♀/Mc 0°18' ⚼	☉/♆ 0°09' ☌	♂/♃ 0°41' ∠	♇/Mc 0°17' ∠
♂/♆ 0°52' ⚼	♀/As 0°38' □	♅/As 0°21' ⚼	♇/☊ 1°01' □	☽/♂ 0°30' ☌
♆/As 0°54' ⚼	♂/♆ 0°57' ☌	♅/Mc 0°41' ☌	☉/♃ 1°20' □	☿/♃ 0°33' □
♅/☊ 1°09' ⚼	☉/♆ 1°04' ⚼	♇/♇ 1°14' ⚼		♇/As 0°37' □
♅ Orb	**☊ Orb**	**As Orb**	**Mc Orb**	**♂ Orb**
☊/☊ 0°04' ⚼	♅/♅ 0°04' ⚼	☽/♀ 0°24' □	♀/♇ 0°36' □	♅/♇ 0°03' □
☽/☿ 0°27' ⚼	☽/☿ 0°22' □	Mc/Mc 0°39' □	As/As 0°39' □	☉/As 0°15' ∠
☉/♇ 1°17' ⚼	☉/♇ 1°21' ☌	☉/☊ 0°46' ∠	☽/♀ 1°03' ☌	☉/Mc 0°34' □
		♆/♇ 0°49' □	♂/As 1°07' □	♄/☊ 0°36' □
		♀/♇ 1°16' ☌	☽/♅ 1°11' □	♃/♃ 0°37' ⚼
♃ Orb	**☉ Orb**	**☽ Orb**		
♄/☊ 0°01' ⚼	☿/Mc 0°05' ☌	♅/☊ 0°20' ☍		
☉/Mc 0°02' ⚼	☿/As 0°24' ∠	☉/♄ 0°21' ☌		
☉/As 0°22' ☍	☽/♃ 0°55' □	♆/As 0°35' ☍		
♂/♂ 0°37' ⚼	♄/As 1°07' ☌	♆/Mc 0°55' ∠		
♅/♇ 0°40' ∠	♆/☊ 1°18' ⚼			

Midpoint Trees: Modulus 45°00' Max Orb 1°30' (3)

♄ Orb	♃ Orb	♂ Orb	As Orb	Mc Orb
♃/♃ 0°22' ☌	☉/♀ 0°18' ∠	♄/Mc 0°20' ∠	♄/Mc 0°02' ∠	☽/♂ 0°16' ☌
☉/♀ 0°40' ∠	♄/♄ 0°22' ☌	♆/♇ 0°20' ⚼	☿/♆ 0°05' ☌	☽/As 0°28' ∠
♂/♃ 1°13' ∠	♂/♄ 0°40' ∠	As/As 0°22' □	♃/Mc 0°08' ∠	☽/♃ 0°34' ∠
♃/As 1°24' ☌	♄/As 0°51' ☌	☿/♆ 0°27' □	♂/♂ 0°22' □	☽/♄ 0°45' ∠
	♆/♇ 1°22' ∠	♃/Mc 0°31' ∠	♆/♇ 0°43' ∠	♅/♅ 0°53' ⚼
♅ Orb	**☽ Orb**	**♀ Orb**	**♇ Orb**	**☿ Orb**
☽/As 0°25' □	♄/♇ 0°04' □	☉/♄ 0°04' ☌	☉/♂ 0°03' □	☉/Mc 0°10' ☌
☽/♂ 0°36' ⚼	♃/♇ 0°15' □	☊/Mc 0°05' ∠	☉/As 0°15' ∠	☽/☊ 0°45' ☌
☽/Mc 0°45' ⚼	☉/♆ 0°49' □	☉/♃ 0°06' ☌	☉/♃ 0°47' ∠	♅/♆ 0°53' ⚼
Mc/Mc 0°53' ⚼	☿/♄ 0°52' ∠	♇/♇ 0°54' ∠	☊/Mc 0°48' □	☉/As 1°21' ∠
♆/☊ 0°59' ∠	☿/♃ 1°03' ∠	☉/♂ 0°58' ∠	☽/☊ 0°50' □	☽/☉ 1°28' ☌
☊ Orb	**☉ Orb**	**♆ Orb**		
♂/♅ 0°02' ∠	♀/♃ 0°25' ∠	♀/Mc 0°35' ⚼		
♅/As 0°13' □	♀/♂ 0°26' ☌	♀/As 0°35' □		
♃/♅ 0°49' □	♀/♄ 0°36' ∠	♀/♂ 0°47' ⚼		
♄/♅ 1°00' □	♀/As 0°37' ∠	☉/☉ 1°13' ⚼		
♅/Mc 1°24' ∠	♆/♆ 1°13' ⚼	♅/♇ 1°29' ∠		

Figure 98B. Princess Diana's midpoint trees: (1) natal chart; (2) solar arc; (3) event chart

Ur/No: Experiences in life shared with others; the commencement of associations; exhibiting enthusiasm for others. Natal Saturn is on the midpoint of Me/Ur: the correct grasp of a difficult situation and the attainment of success and advancement, separating oneself from others, and achieving safety for oneself.

Transiting Uranus is interacting with both these directed axes. It makes a t-square with the dJupiter conjunct Moon opposite Uranus, and a sextile/trine to the directed Sun-natal Saturn opposition. Transiting Uranus is bringing change. It is also opposite natal Venus and conjunct directed Neptune, vaulting her into the spotlight. Transiting Neptune was sextile/trine the directed Jupiter-natal Moon-natal Uranus axis, repeating the theme of a startling public obsession.

In addition, there are four other directions. Directed Neptune is sextile Saturn, which is a further activation of natal Saturn. This suggests that perhaps she didn't have a correct grasp of a bad situation or was hopeful she could overcome the difficulty. It is also the sickness pair, possibly related to mental health. Bringing lots of hope and happiness is the square between directed Jupiter and natal Venus. Passion came from directed Pluto trine Venus. Directed Mercury is square the Midheaven and she would make the news like no other.

Additional transits activated natal points. For more publicity and glamorous public projection, transiting Neptune is conjunct the Ascendant, sextile the Midheaven, sextile Jupiter, and trine Uranus, giving a hope-filled fairy tale. The transiting Jupiter-Saturn conjunction is trine natal Jupiter (natal chart ruler) and square natal Mercury (natal 7th house ruler). Natal Mercury and Jupiter are inconjunct, signifying a need for adaption and adjustment. They are brought together by the chronicators that define a generation and made this particular couple a part of history.

The fast-moving transits are the triggers of the event. Transiting Venus is conjunct natal Pluto giving passion and power. With transiting Mercury square the Midheaven and sextile Venus, she may not have liked being in the news, but she liked the attention, and it made her popular. For a ceremony that was beamed around the world, transiting Sun is opposite natal Jupiter and square natal Neptune, adding more projection and glamor. Transiting Mars is trine her natal Neptune from the 7th, suggesting that she didn't clearly see the man she was about to wed.

In conclusion, the event chart that symbolized the marriage showed it clearly. The synastry with Diana's natal chart and solar arcs indicate a young woman ready for marriage and accepting or coerced into a role required by the once-in-twenty-year conjunction of transiting Jupiter and Saturn that occurred out of element that year in Libra.

As mentioned previously, I don't look at solar arcs or midpoints in the chart. If it seems like a clunky way of dealing with directions, midpoints, and transits—it is. I have gone through this example for readers who might be interested in adding midpoints to a chart but don't want to use a dial. Personally, in the 360° chart, I look at secondary progressions activated by transits in a triwheel. Then I go to the dial and examine the solar arc directions, transits, and midpoints, where these are easier to see. It's funny that many people have told me that solar arcs don't work in a chart, and I agree—for some reason they don't. Nonetheless, they do work on the dial. From here on in, I'll leave midpoints in the chart behind and concentrate on finding them on the dial.

 HOMEWORK: Chose a significant event in your life and look at the active solar arcs, transits, and midpoints in a triwheel.

Chapter 18

Transits and Solar Arcs
on the Dial

The same method we used to find solar arcs and active transits in the chart applies to the dial. The same rules hold as well: The focus is on natal planets that are activated by either a direction or an outer planet transit, as triggered by a fast-moving transit. Midpoint pairs still can't be mixed across levels. We can use midpoints in a transiting chart, midpoints in a directed chart, and midpoints in a natal chart, but not midpoint pairs between these three charts. The exception noted earlier remains valid—when the same planet is in a transiting/natal midpoint or directed/natal midpoint, the pair is active. We still don't pay attention to transits hitting only a directed planet, since the response is always through a natal planet.

In the dial, I add both directions and transits to the natal points to see how they line up. In practice, I toggle between directions and transits, which is easy to do with the Nova software. I first look for directions and note natal planets hit by 8th harmonic aspect. Then I remove the directions and add the transits and note just the directed-natal planets identified. As mentioned in the last chapter, Ebertin found the outer planets and Saturn transits nearly as powerful as directions, so I go around the dial again and note what the outer transits are hitting in the natal chart. These are the main players. Then I look again and see what the fast-moving transits are triggering.

The orb I use for transits on the dial in a timed event is around 1½ °. This is a tight orb, but precise. I look for transits that are nearly exact to show which natal and directed midpoints are important. For example, a transit that is 1° before a natal planet, is hitting any natal midpoint pairs that fall 1° earlier than the natal planet. If the transit is 1° after the natal planet, it is hitting natal midpoint pairs that fall 1° after. I look at the transiting and directed midpoint pairs associated with the natal planet, and if the orb is not exact, I adjust the pointer [turn my attention] from the natal to the nearby directed planet and note its associated transiting and natal midpoint pairs.

If there is an axis with two natal planets in close aspect, unless the aspect is almost exact, <10-20′, I take each planet's directions and transits separately. This point will become clear in the following examples. To summarize, my method is:

1. Look at a timed event in a stand-alone transiting chart and find the major aspects (using the orbs of the chart: for transits 3 to 5°,)

2. Look at the synastry between the transits and the natal chart in a biwheel.

3. Look at solar arcs on the bidial and note the 8th harmonic aspects and associated midpoints.

4. Look at the tridial and find any transits making an 8th harmonic aspect simultaneously to both a natal and directed planet.

5. Look at the event transits on the dial and add any remaining minor 8th harmonic aspects to natal planets and their midpoints.

It sounds more involved than it is. You can use the Predictive Worksheet in Appendix 6 as a guide until the process becomes second nature.

DIVORCE

In the last chapter, we looked at the wedding of the Princess of Wales. Here we'll look at her divorce. After a long and messy separation, the divorce became final on August 28, 1996, at 10.27 a.m. in London. The event chart is shown in Figure 99. The angles are the same signs as those of the marriage chart. Again, a debilitated Mars in Cancer is elevated and conjunct the Midheaven. Neptune is on the Ic, for the ending of a fairytale. The lights, Sun and Moon—the figurative king and queen—are in applying opposition and as far from one another as they can be. The Moon is square Pluto, giving anguish and emotional turmoil. Mercury is trine Uranus, suggesting someone is happy about having their freedom. Venus and Mars are both

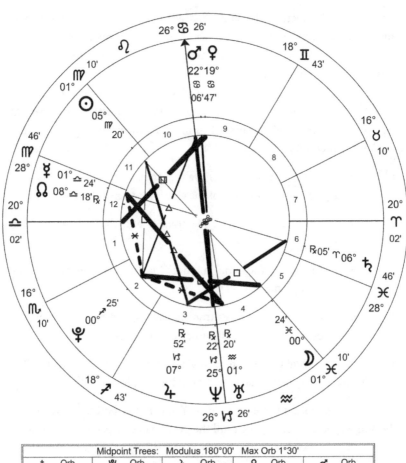

Midpoint Trees:		Modulus 180°00'	Max Orb 1°30'	
♄ Orb	♆ Orb	♃ Orb	♀ Orb	♂ Orb
☿ ⊥ ☊ 1°13' ☍	♄ ⊥ Mc 0°50' ☍	♄ ⊥ ☊ 0°40' ♂	♃ ⊥ ♅ 0°10' ☍	♀ ⊥ Mc 1°00' ♂
	☿ ⊥ ♅ 0°57' ♂			
	♂ ⊥ ♄ 1°19' ☍			
	♆ ⊥ ☊ 1°25' ♂			
	♃ ⊥ As 1°27' ♂			
♆ Orb	Mc Orb	☽ Orb	☉ Orb	
Mc ⊥ Mc 1°04' ☍	♆ ⊥ ♆ 1°04' ☍	♂ ⊥ ☊ 0°11' ☍	♀ ⊥ As 0°26' ♂	
♂ ⊥ Mc 1°05' ☍		♄ ⊥ ♆ 0°19' ♂	♂ ⊥ As 0°43' ♂	
		♀ ⊥ ☊ 1°21' ☍		
		☿ ⊥ Mc 1°28' ☍		

Figure 99. Princess Diana's divorce chart

230

square the Ascendant, perhaps symbolizing public lovers. With Uranus sextile Pluto, there is transformation and change. Reminiscent of the marriage chart, Jupiter and Saturn are now in a closing square—something begun fifteen years ago is in crisis.

In synastry, the transiting Sun is conjunct natal Pluto, as the transiting Moon is opposite natal Mars, pointing to brutality and suffering, and in this context, a loss of power and status. Transiting Jupiter square Saturn is in a t-square with the natal Sun, with transiting Jupiter sextile natal Neptune, showing the royal family standing against her, as her popularity expands. Transiting Neptune is conjunct natal Saturn, opposite transiting Mars and trine natal Venus; the public obsession lay with her and not her husband at this time of final separation. Transiting Pluto is square her Mars, as powerful forces sought to restrict her.

The stand-alone dial of the event is shown in Figure 100. We can see the close hard aspects clearly:

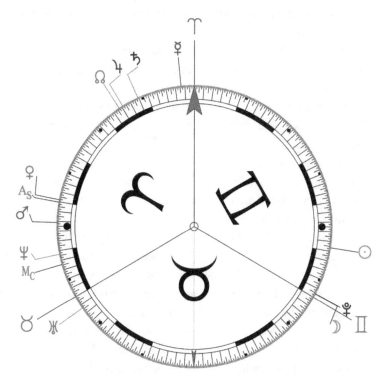

Figure 100. Princess Diana's divorce dial

Ju = No: advantageous associations.

Ve = As = Su: a love affair, niceness, a beautiful body, gracefulness; making an impression through physical beauty.

Ne = Mc: the sense of disappearing ego.

Mo = Pl: extremely emotional life or extreme expression of feeling

Here are the following close midpoints:

Ve = As = Su = Ur/JuNo: popularity; social justice, finding a partner; a happy union with a man (an inheritance [Ur/No = Ju] through a partner i.e., alimony).

Ma = VeAs/Ne: wrong ways of love; being unsatisfied; (awareness of one's personal charm, the ability to use one's charm to advantage, an impulsive attachment, the desire for love).

Ne = VeAs/Ur: the need to renounce love; sadness about romantic loss (sudden notions of love; love at first sight; intense flair; attractiveness to others).

Mc = Ma/Ur: a person putting a metaphorical pistol to someone's head, an act of violence.

Ur = Me/MoPl: violent emotional outbursts, inner shocks, emotional upheavals; wielding powerful influence over the public through speeches.

MoPl = Ma/JuNo: successful enterprises; brilliant successes; people who can tackle big projects; making fortunate decisions guided by intuition, a sense of honor, pride (a successful wife, bride; a happy union, an engagement.

The event chart speaks of marriage and happiness, but also sadness and the loss of love. The tridial shows which midpoints and aspects in the event chart hit Diana's charts directly (Figure 101).

There are three directions:

dPl = Su = MoVe = dMe/Ne = dUr/As: directed Pluto has come to the love axis bringing wrong thinking, faulty judgment and a major new start.

dNe = Sa = Pl/As = dMo/Mc = dVe/Mc: suffering from forcible suppression, subjected to coercion; emotional suffering caused by others; unsatisfied and unhappy in love, soul suffering.

dSa = Ma = Pl/No = dMe/Ur: harmful or destructive energy, hampered or destroyed vitality; death, difficulties to overcome; a heavy injury, violent destruction; demonstrating brutality in the presence of others; disempowerment, exhibiting personal power; tyranny.

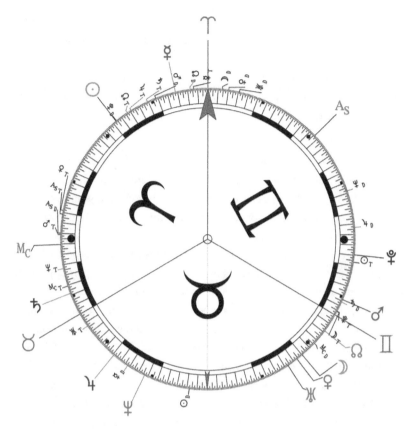

Figure 101. Princess Diana's divorce bidial

The three directions are all extremely difficult, a grim testament to a hard time with no saving grace.

Of these three directions, only the axis of natal Saturn (dNe = Sa = Pl/As = dMo/Mc = dVe/Mc) was activated by the event chart's Midheaven. The suppression affected her life purpose and reputation.

One glimmer of hope came from tJu = tNo = Ur = Sa/As, which appears to be the settlement she got from Charles. Also joy over a separation.

The last remaining transit is the transiting Sun coming to Pluto on the axis of tVeAs. This is a reiteration of the first direction and indicates the destruction of love.

As we can see, none of the loving happy midpoints in the event chart impacted her chart. Presumably, these did affect the charts of others connected with this event.

DEATH

A year after her divorce, Diana died in a car accident in Paris on August 31, 1997. The stand-alone chart at the time of the accident is shown in Figure 102. The transiting Ascendant at 18°Gemini is Diana's Descendant and square the March total Solar Eclipse at 18° Pisces. The transiting Nodes are 1° away from the eclipse. The Moon on the transiting Ic is opposite Jupiter on the Mc in a t-square with Mars in Scorpio. The tension of the opposition is eased through a sextile/trine from Venus in Libra—could be love. However, a debilitated Saturn is opposite Venus and trine the Moon pointing to some form of difficulty and separation. The Sun and a retrograde Mercury are conjunct, with Mercury combust and burning. The pair are sextile Mars and separating from a square with Pluto indicating destruction and brutality. Pluto is sextile Uranus symbolizing transformation and change.

In the biwheel (Figure 103, page 236), transiting Mars is conjunct her Neptune and trine her natal Sun. Transiting Sun-Mercury is sextile both natal points and conjunct Pluto. This complex describes a grievous loss. Transiting Neptune is conjunct natal Saturn, showing sickness. Transiting Saturn, the grim reaper himself, is trine the Ascendant, impacting physical vitality. Transiting Pluto is square natal Mars, reinforcing brutality and destruction.

The stand-alone event on the dial is shown in Figure 104. There is one 8th harmonic aspect, Ur = No, giving an experience of upsets together with others. Here are the midpoints:

Ne = Sa/Ur = Su/As = Ve/Ma: physical debility; emotional struggle or pain; concerns about the blood; bereavement about separation; damage through others, slander, lovers.

Ur = No = Ju/Ne: association with swindlers; coming down to earth with a crash, suddenly realizing a difficult situation.

234

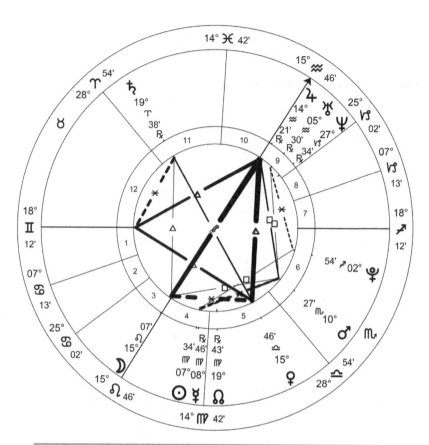

Midpoint Trees:		Modulus 180°00'	Max Orb 1°30'	
♀ Orb	♄ Orb	♂ Orb	♆ Orb	As Orb
♃ + As 0°30' ☍	⊙ + ♆ 0°35' ☍	☽ + ♅ 0°08' ☌	☊ + Mc 0°09' ☌	♂ + ♆ 0°48' ☍
♂ + ☊ 0°40' ☌	☿ ⊥ ♇ 1°12' ☍	♀ ⊥ ♆ 1°07' ☌	♃ ⊥ ☊ 0°51' ☌	☽ ⊥ ♄ 0°49' ☌
As ⊥ Mc 1°13' ☍				
♆ Orb	♅ Orb	♃ Orb	☽ Orb	Mc Orb
⊙ + As 0°18' ☍	♃ + ♆ 0°28' ☌	☽ + ☽ 0°45' ☍	♃ + Mc 0°03' ☍	☽ + ☽ 0°38' ☍
☿ ⊥ As 0°54' ☍	♆ ⊥ Mc 1°10' ☌	Mc ⊥ Mc 1°24' ☌	Mc ⊥ Mc 0°38' ☍	♀ + As 1°13' ☍
			♃ ⊥ ♃ 0°45' ☍	♃ ⊥ ♃ 1°24' ☌
⊙ Orb	☿ Orb			
♄ + ♆ 1°02' ☍	♄ + ♆ 0°10' ☍			
☿ ⊥ ♅ 1°12' ☌	⊙ ⊥ ⊙ 1°12' ☌			

Figure 102. Princess Diana's death chart

235

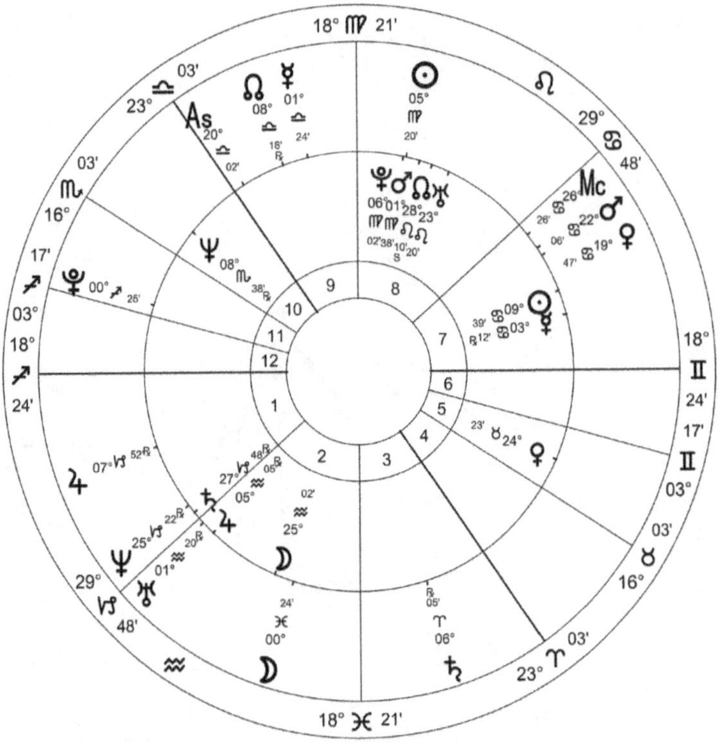

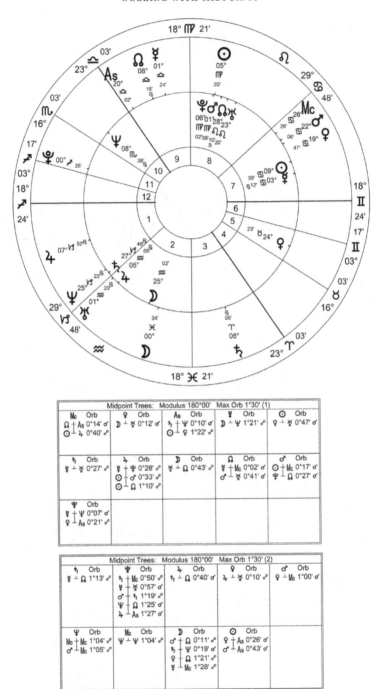

Midpoint Trees: Modulus 180°00' Max Orb 1°30' (1)				
Mc Orb ☊/As 0°14' ☌ ☉/♃ 0°40' ☍	♀ Orb ☽/♅ 0°12' ☌	As Orb ♄/♆ 0°10' ☌ ☉/♀ 1°22' ☍	☿ Orb ☽/♆ 1°21' ☍	☉ Orb ♀/♅ 0°47' ☌
♄ Orb ☿/♅ 0°27' ☍	♃ Orb ☿/♇ 0°28' ☍ ☉/♂ 0°33' ☍ ☉/☊ 1°10' ☍	☽ Orb ♅/☊ 0°43' ☍	☊ Orb ☿/Mc 0°02' ☌ ♂/♅ 0°41' ☌	♂ Orb ☉/Mc 0°17' ☌ ♇/☊ 0°27' ☌
♇ Orb ☿/♆ 0°07' ☌ ♀/As 0°21' ☍				

Midpoint Trees: Modulus 180°00' Max Orb 1°30' (2)				
♄ Orb ☿/☊ 1°13' ☍	♇ Orb ♄/Mc 0°50' ☍ ☿/♅ 0°57' ☌ ♂/♄ 1°19' ☍ ♆/☊ 1°25' ☌ ♃/As 1°27' ☌	♃ Orb ♄/☊ 0°40' ☌	♀ Orb ♃/♅ 0°10' ☍	♂ Orb ♀/Mc 1°00' ☌
♆ Orb Mc/Mc 1°04' ☍ ♂/Mc 1°05' ☍	Mc Orb ♆/♆ 1°04' ☍	☽ Orb ♂/☊ 0°11' ☍ ♄/♆ 0°19' ☌ ♀/☊ 1°21' ☍ ☿/Mc 1°28' ☍	☉ Orb ♀/As 0°26' ☌ ♂/As 0°43' ☌	

Figure 103. Princess Diana's death biwheel

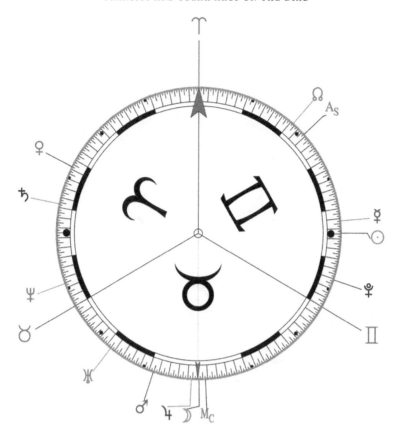

Figure 104. Princess Diana's death dial

Ma = Ur/MoMc: lack of control, acting rashly; acts of violence; accident, injury, operation.

Ju = Me/Sa: a glad farewell, short journeys.

Mo = Ne/Pl = Ju/Mc: strange soul experiences, high sensitivity, changes of mood, immediate reactivity; a peculiar or strange woman, supernatural experiences; the joy of expectation, a harmonious temperament.

Pl = Ve/Sa = No/Mc: unusually strong tension in love relationship, states of chaos; success with associations or partnerships, the use of force

Me = Sa/Ne = Su: a slow or difficult grasp of things, always thinking the worst; a nervous disease; physical illness as a consequence of emotional suffering, lack of vitality, a sensitive physique, illness.

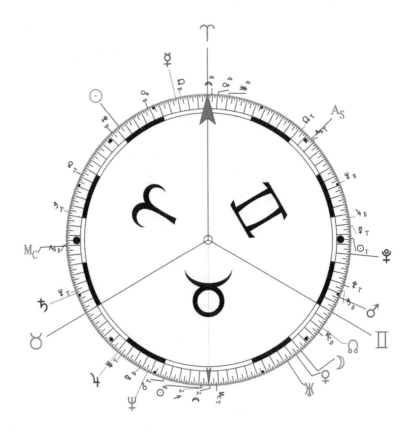

Figure 105. Princess Diana's death tridial with solar arc and transits

As = Sa/Mc = Ma/Ne: suffering from others, being placed in unfortunate situations; sharing anxiety with others, parting from others, sadness;
hospital stay; a weak and unstable person, no energy to advance in life;
sharing grief and sorrow with others, the termination of associations or
unions.

The accident and its severity are evident in the stand-alone dial. To see
how the event impacted the nativity, the tridial is shown in Figure 105 on
page 238. There are six directions: dNo = Me; dPl = Mo; dAs = Mc; dNe =
Sa; dMc = No; and the death pair, dSa = Ma.

On the first axis, there is: dNo = Me = dMoVe/Ma = dMe/Mc = Ma/
Ju = Ne/No. There are no activating transits. The direction of dNo = Me
speaks to an exchange of ideas, making plans, chatter, and gossip. Given the
involvement of dVe/Ma and dMo/Ma, this is likely a lover's getaway. The

midpoint Me = Ne/No means the tendency to make secret arrangements. The midpoint Ma/Ju = No means a happy union, an engagement. We can guess why this axis was not active at this moment by transit.

The second axis also has no transiting activations. On this axis, there is: dPl = Mo = Su = Ve = dMe/Ne = dUr/As. The combination of dPl = Su = Mo means changed circumstances leading to critical phases of development in life, or to separation from others. The midpoint dPl = dMe/Ne indicates widespread news, while dPl = dUr/As shows a quick response to the influence of the environment, the use of force.

The third direction is activated by the transiting Sun-Mercury pair. The axis has dAs = Mc = No/As = dSa/Ne = dSu/No = tSu = tMe = tSa/Ne. Note the number of personal points connected to the axis, as well as the repetition of Sa/Ne by direction and transit. This may explain why death did not occur immediately. There was a requirement of sickness at this place (As), at this time (Mc).

The fourth direction also describes illness. On the axis there is: dNe = Sa = dUr/Mc = Me/Ur = dVe/Mc = tNe = tSa/Ur. With Uranus appearing in three combinations, the axis indicates upset and change. Along with Saturn, it suggests a coming down to earth again, the desire to part quickly, saying good-bye, or being let go from a job. The transiting midpoint of tNe = tSa/Ur sums up the situation: a resolve to resign oneself to the inevitable, abandoning resistance, weakening strength, separation, mourning, and bereavement.

The fifth direction is not activated by transit. On the axis there is dMc = No = Ma/Ur = Me/Mc = dNo/As = VeMo/Ma. Here are the accident pair (Ma/Ur) and the lovers (Ve/Ma). The direction of dMc = No and dNo = As means individual relationships; being recognized; meeting.

The final direction is activated by transiting Pluto. On the axis, there is: dSa = Ma = dPl/As = Pl/No = tPl = tVe/Sa = tNo/Mc. There is no doubt this is the death axis. dSa = Ma = tPl means brutality, destruction; the intervention of Higher Power, bodily injury or harm, murder. The pair dSa = dPl/As gives suffering from forcible suppression, being subjected to coercive measures; suffering caused by other people.

In addition, two axes are activated by transit that are not active by direction. The first has tUr = Ju = tNo = tJu/Ne. While the combination of Jupiter and Uranus gives luck, Jupiter is also often active at the time of death. Given the extent of the injuries, Ju/Ne may have given mercy and compassion, and

239

a quick release from illness. The second axis has tAs = As = Sa/Ne = Ne/
tNe. Here is another indication of sickness (Sa/Ne). The midpoint As = Sa/
Ne means an emotionally depressing environment, oppressive family circumstances, emotional suffering caused by other persons, and limitation of
freedom. The addition of Neptune adds mystery, intrigue, and uncertainty
that surrounded the accident.

EXAMPLE: EBERTIN

In his book *Directions*, (pages 107–108) Ebertin gives a rare example of
tridial, where he examines both solar arcs and transits on the dial (Figure
106). Here the Mean Node is used. This is the horoscope of a woman who

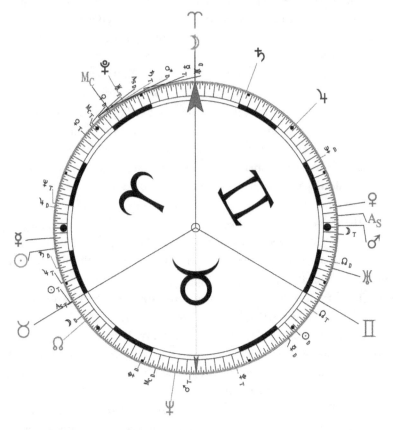

Figure 106. Ebertin's example of a lady in a car accident

drove into a military tank that had gone off the road and had no lights to make it visible in the early morning. She was killed instantly. Her solar arc was 31°43.

He notes that dPl and the dMc had come to the axis of Saturn, which was "a force directed against oneself." In the nativity, Ebertin saw Mars and Uranus conjunct within 4°, and figured these "played a role in the accident." At the time of the crash, directed Mars had reached the Midheaven which is on the midpoint of Ur/Ne. Ebertin remarked the pair is related to stillborn births. The axis was triggered by transiting Mercury, Saturn, and Uranus. He wrote out the points on the axis and gives their longitude degree on the dial:

tUr = tSa = tMe = dMa = dMe = Mc
10°23 10°12 8°46 9°39   25°10 = 10°10 (9°09)

He remarks this axis indicates the Mc is 1° off and should be at 10° and not 9°09. Here he is using an event to rectify a birth time. He interprets this axis to mean "unconsciousness, one's own death through the misguidance of energy (Mc = Ur/Ne) when traveling (Me = Ur/Ne)."

What Ebertin doesn't note are two additional, relevant axes:

dMc = Ur = Sa/Ne = dVe/Sa = tNe: shocking sickness, separation, lifelessness.

dMo = No = Mo/Ur = Sa/As = tAs: feeling depressed due to the environment, separation, unpleasant circumstances.

In this latter axis, the transiting Ascendant is approaching the Node in 2°, or 8 minutes of clock time.

In conclusion, using transits to identify the activated directions triggered at a timed event is a means to quickly pinpoint the important axes that astrologically describe the event. Using this method we can zero in on what is significant at any astrological moment.

 HOMEWORK: Pick another significant event in your life and examine the directions and transits on the dial. If you don't have a precise time, use the diurnal transits.

CHAPTER 19

Carl Jung: A Case Study

W e've covered a lot of material so far, and I'll wrap it up in this chapter with a case study of one of my favorite people, Carl Jung. Throughout this book we have progressed step-by-step; if anything got muddled or was unclear, I hope this chapter brings clarity. As always, it is best to print out the charts and dial and do the analysis yourself first and then compare your work with mine.

To recap, my process in an in-depth study is to start with the natal chart. (If I'm looking at someone in the news, I typically glance at this briefly.) I look at the rising sign, chart ruler, planetary dignity, planets conjunct the angles, and the tightest aspects. The orbs I use in the natal chart are:

- Sun, Moon, Ascendant, and Midheaven: 5°
- Mercury, Venus, and Mars: 4°
- Jupiter, Saturn, Uranus, Neptune, Pluto, and Nodes: 3°

Then I go to the dial. I find the minor 8th harmonic aspects and the midpoints. I jot down what they mean. The orb on the dial is:

- minor aspects and the midpoints: 1½°

With that done, I turn to events. If I have a timed chart, I use its time and place and look at the stand-alone chart using Solar Fire software. If I don't have a timed chart, I use a natal diurnal chart time, if possible. For a chart of an eclipse, ingress, or lunation, I use the current place of residence. If I am looking at a return chart, I set it for the birthplace. I briefly delineate the stand-alone chart, glance at the synastry in the biwheel, and then move to the dial. Here I look at the stand-alone event, adding the minor aspects and midpoints. I begin filling out the form in Appendix 6.

Next, I look at the bidial and note the directions. There are typically 4 to 5 at any given time. Then I look at the transits on the bidial and see which transiting points are activating natal placements, especially those already active by solar arc.

I use smaller orbs in an event dial than I use in the natal chart. For transit-to-transit aspects, or transit-to-natal, I use <1°. My orb for a solar arc is 1° applying and separating. My orb for all directed midpoints is < 1½°.

I only use occupied midpoints and I don't mix levels. This means I exclude the incomplete natal midpoints and incomplete directed midpoints. A transiting midpoint has to be completed in the transiting chart. I don't use transiting pairs that are completed by a natal planet. I only use transit-to-directed combinations that are on a natal axis that contain a natal planet at the focal point (e.g. transiting Saturn conjunct directed Pluto conjunct natal Sun.) I keep the integrity of the midpoints across all levels. This method minimizes the amount of material, without losing valuable information.

CARL JUNG NATIVITY

Here is a brief biography of Jung's life, some of which previously appeared in my book on the nodes.

C.G. (pronounced Say-Gay) Jung was a medical doctor, psychiatrist, and depth psychologist. He married Emma, an heiress, and had five children. The son of a poor pastor and a fey housewife, he grew up in the countryside close to nature, and had a rich and vivid imagination. He said he was born knowing that dreams were important. As a boy, he was aware that he had two personalities whom he named Number 1 and Number 2. He wrote in his autobiography *Memories, Dreams, Reflections* that "No. 1 was the son of my parents who went to school and was less intelligent, attentive, hard-working, decent and clean than many other boys. The other (No. 2) was grownup —old, in fact —skeptical, mistrustful, remote from the world of [people], but close to nature, the earth, the sun, the moon, the weather, all living creatures, and above all close to the night, to dreams, and to whatever "God" worked directly in him…. In my life No. 2 has been of prime importance, and I have always tried to make room for anything that wanted to come to me from within."

Jung recalled a dream where he was in dense fog, cupping a candle, and being pursued by a "gigantic black figure." He knew whatever happened, he had to keep the candle lit. When he awoke, he realized "that this little light was my consciousness, the only light I have. My own understanding is the sole treasure I possess, and the greatest. Though infinitely small and fragile in comparison with the powers of darkness, it is still a light, my only light." The dream told him "that No. 1 was the bearer of light and … in the role of No.1 [he] had to go forward—into study, moneymaking, responsibilities, entanglements, confusions, errors, submissions, defeats…."

He went to medical school and then worked at an asylum, studying the new field of the unconscious. He conducted word association experiments to compare the responses between normal people and neurotics. His initial idea was to conduct statistical tests, but he was averse to math and quickly became interested in individual responses as he tried to "catch the intruder in the mind" and prove the validity of the unconscious.

Freud was the leader in the field, and the two met in 1907 and began to collaborate. Freud believed that sex was the ultimate motivation of behavior and the cause of mental neurosis, but he was reluctant to present his views openly in public and wanted Jung to do it for him. From the beginning Jung did not accept Freud's view of the supremacy of sexual motivation: "Above all, Freud's attitude toward the spirit seemed … highly question-able… [Any] expression of spirituality [he saw as] repressed sexuality."

By 1911, Jung had discovered astrology and was using it for insight into the psyche of his patients. In a letter to Freud, he wrote, "My evenings are taken up very largely with astrology. I make horoscopic calculations in order to find a clue to the core of psychological truth. Some remarkable things have turned up which will certainly appear incredible to you. For instance, it appears that the signs of the zodiac are character pictures, in other words, libido symbols which depict the typical qualities of the libido at a given moment."

In another letter, he wrote, "I am looking into astrology, which seems indispensable for a proper understanding of mythology. There are strange and wondrous things in these lands of darkness. Please don't worry about my wanderings in these infinitudes. I shall return laden with rich booty for our knowledge of the human psyche. For a while longer I must intoxicate myself on magic perfumes in order to fathom the secrets that lie hidden in the abysses of the unconscious."

Freud was not impressed with Jung's "dabbling in spookery," and despite Emma's efforts to smooth out their differences, the two men grew estranged. They split at the onset of World War 1. As Jung wrote in his auto-biography, "After the break with Freud, all my friends and acquaintances dropped away. My book was declared to be rubbish; I was a mystic and that settled the matter... I had known that everything was at stake and that I had to take a stand for my conviction. I realized that the chapter "The Sacrifice" meant my own sacrifice."

Jung was sidelined and black-balled by the psychological community with Freud leading the charge. Jung opened a private practice in his home and was seeing patients, but by the autumn of 1913, he was "menaced by psychosis," besieged by visions and dreams he could not understand. In the *Tao of Jung*, David Rose wrote, "Jung courageously began to live what was to become the core of his psychology; death of the false self and birth of the true self." According to Jung, "he felt as if he had fallen into an immense hole ... and the single most important achievement in his life was that he saved [himself] from that hole and didn't drown in it."

Although Jung became suicidal, he considered those years as the "most important time of [his] life—everything else can be derived from it. My whole life consisted of reappraising what had broken free of the uncon-scious back then and flooded me like a mysterious stream and threatened to destroy me."

Jung began treating himself as if he were his own patient, observing himself, noting his meditations, and keeping a detailed daily diary. He had many visions, conducted numerous inner dialogues, and spent hours in the garden conversing with an imaginary old man of "simply superior knowl-edge" who was teaching him and "almost seemed real." This old man was No. 2, who "represented a force which was not myself ... I held conversa-tions with him, and he said things which I had not consciously thought... He said I treated thoughts as if I generated them myself, but in his view, thoughts were like animals in the forest, or people in a room ... If you should see people in a room, you would not think that you had made those people, or that you were responsible for them. It was he who taught me psychic objectivity, the reality of the psyche."

In the midst of the break-up with Freud, Emma gave birth to their fifth child. Two weeks later, Jung began his affair with a former patient, twenty-six-year-old Toni Wolfe. Explaining his adultery, he says, "back then I was in the midst of the anima problem. What could you expect from me? —the anima bit me on the forehead and would not let go."

The marriage became strained. Toni became Jung's professional assistant and Emma was sidelined. Although three times she threatened to end the marriage, Jung always fell sick and she could not leave. Jung was dependent on her money, and although Swiss law would give him the children, Emma did not want to lose them.

When Jung came out of seclusion in 1917, his private practice grew to the point where appointments had to be made a year in advance. He lectured, traveled, and was the only psychoanalyst to rival Freud. Jung founded the Psychological Club in Zurich, which hosted guest speakers and enabled analysts to keep up with current theories. Over the years he met many influential people: Albert Einstein, Hugh Walpole, H.G. Wells, F. Scott Fitzgerald, and James Joyce. He treated Herman Hesse and James Joyce's psychotic daughter.

In 1929, after reading Richard Wilhelm's alchemical text, Jung developed an interest in alchemy, which to him symbolized the evolution of inner growth. In 1931, Jung treated a patient for alcoholism. He saw drinking as a disease of the spirit and gave the later-formed Alcoholics Anonymous organization their major key to recovery.

World War II came. Jung turned the front yard of his house into a garden to grow food. He was forced to work as a physician. During this time he was accused of being a Nazi sympathizer, although he said he was on their hit list. After the war, he returned to counseling, writing, and traveling.

In 1948, the Jung Institute opened in Zurich, where Jung, Emma, and Toni taught and trained other analysts. By 1950, Jung was cementing his ideas of synchronicity that had interested him for twenty years. He renewed his former interest in astrology, which he considered to work through synchronicity: "Acausal orderedness occurs in an ongoing way in nature, but synchronistic events are acts of creation at specific moments in time." He realized he needed astrological help from people who knew more astrology than he had time to learn, and he recruited four volunteers, one of whom was his daughter Gret.

For three years Jung conducted astrological research. He published the results in *Mysterium Conjunctionis,* even though he knew he would be criticized for the astrology, "which American readers would never take seriously." He considered the book to be "nothing less than a restoration of the original state of the cosmos and the divine unconsciousness of the world …" It was an alchemical text, which outlined three stages of individuation. The first stage entailed becoming conscious of the Shadow: "the darkness gives birth to light." In the second stage, the opposites (the male—the highest heaven; and the female—the lowest earth) were united. This led to the third stage, and the connection of the ego to the self, which he called actualization, and was equivalent to spiritual wholeness.

The goal of Jungian analysis is to increase consciousness by becoming aware of the unconscious. To Jung, the psyche was comprised of the conscious and the unconscious. The ego stood at the center of consciousness, while the self stood at the center of the psyche. He thought the unconscious had two parts, which he termed the "personal" and the "collective." The personal unconscious (the Shadow) contained the unwanted and unrecognized parts of the personality that were rejected, and either buried or projected. Part of his therapy involved learning to accept the discarded pieces so that they were less likely to be acted out inappropriately or projected onto others.

He viewed the collective unconscious as the archetypal realm that was represented in myths and dreams, which could not be understood with reason, but through feelings and symbols. It was also the domain of spirit, of "God," but since "God" was too unscientific a term, Jung called it the collective unconscious. To him, they were one and the same.

Jung's model of the psyche is that of psychological astrologers. The Sun is the ego, the center of consciousness; Pluto is the Shadow, the personal unconscious; Neptune is the collective unconscious; and Uranus is the urge to be true to the inner higher self. The astrological chart as a whole represents the psyche, with the higher self at the center.

In late 1957 at the age of eighty-two, in an effort to describe his inner world, Jung began writing his autobiography. Of the outer world, he thought only two things had happened of great importance: a trip to India and a heart attack. At the end, he wrote, "I am satisfied with the course my life has taken… Much might have been different if I myself had been different. But it was as it had to be; for all came about because I am as I am."

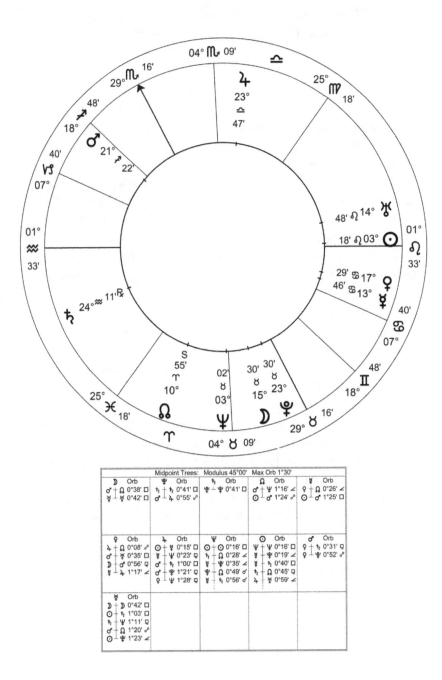

Figure 107. Carl Jung's natal chart

NATAL DELINEATION

Jung's natal chart is shown in Figure 107, his 45°-midpoint trees in Figure 108, and his dial in Figure 109. I suggest you fill out his natal worksheet (shown in Appendix 3) before reading on. By the time you are done, you should have a feeling for the important planets and what they are doing. I'll go through the planets one by one, delineating their condition and midpoints on the dial. The text is adapted from the COSI unless otherwise noted.

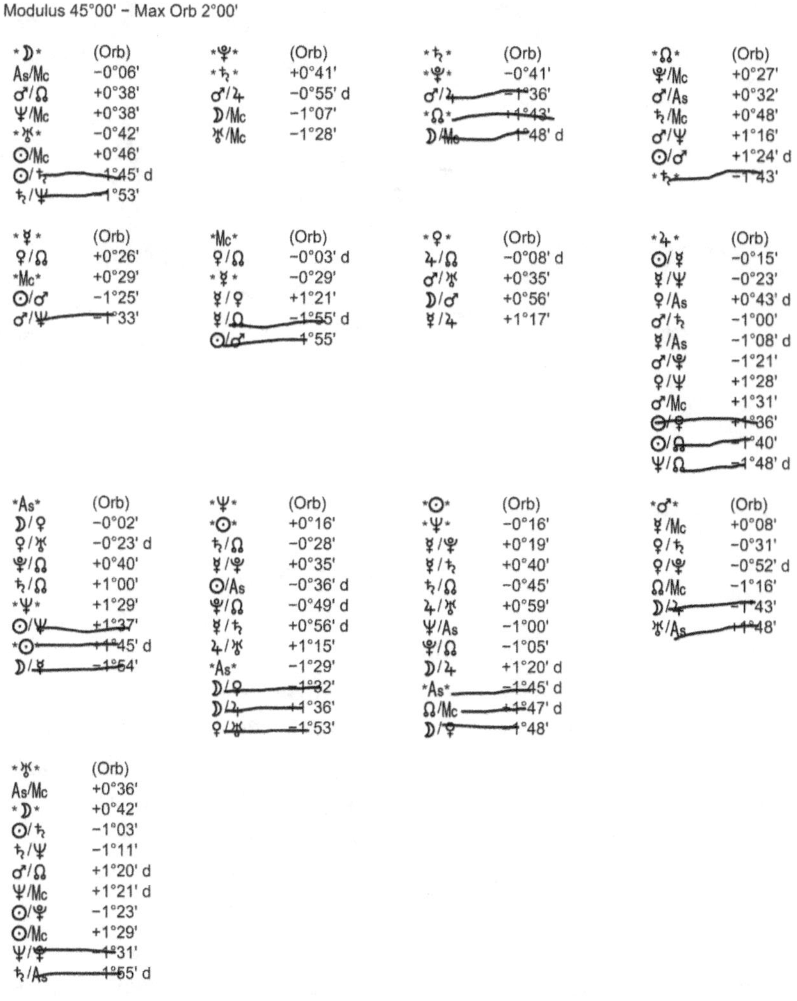
Modulus 45°00' – Max Orb 2°00'
☽ (Orb)
As/Mc −0°06'
♂/☊ +0°38'
♆/Mc +0°38'
♅ −0°42'
☉/Mc +0°46'
☉/♄ 1°45' d
♄/♆ 1°53'
♇ (Orb)
♄ +0°41'
♂/♃ −0°55' d
☽/Mc −1°07'
♅/Mc −1°28'
♄ (Orb)
♇ −0°41'
♂/♃ 1°36'
☊ 1°43'
☽/Mc 1°48' d
☊ (Orb)
♇/Mc +0°27'
♂/As +0°32'
♄/Mc +0°48'
♂/♆ +1°16'
☉/♂ +1°24' d
♄ 1°43'
☿ (Orb)
♀/☊ +0°26'
Mc +0°29'
☉/♂ −1°25'
♂/♆ 1°33'
Mc (Orb)
♀/☊ −0°03' d
☿ −0°29'
☿/♀ +1°21'
☿/☊ 1°55' d
☉/♂ 1°55'
♀ (Orb)
♃/☊ −0°08' d
♂/♅ +0°35'
☽/♂ +0°56'
☿/♃ +1°17'
♃ (Orb)
☉/☿ −0°15'
☿/♆ −0°23'
♀/As +0°43' d
♂/♄ −1°00'
☿/As −1°08' d
♂/♇ −1°21'
♀/♆ +1°28'
♂/Mc +1°31'
☉/♀ 1°36'
☉/☊ 1°40'
♆/☊ 1°48' d
As (Orb)
☽/♀ −0°02'
♀/♅ −0°23' d
♇/☊ +0°40'
♄/☊ +1°00'
♆ +1°29'
☉/♆ 1°37'
☉ 1°45' d
☽/☿ 1°54'
♆ (Orb)
☉ +0°16'
♄/☊ −0°28'
☿/♇ +0°35'
☉/As −0°36' d
♇/☊ −0°49' d
☿/♄ +0°56' d
♃/♅ +1°15'
As −1°29'
☽/♀ 1°32'
☽/♃ 1°36'
♀/♅ 1°53'
☉ (Orb)
♆ −0°16'
☿/♇ +0°19'
☿/♄ +0°40'
♄/☊ −0°45'
♃/♅ +0°59'
♆/As −1°00'
♇/☊ −1°05'
☽/♃ +1°20' d
As 1°45' d
☊/Mc 1°47' d
☽/♀ 1°48'
♂ (Orb)
☿/Mc +0°08'
♀/♄ −0°31'
♀/♇ −0°52' d
☊/Mc −1°16'
☽/♃ 1°43'
♅/As 1°48'
♅ (Orb)
As/Mc +0°36'
☽ +0°42'
☉/♄ −1°03'
♄/♆ −1°11'
♂/☊ +1°20' d
♆/Mc +1°21' d
☉/♇ −1°23'
☉/Mc +1°29'
♆/♇ 1°31'
♄/As 1°55' d

Figure 108. Carl Jung's 45° trees

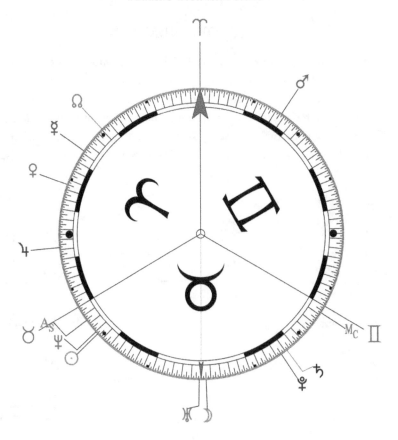

Figure 109 Carl Jung's dial

Sun

Sun in Leo on the 7th cusp, ruling the 7th house, square Neptune, at the midpoint of Me/Pl, Me/Sa, Sa/No, Ju/Ur, Ne/As, Pl/No, Mo/Ju.

Sun in Leo: domineering people, self-confident, self-assured, energetic, creative, desiring ownership and possessions, a wealth of ideas, organization, leadership, able to rise and advance , patronage, protection.

Sun in 7th: harmony, public spirit, sociable, adaptable, vain, the need to be important, love of the arts, good manners. Lack of firmness, consistency, and constancy. Associations are important.

Sun = Neptune: sensitive, illness, impressionable, imaginative, enthusiastic, inclined to mysticism, cultivating an inner life, abundant experience in psychic realms, mystical experiences, travel to distant places, success through sympathetic understanding, chaos, entangled in scandals.

Su = As: judging the intellect of others, striving for public recognition, the desire for social esteem and importance, self-confident. Disharmonious relationships. Over-accentuated or misplaced self-confidence. Endeavor and industry, the need to become important. Meeting and contact with others, advancing personal interests, public relationships; disadvantaged or harmed by others, separations.

Su = Me/Pl: a persuasive speaker, a keen observer, circumspection or discretion, gaining recognition.

Su = Me/Sa: stagnated or underdeveloped mental ability, a love of traveling, changes, separations, repeated changes of residence, moves (a serious writer and thinker).

Su = Sa/No: the desire for seclusion, feeling uncomfortable or hindered in the presence of others.

Su = Ju/Ur: good intellectual grasp, an inventive mind, taking the long view, physical agility or mobility; sudden happiness, birth; optimism, a lucky chance, blissful realization; the big break; success or going it alone to find better opportunities.

Su = Ne/As: creative, artistic, sensitivity used for gain.

Su = Pl/No: imposing one's will on others with ruthlessness, being subjected to others' ruthless will.

Su = Mo/Ju: optimism, happiness and contentment, pacifism, social outlook, learning and scholarship.

In summary, this is a dignified Sun, strong by sign and angularity. Jung has drive and self-confidence, and a need to be successful and important. There is luck, optimism, and a big break. Also, creativity, imagination, mysticism, insecurity, the need for solitude, and the potential danger of exploitation and harm from others.

Moon

Moon in Taurus in the 3rd ruling the 6th, in mutual reception with Venus, square Uranus, sextile Mercury, sextile Venus, at the midpoint of As/Mc, Ma/No, Ne/Mc, Su/Mc.

Moon in Taurus: constancy, tenacious clinging to possessions, being steadfast and firm, understanding and appreciation of beauty, enjoyment of life, shifting material circumstances.

Moon in the 3rd house: powerful expression of feelings in many vivid ways, changes of mood, mental and physical mobility, multiple interests, abundant wishing and hoping, easily despondent, superficial, many ups and downs, changes, associations.

Mo = Ur: emotional tensions. A sudden manifestation of subconscious (I would say unconscious) forces.

Mo = Me: thinking influenced by feeling, perception, an active mind, author, extensive intellectual study, journey or travel, exposure to criticism, gossip, slander.

Mo = Ve: feelings of love, devotion, affection, artistic, good judgment and appreciation of value, cheerfulness, graceful, moody, intensely emotion, the joy of living, a marriage with many children, conflicts in love.

Mo = As/Mc: a life governed by feeling, cordial relationships with others, a person guided by instinct; indicates attitude to women in general, association with women.

Mo = Ma/No: soul contacts, relationships based on soul connection, an emotional attitude toward others, associations or organizations consisting of only women members.

Mo = Ne/Mc: fanciful imagination, intense imagination, dreamy, a misinterpretation of observations and perceptions, peculiar feelings.

Mo = Su/Mc: subconscious stirrings, an instinctive understanding of life goals, the "I" as it relates to the "Thou," attitudes toward the opposite sex, the recognition of the "Thou" in oneself.

In summary, this is an exalted Moon, making both lights in the chart dignified. It is practical and determined, and seeks stability, but is hampered by the square to Uranus. His instincts are strong. The unconscious leaked into his daily life. It's interesting to see stated outright, the notion that the other is in oneself. To this I would add, the self is also seen (projected) in the other. The impact of the mutual reception between the Moon and Venus can't be overstated. He had empathy and feeling for women, which was mutual.

Mercury

Mercury in Cancer in the 6th ruling the 5th and 8th, conjunct Venus, sextile the Moon, square the Nodes at the North Bending, sesquisquare the Mc, at the midpoint Ve/No, Su/Ma, Ma/Ne.

Mercury in Cancer: intellect, sound judgment, critical ability, dexterity in expression and writing, diplomatic.

Mercury in the 6th: hungry for knowledge, practical, patient, well-grounded expert knowledge, good collaborator, teamwork.

Me = Ve: appreciation of beauty, thoughts of love, authors, artistic talent.

Me = Mo: thinking influenced by emotion.

Me = No: the exchange of ideas, common or joint plans, forming associations to pursue common interests.

Me = Mc: one's outlook on life, self-knowledge. Pursuing and attaining life's goals, and career advancement, vocational changes, deep thinking, much meditating or reflecting, forming one's own opinion.

Me = Ve/No: the urge to discuss love life with others, the need for social contact; connecting through shared feelings of love, association with others through common interests or love.

Me = Su/Ma: bringing plans to fruition; the mental fighter or leader, both in physical struggle or at work.

Me = Ma/Ne: thoughtless, nervous weakness (as a consequence of drugs or misuse of energy), weakness of mind, sensitive nerves (a receptive mind); many plans with no chance of realization (Tyl: Imagination may lose anchor; difficulty coping).

On the Mercury axis there is self-knowledge, exchange of ideas with others, enjoyment of discussing relationship upsets, a lot of thinking and formulating opinions. There is also fanciful thinking and over-thinking.

Venus

Venus is in Cancer in the 6th house, ruling the 3rd, sextile Moon, conjunct Mercury, at the midpoint of Ju/No, Ma/Ur, Mo/Ma, Me/Ju.

Venus in Cancer: a deep-seated feeling of love, a strong urge to lean on others, appreciation of family and home, art, and music.

Venus in the 6th: a moral sense, the desires of the heart superseded by practicality, indecisive in love, the striving for moral purity.

Ve = Mo: love, devotion, art.

Ve = Me: thoughts of love, inspiration, writers and authors, artistic genius, artistic successes.

Ve = Ju/No: friendly and pleasant social demeanor, popularity; affectionate care of another, a love relationship.

Ve = Ma/Ur: passionately excitable; assertive in matters of love, a surge of energy in love matters (birth); medical intervention of a woman.

Ve = Mo/Ma: passionate, sexual desire; the desire for having children, creative, the desire to create, shape or mold something.

Ve = Me/Ju: reveling in something or rapture, being enamored with another, being in love, appreciation of beauty, interest in art, cheerfulness.

Not surprisingly, the Venus axis speaks of high passion and a need for love, and to be creative and caught up in passion.

Mars

Mars in Sagittarius in the 11th, ruling the 9th and 10th, sextile Jupiter, sextile Saturn, at the midpoint of Me/Mc, Ve/Sa, Ve/Pl, No/Mc. (At a declination of - 27.53, it is wildly out of bounds.)

Mars in Sagittarius: the need to convince others of one's ideas, love of contest and sport, enthusiastic in work, mobility, frankness, candor, rashness, love of adventure.

Mars in the 11th: deliberation, love of freedom, implementing new work methods, the urge to reform, teamwork, organization, independent.

Ma = Ju: successfully creative, pride, a sense of honor, living an active life, strong focus on aim or goals, energy, ambition, able to cope with every situation.

Ma = Sa: harmful or destructive energy, endurance, the power of resistance, periods of impotence and weakness alternating with periods of brutality or ruthlessness, progress and advancement in life.

Ma = Me/Mc: open-minded and frank, able to understand clearly, a clear sense of one's life goals, outstanding thoughts and acts, aware of one's viewpoints.

Ma = Ve/Sa: jealousy, violence, weakened powers of procreation; actions dictated by emotional inhibition or new sobriety, discussions or dispute, separation.

Ma = Ve/Pl: strongly sensual, the desire for many children (rape), a brutal and coarse emotional expression (Tyl: the sex drive dominates expression).

Ma = No/Mc: comradeship and team spirit, strong teamwork, an association or organization fighting to uphold a common cause; inner attachment and physical attraction.

This out-of-bounds Mars is beyond the pale, which was reflected in his far-reaching philosophy of the psyche and his long-lasting public influence. It gained expression through the career and working with others and achieving goals. Extreme sexualization is also in evidence.

Jupiter

Jupiter in Libra in the 8th, ruling the 2nd and 11th, sextile Mars, trine Saturn, at the midpoint of Su/Me, Me/Ne, Ve/As, Ma/Sa, Me/As, Ma/Pl, Ve/Ne, Ma/Mc.

Jupiter in Libra: a sense of justice, good conversationalist, popularity, finding joy in social contacts, public work, easy-going nature, dependence or reliance on others.

Jupiter in the 8th: ruthlessly avaricious [greedy or hedonistic], materialistic, overly pronounced sexual life.

Ju = Ma: successful creativity, a fortunate decision.

Ju = Sa: industrious, success through perseverance, clear objectives and goals.

Ju = Su/Me: doctors; optimism, expanding one's horizon and mental focus; a good thinker, speaker and organizer; good connections, protection and sponsorship, travel.

Ju = Me/Ne: rich imagination, fantasy, poet, actor; having great hopes.

Ju = Ve/As: appreciation of luxury, beauty, and art; sociable; affectionate with others, happy in love.

Ju = Ma/Sa: total focus on one objective to the exclusion of all else, the ability to completely destroy or eliminate; improvement during an illness, a fortunate separation, a quick dissolution (of the body), an easy death.

Ju = Ve//Ne: rich imagination, romantic, love of comfort, beauty and art, reveling in illusions, unreal or apparent happiness in love, keeping up a good front.

Ju = Ma/Mc: a good organizer, independent, prudent, far-sighted, clear objective in life; luck in enterprise or business ventures, great successes; happy attachments, becoming engaged, great joy.

Jupiter in Libra again points to the importance of relationships. In the 8th house, he was studying unconscious influences that marred and impacted partnerships. We know this study led him to analyze the partnerships within the self and his realization that unrecognized parts that were rejected by the self were projected onto others and seen as coming from the outside, rather than the inside. Jupiter is well supported and on the axis we find luck, sponsors, happiness, the ability to recover from illness, popularity, great joy, and success.

Saturn—the Chart Ruler

Saturn in Aquarius, in the 1st, ruling the 1st and 12th, retrograde, square Pluto, sextile Mars, trine Jupiter, at the midpoint of Ma/Ju (wide 1°36).

Saturn in Aquarius: harmonious associations, reliable partner, plans that come to fruition, social aspirations; over-expectations leading to disappointment.

Saturn in the 1st: diligent, industrious, ambitious, endurance, obstinacy, self-will, defiance, self-restraint, modest, focused on work.

Sa = Pl: Hard labor; cruelty. Tenacious and tough, enduring, putting in the hard work necessary to accomplish goals, making the best effort possible, efforts of the highest order, able to perform difficult tasks with discipline; self-denial, renunciation; fanaticism, stubborn, cold-hearted, severity, violent tendencies. Also magicians and adepts.

Sa = Ma: endurance, resistance, destructive energy, periods of weakness alternating with periods of ruthless attainment.

Sa = Ju: creative activity, active life, energy, ambition, pride, a sense of honor, strong focus on objectives, able to cope with a variety of situations.

Sa = Ma/Ju: inhibited decision-making, indecisive, letting opportunities slip away; the termination of a relationship, a difficult birth. Also success in real estate.

The retrograde dignified Chart Ruler bestows hard work, tenacity, and self-discipline. There is significant struggle at work. Symbolizing magicians and adepts, the axis speaks of an occult influence. The square to Pluto describes his impoverished upbringing, and fear of destitution, but also his unfailing hard work and resilience.

Uranus

Uranus in Leo in the 7th, square Moon, at the midpoint of As/Mc, Su/Sa, Sa/Ne, Ma/No, Ne/Mc.

Uranus in Leo: enterprising spirit, bold, determined, love of freedom, gambling or speculation, the love of adventure, licentiousness.

Uranus in the 7th: inspiration, empathy, artistic talent, creativity, social reform, peculiar views on marriage.

Ur = Mo: emotional tension, a sudden manifestation of subconscious forces.

Ur = Ma: unusual achievement through focused effort; danger or peril.

Ur = As/Mc: excitability, emotional, snap judgment; sudden experiences, upsets, spoiled plans (I would add inspiration).

Ur = Su/Sa: fluctuating life goals, sudden inhibition, emotional tension, nervous; unusual events, crises, separation, mourning, seclusion.

Ur = Sa/Ne: irritable, excitable, emotional upset, peculiar drives; upsets resulting in illness, weakness or illness coming on suddenly.

Ur = Ma/No: active cooperation, an organizing activity; sudden partnerships and associations, sudden group experiences, social or organizational upset.

Ur = Ne/Mc: emotional irritability, occasional lack of clarity and certainty, manifesting ideas no matter what; sudden inner experiences, confusion, schizophrenia.

The Uranus axis points to medical research and the institute he built. He was irritable and had irritable patients. Uranus was key to his understanding of individuation. We have to get as far away (7th) as we can from the ego to grasp the concept of a higher self that is unique, and different from early conditioning and societal expectation.

Neptune

Neptune in the 3rd in Taurus square the Sun and square the Ascendant and at the midpoint of Sa/No, Me/Pl, Su/As, Pl/No, Me/Sa, Ju/Ur .

Neptune in Taurus: moody, good taste, a sense of tact, strange source of income, ability for creative design.

Neptune in the 3rd: impressionable, understanding, easily inspired, fantasy and imagination, mystical, aspirational, love of nature.

Ne = Su: sensitivity, weakness, illness, addiction. Impressionable, open to ideas, imaginative, enthusiastic, mystical interests, cultivation of inner life.

Ne = As: impressionable, drawn to peculiar people. Also an abuse or betrayal of confidence, deceit, falsehood, disappointment, and disillusion.

Ne = Sa/No: feeling neglected, being misunderstood or lonely, emotional distress due to falsehood, deception, fraud, separation, illness.

Ne = Me/Pl: overly receptive, nervousness, pursuit of peculiar ideas, cunning, falsehood, slander, libel, defamation.

Ne = Su/As: hyper-sensitivity among others, easily influenced, easily angered or upset; damage through others, disappointment, slander, degradation.

Ne = Pl/No: social climbing using lies and fraud, disadvantages, and losses.

Ne = Me/Sa: depression, distrust, emotionally inhibited. Also, travel by sea or air, desire for long-distance travel, home-sick.

Ne = Ju/Ur: being led by false perceptions, quick disappointment, a lack of foresight and caution, unearned gains, gains after losses (e.g., an inheritance after a death or new job offer after termination).

Ebertin's negative view of Neptune comes through clearly in these delineations. If we look at Neptune as the unconscious mind and myth, the midpoints assume a more relevant meaning. Jung studied depression and upset through the lens of unconscious factors. He investigated both the personal and collective unconscious and dealt with people who were swamped by their unconscious. He attained success in the medical field through this work. His luck can be in part attributed to his understanding of the mind. He brought the otherworld into the manifest realm through communication. Using active imagination, he communicated with the unconscious in a manner that gave the unknown a voice.

Pluto

Pluto in Taurus in the 3rd, square Saturn, at the midpoint of Ma/Ju, Mo/Mc, and Ur/Mc.

Pluto in Taurus: urge to acquire, striving for possessions, great dependence on money and property, the influence great gain or loss has upon future plans.

Pluto in the 3rd: Intellectual power of assertion as a scientist or speaker, organizer, adventurer. Ruthless behavior toward society and the generally accepted status quo. Influencing the masses.

Pl = Sa: cruelty, hard labor, tenacious and tough, endurance, strength of will, working difficult tasks with extreme self-discipline, self-denial, and renunciation; unfeeling cold-hearted, severe, a tendency to violence, fanatical and stubborn ideals. Also, magicians and adepts.

Pl = Ma/Ju: unusual enterprising spirit, brilliant successes, great creativity, capable of tackling big projects.

Pl = Mo/Mc: deep depression, a peculiar or strange soul life, inner (or spiritual) growth hampered by mother or wife; emotional shock and upheaval.

Pl = Ur/Mc: restless pursuit of goals, ambition to the point of fanaticism; a nervous breakdown.

Pluto brought Jung success and professional drive. It also brought him to the dark side along with deep depression.

Nodes

The North Node is in the 2nd in Aries, square Mercury, and at the midpoint of Pl/Mc, Ma/As, Sa/Mc, Ma/Ne, Su/Ma. The Nodes were stationary, which to Vedic astrologers denotes a person of consequence.

NN in Aries: associations, striving for social leadership, the cultivation of personal connections.

NN in 2nd: permanent unions, the consolidation and preservation of alliances, the fostering and developing of communal establishments. Seeking advantages through others.

No = Me: the exchange of ideas, common or joint plans.

No = Pl/Mc: gaining social leadership by force. The power to wield influence over others.

No = Ma/As: comradeship and good fellowship, teamwork, the guidance of others; relationships based on physical attraction.

No = Sa/Mc: sympathy and compassion; being bound to others through bad circumstances or mourning; people in mourning.

No = Ma/Ne: nursing, retirement home; hospitalization; dissolving associations due to lack of stability, unreliability; weakness of will or negative attitude; association with weak or sick persons.

No = Su/Ma: the cultivation of fellowship, teamwork, joint plans or undertakings, and collective work or fighting for objectives.

The Nodal axis shows Jung's groups. He wants to work with others, but in a leadership mode. His work in the mental hospital is in evidence.

Ascendant

The sign on the Ascendant is Aquarius, opposite the Sun, square Neptune, at the midpoint of Mo/Ve, Ve/Ur, Pl/No, Sa/No.

Ascendant in Aquarius: An environment keyed to reform ideas, one's own ideas, a knowledge of human nature; innovative, wide-ranging interests, adaptable, an intense soul life.

As = Su: being intellectually judged by others, intellectual judgment of others, the need for public recognition, gaining social esteem and importance, self-confidence.

As = Ne: impressionable; dominated by or under the influence of others, making strange or peculiar contacts with others. Abuse or betrayal of confidence, falsehood, deceit, disappointment and disillusion.

As = Mo/Ve: love of conversation; an active exchange of thoughts; an acquaintance dating from one's youth.

As = Ve/Ur: social demonstrations of love; a sudden meeting or contact.

As = Pl/No: the need to wield public influence.

As = Sa/No: inhibited with a desire for seclusion, suffering difficulties with others; separation.

The Ascendant axis repeats the need for public success and recognition. We see here his daily environment in one-to-one consultation in "talk therapy." His patients matter to him, and he is sensitive to their suffering.

Midheaven

The last degree of Scorpio culminates on the Mc, sesquisquare Mercury, at the midpoint of Ve/No and Me/Ve.

Mc in Scorpio: ambition coupled with great exertion and hard work, industry, perseverance, sympathetic understanding of others, able to grasp the gist of every situation, a strong sense of acquisition, ruthless.

Mc = Me: One's outlook, self-knowledge.

Mc = Ve/No: one's attitude to love unions or to the arts; deep feelings of love.

Mc = Me/Ve: an understanding of art, pursuing artistic aims, a sense of beauty, "the wings of artistic genius and inspiration," light-hearted living, artists, writers.

The life goal is stated clearly: self-knowledge. This is shared with others through his books and his art.

In sum, this is a remarkable chart that mapped out the life of an astonishing man. His work shed light on the makeup of the psyche and the complexity of the mind. He studied the forces operating behind the scenes that were up until then, largely unknown. He also realized there was a great spiritual purpose and reason driving daily life and experience. He accepted astrology and used its wisdom as he studied various pieces of the mind. This delineation gives us a well-rounded sense of the man that is in agreement with his biography. We see all areas of his life, both problems and successes, displayed in high relief. We'll now look at solar arcs and transits to see when these various axes were active during significant events.

ADOLESCENT TRAUMA

Jung experienced his first psychosis when he was twelve, after being bullied by classmates. He fell and banged his head, losing consciousness. When he recovered and was forced to return to school, he had fainting spells. The bullying made him physically ill and prevented him from returning to school. The episode lasted six months until he overheard his father bemoaning the financial burden of a sick child. Jung recognized he had "asked" for the neurosis and realized he could think himself well. He did so and returned to school determined to work hard. He never fainted again.

Although the exact date is uncertain, Jung states in his autobiography that the incident happened during early summer. We'll look at his solar return for July 26, 1887, at 17.06. pm, set at his birthplace (Figure 110). In the solar return, the Moon in Libra is conjunct the Midheaven, a difficult placement because the emotions are on public display. The Sun is conjunct the 8th house and sextile Pluto on the cusp of the 6th. He is going into the underworld. There is a partile square between Mars in fall in Cancer and

261

Uranus in Libra, symbolic of an accident associated with a fall (or a shove). Jupiter is in partile square to Saturn, also debilitated in Cancer, indicating social change, not for the best.

In the biwheel (Figure 111), return Neptune has come to the natal IC— his rational mind was swamped by unconscious forces. The natal 11th house is rising in the return, highlighting friends, in this case, ones who are violent.

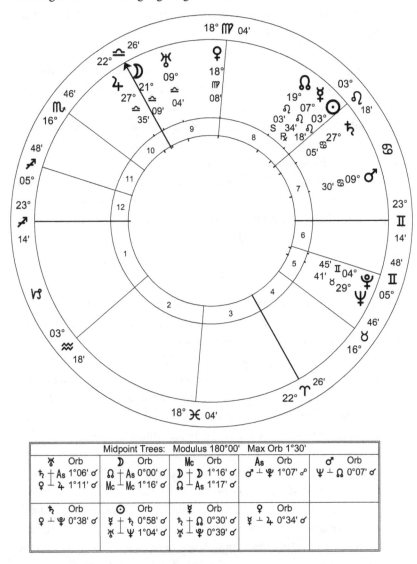

Midpoint Trees: Modulus 180°00' Max Orb 1°30'					
♅ Orb	☽ Orb	Mc Orb	As Orb	♂ Orb	
♄ + As 1°06' ♂	☊ + As 0°00' ♂	☽ + ☽ 1°16' ♂	♂ ⊥ ♆ 1°07' ♂⁰	♆ ⊥ ☊ 0°07' ♂	
♀ ⊥ ♃ 1°11' ♂	Mc ⊥ Mc 1°16' ♂	☊ ⊥ As 1°17' ♂			
♄ Orb	☉ Orb	☿ Orb	♀ Orb		
♀ ⊥ ♆ 0°38' ♂	☿ + ♄ 0°58' ♂	♄ + ☊ 0°30' ♂	☿ ⊥ ♃ 0°34' ♂		
	♅ ⊥ ♆ 1°04' ♂	♅ ⊥ ♆ 0°39' ♂			

Figure 110. Carl Jung's Solar Return age 12, July 26, 1887, 17:06 pm, Kesswil, Switzerland.

The return on the dial is shown in Figure 112 on page 264. The three major 8th harmonic aspects mentioned are evident: Ma = Ur; Mo = Mc; Ju = Sa. In addition, there are two minor aspects: Su = Ve and Mo = Pl.

These are the close midpoints in the stand-alone dial:

Ma = Ur = Ne/No: passing a test of nerves, struggling for survival, an accident, an injury; disharmony with others, unable to adapt or adjust to

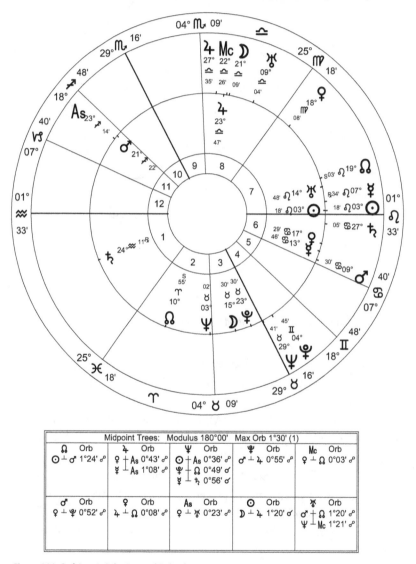

Midpoint Trees: Modulus 180°00' Max Orb 1°30' (1)				
☊ Orb	♃ Orb	♆ Orb	♇ Orb	Mc Orb
☉⊥♂ 1°24' ⚹	♀＋As 0°43' ⚹ ☿⊥As 1°08' ⚹	☉＋As 0°36' ⚹ ♇⊥☊ 0°49' ♂ ☿⊥♄ 0°56' ♂	♂⊥♃ 0°55' ⚹	♀⊥☊ 0°03' ⚹
♂ Orb	♀ Orb	As Orb	☉ Orb	♅ Orb
♀⊥♇ 0°52' ⚹	♃⊥☊ 0°08' ⚹	♀⊥♅ 0°23' ⚹	☽⊥♃ 1°20' ♂	♂＋☊ 1°20' ⚹ ♇⊥Mc 1°21' ⚹

Figure 111. Carl Jung's Solar Return biwheel

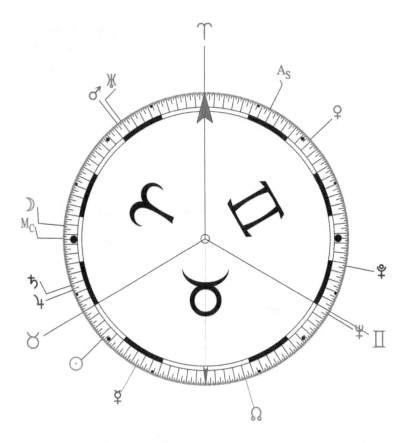

Figure 112. Carl Jung's Solar Return on the dial

circumstances; too self-willed to integrate into a community , getting upset over the anti-social conduct of others; sudden undermining or destruction of relationships.

Mo = Mc = Su/MaUr = No/As: putting one's needs out in the open (Tyl); striving for cooperation with others; accepting responsibility, attaining success; the impact of sudden events or emotional upheavals.

Sa = Ju = Su/Ma = Su/Mc: defeat (in a fight or contest), separation, suffering or worries; striving for power; successful activity; a negative outlook, the negation of life, reserve, inhibitions; withdrawing or retiring, sadness, needing to make consequential or difficult decisions; attaining one's objective.

Su = Ve: harmony, happiness.

Me = As = JuSa/No = MaUr/Pl: force, violent interventions; disharmonious or unfriendly attitude toward others; difficult social experiences; thoughts of separation, estrangement or alienation, news of loss; inhibition and a desire for seclusion, suffering difficulties with others or kin; separation.

Ne = Mo/MaUr = Me/As: a negative attitude, weak willpower, the tendency to worry, anxiousness, and grief; circumstances detrimental to family-life; lack of energy, weakness, wrong-headed or confused aspiration; nervous, exhausted; sudden disappointment; falsehood, deception, slander or libel, thinking badly of others, disappointment, being deceived by others.

Mo = Pl: violent outbursts of feeling, inner shocks, or emotional upheavals.

In the stand-alone return, the emotional trauma and its effects are evident, as is the promise of overcoming it. Although not specified, the circumstance surrounding the event is clear, though unnamed. We see the violence and its emotional impact, but not a gang of bullying thugs causing harm.

The tridial is shown in Figure 113 on page 266. The solar arc is 11°29 and there are three directions:

dUr = No: sharing experiences with others.

dSu = Ur: sudden adjustment to new conditions; excitement or upset; accidents.

dNe = Ur: elimination of the waking consciousness.

No solar return transits activated these directions.

However, the solar return transits activated several natal planets (axes). The difficult and problematic natal Saturn-Pluto is activated by tMaUr. On the axis, there is tMaUr = SaPl = tNe/No = tAs/Mc. We saw in the previous section this transiting axis pertained to disharmony and injury, as well as upset over the anti-social contact of others. Together, this manifests as self-destructive energy.

The happy natal axis of Ju = Ve/As is activated by the solar return Midheaven. His happiness is spoiled by the incident. Still, out of school, he spent many happy hours in nature on his own, pursuing his own interests.

As a solar return chart, the transiting Sun has come to the natal Sun, along with the transiting midpoints of tMe/JuSa. On this axis, there is tSu

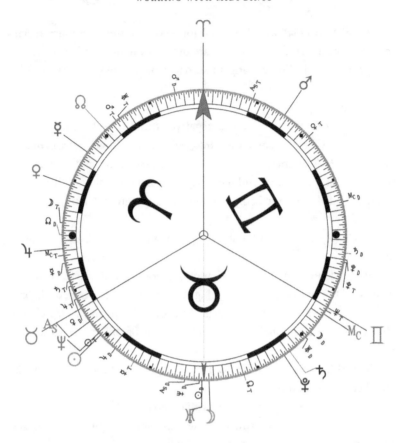

Figure 113. Carl Jung's tridial age 12 with directions and Solar Return

= Su = Ne = tMe/JuSa. This is sensitivity, a desire to withdraw from other people; depression, distrust, and emotional inhibitions.

The natal Midheaven on the midpoint Ve/No is activated by tNe that is on the midpoint of Pl/tPl and tSu/As. Taken together, this shows, sensitivity to others; supernatural experiences; criminal offenses; shyness, feelings of inferiority, a depressing environment, emotional suffering through others; separation caused by disagreements, , the inclination to feel depressed, oppressed, inhibited, frustrated or slighted by others; suffering from others' actions, the gaining of experience.

In sum, the synastry with the natal chart reiterates the feeling of the stand-alone dial. It would have been a difficult summer for a twelve -year-old boy. The solar return shows clearly the effect of the bullying and describes the ensuing trauma, as well as the stimulation of unconscious psychic factors.

Of this period, Jung wrote, "Nature seemed to me full of wonders. . . . Every stone, every single thing seemed alive and indescribably marvelous." He also realized, "that I myself had arranged this whole disgraceful situation. That was why I had never been seriously angry with the schoolmate who pushed me over. I knew that he had been put up to it . . . and that the whole affair was a diabolical plot on my part" (*Memories, Dreams, Reflections*).

FATHER'S DEATH

Jung lived at home while attending the University of Basil. Driven by a need for financial security rather than a love of the profession, he enrolled in a program leading to medical school. He was twenty, in his second year of university, when his father got seriously ill and died unexpectedly. This nearly ended Jung's medical career for he had to support his mother and younger sister as there were no family savings, no pension, and no money for schooling. However, help came from an uncle whose financial aid enabled Jung to stay in school.

Jung's father died on January 28, 1896. Are the death and upcoming hardship shown in the Capricorn Ingress? The ingress chart is shown in Figure 114. Mercury is out-of-bounds and combust the Sun. This is disturbing news or a focus on studies. Venus in detriment is conjunct Saturn, which shows sadness and financial difficulty. The Pisces Moon is conjunct the North Node, indicating attention on his emotions, family, or mother. There is a t-square between Mars opposite Pluto square Moon-Node, with Mars at the South Bending (ruling the natal 9th and 10th), suggesting difficulty at university and with his mother. Mars gets help from a trine to Jupiter, the mundane significator of an uncle.

In the biwheel, transiting Saturn is opposite the Moon, indicating a depressing time. Transiting Venus and transiting Saturn are square natal Uranus, signifying a sudden upset or change. Venus rules the natal 4th house and Saturn rules the nativity, bringing together the symbolism of Jung and his father. The Ingress Mc is conjunct the Descendant and the natal Sun, while the IC, the cusp of endings and the father, is rising. Moreover, transiting Venus, ruler of the natal 4th, is trine natal Mercury, ruler

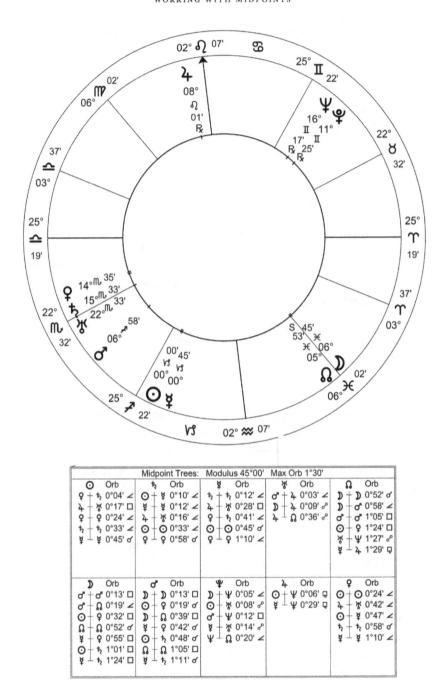

Figure 114. Carl Jung's Father's death Capricorn Ingress 1895 chart

8th, depicting the death of the father. Transiting Uranus is opposite Pluto, describing a change in fortune.

The stand-alone dial of the ingress is shown in Figure 115. In addition to the major 8th harmonic aspects of Su = Me, Ve = Sa, No = Mo = Ma, there are the minor 8th aspects of Pl = As, Ne = Mc, and SuMe = VeSa. These are Ebertin's delineation of the close aspects and midpoints:

Su = Me = Ve = Sa = MoNo/As = Ju/Ur: dutiful, thrifty, economical, sober thinking, confronting stark reality; luck; the tendency for depression, tackling serious problems, thoughts of separation; mourning and bereavement.

Pl = As: a drastic or radical change of one's life.

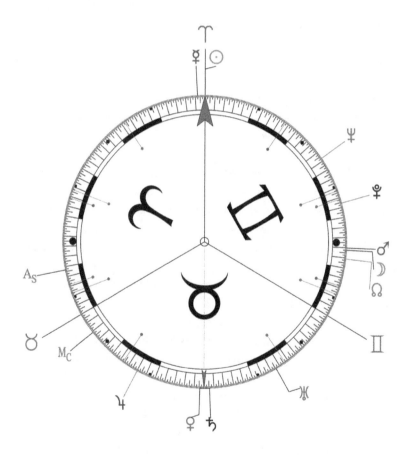

Figure 115. Capricorn Ingress 1895 in dial

269

Ne = Mc = Ju/As: depression and psychoses; insecurity, lack of self-confidence; interest in the occult, interest in the unconscious and the supernatural; inclined to taking chances, finding good fortune, successful in making contacts with others.

Ju = Su/Ne = Me/Ne = Ve/Mc: achieving success, having great hopes, easily gaining the affection of others.

Ur = MoMa/Ju: active resistance to guardianship or tutelage, ambition, quick determination; love of enterprise; sudden good fortune.

MoMa = Su/Ve: a strong feeling of love, (a mother and a sister).

Pl = MoMa/Ne = SuMe/Ur: failure due to lack of planning, emotional shock or upheaval; sudden physical restrictions; hasty realization of plans.

The stand-alone Capricorn Ingress points to sudden change. The Venus-Saturn influence shows a lack of money, while the Jupiter contacts indicate success. With the uncle's help, Jung ended up selling antiques to support his mother and sister.

The tridial of the Capricorn Ingress is shown in Figure 116. There are two active directions: dMa = No and dMe = SuNe = dMc. On the first axis, there is dMa = No = Sa/Mc: the stage of entering into union with others; a link with others through bad circumstances or mourning; people in mourning; leadership gained by force.

On the second axis, there is dMe = dMc = Su = Ne = Me/SaPl = Ju/dJu: a negative outlook; periods of depression, hyper-sensitivity or mental and emotional stress; nerve weakness; deception or illusions; a desire to solve difficult problems; privation; optimism, success.

Taken together we see a difficult time and Jung's plan to deal with poverty, which was to sell antiques.

Turning to the transits, the ingress planets did not activate either direction. In synastry there is:

tSu = MoUr = tVeSa = As/Mc: emotional tension; sudden appearance of sub-conscious forces; making sacrifices for others; quick determination; sudden experiences, excitement or upsets, a spoiling of one's plans.

tNe = As = Ve/MoUr: unable to maintain one's position in the world, easily influenced by others, moody; a sudden meeting or contact.

tUr = SaPl = Ma/Ju = tMaMo/Ju: able to make quick decisions in difficult situations; enterprising spirit; good cooperation with others.

In sum, the season of the ingress depicts mourning, loss, upsets, tension, money problems, but also beneficial associations, and success.

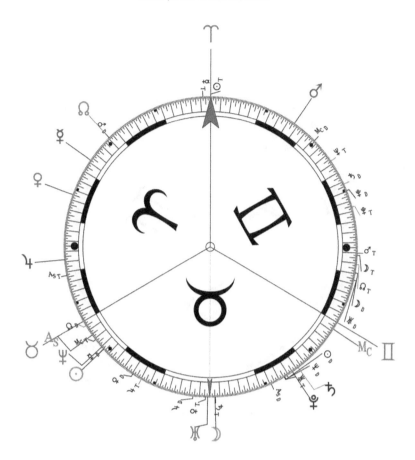

Figure 116. Carl Jung's tridial with Capricorn Ingress 1895

His father died a month after the ingress. While there was no indication of this in the predictive chart, the circumstance resulting from the death was evident. The bidial of Jung's father's death is shown in Figure 117 on page 272. The event chart was set at noon in Kesswil. (I don't know why, but the diurnal charts for Jung are so far off the mark I find them unusable. In an untimed chart, I ignore the angles and the Moon.)

The two directions we looked at are still in play. Now, on the day of the death, the dMa = No is activated by transiting Mercury at the midpoint of tSa/No, giving the axis of dMa = No = tSa/No: death of relatives, association with elderly or experienced persons, also sponsorship through such people; suffering caused by others; unforced separation, family bereavement.

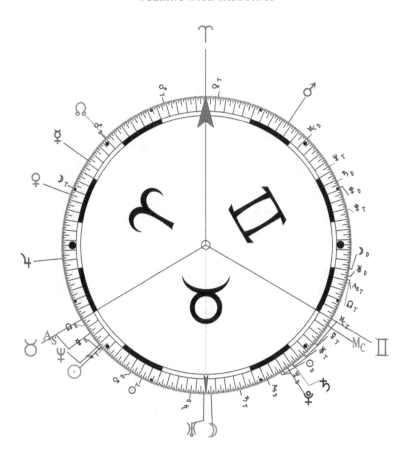

Figure 117. Carl Jung's transits and directions at the time of his father's death

The direction of dMe = dMc = Su = Ne is triggered by transiting Jupiter. The contact of tJu = Su can signify an easy death of the father. At this time, Jung's continuation at university is uncertain.

Another transit in play is tUr = Sa = tJu/Ne, indicating a break from the past, feeling abandoned by luck, and recognizing a difficult situation.

It's interesting that the axis of Ma = Sa in the transiting chart does not connect with Jung's chart. The chart it does connect with is the natal chart of his father (12/21/1842; time and place unknown), who had natal Saturn at 18° Scorpio opposite transiting Saturn at 18° Taurus at the time of his death. Natal Mars at 4° Capricorn was square transiting Mars at 4° Aries. In the dial, 4° cardinal is on the axis of 19° fixed, bringing these axes into alignment.

INSANE ASYLUM

Before and during college, through his mother's side of the family, Jung became involved with the occult and attended séances. The title of his medical dissertation was: *On the Psychology and Pathology of the So-Called Occult Phenomena*. Jung finished medical school and met Emma, but his affections were not reciprocated. She moved to France, while he (to the dismay of many) moved to Zurich and began an internship at the Burgholzli Mental Hospital, specializing in psychiatry, "the most despicable branch of medicine." He was twenty-five.

Of his early experiences there, he wrote, "... life took on an undivided reality—all intention, consciousness, duty, and responsibility. It was an entry into the monastery of the world, a submission to the vow to believe only in what was probable, average, commonplace, barren of meaning, to renounce everything strange and significant, and reduce anything extraordinary to the banal. Henceforth there were only surfaces that had nothing, only beginnings without continuations, accidents without coherence, knowledge that shrank to ever smaller circles, failures that claimed to be problems, oppressively narrow horizons, and the unending desert of routine."

For six months Jung lived like a recluse, never leaving the hospital. He had no money for entertainment or clothes and was overworked by the hospital director. In the early days ... "'he was "deeply humiliated" to see how Bleuler [the director] and his only other assistant doctor moved so confidently about their duties, while he was all the time "more and more" baffled and plagued by such "feelings of inferiority that [he could] not bear to go out of the hospital."' Jung was sending his whole salary to his mother and had no money to socialize. During this period, he resented his parents "intensely for their poverty and the resulting shame he felt about his lack of experience in life."

Jung began work at the mental hospital in Zurich in early December. There was a Solar Eclipse on November 22, 1900, at 29°Scorpio (Figure 118 on page 274), conjunct Jung's natal Midheaven. (The chart is set in the place of the impending residence, giving angles 1° earlier than the natal location.) Briefly, the lights are square Mars conjunct the royal star Regulus, ruling the natal and eclipse 10th; a portentous sign to start a career. Mars is sextile Neptune, which describes work with the collective unconscious. Study of the personal unconscious is given by the opposition of Jupiter and Pluto.

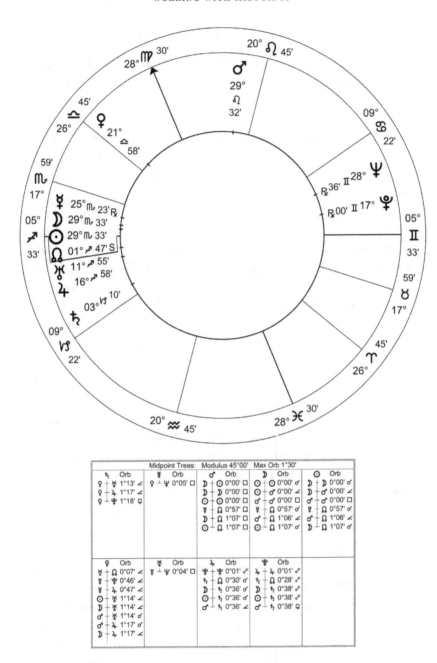

Figure 118. Solar Eclipse chart before Carl Jung started work at asylum

In synastry, transiting Saturn is sextile Neptune, highlighting the focus of study. Transiting Venus is sextile Mars, likely desire to win Emma over. There is a t-square formed with transiting Mercury square natal Saturn opposite natal Pluto, suggesting a difficult period of hard work and no money. Still, transiting Venus was conjunct natal Jupiter, adding hope and happiness. The eclipse Midheaven is conjunct the cusp of the natal 8th house, dealing with the personal unconscious and deep emotional matters that send people to therapy.

The dial of the eclipse is shown in Figure 119. There are no minor 8th harmonic aspects, and the major 8th aspects are evident: Ne = Mc; Ju = Pl; and Su = Mo = Ma. These are the close midpoints:

Ve = Ur/No: heightened feelings among others, sudden attachments, falling quickly in love quickly.

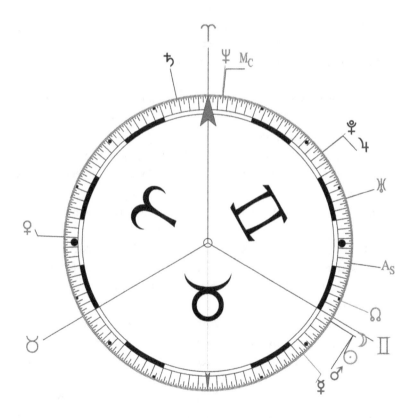

Figure 119. Solar Eclipse dial before Carl Jung started work at asylum

Me = Ve/NeMc: announcing one's relationship, reveling in romance, a dreamy nature.

Su = Mo = Ma: making ideals and wishes reality, sexual attraction between couples, impulse to marry, desire for children, joint objectives, sexual union, marriage.

No = As/SuMoMa: amiable and obliging; desire for a personal relationship; becoming close by living together; teamwork, the guidance of others.

As = Ur/SuMoMa = Me/JuPl: energetic and excitable woman; sudden experiences, new associations, an upsetting experience (Tyl: consideration of geographic relocation); the gift of oration, the desire to influence many people. A propaganda campaign, persuasion, influence, promotion of cause.

Ur = Me/NeMc: a stepped-up imagination, ideas, inventions, inspirations, ambition; a sudden shifting of focus onto a different goal, getting excited or upset, sparked into sudden action.

JuPl = As/NeMc: desire for power; loss of luck or good name; depressed by one's environment; harmed by deceit or libel, malice from others; popularity; joy and success; the power to wield influence.

NeMc = Ve/As: devoted to peculiar goals, an undermining activity, falsehood, disappointment in love. Union with another through love.

The axes and associated midpoints in the stand-alone dial clearly point to love, vocation, and the power to influence people (patients in the asylum).

The tridial with the solar eclipse is shown in Figure 120. The solar arc is 24°18" and there are three directions: dAs = No; dUr = Ju; dSaPl = SuNe. These give:

dAs = No = dMo/Ve: a love-contact, the commencement of associations, the sharing of experiences in life together with others.

dUr = Ju = No/dNo: luck, fortunate turns in life, a sudden change of destiny, sudden recognition, successful speculation (also good for scientific inquiry), and the ability to show oneself cheerful, gay, and hopeful in the presence of others.

dSaPl = SuNe = Me/Pl = No/SaPl: renunciation, privation, a physical separation; persuasive speaking, a keen observer, circumspection or shrewdness and vision, the need for recognition; a nervous sensitivity, pursuing peculiar plans; sharing a common suffering with many others.

The axis brings the planets of the unconscious, Neptune and Pluto, together with Mercury and Saturn—deep mental work, that he threw himself into (Sun).

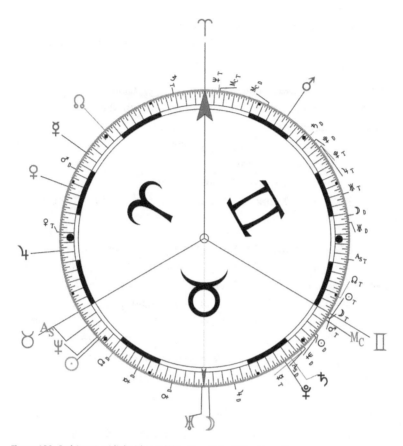

Figure 120. Carl Jung's tridial with natal/directions/Solar Eclipse transits

Only the first direction was triggered by the eclipse, as transiting Mercury landed on the axis of the Node, adding: longing for love, erotic thoughts, reflecting on love problems. The midpoint tVe/NeMc is also on the axis, giving: a disappointed hope, an unhappy union, deep bonds of love, personal attachment, a love affair, the vow of love.

There are three other active transiting axes:

1. tNo = Ve = Ju/No = tAs/SuMoMa: friendly and pleasant personality, popularity; affectionate caring for another, a romantic relationship; obliging manner; one's attitude to others; wanting personal relationships with women; closeness through living together; teamwork, the guidance from others.

Putting these together we get a sense that while Jung pined away for Emma, he was making friends in the asylum and expressing a caring attitude.

2. tJuPl = As = Mo/Ve = tSa/SuMoMa: attaining leadership, shrewd, forward thinking and prescient, a talent for organization, the desire for power, personal advancement, tunnel vision; a happy love life, affectionate and optimistic; sudden amorous intensity; separation from someone, loss of social standing, development inhibited by illness.

This is an interesting axis because it summarizes his job with its low prestige, his love for Emma and her absence, as well as his all-consuming focus on work.

3. tSuMoMa = Mc = Me = Ve/No: bringing goals to fruition, sexual attraction between partners, the desire for children, the urge to marry, joint objectives; adhering to work as a labor of love, gladly taking on responsibility, masculine expression, attaining success, a fighting character, marriage, demonstrating one's feelings to others, open discussions of love problems, need to form contacts with others; personal associations with shared interests or love; sending a love letter; deep feelings of love.

This axis seems dedicated to his feelings and longing for Emma.

In sum, repeatedly, the primary theme of the solar eclipse was love and problems with love. The job and work are evident, but not as prominent.

Jung started work on December 10, 1900. I arbitrarily set the chart at 9.00 a.m. in Zurich and the tridial is shown in Figure 121. I will ignore the position of the transiting angles and the Moon.

The directions are unchanged, and the transiting Node is still on the axis of Venus, and transiting Pluto (minus tJu) is on the axis of the Ascendant. Now, appropriately, transiting Jupiter has come to Mars, symbolizing his job. On the axis, there is tJu = Ma = tMa/Sa = No/tNo = Me/Mc. This gives the complete concentration on a singular objective, regained sobriety, separation; cooperation in the technological arena; fortunate rearrangements of the environment, optimism, successful teamwork; unusually tense romantic relationship, good cooperation with others; a clear consciousness of life goals, outstanding thoughts and acts, self-awareness of viewpoints, an abundance of thoughts, optimism, ability of self-knowledge and recognition of good fortune.

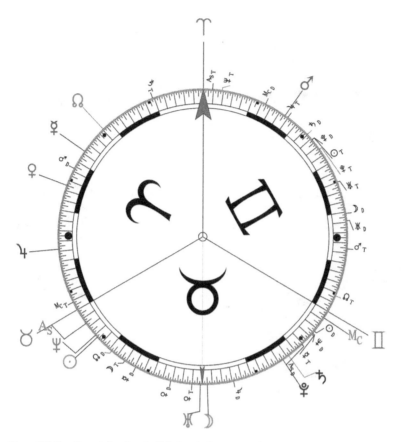

Figure 121. Transits and directions in dial when Carl Jung started at asylum

The transiting Sun had come to the axis of the natal Sun giving tSu = Su = Ne = tSa/No: successes through a sympathetic understanding of other people, a person exploited by other people; great disappointments, chaotic conditions; feeling uncomfortable in the presence of others.

The final transit involved tVe = Ur = Su/Sa: arousing of love, suppressed feelings, reserve; inhibited love life, the separation of lovers, being love-sick; emotional tensions, sudden inhibitions, nervousness; unusual situations, crises, separation, mourning, seclusion.

In the event chart, there is more focus on work, but relationship angst is still prominent.

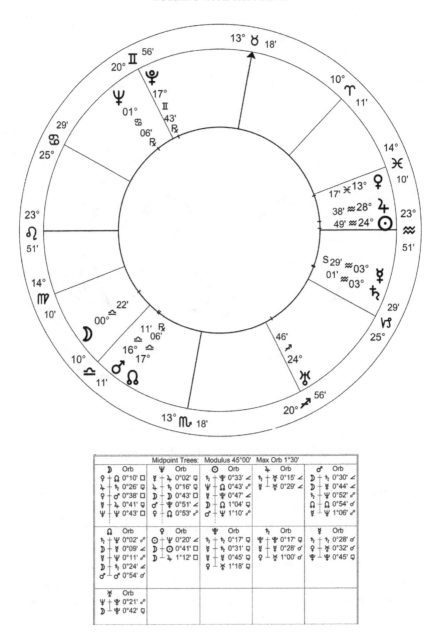

Figure 122. Carl Jung's marriage chart

LOVE AND MONEY

Three years later, on Valentine's Day, in 1903, after a long courtship and an initial refusal, Jung finally won Emma's heart (with help from her mother). He married an heiress whose family was one of the richest in Switzerland. Her wealth brought a practical end to his financial difficulties.

Up until then, Jung was "properly timid with women, he had not had an adventure before, so to speak." As he later told Freud, as a boy he was "a victim of sexual assault by a man he once worshiped," and his feelings had hampered him ever since. He found close relationships with men "downright disgusting" and he had problems with male friends throughout his life. He would also have trouble with women and in his marriage. Freud interpreted several of Jung's dreams from this period as portending the "failure of a marriage for money."

The marriage took place on 2/14/1903, time unknown. I set the chart for 5.31 pm in Kesswil, a somewhat diurnal chart that places the Sun correctly in the 7th house. It seems like a reasonable time to get married. However, I will ignore the position of the angles and the houses.

The stand-alone chart is shown in Figure 122. Mars is in detriment in Libra and gains strength from its conjunction with the Node. Mars is trine a retrograde Pluto, adding potential nastiness and brutality. Sadly, a stationary direct Mercury is conjunct a strong Saturn. More sadly still, the pair is trine the Moon (if the time is close). Happily, there is a Sun-Jupiter conjunction. However, the Sun is in detriment. There is an exalted Venus in Pisces squaring Pluto, adding passion.

The dial of the event is shown in Figure 123 on page 282. The major 8th harmonic aspects are evident: Ma = Mo/Ne, and Me = Sa. There is one minor aspect of Pl = MeSa. Adding midpoints gives:

Ne = Mo = Ve/No = Ve/Ma = Ju/Sa = Me/Ju: shyness, feeling inferior in love life, disappointment; abnormal sexual craving, denying one's feelings of love, inclination to perversity; disappointment in sexual relationship; pessimism, feeling abandoned, begrudging the good fortune of others; intolerable loneliness, swindling or misleading others, losing confidence during speaking, trusting in good fortune, successfully deceptive.

No = Ma = Sa/Ne: joint or shared successes, being in union with others, being inhibited or depressed with others, shyness, feelings of inferiority; weak or sick persons, a hospital stay, weak procreative powers.

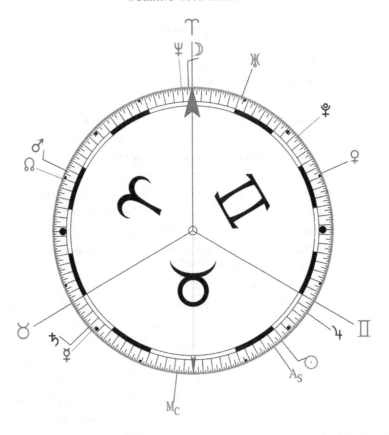

Figure 123. Carl Jung's marriage dial

Sa = Me = Pl = Ve/Ur: quarrelsome, nagging, irritable, skeptical; irritable from overwork, the target of bitter attacks; able to stimulate ideas in others, the sudden feelings of love; controlled sensuality, suppressed tensions in love, occasional sexual and emotional inhibitions; coming to senses after being drunk in love, estrangement, separation; highly excitable.

Su = Ne/No = Sa/Pl = Me/Pl: physical toil and over-exertion, putting everything into one's work; renunciation, privation; difficulty establishing contacts with others, unable to articulate ideas, unable to reach understanding with others; being tormented, disappointed or let down by others; a persuasive speaker, a keen observer, wary, or prudent, the desire for recognition.

Ju = Sa/Ur = Me/Ur: easily adapts to any situation, release from tension; sudden turn in destiny, fortunate ideas, the gift of gab (quick wit), optimistic and confident, positive outlook, ability for long-term planning, a clear grasp of things, a fortunate turn.

Ve = Su/Ne: chastity, a weak constitution, being reserved in love or with affections, disappointments, aberrations in love or sexual expression.

Ur = Ne/Pl: a flair for eccentricity, adventurous, mystical, supernatural experiences; hyper-sensitive; making peculiar discoveries, experiencing unusual catastrophes.

These are quite interesting midpoints transpiring on a wedding night. They point to what may not have been a good night to remember. Nonetheless, the fortunate turn in life is in evidence.

The tridial is shown in Figure 124. There were four directions:

dMa = Ve: the traditional marriage indicator where Venus is combined with Mars.

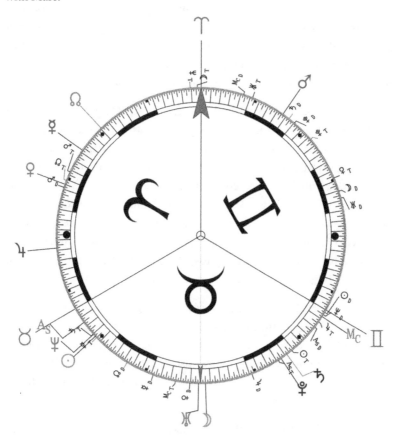

Figure 124. Carl Jung's tridial at time of marriage, with natal/directions/transits

dAs = Me: meeting others, the exchange of ideas, making acquaintances; receiving documents, letters.

dSuNe = Mc: disappointments, confusion, lack of clarity. (Tyl: something threatens ego definition).

dSa = Ma: harmful or destructive energy, inhibited or destroyed vitality; death, difficulties to overcome.

If we add the wedding transits, we get:

1. dMa = Ve = tNo = tMeSa/Ne = Ju/No: impulse to love, passion; magnetic sexual personality; sexual unions; the ability to enter into associations with others and the power to connect imaginative elements or factors; discussion of joint plans and ideas; rapturous imaginings, expectations of love too high, strong but short-lived attractions; bringing plans or inventions to fruition, deliberate action based on experience; inhibited sex life, lack of energy and initiative, faintness or feebleness; weak powers of procreation; friendly and pleasant with others, becoming popular; taking affectionate care of another, a love relationship; a good colleague or coworker, a happy partner; happy physical union, engagement, procreation; successful teamwork.

2. dAs = Me = tJu = Mc = tMeSa/Ur = Ve/No = dSu/As = Mo/dMo: sociable, lively exchange of ideas, cheerful, participating in pleasurable entertainments; successful discussions, negotiations, transactions; happy and harmonious relationship to one's social environment; coming into pleasant contact with others, making contacts with other others easily, a festivity; adaptable to every situation, fortunate release from tension; sudden turn in destiny; good companionship, self-confident in meeting new people, hopeful expectation in new relationships; a rich or happy (and fortunate) love life; optimism, taking joy in the pleasant things in life, achieving success; associations with weak or sick persons, a stay in the hospital.

3. tNe = SuNe/Mc = tMeSa/Ju = MoUr: being misunderstood, lack of confidence; disappointments; annoyance from a female source, changing relationships to women; feeling abandoned, begrudging others their good fortune; subconscious stirrings, good instincts for life goals, the "I" in relation to the "Thou," the recognition of the "Thou" in oneself; attitudes to the opposite sex.

4. tMe = tSa = Su = Ne = tPl: inhibited thinking, dark or depressing thoughts, taking on serious problems; research; psychical or inner peculiarities, lack

of vitality; a mental, emotional, or physical crisis; (Tyl: delusions within a relationship); dark forebodings, pessimism, self-torment; emotional suffering; thinking and acting while under strange influences, over-sensitivity, plans incapable of realization.

5.tSu = Sa = Pl = tNo/Ne: difficult struggle advancing in life; unable to develop one's ideas, unable to come to an understanding with others; torment, disappointment, being let down by others; socially emotionally inhibited, disadvantages, painful and grievous losses due to others, separation through deceit, treachery or untruthfulness, emotional suffering caused by a partner.

In conclusion, there were difficult directions and transits at the time of the wedding, which would reflect a difficult marriage. He had multiple affairs and a long-time lover who behaved as a co-wife without the shackles of a house and children. Although in their later years, they were apparently happy, when Emma died, she left her fortune to her children, leaving her husband only the minimum required by law.

FAMILY LIFE

During the first year of his marriage, Jung was hard at work at the asylum, acting as "director, senior physician, and first assistant," and losing fourteen pounds in the process. But he was happy, "For what satisfies us in life more than real work?" The Jungs lived in an apartment near the asylum and Emma helped him at the hospital for a year until she became pregnant with Agathe, the first of Jung's five children. His second daughter, Gret, was born a year later. His relationship with his two daughters was vastly different. Let's briefly look at what the astrology shows.

The tridial at the time of Agathe's birth is shown in Figure 125 on page 286. There is no time and so the chart is set at noon in Zurich. At the time of Agathe's birth, there were two directions: dVe = Mo and dSaPl = Ma. We'll look at each axis in turn.

dVe = Mo = As/Mc = dJu/No = As/dAs: personal feeling about life, association with females; , emotional, quick determination; sudden experiences, excitement, birth, happy relationships with others.

dSaPl = Ma = Me/Mc = Ve/SaPl: a clear understanding of everything, a clear consciousness of aims, outstanding thoughts and acts, jealousy,

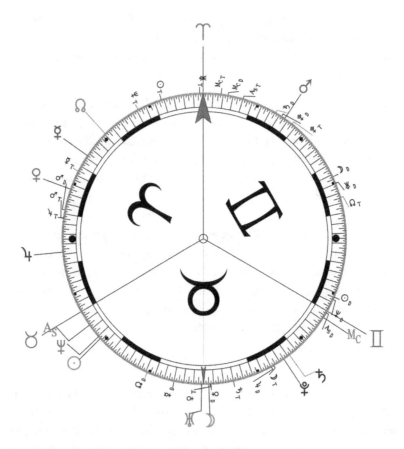

Figure 125. Agathe's birth tridial with natal/directions/transits

weakened powers of procreation; strongly sensual nature, the desire for many children.

Both directions were activated by transits, and these were the only transits that connected to his natal chart. On the first axis of Moon-Uranus-dVenus, there is transiting Venus-Uranus (no transiting midpoints) activating the direction across the axis. Here is another birth pair that is active and descriptive of the moment.

This second axis is activated by transiting Pluto. The combination of tPl = Ma gives exceptional ability; superhuman power. This may apply to Emma giving birth, or Jung throwing himself into his work. Outwardly, it did not express as brutality and meanness.

Gret was born less than fourteen months later. Her tridial is shown in Figure 126. The time is set for 1.25 pm and the chart has an A rating. There are two directions: dSuNe = Ve and dJu = SaPl. We'll look at them both.

dSuNe = Ve = Ju/No = tSa = MoUr/Ma: weak constitution, reservation in love or affections, aberrations in love; emotional inhibitions in partnerships, disappointments, indecision or vacillation, instability, unreliability; a stalled venture, difficulties; a negative attitude, weakness of will, a tendency to worry, fretfulness and grief, misdirection of energy; renunciation; detrimentally undermining circumstances affecting the family; suppressed feelings, dissatisfaction, lack of interest, quarrel.

dJu = Sa = Pl = tNe = Mo/Mc = tVe/Mc = tSu/Ju: dark forebodings, pessimism, self-torment; emotional suffering, hard labor; cruelty, compulsively

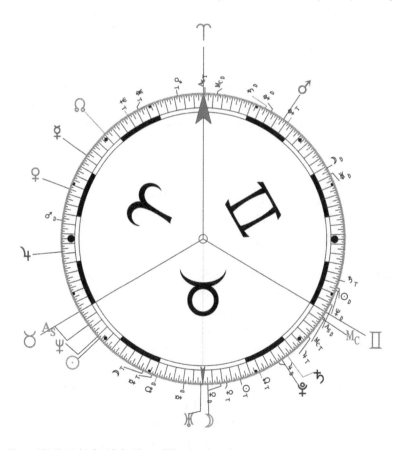

Figure 126. Gret's birth tridial with natal/directions/transits

self-destructive; emotional tension and inhibition, discontent; suppression of pessimism and self-destructive thoughts; secret desire to harm others, deep depression, difficult growth or development; repressed love, estrangement, separation; a peculiar attitudes toward love, inexplicable dislikes or aversions; renunciation, dissatisfaction and unhappiness; disinclination to action due to negativity.

The transits add:

tAs = MoUr = tMe/No = tNe/Pl = As/Mc: quick response to one's environment; upsetting experiences; stimulating ideas coming from others; hyper-sensitivity; peculiar discoveries, being placed in a peculiar environment, unexpected catastrophes; surrounding oneself with an air of mysticism.

tMc = Me = Mc = Sa/tSa = Ve/No: pessimism, melancholy, a love of solitude and meditation, separation, mourning; difficulties or worries in love; sharing common interests with others.

tPl = Ma = tSa/Ne = Ve/Sa = Me/Sa: superhuman power, force, brutality; deep depression, difficult development; action inhibited by emotion; unusually strong tension in love; incompatibility, unrest, the need to quarrel, treating others badly, disputes and arguments resulting in separation.

In conclusion, Jung's synastry with each of his two daughters is vastly different. According to Deirdre Bair who wrote the biography *Jung*, he was afraid Gret was "slightly unwell." As a child she was different from her sister who was "a large, sunny blond child, independent, outgoing, and easy to raise; [whereas] Gret was dark and thin, cranky, irritable and obstreperous." Jung had a difficult relationship with her throughout his life. "The truculent Gret was 'the family problem.' [She] exasperated [Jung] so terribly that he would beg the others not to let her near him, as 'she puts such pressure on one' that he could not sleep after their daily battles." Gret was an astrologer, and she was especially incensed when she found an "astrologically fortuitous day" to marry, and Emma insisted she delay the marriage until after Jung returned from Africa. Later, when he was sick, she wanted to move into the house and take care of him, but "because of the lifelong tension between her father and herself, she was the least likely candidate. Gret was a marvelous cook, but their relationship was so quarrelsome that each time she cooked one of her superb meals for him, he claimed she ruined his digestion." In their synastry, Gret's greater benefic Jupiter magnified the destructive Saturn-Pluto in Jung's chart.

THE FREUD YEARS

Jung read Freud's *Interpretation of Dreams* when it was first published in 1900, but did not grasp its significance until 1903. "What chiefly interested me was the application to dreams of the concept of the repression mechanism .... I had frequently encountered repression in my experiments with word association; in response to certain stimulus words the patient either had no associative answer or was unduly slow ... such a disturbance occurred each time the stimulus word had touched on a psychic lesion or conflict ... the repressive mechanism was at work here."

In 1906, Jung published *Diagnostic Studies* and sent a copy to Freud who promptly responded with praise for the book. They agreed to meet. According to Jung, before their first meeting, he felt "a 'knowledge' inside him ... that 'something unconsciously fateful' ... was bound to happen. It belonged somewhere in his future, and he already knew about it 'without knowing about it.'"

Jung met Freud at his house in Vienna on March 3, 1907, at 10.00 a.m. Previously, a 1 p.m. time was assumed for this event chart, but recent diaries indicate the men met in the morning on that Sunday, at a time Freud recorded as 10.00 a.m. (*Working with Astrology*, p. 113). The event chart of that first meeting is shown in Figure 127 on page 290. The corresponding dial is shown in Figure 128 on page 291. Notably, the event IC at 8 Leo is the degree of the previous Lunar Eclipse within 2 minutes. The hard aspects in the chart are visible on the dial. Mercury is square Jupiter (intellectual communication), and Uranus is opposite Neptune (elimination of the waking consciousness). The wide t-square of Sun-Saturn square Mars square Ascendant is evident in the mutable sector of the dial. In addition, the separative aspect of Sa = No is active. Their coming estrangement was baked in from the start, but this first meeting is pleasant and harmonious, given Sun semisquare Venus (power of attraction, popularity).

Here are the midpoints:

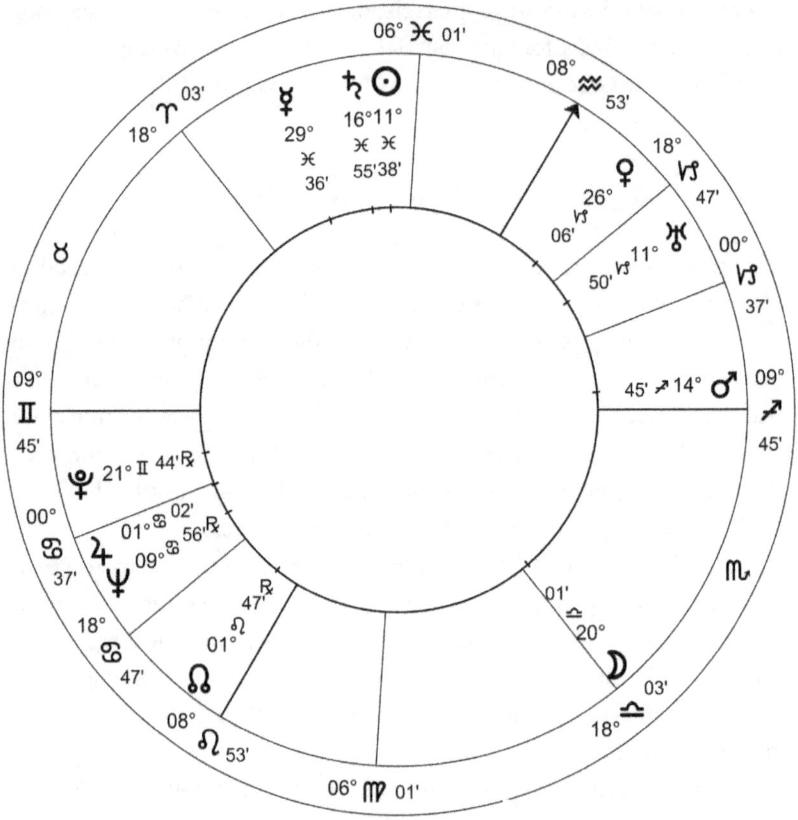

Midpoint Trees: Modulus 45°00' Max Orb 1°30'				
♃ Orb ♆ ┼ ♇ 0°12' ☌ ☽ ┼ ☉ 0°13' ☍ ♅ ┼ ♇ 0°44' □ ☽ ┼ ♂ 1°20' ⚼ ☿ ┴ ☿ 1°26' □	♆ Orb ☽ ┼ ☿ 0°07' ☍ ♄ ┼ ☊ 0°34' ∠ ☽ ┼ ♃ 0°35' ∠ ♀ ┴ ♇ 1°00' □	♅ Orb ♇ ┼ ☊ 0°04' ☍ ☿ ┼ ♀ 1°01' ∠ ☽ ┴ ♃ 1°18' ⚼	☽ Orb ♆ ┼ ☊ 0°50' □ ♀ ┴ ♅ 1°02' □	♀ Orb ☽ ┼ ☊ 0°12' ⚼ ☉ ┴ ☉ 0°31' ∠
☉ Orb ♀ ┼ ♀ 0°31' ∠ ☽ ┴ ☊ 0°44' ☍	♂ Orb ☉ ┼ ♄ 0°28' □ ♀ ┴ ☊ 0°48' ∠	☊ Orb ☉ ┼ ♇ 0°06' □ ♄ ┼ ♄ 0°07' ⚼ ♂ ┼ ♄ 0°57' ☍ ♂ ┴ ♇ 1°27' ∠	♄ Orb ☊ ┼ ☊ 0°07' ⚼ ☉ ┼ ♇ 0°14' ∠ ♂ ┴ ♇ 1°19' ☍	♇ Orb ☉ ┼ ♃ 0°23' ∠ ☿ ┼ ♂ 0°26' ⚼ ☉ ┼ ☿ 1°06' □ ♂ ┴ ♃ 1°09' □
☿ Orb ♄ ┼ ♅ 0°13' ∠ ♄ ┼ ♆ 1°10' ∠ ☽ ┼ ☉ 1°13' □ ♆ ┼ ♇ 1°13' □ ♂ ┼ ♅ 1°18' □				

Figure 127. Carl Jung met Freud chart

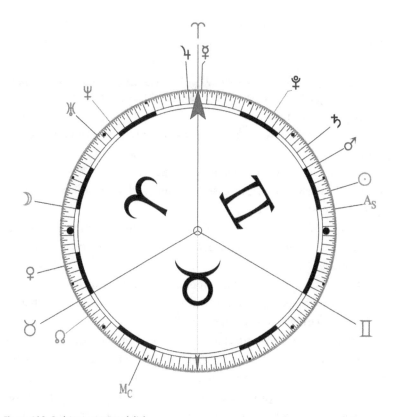

Figure 128. Carl Jung met Freud dial

Me = Sa/Ur = Mo/As: intervention in destiny, limited freedom, adaptable, sociable, entertaining, cultivating an exchange of thoughts.

Ju = Ne/Pl = Su/Mo: peace-loving, religious, strong inner cognition and perception; happy soul experiences, success in metaphysical research; seeking joint endeavors; happy relationship, joint success.

Ne = Mo/Me = Mo/Ju = Su/Mc: active imagination, fanciful thinking, wrong thinking, a lie; a deceived girl, happiness, kindness (or a good heart); social success, large-scale enterprises, material advantages, travel to foreign countries; goals or objectives in life; ego recognition.

Ur = Ma/Mc = Pl/No: the desire for quick advancement, acting rashly or without thinking; new associations that may have future importance.

Mo = Ju/Mc: a cheerful soul, confident, the joy of expectation, harmonious disposition.

Ve = Su = Mo/No: popularity, harmony, the ideal; a spiritual attitude to friendships; marital harmony; entering into relationships with others; affectionate behavior in relationships; forming attachments to others.

No = Sa = Su/Pl: association with those who are elderly or more experienced, also patronage from such people; ruthlessly overcoming obstacles and difficulties; fateful associations.

Mc = Ju/Sa: philosopher, conscious objectives, tenacious pursuit of plans.

As = Ne/Mc = Ur/Mc: sensitivity; an interest in the occult, living in a world of illusion and unreality; easily excitable; sudden experiences, adjusting to new conditions in life.

Ma = Su/Sa = Mo/Mc: crises of the soul caused by inhibitions; devoting body and soul toward a goal; actions based on emotions; industrious, conscientious activity.

Pl = Su/Ju = Me/Ma: the pursuit of happiness, the expectation of luck, acquiring wealth, being fanatically critical, over-zealous orator, sharply analytical; suffering attacks from others.

How did this energy impact Jung? The tridial with his natal placements is shown in Figure 129. Jung's solar arc is 30°21. He is almost thirty-two years old and had been a practicing physician at the mental hospital for seven years. According to Deirdre Bair, at this time, Jung's marriage was in trouble. Jung may have been having an affair. Emma demanded a holiday and Jung squeezed in a visit to Freud on the way. It turned out to be a juggling act to set the traveling schedule. Nonetheless, it was a successful meeting. The two men spoke for hours—until 1 a.m. the following morning. Immediately, Freud anointed Jung as his scientific "son and heir."

There are three solar arc directions: dMc = dMe = Ur; dAs = Ve; and dJu = SaPl. These are the directed axes:

dMc = dMe = Ur = dVe/No: ambition; channeling thoughts in a new direction, excitement, impelled to sudden action, a pleasant meeting, emotional meetings, connecting on a soul level, soul affinity, an emotional attitude.

dAs = Ve = dMo/Ve = Ju/No: females, a love affair, being friendly and pleasant manner, becoming popular; desire to be influential.

dJu = Sa = Pl = dMe/SuNe: professors and teachers, development of innate gifts.

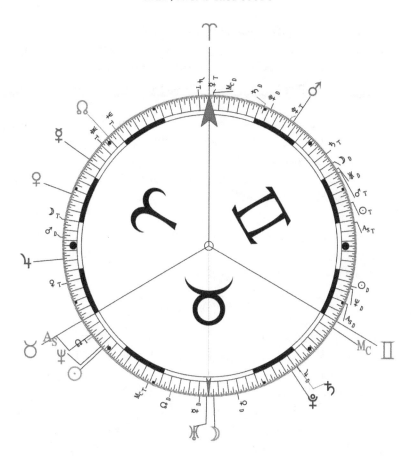

Figure 129. Carl Jung met Freud tridial with natal/directions/transits

The first direction was triggered by transiting Mercury and transiting Jupiter, describing the purpose of the meeting: a discussion, professional (Jupiter) in nature (dMc) and exciting (Ur). The transiting midpoints on the axis included:

tMe = tSa/Ur (tension and mentally coping).

tJu = tNe/Pl = tSu/Mo: intuitive cognition and perception; grounded both intellectually and emotionally, desire for joint pursuit, expansion and possessions; happy relationship.

In this set up, transiting Mercury was aligned with natal Uranus, and transiting Jupiter was on the axis of the natal Moon, activating the natal planets and their attendant midpoints.

In addition, several natal placements are activated by transits. The natal Node combined with transiting Uranus and transiting Neptune, which Tyl defined as meeting with people who care about one's future.

Transiting Neptune had come to the axis of Saturn on the transiting pair of tAs/Mc. Ebertin considered one psychological interpretation of Sa/Ne as a dual character, a struggle between the lower and the higher nature (Freud's id and superego). Neptune with Saturn is also the influence the unconscious mind has on physical reality.

Lastly, the transiting midpoint of tPl = tSu/Ju is on the axis of natal Mars, an indication that through work Jung would achieve success and good fortune.

In summary, the meeting, difficult to schedule, went well and marked the start of a collaboration of two pioneers working in the field of mental health and the influence of the unconscious mind.

OCEAN VOYAGE

Later that year, Jung's third child was born, and Jung resigned from the mental hospital to start a private practice in the home on Lake Zurich that he and Emma had recently built. There was gossip that he was having an affair with a patient, which Jung denied, and about which Emma sought Freud's advice. The collaboration between Jung and Freud reached its peak during their 7-week trip to the United States, where they analyzed each other's dreams every day—and Jung realized Freud was no expert in dream interpretation. While he was still a father figure to Jung, Freud would soon lose "much of his authority for me." (*Memories, Dreams, Reflections*, p. 187).

The two men embarked on this voyage from Bremen, Germany, on August 21, 1909. The tridial is set for noon (Figure 130). I will ignore the transiting angles and the Moon. Can we see in this chart the seeds of their coming bitter estrangement? There are three directions: dJu = No; dMa = Ju; and dMo = SuNe. The last two are triggered by transits, while the first, which is separating, is not. This suggests that the influence of the first direction is ending. For a year and a half, despite their differences, Jung had enjoyed the benefits of dJu = No: good relationships and connections, agreeable or pleasant contact. This benevolent influence was coming to a close.

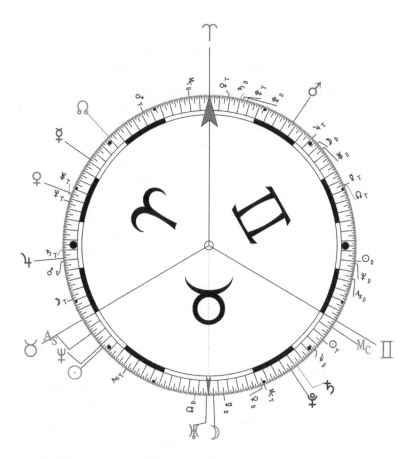

Figure 130. Carl Jung's voyage with Freud tridial with natal/directions/transits

Jung did have dMa = Ju which denotes successful enterprises, fortunate business deals, and successful professional results. However, transiting Saturn is hitting the axis like a wet blanket: dMa = Ju = tSa = dVe/Sa = Ma/Sa = dMe/Mc: termination of a relationship; jealousy, emotional inhibition or regaining one's senses, discussion or dispute, separation; thorough destruction or elimination of something; a fortunate separation; self-knowledge.

The last directed axis contained: dMo = dUr = Su = Ne = tJu = Me/SaPl = Ju/Ur = dAs/Mc: sound mental and emotional faculties, seeking a joint endeavor happy relationship; inner discontent, tormenting oneself, getting easily upset; shared suffering, mistake, misunderstandings, illusions or deceptions, the undermining of associations; depression, distrust, travel by sea, longing for distant places; philosophical thinking, the application of method, thoroughness, industrious; successfully handling difficult or bothersome work, a fortuitous separation, a happy farewell; opportunity for wide-ranging experience, absorbing and digesting multiple impressions; persuasion, teaching ability, diplomacy, public recognition, success; a nervous sensitivity, pursuing unusual plans, cunning, falsehood, verbal attacks (libel, slander, defamation); speaking from the heart to sway others, quick thinking, verbally glib; fanatical pursuit of plans; sudden upsets, nervousness, convulsions; a sudden weakness, emotional crisis; the emergence of the unconscious; intellectually sharp, an inventive mind, foresight; intuitive, optimistic, prudent; unearned gains, an upturn in fortune after losses, good prospects for a new job.

In addition, transiting Uranus and transiting Neptune had come to the axis of Venus: tUr = tNe = Ve = MoUr/Ma = tMo/Ma = tVe/As: elimination of the waking consciousness; high sensitivity, unusual art, unrequited love; a peculiar love; quickly irritable, quick-tempered, sudden violence, anger or reaction that is easily provoked, irascibility, negativity, weak-willed, worried, anxious, misdirected energy and emotion; cunning and deceitful, underhanded and mean, harming others, bad intentions; swooning or fainting on overexertion, a fit of rage (also raving madness); quick at verbal comebacks, good responses under challenge, propagandist, resourceful orator; powerful imagination, the tendency to swindle or mislead others, loss of solid ground while speaking, trusting in luck.

In the directions and transits of the time, stress and irritability are present. The ebbing influence of the separating Jupiter-Node may also explain the loss of good feeling both men likely had for each other.

BREAKUP

Three years passed and the relationship became increasingly untenable. It ended, as Jung suspected it would, with the publication of his book *Symbols of Transformation* (originally titled *The Psychology of the Unconscious*) where Jung used myth to explain psychology. Freud rejected the validity of the collective unconscious and considered the book "nothing more or less than the record of Jung's own fantasy life, recklessly projected onto ancient symbols and myths."

Their association ended in January 1913, when Jung received a letter from Freud: "I propose that we abandon our personal relations entirely. I shall lose nothing by it, for my only emotional tie with you has long been a thin thread—the lingering effect of past disappointments... Take your full freedom and spare me your suppressed tokens of friendship." Jung replied to the letter on January 6th, writing "he would never 'thrust' his friendship on anyone, and "the rest is silence.""

From then on, Freud did everything in his power to discredit and undermine Jung. According to Bair, Jung "was racked by feelings of loss, trepidation over the magnitude of what had transpired, and fear for his immediate professional future. "After all," Blair recounts, "I knew nothing beyond Freud, and yet, I dared to take the step into darkness." Later, Jung described it as "falling out into that which is not known." He thought he was "experiencing a psychological disorder." In other words, he was having a nervous breakdown.

Jung received this letter on January 6, 1913. The tridial shown in Figure 131 on page 298 is set for noon. There are five directions, four of which are triggered by transits. We'll look at each of them.

dSa = dPl = Mo = Ur = tJu = tPl = As/Mc = tSa/Ur = tVe/Ur = tMe/No: cruelty, self-destruction, termination of relationships, separation, hardship, loss, tension and upset, the need for self-reliance, the need to rise up and go on alone; anxiety, mental and emotional suffering; quick developments, adjusting to new circumstances; estrangement.

dSu= dNe = Ju = dMe/Pl = tNe = tSu/Ur: sensitivity, weakness, loss of ego; emotionally ill; prone to depression; narrow-minded, egotistic; unable to act, detrimental zealousness; unexpected events.

dVe = Sa = Pl = dJu/No = tNo = MoUr/Mc = tSu/Ju: estrangement and alienation; difficulty in teamwork, a stalled venture, termination of a relationship; quick partings and goodbyes, loss of job position; nervous breakdown; restriction, separation, taking destiny into one's own hands.

dJu = Mc = dSu/Me = Me = Ve/No = tVe: doctors; optimism, expanding horizons and mental focus; a good thinker, speaker, and organizer; protection, and sponsorship; mental development, steadfast convictions, speaking up for oneself; contacts with others, good connections, common interest associations. (This axis seems related to Jung's private practice).

dMo = Ma = dUr = Ve/Sa = Ve/Pl = Me/Mc = dAs/Mc: ambitious, lack of control, acting rashly; setting big goals; tense relationships; quarrels,

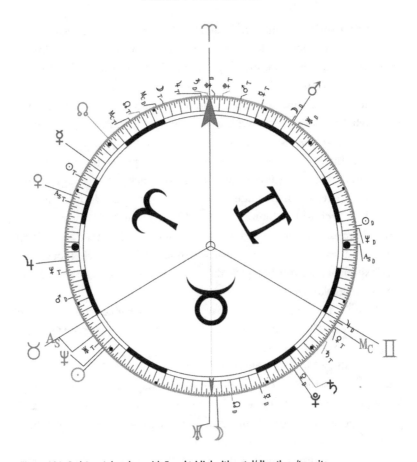

Figure 131. Carl Jung's breakup with Freud tridial with natal/directions/transits

separations; irritability, refocusing mental attention, excitement or upset, sudden actions; clarity of understanding, clarity of life goals, awareness of personal viewpoints.

In addition, there are two significant transits:

tUr = Su = Ne = SaPl/No = tSa/No = tVe/No: sudden upset, nervousness, convulsions; sudden weakness or illness, emotional crisis, mourning; need for seclusion, feeling obstructed by others; feeling neglected, being misunderstood, a violent dispute, loneliness, falsehood, deception, fraud, separation; unwillingness to bend to another's will; liberation from stress.

Finally, transiting Saturn's approach to the Midheaven indicates tenacious grasp of objectives and aims, being self-occupied, feeling inferior;

lack of courage, despondency; mental illness; disintegration of the personality; struggling against difficulties or odds; separation, difficulties in career.

In summary, the directions and transits at the time of the break clearly show the event at hand. They also emphasize the importance of the three pairs in Jung's natal chart—SuNe, MoUr, SaPl—that are joined to each other at the midpoint of MoUr.

A FALL

Let's skip forward twenty-seven years and look at another accident chart. In 1944, when Jung was 69, he fell and broke his leg during his daily afternoon walk. Ten days later, emboli caused by the fracture broke loose and blood clots lodged in his lungs and heart. The ensuing heart attack kept him hospitalized for four months. During this time, he was treated with oxygen and camphor, which elicited a near-death experience as well as sensations of being at the "'outermost border,'" somewhere between "a dream and an ecstasy.'" He was disappointed when he recovered and was sent home. "But there have been protests against my leaving (planet Earth) and I must return," he wrote in his autobiography. He became depressed and it took him three weeks to will "himself to live again."

The accident occurred on February 11, 1944; the chart is set for 4.00 p.m. The tridial is shown in Figure 132 on page 300. The solar arc was 66°23. There are five directions, two of which are triggered by transits. We'll start with those:

dMc = Ma = dMe = tNo = tPl = Ve/SaPl = No/Mc = tSa: rising up from difficulty through tenacity and endurance, severity, one-sidedness; a fighter; separation from the astral body; association with elderly or needy persons such as a retirement home (sounds like a hospital), harmful or destructive energy, hampered or destroyed vitality; death, difficulties; powerless in the face of overwhelming force, force majeure (as through Higher Power), operation; separation; suffering violent assaults, injuries.

dNo = Su = Ne = tMo = tSa = tAs = tSuJu/Ve = Ju/Ur = Ur/dUr = dMa/As: negativity or weakness in the presence of others, association with those who are sick or weak, sickness, a hospital stay; profound inner experience, emergence of the unconscious; held back by illness or debility, emotional affliction; illness, poor or blocked vascular circulation, unhealthy blood,

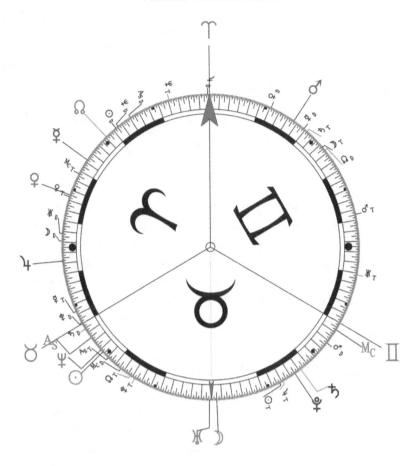

Figure 132. Carl Jung's fall tridial with natal/directions/transits

heart failure; elimination of waking consciousness; growth of subconscious powers, inner vision, illumination and enlightenment; peculiar psychic states, inspiration, spiritual awareness; long journeys; a sudden change of destiny; luck; success in the spiritual sphere; inhibited, lonely and sad people; a tendency to shun others; depression, joylessness, anxiety; peculiar and depressing circumstances; unfortunate circumstances; sharing anxiety with others.

These two axes alone described the aftermath of the fall. We'll look at what else is in play by direction:

dJu = Mo = Ur = dSuNe/Me: luck; success; incoherent and erratic thinking, sudden ideas, inventions, inspirations, talent in science and technology, organization and reform, adjusting to new life circumstances; imagination and fantasy, pictures and ideas emerging from the subconscious, an impressionable mind, receptivity, sympathetic understanding.

dAs = Sa = Pl = dMoUr/Ve: cumbersome and difficult circumstances; separation, mourning, bereavement; an unhappy, sad, or sick woman; separation from or loss of the husband.

dSu = dNe = Sa = Pl = dAs: illness, low energy, a sensitive physique, disease; depression or depressing environment, stunted or under-developed reasoning; oppressive family, emotional suffering, restricted freedom; being placed in complex or difficult circumstances; separation; danger through water, poison or gas; afflictions rising from emotional or physical suffering, highly sensitive, a tragic deception or illusion, blood transfusions; in the company of weak or sick individuals, a hospital stay.

There were a few transiting connections. The pleasant tVe = Ve = Ju/No gave affectionate care. The trMo = SuNe gave deep inner experiences, the emergence of the unconscious. A brutal event is evident in the tPlNo = Ma: misfortune to be placed in somebody else's hand and power.

In summary, the accident is clearly shown in the directions and the transits.

EMMA'S DEATH

The Jungs celebrated their 50th wedding anniversary on Valentine's Day in 1953. The following month, Toni Wolfe, a long-time chain smoker, died in her sleep at age sixty-five. By this time, she had made amends with Emma and was more comfortable in her company than in Jung's. He was too emotional to attend her funeral and Emma went in his place.

But Emma was also not well. She had stomach cancer. Her symptoms first appeared in late 1952, but she ignored them and did not see a doctor for almost a year. By then, she had developed a backache that made walking difficult. In 1954, she had surgery, chemotherapy, and radiation. Her adult children were told she had back trouble. In the summer of 1955, Jung publicly celebrated his eightieth birthday and Emma was well enough to attend. By November, she was bedridden. The cancer had spread to her spine and brain, and her kidneys were failing. She died on November 27, 1955. The chart is set for Zurich at noon. The tridial for Jung is shown in Figure 133.

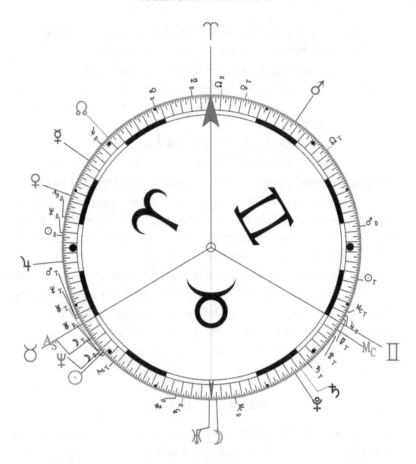

Figure 133. Emma's death tridial with natal/directions/transits

There are two directions, one of which is triggered by transits. For the first:

dMo = dUr = Su = Ne = tNo = tUr = dAs/Mc = SaPl/No: sudden upsets, nervousness, emotional crisis, mourning, sick or weak people, blood relatives; shared suffering; self-torment; shared upsets, sudden conflicts, separation of partners; emotional tension; exhaustion; sudden disappointment; restlessness and agitation around others; ambitious or nervous women; desire for seclusion, uncomfortable or shut-down around others; liberation from great stress at all costs, a violent dispute, sudden separation, bereavement; feeling neglected, feeling misunderstood, lonely; emotional distress from falsehood, deception, fraud, separation, illness; being a widow.

The second direction is separating, but shows the circumstances in the months leading up to Emma's death:

dMa = Ju = dMe/Mc = Ve/As = dVe/SaPl: emotionally inhibited from taking action; regained sobriety; suffering in love; intense thinking, meditating or reflecting; hope for positive outcomes.

There are two active transits on the day:

tPl = Me = Mc = tVe/Ur: highly excitable; sudden thoughts of love; overtaxing one's strength, disturbances of the nervous system.

tSa = SaPl = tUr/No = Ma/tMa: fighting for life; death; excitable in the presence of others, quarreling, difficulty exercising self-control; difficulties shared with others; upsetting experiences shared with others.

In summary, in these directions and transits we can see the specter of death, and the effect of Emma's death on Jung.

JUNG'S DEATH

Jung died six years later. In the last years of his life, he was plagued with worry. Emma had managed the money throughout the marriage and, after she died, Jung was left to deal with the finances. Though Emma had great wealth, she left Jung only that which was required by law. Though far from poor, Jung fretted about money. Afraid he would lose his house, he had an architect draw up designs for apartments he could rent out. He minimized the household help and chastised those who remained for leaving on lights and turning up the heat. He started hiding money. He fell into a depression that lasted five months. He retired to his home in Bollingen (just a few miles down the lake) and began carving stones. He wondered why he had survived and what purpose he had to fulfill before he could die. At eighty-two, he began writing his autobiography. In the spring of 1961, he suffered a number of heart attacks and a stroke that left him unable to speak. He died June 6, 1961, only weeks before his 86th birthday: "a quiet death ... after a long slow sunset and gradually fading light." I set the chart for 8.10 p.m. in Zurich, which was when the transiting Sun was setting. The tridial is shown in Figure 134 on page 304.

Jung's solar arc at his death is 83.32.01. His is a summer birth, with a slow-moving Sun and a solar arc that, at the time of his death, is lagging 2½ degrees behind his age in years. There are three directions, only one of which is triggered by transits:

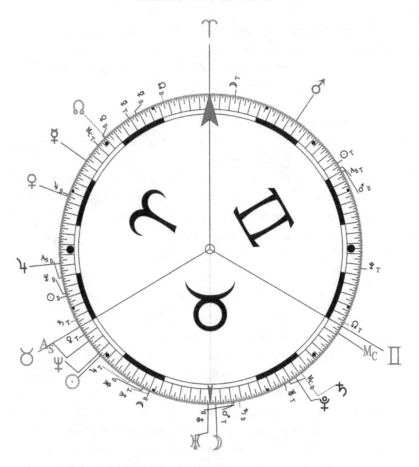

Figure 134. Jung's death tridial with natal/directions/transits

dMc = Sa = Pl = dMe = tUr = Mo/Mc = tSu/Sa: a magician or adept; flight; unafraid of danger, sound decision-making in difficult situations; defective speech; separation, mourning or bereavement; peculiar or strange soul (Tyl: tremendous thrust forward); illness; ambivalence toward life, emotional tension, sudden inhibitions, nervousness; unusual circumstances, crises, seclusion.

dVe = No = Ma/As = Pl/Mc = dJu/No: love relationship; pleasant meetings; attaining one's objective; passionate.

dJu = Ve = Ju/No = dMe/SuNe: gaining quick popularity; joy; friendly and pleasant among others; doctors, travel; great powers of fantasy and increased imagination.

And by transit:

tVe = As = tSu = Mo/Ve: harmonious disposition, graceful; love, devotion; affection toward others, association with women, marriage.

tJu = Ma = tMe/Pl = tSu/Mo = tNo/Mc: successful (profitable) business; public recognition; camaraderie and team spirit, a strong collegial working relationship; love of parties and entertainment, social gatherings in cozy atmosphere; happy communion of souls.

In summary, the presence of the death pair (Ma/Sa) is not active, not natally, not by direction, not by transit. What I find fascinating is the high quality of directions and transits at the end of his life. The atmosphere seems like a party, jovial and happy, and filled with people, perhaps not of this plane. It makes me wonder if these significators are describing his afterlife experience. To be sure, Jung had a remarkable life matched by a remarkable chart.

One reason I went through this number of charts in this detail was to demonstrate how to find the active axes in an event and how to delineate them. If you went through the dials yourself, you may have noticed that you included some planets and midpoints that I did not. When the directions and transits are exact, it's easy to see what is activated. When there is an orb, and multiple planets together, deciding which midpoints and planets to include requires personal judgment, which may differ between individuals. In any case, the repeating themes stand out in stark relief. The main discriminating factor is the use of completed midpoints, natally, by direction, and transit.

 HOMEWORK: Examine significant events in your life using the tridial.

Chapter 20

Working with Clients

If you have a busy practice, running a series of predictive charts throughout the year is time-consuming and impractical. For clients who return yearly for an update, I recommend looking at the directions and associated midpoints at the time of their upcoming birthday on the dial. The outer planet transits, and transiting outer planet midpoint pairs, can be viewed separately on the 45° graphic ephemeris for the year.

I using the transiting pairs as a guide only. The line of a pair in the graph shows their midpoint degree. When the midpoint degree of a transiting pair comes to a natal point, the pair is primed. At this stage, a fast-moving transit connecting with the natal point by aspect will simultaneously trigger the transiting pair and form a completed transiting midpoint. Due to the fast-moving inner transits and angles, these transiting pairs will be activated numerous times during the period their midpoint degree is in orb to a natal planet.

I'll illustrate these points with an example of a client who came for an update near her 68th birthday. Her dial with the birthday directions is shown in Figure 135. There are five directions:

dMa = Ju = dMe = Pl/Mc: successful creativity, a love of work, the joy of living, an active life, pride, a sense of honor; excelling in a profession.

dSa = Ne: illness, diseases of unknown cause or difficult to diagnose

dNo = Pl: new associations or connections.

dVe = Mc = dSu = Ma/Pl: powerless in the face of overwhelming factors, victim of force majeure (Higher Power), surgery; passionate; hard-working, indefatigable in work, work till collapse or complete breakdown, injury, accident, violent measures, shock or upset.

dNe = Me = Mc/MoUr = As/dAs: highly sensitive; excitable, energetic, ambitious goals, determined, prepared to take action; a tendency to meddle or interfere; inclined to illusion and unreality, pursuit of wrong ideas, acting

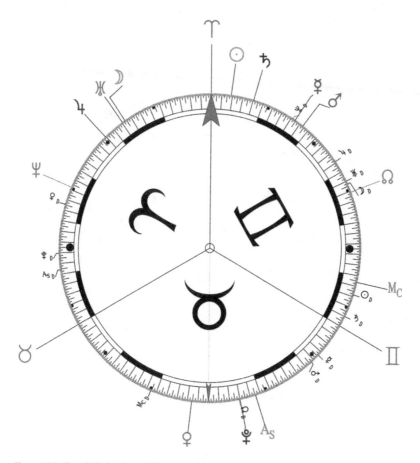

Figure 135. Client bidial with natal/directions

and pretense; prone to deception; following a wrong life path, wrong objectives, uncertainty or insecurity.

The directions are mixed. The 1st, 3rd, and 4th may pertain to her mail-order business. She is a very creative person and does a lot of handicrafts, which she sells online. She had recently been sick, as had her husband, which seems related to the 2nd, 3rd, 4th, and 5th directed axes. She doesn't trust doctors and doesn't heed their advice. Nevertheless, I encouraged her to take it easy, not push herself, visit her doctor, and don't let her husband do too much.

The outer planet transits and the node are shown in the 45° graphic ephemeris in Figure 136. Notice the June solar eclipse on the line of Jupiter,

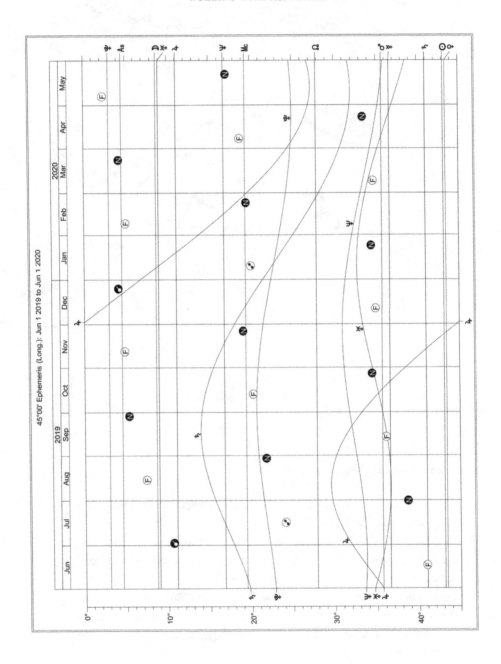

Figure 136. Client graphic ephemeris transits

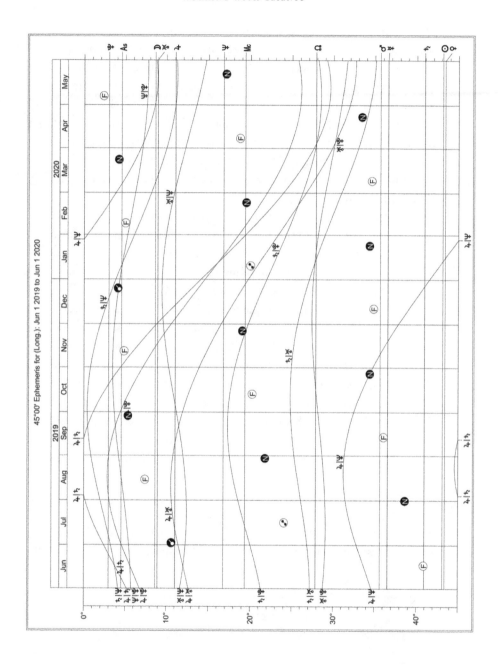

Figure 137. Client graphic ephemeris transiting midpoint pairs

likely corresponding to a profitable and successful time in her business. The winter eclipses hit both her angles, indicative of a significant period that would likely be remembered. Her birthday began with transiting Saturn and the transiting Node near her Neptune, already activated by directed Saturn. At the time, her husband was not feeling well, and she was feeling tired. Transiting Uranus was near the natal Mercury-Mars line, and she didn't have the energy she felt in the past. The nearby transit of Jupiter brought hope that her condition would improve. Near her next birthday, transiting Neptune was approaching the Mercury-Mars line, which could mean a further loss of energy.

The transiting midpoint pairs for the year are shown in Figure 137. We can see the summer solar eclipse attended by tJu/Ur, adding to her own Jupiter, signaling a pleasant time. Some of her children and grandkids came for a long visit. The transiting pair of Jupiter/Neptune coming to her natal Mercury/Mars line indicates idealism and hopeful thinking. In December, the solar eclipse on her Ascendant occurred near transiting Sa/Ne, the sickness pair. The solar eclipse was in opposition to the Descendant, and her husband's condition grew drastically worse. In January, the crossing of tSa/Ur and Ur/Pl on her natal Node indicated major transformation and change. That month her husband declined hospice care. He died on the Full Moon that landed on her Ascendant in February.

Toward her next birthday, as transiting Sa/Ur came to natal Mercury and Mars, along with transiting Uranus and transiting Neptune, there was more disappointment and disillusion—she received a diagnosis that her cancer had returned.

In summary, using directions on the dial, and transiting outer planets and their midpoints in the 45° graphic ephemeris, is a quick and accurate method of assessing the upcoming astrological weather.

 HOMEWORK: Use this method to review a previous year or an upcoming year.

Chapter 21

Ebertin's Method

E
arlier we looked at some of Ebertin's examples given in his texts. The previous example is typical of how Ebertin dealt with prediction. However, we have our differences. I'll go through a few more of his examples to demonstrate his process in detail and point out where and how our methods diverge.

In *Applied Cosmobiology,* page 177, Ebertin examines the dial of a man who won 1000 DM. This was apparently a good win for 1957. Ebertin looked at the dial, solar arcs, and transits of the win (Figure 138 on page 312), and the two months bracketing the win on the transiting 45° graphic ephemeris.

There was no time given for the transits and I used the diurnal time of 5.45 a.m. I am not sure what time Ebertin used, as he did not include the Moon or angles in his tridial. Since Ebertin used the Mean Node, I use it in these examples as well.

In his introduction to this example, Ebertin wrote that lottery winners have Jupiter-Neptune in some combination, which shows "gain through speculation." This winner had the combination in the natal midpoint Ne = Ju/As. Here Neptune is connected to Jupiter through an angle. He did not mention Neptune is also on the lucky Ju/Ur and successful Su/Ju.

The solar arc at the time of the win was 34°28. Ebertin wrote the directed Sun was approaching Jupiter, signaling "a lucky chance is quite possible." The directed Sun was applying in just over ½°.

Jumping to transits, he saw transiting Jupiter approaching the axis, and on the opposite side, transiting Pluto. He interpreted this as indicating that "only some days later did the young man get the most pleasure from the money." He remarked the tMa/Ju = Mc axis was significant, which he defined as "personal success, personal happiness." Another notable midpoint "exact to the minute" is tJu/Ur = Su "with an indication of sudden happiness."

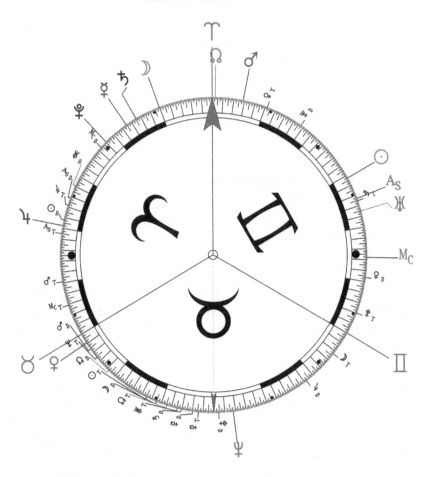

Figure 138. Ebertin's example of a woman's son lotto winner's dial

Note that in these last two midpoints, he used incomplete transiting pairs that are occupied by natal points. It appears that Ebertin used transiting pairs that transiently occupy a natal point. To me, this is a mixing of levels. I call these mixed midpoints and I don't use them.

Additionally, Ebertin remarked that transiting Saturn's connection with the natal Ascendant "does not seem to be the aspect to signify gain." However, in the natal chart, Saturn rules the 5th house of games and speculation, making it relevant to the event—though Ebertin ignored house rulership.

Next, Ebertin turned to the 45° graphic ephemeris (Figure 139 on page 314). There he drew attention to the transiting Jupiter line that was connecting with the transiting Pluto line as an "especially favorable cosmic condition." Given their approach to natal Jupiter, "one may deduce that shortly before this transit over Jupiter and MC of the birth chart, a largish success or advantage may be predicted."

He also noted that transiting Uranus was stationing over natal Mars. Typically, this might be seen as an accident waiting to happen, but Ebertin wrote that for this winner, Mars was lucky because it was at the midpoint of Ju/Mc. Thus, transiting Uranus stationing over this midpoint was fortunate. He concluded, "this example shows that not only the directions and transits are significant, but the midpoints also have to be included."

This is a neat and tidy example, except Ebertin ignored aspects and midpoints that ran counter to his narrative. Here is a comprehensive list of the axes activated this day by diurnal transits and/or directions:

dMc = Pl = dMa/Ne = tMo = Ur/tUr = tSa/No = Su/tSu

dSu = Ju = Ve/Sa = Ne/dNe = dVe = Me/Ve = tAs

dMa = Ve

dSa = Ma = Pl/As = tUr = tMe/No = Su/Me

dPl = MN = Ju/Ur

tMc = tSa = As = Sa/Ne = Me/Ne

This illustrates another difference between our techniques. In many examples given in his books, Ebertin selected axes to delineate. He used no systematic method to determine which natal axes were activated. Instead, he cherry-picked axes that described the event. While this can be done when an event is known, it is not a good strategy in forecasting. It's possible Ebertin was looking at more that was behind the scenes than what he wrote down, but we are left with only what he wrote.

In another example, given in his book *Directions*, page 105, Ebertin examines the dial of a friend, a well-known writer, who had a serious car accident. A few days before the accident, Ebertin told his friend, "You will soon be subjected to potential tension of a severe kind and may come to harm if you do not positively adapt to the pending cosmic tendencies. This period will bring you success in the scientific field; however, it also contains a warning to be extremely cautious."

The bidial is shown in Figure 140 (page 315). The friend was born in Vienna, Austria, on May 2, 1916. Using the angles given in the book, I derived a time of 1.38 p.m. This puts both angles in the degrees used by Ebertin, but the minutes are off. The Moon's placement is the same.

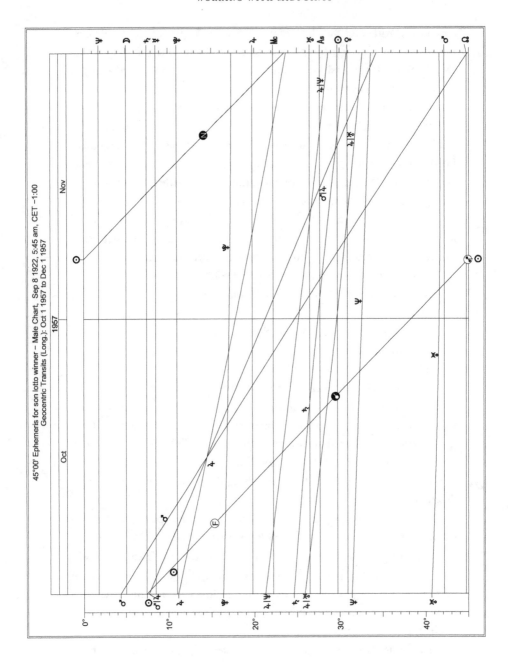

Figure 139. Ebertin's example of woman's son lotto winner's graphic ephemeris

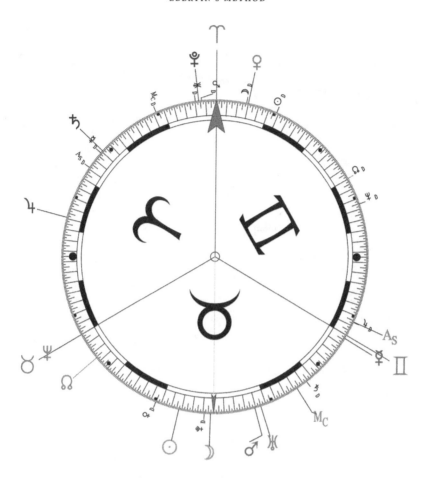

Figure 140. Ebertin's example of friend's car accident bidial of natal/directions

The accident occurred on July 12, 1960, when the friend was forty-four years old and had a solar arc of 42°17. Ebertin notes five active solar arcs:

dMaUr = Pl: which he called a "genuine accident direction."

dSa = Mc: "hindered growth or development and the necessity to struggle against difficulties."

dMe = Sa: "depth of thought, mental work, serious writing."

dMo = Ve = Su and dJu = As: two axes Ebertin lumped together and considered positive. The recuperation period enabled the writer to do a lot of work.

Ebertin did not describe any directed midpoints in this example, although they are present. After noting the directed aspects, he turns to the

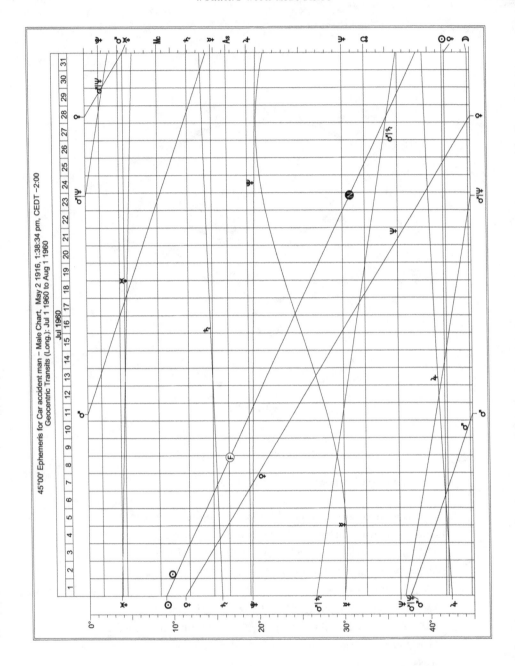

Figure 141. Ebertin's example of friend's car accident graphic ephemeris

graphic ephemeris to look at the transits (Figure 141.) He added the transiting midpoint pairs of Ma/Sa (death) and Ma/Ne (illness, weakness) to his list of transits. He drew attention to transiting Uranus coming to natal Mars and Uranus, as well as transiting Mars coming to natal Pluto. He writes that transiting Saturn coming to natal Mercury "corresponds" to the direction of Mercury coming to natal Saturn. He is reiterating the importance of repeated combinations, which I call a "double-whammy." He further notes tMa/Sa crossing the Neptune line, which indicates a danger to life. Here he is looking at an unoccupied transiting midpoint completed by a natal planet. He takes the aspect tJu = Su as a positive influence. He ends with tMa/Ne = Su as weakness and illness, here again completing a transiting pair with a natal planet.

We can see from this example that Ebertin completed transiting pairs with natal points. Did he do the same with directions? Again, on occasion, he did. In another example, Ebertin examines the solar arcs of a 14-year-old Polish girl (*Directions*, p. 19). The bidial shown is shown in Figure 142 on page 318. There are four directions:

dPl = Me = dMc = Mo/Sa: the natal midpoint of Me = Mo/Sa "indicates contemplation and brooding, whereby a separation or a farewell may have been the cause. Pluto entering the picture would mean the possible triggering of the negative side, and bereavement or a state of depression might be the result."

dNe = Mc = Ur/Ne = Ne/No: Here he notes that the direction of Neptune has passed the Midheaven by about four months. He calls Mc = Ur/Ne = Ne/No: "lack of resistance, grief, dissolution, and emotional suffering. The significant fact here is that the personal point, the Midheaven, is also involved. Neptune's transit over the Midheaven corresponds to a period of insecurity, of personal disappointment, or even suffering and pain."

dVe = Ur = dSu: he writes this could be a first love, if not for the other directions.

dUr = dAs = Su/Sa: he considers the complex points to "faulty development due to illness or emotional suffering, and that separation plays a significant role."

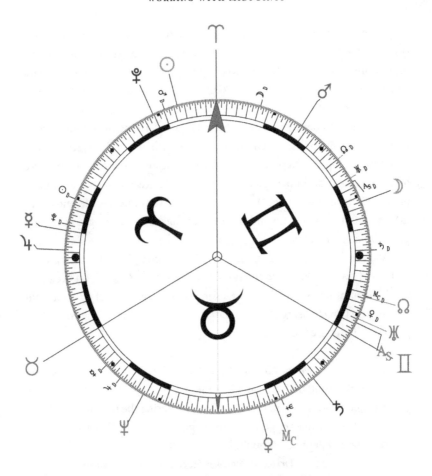

Figure 142. Ebertin's example of a 14-year-old Polish girl bidial of natal/directions

Note that in this last direction, he is using an incomplete pair. This is the example mentioned earlier in the text where he urged caution in using unoccupied natal pairs (here, Su/Sa). He wrote that he used them because they were supported by other factors. What happened to the girl at this time? Four months before her birthday, her father died.

Let's take one last example from Ebertin and examine the solar arcs at the time of President John F. Kennedy's marriage, described in *Directions* a few pages later (p.35). JFK got married on September 12, 1953. The solar arcs at this time are shown on the bidial in Figure 143. While the birth time used by Ebertin (stated in Astro Databank as 3.00 p.m.; the time shown in *Directions* corresponds to 3.04 p.m., which I use here).

At the time of the marriage, the solar arc is 34°40. There are three directions:

dSu = No, dVeMo = As, and dNe = Su.

For the axis involving the first direction Ebertin gives: dSu = No = Pl/As = Su/Ma = dAs/Mc, which means "spiritual or physical relationship... entering into a fateful relationship ... the husband, maintaining fellowship, desire for achievement through joint effort ... (presidential campaigning done by both), marital connection ... coming together, establishing contact."

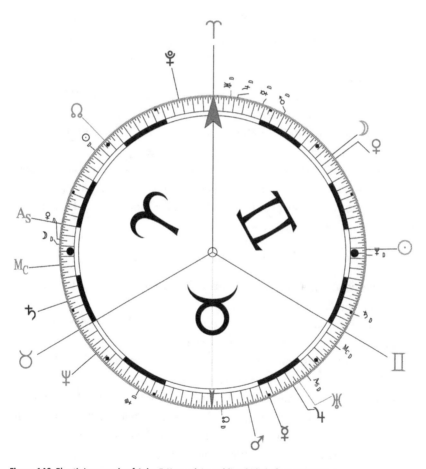

Figure 143. Ebertin's example of John F. Kennedy's wedding bidial of natal/directions

319

He combines the second and third directions, noting that while directed Moon and Venus had passed the Ascendant, they are approaching the natal Sun and directed Neptune on the far side of the axis. The combination gives dVe = dMo = As = Su = dNe, which he defines as affectionate behavior, relationship with a woman, expression of love, conjugal love, love going astray, and renunciation. He thought the main direction was dNe = Su, which denoted a sick man, which Kennedy was at the time of his marriage and on up to his death.

So far, we are using the same technique. But Ebertin goes further, branching out, adding axes with unoccupied midpoints. First, he finds select directions he combines with natal pairs:

dMc = Su/Ju = Su/Ve = Pl/Mc (ignoring dMa/Pl and Sa/Pl)

dMe = dMa/Ju = dMa/Ur = Mo/Pl = Su/No = Sa/Ur = Ju/Sa = Ur/Mc.

To these he adds three more axes obtained by combining a directed pair completed by a natal point:

As = dMa/No (omitting = JuUr/MoVe = Ma/dMa = dMe/Ma)

Mc = dSu/Pl = dMa/As (omitting dMe/As = Ju/dJu)

Ju = Ur = dNo/Mc = dMe/Ve = dMo/Me (omitting dNe/Pl)

Again, he is picking pairs that support the event he is investigating. This is typical. Throughout his books, Ebertin mentions there are too many midpoints to list and delineate. He is afraid of boring the reader and for this reason, states that he only looks at the main configurations. He examines only those midpoints he considers most relevant.

To summarize Ebertin's method

In the natal chart, he only used completed midpoints. To do otherwise would be meaningless.

In directions, he advised using incomplete midpoints with caution. At times he included them, other times he did not.

With transits, Ebertin's preferred method was to use the 45° graphic ephemeris. This shows transits to the natal chart over time and is not geared to looking at either completed transiting midpoints or transiting midpoint pairs. For the latter, Ebertin went looking for them on the dial, specifically on the axes he was investigating. At times he added select pairs to the graphic ephemeris. He used transiting pairs completed by a natal planet, as well as a transit completing a natal pair.

He never examined all active axes in a dial. If he knew the nature of an event, he went looking for the pairs that described it.

As I pondered Ebertin's methodology during the writing of this book, I often came back to the last page of the COSI, to the last paragraph of the last addendum, and the last sentence (Note 95) where he wrote: "The midpoint As/Mc should always be examined as this frequently has a bearing on the whole personality and because direction over this point may result in a change of life and circumstances." What did he mean by this? We should look at the degree of the natal midpoint of the As/Mc and watch directions to this degree. Even if this degree is unoccupied? Ebertin doesn't say. I do know that examining As/Mc is a far cry from his warning to use an unoccupied midpoint with care. It is not a far cry from Uranian astrology. In fact, any Uranian astrologer would find the As/Mc midpoint pair extremely significant. And this makes me wonder if Ebertin didn't circle back in his later years and return to using some Uranian techniques. In the next chapter we'll look at the similarities and differences between Cosmobiology and Uranian astrology.

 HOMEWORK: Find an important event in your life and look at the incomplete transits and directions on the dial that are completed by a point in another chart (e.g., tSu/Mo = nSa). Note especially the directions of and to As/Mc and Su/Mo. Are these midpoint pairs active?

Chapter 22

Uranian Astrology

E bertin began his foray into midpoints as a student of Alfred Witte (March 2, 1878–August 4, 1941, Germany), studying Uranian astrology. Ebertin eventually abandoned it because he thought the TNPs (trans-Neptunian planets) were unnecessary, and he didn't like to work with houses because he thought house cusps were ambiguous. So, he discarded house symbolism and the traditionally important concept of house rulership. He kept the dial, 8th harmonic aspects, and midpoints.

Cosmobiology and Uranian astrology both use midpoints. How each defines midpoints is largely interchangeable. To each school, the planets and points mean the same thing. However, there are important differences.

The Uranian system deals with axes of symmetry. Uranians recognize two types of axes, type 1 and type 2. Type 1 resembles the axes we have been using throughout this book where there is a focal planet on an axis, configured with one or more midpoint pairs. A type 2 axis has no focal point planet and comprises at least two midpoint pairs—it is an axis of symmetry. For a type 2 axis to be active, at least one planet on the axis has to be a personal point. Uranians use six personal points: Su, Mo, As, Mc, No, and the AP (Aries Point).

The ancient Arabic Part, the Part of Fortune (PoF), is an axis of symmetry. As Michael Harding and Charles Harvey write on page 9 of their book, *Working With Astrology*, "We can equally consider Fortuna to mark the precise zodiacal position which brings the Sun, Moon, and Ascendant into an exact symmetrical relationship with each other." The formula for the Part is: As + Mo —Su = PoF. Algebraically, this rearranges to As/Mo = Su/PoF. In other words, these four points share a single axis. The axis for Jung (Figure 144) has no focal point. Mars is nearby, but at too wide of orb to consider. Therefore, it is a type 2 axis. The axis marks the midpoint degrees of Mo/As, Su/PoF, Ur/Ne, Ju/SaPl, and Ve/Mc. For Uranian astrologers, this

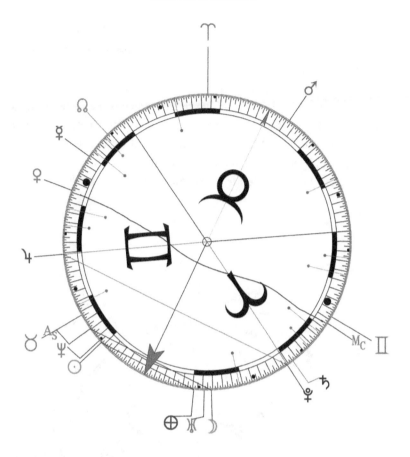

Figure 144. Common Axis of Jung's As/Mo = Su/PofF

would be a primary axis to watch as it combines four of the six personal points.

AXIS ACTIVATION

In the Uranian system, in a type 1 axis, any transit or direction coming to the focal point triggers everything on the axis. However, there are additional ways to activate a type 1 axis that does not involve the focal point, but rather the axis itself. This occurs if a transit or direction forms a midpoint pair on the axis (t/t or d/d), or a transit or direction combines with a natal point (t/n or d/n) to form a midpoint pair on the axis, or a transit combines with a direction (t/d) to form a midpoint pair on the axis. In the Uranian

323

system, mixing levels of midpoints across charts is fine. These types of mid-points I call mixed-level midpoints to reflect midpoint pairs that are formed by mixing levels of charts.

Let's see how the Uranian system (minus the TNPs) would handle a single axis on the tridial shown in Figure 145, which is the event of Jung's break-up with Freud. If we look at the Mc axis, it is activated by a direction of Jupiter and transiting Venus. In our method, if we use only occupied midpoints completed in one level, we have on the axis:

dJu = Mc = tVe = dSuNe/Me = dMa/Sa = tMe/Ur = tMa/Ur

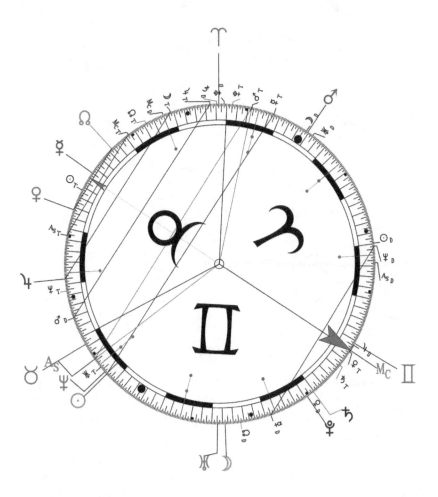

Figure 145. Jung's Type 1 Mc axis in dial

324

To this, Uranians would *add* the unoccupied pairs and midpoints formed across levels that align with the Mc axis, giving, in addition, to the above:

= nSu/tMe = nNe/tMe = nAs/tMa = dMa/tJu = nJu/tMo = tNe/dMc

Furthermore, the Uranian system adds all combinations formed with the eight TNPs, and the Aries Point. This would generate a complex axis that would be unreasonably long for delineating as a whole. In this case, only the most important midpoints would be interpreted.

How is a type 2 axis activated? Like type 1, a type 2 axis can be stimulated by a transit or solar arc direction coming to the unoccupied focal

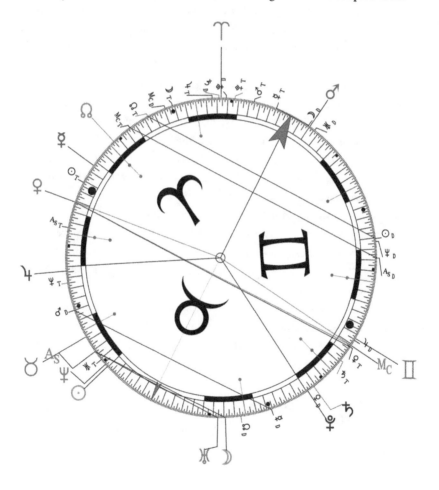

Figure 146. Jung's Type 2 axis in dial with axis at Ve/Mc

point of the axis. A type 2 is also activated by transient midpoints pairs aligning on the axis as outlined above. The pairs could be in the form of a transit or direction combining with a natal planet (n/t, n/d), a transiting pair (t/t), a directed pair (d/d), or a transiting/directed (d/t) pair.

To find a type 2 axis in the Nova software, select two points and find their midpoint and see if there is another pair on the same axis. Jung's natal Ve/Mc axis shown in Figure 146 is a type 2 axis. There is no planet at either end of the pointer, but As/MoUr is on the axis, giving an axis of symmetry. There are three personal points on the axis, which highlight its importance. At the time of the breakup, another personal point, the directed Sun, had come to the axis forming a pair with another personal point, the transiting Node (dSu/tNo). In addition, dNe/tNo and dMo/tMe activate the axis. The nUr/tUr is also on the axis. In total we have: Ve/Mc = As/MoUr = dMe/Ma = Ve/dJu = tAs /tVe = tAs/nMc = tNo/dSu = tAs/dJu = tNo/dNe = dMo/tMe. Presumably, adding the TNPs would provide further information about the ending of a significant relationship.

In these Uranian examples, we can see shades of Ebertin's technique. However, he never used type 2 axes (he did use type 2 in transits). In the natal chart, he stuck to type 1. In using solar arcs, he looked at a direction activating a natal planet by hard aspect. This is analogous to the direction coming to an axis at the focal planet. He never looked at mixed-level pairs on the axis formed by a natal/directed combination. The same for transits. When he looked for transiting midpoints on the dial, these were type 1 coming to the axis of a natal planet. He never mixed midpoint pairs across levels of charts. They were of the form of a transit/transit pair and occasionally a directed/direct pair.

In sum, Ebertin appears to have employed a restricted portion of Uranian technique, focusing on type 1 axes and excluding type 2 axes. To recap: the only difference between the two is that a type 1 axis has a planet at the focal point, and a type 2 does not.

 HOMEWORK: Find a type 2 axis in your natal dial. Was it active during a significant event in your life by direction or transit?

Chapter 23

Occupied vs Unoccupied Midpoints

As we near the end of this text, it brings me back to the beginning of my study, which began with an observation of the activation of my natal Sun/Moon and Mars/Saturn axis by the transiting Sun when my dog died. In my chart though, this is a type 2 axis, and while it is a completed picture in Uranian astrology, these are unoccupied midpoints.

For years I used unoccupied midpoints. Many astrologers do. It was only in writing this book that I saw how many of them there were that needed to be typed out and delineated. I began to look for a method to narrow down the number. Using only completed midpoints was a way to accomplish this.

I wrote in the first chapter that midpoints are written in the form X = Y/Z, where X is the midpoint of Y/Z. Regardless of whether or not there is a planet or angle at X, it remains a degree of longitude and therefore is the midpoint of the pair Y/Z. The seminal question is whether X is occupied by a planet at, or in hard aspect to, that degree. In my view, this ambiguity has created confusion that persists to this day. Every pair of planets has a midpoint. What matters is: Is that degree occupied?

I consider an unoccupied pair to be similar to this analogy: Everyone has a Sun and Jupiter in their chart. The important consideration becomes whether or not the two are connected by aspect. Similarly, everyone has a Su/Ju midpoint in their chart. Here, the important thing is whether or not the midpoint is occupied. In prediction, the natal promise unfolds over time. Major events occur with the activation of natal aspects and configurations. If something is not there to begin with, a transient formation won't be expressed as a significant event.

We know that aspects work across charts. If transiting Pluto makes a conjunction to our Moon, we feel it. However, Pluto will simultaneously trigger any of the Moon's midpoints, as it connects with the Moon. It is not transiting Pluto activating the pairs per se; it is transiting Pluto activating the entire complex. While we might interpret Pl = n/n, we recognize this is because Mo = n/n and tPl = Mo.

If the rule is that midpoint pairs can't be formed across charts, is it possible to form them between charts using a focal point from a different chart? The Uranians say yes. Ebertin says yes, if there is other supporting evidence. I say—for reliability—the midpoints should be completed within a single chart. This vastly narrows the range of midpoints obtained from three charts in a triwheel. Those that are formed, matter.

What about a directed planet or transit coming to the unoccupied midpoint of a natal aspect? For example, Jung has Jupiter trine Saturn in his chart. Their unoccupied midpoint is at 24° Sagittarius, sextile to them both. Mars is nearby but beyond orb. In the dial, the axis has Ju/SaPl, a combination that means the inclination to sacrifice oneself for others, religious and social fanaticism, and difficulties caused by illness. Was this midpoint occupied at the time of Jung's break up with Freud? The separation came from the publication of Jung's book on mythology and spiritual awareness. The estrangement gave Jung a near nervous breakdown. The answer is no. There was no direction or transit at or near this unoccupied natal midpoint. Nor was the directed aspect in contact with a natal point or a transit. To me, the chart is saying loud and clear, ignore this and look elsewhere.

What about the important Su/Mo and As/Mc axes? For Jung, the midpoint degree of Su/Mo is 24° Gemini. It is an unoccupied midpoint (see Figure 144 on page 323). At the time of his breakup with Freud, it was not triggered by a direction or a major transit. What about As/Mc? Natally, Jung has this completed by the Moon and Uranus, such that Mo = Ur = As/Mc. At the time of their breakup, directed Saturn and directed Pluto had come to the axis, and transiting Jupiter was separating from the axis, quite descriptive of the traumatic event. Here we can see the activation of an important occupied natal midpoint, and the inactivity of an unoccupied, but relevant natal pair.

Ebertin was not alone in looking at incomplete midpoints. Other astrologers also do this. Noel Tyl used them in directions, and Michael Harding and Charles Harvey used them in transits. Michael Munkasey included incomplete midpoints in his algorithm to rank natal pairs in Solar Fire.

Using incomplete midpoints in transits raises the subject of what to do when a pair such as Ju/Sa is completed by a planet that is contained in the pair, such as tSa = Ju/Sa. Tyl said these had to be ignored, while Harding and Harvey said they should be included. Ebertin's view evolved. He initially thought they should be ignored, and later said they were important. However, this question is moot if we retain the integrity of midpoints, and never mix levels. We interpret the completed midpoints individually.

It appears many current astrologers use midpoint pairs, anticipating an accident with Ma/Ur or sickness with Sa/Ne. Are these incomplete midpoint pairs significant? They are to Uranian astrologers. Are they to Cosmobiologists? I don't know. Just because I don't consider them in this text, doesn't make them irrelevant.

For anyone with the natal As/Mc or Su/Mo pair completed, these will be significant midpoints in the chart. If these pairs are not completed, maybe not so much. You can verify this for yourself. If they are not occupied in your chart, study major events in your life and see if these pairs are active. In my experience, I have found them to be active during insignificant times, and inactive at significant times. In my view, this renders them unusable. Inconsistency is the death knell of accurate predictive astrology.

Given Ebertin's background in the Uranian system, I suspect that when he was researching events and noticed relevant midpoint pairs, he noted them, regardless of whether they were occupied or not. After all, in the Uranian system, they would be noted. Just because they are not typically used in Cosmobiology, doesn't invalidate them. Ebertin didn't use sextiles and trines, but that doesn't mean they don't work.

Ebertin also sought specific midpoint pairs that were pertinent to his inquiry. This cherry-picking is a technique my Uranian teacher used—figure out the midpoint pair that symbolizes what you're looking for and go straight to it. If you're looking for the birth of a baby, go to the Ve/Ur or Ma/Ur pair and see what is activating it and when. If you don't find anything, look at dVe/Ur or dMa/Ur. If a baby is coming in the near future, one of these will be active.

Ebertin's favorite method of assessing transits was using the 45° graphic ephemeris. However, this is not suited to showing either midpoints or midpoint pairs. At times he drew in relevant midpoint pair lines, but most of the time he looked to see when an outer transit was crossing a natal point (with its midpoints) that was simultaneously activated by a direction (with its midpoints). He often looked at transiting pairs. It's important to keep in mind that a transiting midpoint pair will be completed by the transiting Midheaven and transiting Ascendant multiple times a day. It may be for this reason that on the dial, Ebertin used transiting pairs (i.e., unoccupied transiting midpoints). This is not the case with directions, which may explain why he used directed pairs with caution.

In summary, cosmobiologists and Uranian astrologers use the same tool (90° dial) in different ways to get a similar result. I don't know if using unoccupied natal midpoints with directions and transits is a valid Cosmobiology technique, but it is in Uranian astrology. I don't know Ebertin's opinion on the matter as I find examples of both in his work. I do know that it's easier as well as accurate to look only at completed midpoints. We can ignore the unoccupied pairs without sacrificing accuracy. Still, unoccupied pairs work in forecasting. All I can say is, note them if you see them, and don't worry if you don't. The information arising from occupied midpoints is sufficient to grasp the nature of an event.

 HOMEWORK: Look at an event in your life using only completed midpoints. Then, look at the same event using incomplete natal, directed, and transiting pairs. Does the latter add information lacking in the former? Pick another event and look at it through the lens of incomplete midpoints. How clear is the picture?

Conclusion

I f you have read this far, then you will appreciate the wealth of information that midpoints add to a chart. I hope I have addressed the question asked at the onset—Why use midpoints?—and provided a satisfactory answer. Midpoints modify a planet's expression in unexpected ways. In my view, there is no other branch of astrology that furthers an understanding of the natal chart or casts a clearer light on the future than that of midpoints.

I am reticent to call this a textbook of Cosmobiology because I do not know exactly what Cosmobiology is. I have never seen a definition for it. At one time I thought it was Uranian, absent the TNPs, but it is definitely not that. Does Cosmobiology use type 1 axes without mixing midpoint pairs across chart levels? Does it allow the use of unoccupied midpoints in transits and directions that are completed by an outside chart? If so, are these exceptions or standard practice? I don't know.

Thus, I consider this text a study on completed midpoints. In the method outlined here, I use occupied midpoints only—those that are formed within a single chart. Using completed midpoints negates the need to cherry-pick. The directions and transits point to what is important at any given moment. Aspects between charts operate as usual. A direction or transit aspecting a natal planet triggers the natal planet's axis in its entirety. The midpoints associated with the directions, the transits, and the natal planet all add energy to the event. While an axis may contain many midpoints, I interpret each midpoint individually, as opposed to considering the entire axis. In this manner, the variants contained in any three-planet combination are easy to see. This is not possible when taking an axis as a whole. The use of variants expands the range of midpoint possibilities. If the fortunate Ju/Ur is unoccupied, it may appear in a variant, such as Ju = Ur/Pl or Ur = Ve/Ju.

Midpoints are also ideal for rectification and synastry. However, because these are not my area of expertise, I did not include these topics in this text. However, for those interested in these areas, midpoints add pertinent and precise information to charts under examination.

In closing, this was a difficult subject to study, and a difficult subject to write about. It is not a difficult technique to use. For years I was overwhelmed by the amount of information obtained from delineating incomplete midpoints across three different charts. These numbered in the hundreds. Every meaning and potential seemed to be in evidence. I typed out pages and pages of delineations hoping to find repeated themes. In the end, I felt I was condensing random parts of the COSI with no unified underlying story. I wanted to find a way to identify what was most important. Using only completed midpoints was the answer to the problem.

It is my opinion, that over many decades, Ebertin's simplified use of midpoints became conflated with Uranian techniques. The impact of the merging of the two systems on midpoint theory has led to unnecessary complications. Keeping in mind that if only what is promised in the natal chart can be expressed in life, only completed midpoints in the natal chart are active. For this reason, I found using midpoint pairs alone to be a distraction that gave inaccurate results.

When I was stuck, as I often was in the six years it took to research and write this book, I went back to Ebertin and reread his books. I noted what he said, and followed what he did. At times, these were not the same. He had theoretical information and practical application. In the end, I did my own research, and I suggest you do yours. When you look at events in your own life, you come to understand the nuances of meaning offered by the midpoints, and what your own planetary placements mean. You can determine for yourself what works and what doesn't. Astrology is an empirical science. It can be studied objectively. What I have written in this book, works. I hope that as more people use midpoints and publish their results, we will advance and grow our understanding of this amazing and powerful technique.

Midpoints are invaluable. They are also invisible. They fill a vast and empty space in the chart with hidden information that is not readily apparent. Making the unseen visible is an act of magic that sheds light on the unknown. The activation of midpoints hidden in a chart helps explain the machinations underlying observable astrology. At times, midpoints reveal what traditional astrology fails to see. While midpoints don't name an event specifically, they reveal its circumstance, effect, and emotional response. Midpoints tell a story. Let them speak and they add a powerful narrative to a planetary plot line.

 HOMEWORK: Work with midpoints.

APPENDICES

1: Planetary Keywords

Sun: me, basic energy, vitality, health, leadership, self-expression, what makes you shine, leadership, men, husband, father, hero of the journey, individual personal achievement, ego, will power, assertive power, identity, illuminating

Moon: emotional responses, nurturing, caring, care-taking, desire for comfort, basic and personal needs, motherliness, mother, women, domesticity, memory, 'the people' intuition, the past, the public, habits, reigning need

Node: union with, manifestation of, alliance with, associations with others, connections, event, expression of, emotional connection with, close connection with people, things, objectives, public appeal, relationships and connections with the public, energy can flow in or out of your life

Mc (Midheaven): future, time, plans, where you're going, what you are driven to do, aims, goals, the heights you aspire to, consciousness, career, how you establish yourself outwardly, now, at this time, the minute, your life's direction, what you want to be, what you ambitiously are called to realize, reputation, self-esteem, yourself in the world, public image, answers: what you do for a living, status in the world, life objectives

As (Ascendant): place, your environment, how you respond to environment/stimuli, others in your environment, the vehicle in which you drive (your body), at this particular place, personality, partner

Mercury: the mind, communication, travel short term, flight, intellect, critical analysis, writing ability, talking, thinking

Venus: what and how you love, what you attract, relationships, what you value, sense of art and beauty, physical attraction, positive outlook, happiness, friendship, grace, peace, harmony, balance, relationship needs, devotion, tenderness, affection, girls, women

Mars: ability to assert yourself, drive, aggression, anger, what you pursue, work, energy of action, will power, battle, fighting, determination, ruthless, brutal, military, athletic, strife, attack, brave, cowardly, physical energy, sports

Jupiter: success, expansion, philosophy, religion, royalty, pomp, excess and excessive, optimism, law, ownership, possession, justice, morality, wealth, craving pleasure, business, science, improvement, reach out and extend influence, unlimited, boundless, royal planet of power and authority, situational improvement

Saturn: separation, grounding, realism, down to earth, sadness, mourning, burden, difficulty, social conscience and responsibility, professional, limitations, losses, authority, inhibition, concentration, serious, frugality, melancholy, perseverance, structure, reality, restriction, challenges, focus of ambition, building infrastructure, sadness, authenticity, necessary controls, caution, reserve, rules, standards, task-master, fear of failure, social-standing, self-questioning, doubt, conservative, separate or stabilize, seriousness, setbacks, blockages, mastery, discipline, control, glues things together and binds them, obstacles, oppression, negates, stresses duty,

Uranus: awakening, freeing, releasing, eruption of energy, true-and-personal, revolution, peculiarity, independent, easily excited, sense of rhythm, perceptive foresight, impulsive, innovative, sky, future or forward looking, invisible order, erratic, upsets, unexpected, sudden intervention, sudden, unreservedly, radical thoughts, breaks with tradition, mind of god, eruptions from the unconscious, the great idea, individualism, overturning status quo, tension

Neptune: risk of confusion, deception, dissolving, transcending, spiritual, healing, musical, enlightening, receptive, fantasy, imagination, sensitive, compassionate, collective unconscious, making sacrifices, alcoholism, mysticism, symbology, unknown, ocean, invisible realm behind the scene, illusion, inspirational, glamor, mythic, bewildering, fame, disappointment, visualization, foreign places, photography, film, oceans, fish, hopes dashed, dissolving, nebulous, limitless, confusing, inner vision and inspiration, vague, deceit, mystique, cheat, devious, flight, foreign things

Pluto: force majeure, invisible forces, death and transformation, evolution, growth and change, profound, powerful, extremely emotional, disturbing emotions, unconscious forces, control issues, fated events, influencing the masses, inclination to incite, agitate, personal unconscious, the underworld, regeneration, emotional angst, grand change, outer force, catastrophes, experiences of death and rebirth, catharsis, sweeping change, covert, subversion, private, hidden, DNA, power and force, fanatic, brings passion, possessiveness and jealousy

2: Special Midpoints

Su/Mo: heart and mind, body, and soul

As/Mc: in this time and place

Su/Ju: success

Me/Ve: writer's midpoint

Me/Ur: astrology midpoint

Ma/Sa: death

Ma/Ur: accident

Ma/Ne: infection, weakness, alcoholism

Ju/Ur: luck, "thank the lord"

Ju/Ne: speculation

Ju/Pl: millionaire's midpoint

Sa/Ne: sickness, applied spiritual reality

Sa/Pl: alarming, tenacity, threat of loss, hard, hard, work

Ur/Ne: ends things, bad for health, genius on the edge, loss, awakened spirituality

Ur/Pl: upheaval, reversal, change

Ne/Pl: miracles, occult

Here are the remaining angle-angle midpoints and their meanings:

No/As: personal relationships, good contacts with others; also estrangement, separation, to which I would add: a connection to the place.

No/Mc: a group of people who share same objectives, difficulty in teamwork; to which I would add: the manifestation of career goals.

3: Natal Worksheet

Name_____

Planet	Sign	House	Dignity	Aspects	Midpoints
☉					
☽					
☿					
♀					
♂					
♃					
♄					
♅					
♆					
♇					
☊					
Asc					
Mc					

Standout Features

4: Life Events Table

Year	Age	SA	Event
	0		
	1		
	2		
	3		
	4		
	5		
	6		
	7		
	8		
	9		
	10		
	11		
	12		
	13		
	14		
	15		
	16		
	17		
	18		
	19		
	20		
	21		
	22		
	23		
	24		
	25		
	26		
	27		
	28		
	29		
	30		

	31		
	32		
	33		
	34		
	35		
	36		
	37		
	38		
	39		
	40		
	41		
	42		
	43		
	44		
	45		
	46		
	47		
	48		
	49		
	50		
	51		
	52		
	53		
	54		
	55		
	56		
	57		
	58		
	59		
	60		
	61		
	62		

	63		
	64		
	65		
	66		
	67		
	68		
	69		
	70		
	71		
	72		
	73		
	74		
	75		
	76		
	77		
	78		
	79		
	80		
	81		
	82		
	83		
	84		
	85		
	86		
	87		
	88		
	89		
	90		

5: Linear Diagram

0	0 15											0
1	1 16											1
2	2 17											2
3	3 18											3
4	4 19											4
5	5 20											5
6	6 21											6
7	7 22											7
8	8 23											8
9	9 24											9
10	10 25											10
11	11 26											11
12	12 27											12
13	13 28											13
14	14 29											14
15	15 30 0											15
16	16 1											16
17	17 2											17
18	18 3											18
19	19 4											19
20	20 5											20
21	21 6											21
22	22 7											22
23	23 8											23
24	24 9											24
25	25 10											25
26	26 11											26
27	27 12											27
28	28 13											28
29	29 14											29
30	30 0 15											30
31	1 16											31
32	2 17											32
33	3 18											33
34	4 19											34
35	5 20											35
36	6 21											36
37	7 22											37
38	8 23											38
39	9 24											39
40	10 25											40
41	11 26											41
42	12 27											42
43	13 28											43
44	14 29											44

6: Predictive Worksheet

Name	Date	Event

Event chart:

As_____Mc_____Mc_____ Past Eclipses_____

Angular planets   Midpoints

Closest aspects

Special features

BiWh: Natal H rising   Special features

Angular planets

Synastry   Declination

Notes

Dial SA	Tr-n	Tr-d-n

Active Axes

Resources

Software:

Solar Fire: available from Astrolabe. *https://alabe.com/solarfireV9.html*
This is the daily astrological program I use.

NovaChart Wheel: available from Astrolabe. *https://alabe.com/novacw.html*
A program designed for Uranian and Cosmobiology I use for the dial.

PlanetDance: This free program has a midpoint option.
Available for download from *https://jcremers.com/*

AstrologicPC: Available from Witte-Verlag.
https://witte-verlag.com/produkte/astrologicpc-english.html
Michael Feist has developed Uranian software that contains a dictionary of midpoints

Websites

www.Astro.com
An invaluable online resource that provides charts and midpoints, as well as the birth data of numerous famous people.

https://uranianastrologybooks.com
For dials: These can be purchased through Penny Bertucelli at this site.

Bibliography and Recommended Reading

The books listed below can be purchased wherever books are sold. Some are rare and hard to find and may be found at *UranianAstrologyBooks.com* and through used book sites.

The Combination of Stellar Influences, Reinhold Ebertin, 1st edition, 1940
Applied Cosmobiology, Reinhold Ebertin, 4th edition, 1972
The Annual Diagram, Reinhold Ebertin, 1973
Directions, Reinhold Ebertin, 1976

Man of the Universe, Reinhold Ebertin, 1973

Transits, Reinhold Ebertin, 1971

Rapid and Reliable Analysis, Reinhold Ebertin 1990

Cosmobiology II, The Life Blueprint, Jane Reynolds,1978

Midpoint Interpretation Simplified, Karen Ober Savalan, 1978

Working with Astrology, Michael Harding and Charles Harvey, 1990

Dial Detective, Maria Kay Simms, 2nd Edition, 2001

Fundamentals of Cosmobiology, Eleonora Kimmel, 1979

Patterns of Destiny, Eleonora Kimmel, 1985

Altered and Unfinished Lives, Eleonora Kimmel, 2006

Solar Arc Directions, Carole DeMott Devine, 2000

Solar Arcs, Noel Tyl, 2001: (both Tyl books have a midpoint dictionary in the appendix)

Prediction in Astrology, Noel Tyl, 1991

Cosmobiology: A Modern Approach to Astrology, Doris E. Greaves, date unknown

Cosmobiology Beyond 2000, Doris Greaves, 1999

The Concept Dictionary, Michael Munkasey, 1991

Midpoints, Unleashing the Power of the Planets, Michael Munkasey, 1991

Can Assassinations Be Prevented: E. Ebertin, translated by J. Zahrt, 2017

Midpoints, Don McBroom, 2007

The Language of Uranian Astrology, Roger A. Jacobson, 1975

Rules For Planetary Pictures, Alfred Witte, 1973

Phoenix Workshop, Uranian Astrology Manual, Penelope Bertucelli, 1995

The Mountain Astrologer, "Introducing Uranian and Cosmobiology," #123, Oct/Nov 2005

NCGR Journal, Winter 1991/1992, Uranian/Cosmobiology issue

Predictive Astrology: The Eagle and the Lark, Bernadette Brady, 1999. Uses midpoints in delineating Saros Series Solar Eclipses

When Worlds Collide: Another Look at the Lunar Nodes, Kathy Allan, 2012

Horoscope Symbols, Rob Hand, 1981, pp.149–165

Chart Data

Example 1 Natal Chart: February 8, 1896 NS, 8.30 a.m. LMT, Jersey City, NJ, USA

Example 2 Natal Chart: October 7, 1900, NS, 3.30 p.m. CET, Munich, Germany

Example 3 Natal Chart: September, 21, 1947, 1.30 a.m. EDT, Portland, Maine, USA

Evangeline Adams Natal Chart: February 8, 1896 NS, 8.30 a.m. LMT, Jersey City, NJ, USA

Evangeline Adams Move: March 16, 1899 NS, 8.00 p.m. EST, New York, NY, USA

Evangeline Adams Trial: December 11, 1914, 8.30 a.m. EST, Jersey City, NJ, USA

Stephen King Natal Chart: September, 21, 1947, 1.30 am. EDT, Portland, Maine, USA

Stephen King, publication of *Carrie*: April 5, 1974, 12.00 p.m. EDT, Portland, Maine, USA

Stephen King Quits Drinking: September 22, 1987, 1.30 a.m. EDT, Portland, Maine, USA

Stephen King King Accident, left home: June 19, 1999, 4.00 p.m. EDT, Bangor Maine, USA

Stephen King King Accident, hit: June 19, 1999, 4.30 p.m. EDT, Bangor, Maine, USA

Brigette Bardot Natal Chart: September 28, 1934, 1.15 p.m. BST, Paris, France

Brigette Bardot Crisis: September 29, 1960, 1.15 p.m. CET, Paris, France

Stephen King Solar Return: September 20, 1998, 9.37.54 a.m. EDT, Portland, Maine

Stephen King Lunar Eclipse: January 31, 1999, 11.06 a.m. EST, Bangor, Maine

Stephen King Aries Ingress 1999: March 20, 1999, 8.45.49 p.m. EST, Bangor, Maine

Stephen King Lunar Return: May 30, 1999, 6.25.14 p.m. EDT, Portland, Maine

Stephen King New Moon: June 13, 1999, 3.02.51 p.m. EDT, Bangor, Maine

Diana, Princess of Wales, Natal Chary: July 1, 1961, 7.45 p.m. BST, Sandringham, England

Diana, Princess of Wales, Marriage: July 29, 1981, 11.17 a.m. BST, London, England

Diana, Princess of Wales, Divorce: August 28, 1996, 10.27 a.m. BST, London, England

Diana, Princess of Wales, Death: August 31, 1997, 00.27 a.m. CEDT, Paris, France

Car Accident Lady: January 15, 1921, 5.17 a.m. CET, Celle, Germany

Carl Jung Natal Chart: July 26, 1875 NS, 7.31.58 p.m. LMT, Kesswil, Switzerland

Carl Jung Solar Return: July 26, 1887, 4.59.13 p.m. LMT, Kesswil, Switzerland

Carl Jung Capricorn Ingress: December 22, 1895, 2.38.45 a.m. CET, Kesswil, Switzerland

Carl Jung, Father's Death: January 28, 1896, 12.00 p.m. CET, Kesswil, Switzerland

Carl Jung New Moon: November 22, 1900 NS, 8.17.07 a.m. CET, Zurich, Switzerland

Carl Jung, Jung Starts Work: December 10, 1900, 9.00 a.m. CET, Zurich, Switzerland

Carl Jung Marriage: February 14, 1903, 5.31.59 p.m. CET, Kesswil, Switzerland

Agathe Jung Natal Chart: December 26, 1904, 12.00 p.m. CET, Zurich, Switzerland

Gret Jung Natal Chart: February 8, 1906, 1.25 p.m. CET, Zurich, Switzerland

Carl Jung Meets Freud: March 3, 1907, 10.00 a.m. CET, Vienna, Austria

Carl Jung/Freud Voyage: August 21, 1909, 12.00 p.m. CET, Bremen, Germany

Carl Jung/Freud Split: January 6, 1913, 12.00 p.m. CET, Zurich, Switzerland

Carl Jung's Fall: February 11, 1944, 4.00 p.m. CET, Zurich, Switzerland

Emma Jung Death: November 27, 1955, 12.00 p.m. CET, Zurich, Switzerland

Carl Jung's Death: June 6, 1961, 8.10 p.m. CET, Zurich, Switzerland

Client Natal Chart: June 19, 1951, 11.12 p.m. PDT, Glendale, CA, USA

Son Lotto Winner Natal Chart: September 8, 1922, 5.45 a.m. CET, Kamen, Germany

Car Accident Man Natal Chart: May 2, 1916, 1.38 p.m. CEDT, Vienna, Austria

Female Poland Natal Chart: June 26, 1919, 9.00 a.m. CET, Stettin, Poland

John F. Kennedy Natal Chart: May 29, 1917, 3.04.30 p.m. EST, Brookline, MA, USA

Kennedy Marriage: September 12, 1953, 3.04 p.m. EDT, Brookline, MA, USA (Ebertin's time)

Acknowledgments

I owe my start of working with midpoints to my South Florida astrology groups, the Atlantic Chapter of NCGR, and the South Florida Astrological Association (SFAA). During the school year, twice each month on Saturday, for twelve years, I made the two-hour trip from my home in Fort Pierce to Fort Lauderdale to hear a myriad of renowned astrology speakers. It was here I was first exposed to Uranian astrology. With this background, I was able to understand Maria Kay Simm's book, *The Dial Detective*, and learned much from the Oct/Nov 2005 issue #123 of *The Mountain Astrologer*, dedicated to Cosmobiology and Uranian astrology. At the time I was studying the stock market and thought midpoints might help. They did and they didn't. Midway through my study, I moved across the country, leaving the ocean for the high desert of southern New Mexico. Suddenly cut off from the world, I hiked and worked with midpoints. I read every book on midpoints I could find, including all of Ebertin's. I erected every dial he drew and examined each midpoint axis he described. Early on I could see the main problem was there was too much information—too many midpoints to deal with. Ebertin agreed. As I worked, at times I could feel him beside me, whispering in my head, *zu viel*—"too much." I paid attention. I hope he would be happy with how this text turned out. And I hope this book will stoke the interest of predictive astrologers who will add midpoints to their technique and help advance this wondrous starry field.

On a personal note, I am grateful to Eugene "Spiritweaver" Vidal for introducing me to astrology, and to my first teacher, Terri McCartney. I am indebted to the members of my astrology groups, and clients and students in South Florida whose stories, confidences, companionship, and knowledge, I treasure. I am especially thankful to Tem Tarriktar who was an early supporter and became a good friend. I am thankful to Scott Silverman, for our many conversations over many years on Uranian astrology and Cosmobiology. I thank Kathryn Sky-Peck, an amazing editor, whose efforts made this a much better book. Finally, I am blessed to have found on this remote mountain range a kindred spirit who shares my love of dogs and astrology. Lora Lisbon was an answer to a prayer.

About the Author

Kathy Allan has been studying astrology for over twenty years. She is certified at the professional level by the American Federation of Astrology. She has taught astrology classes at all levels, has lectured nationally, and has been a contributing writer for *The Mountain Astrologer* since 2008. She is a board member of the AFA. Her book *When Worlds Collide: Another Look at the Lunar Nodes* was published in 2012. She has a PhD in Molecular Toxicology and did postdoctoral research in Infectious Immunology. She is married with two grown (amazing) sons and has three rambunctious dogs. A long-time resident of Nairobi, Kenya, and then South Florida, she currently lives in southern New Mexico in the high mountains, close to the stars.